HIPPOCRENE CONCISE DICTIONARY

CATALAN-ENGLISH/ ENGLISH-CATALAN Dictionary

D1148813

HIPPOCRENE CONCISE DICTIONARY

CATALAN-ENGLISH/ ENGLISH-CATALAN Dictionary

M.S. Sabater
J.A. Freixinet

HIPPOCRENE BOOKS

New York

Originally published in 1990 by Arimany.

Hippocrene paperback edition, 1993.

Second printing, 2001

All rights reserved.

ISBN 0-7818-0099-4

For information, contact:
HIPPOCRENE BOOKS, INC.
171 Madison Avenue
New York, NY 10016

Printed in the United States of America.

FOREWORD

This Catalan-English dictionary consists of some 9,000 words, selected from those words most frequently used.

The entries are shown in bold type and their different equivalences in normal type (ex. **decoració** f. decoration / scenery, set.).

As a phonetic aid to the user, we have shown the stressed vowel in the Catalan entry in normal type and, in their English equivalents, the stressed vowel or group of vowels is in bold type.

In the Catalan entries we have shown the gender of the word (ex. **magistrat** m. magistrate.).

In contrast to most bilingual dictionaries of this size, we have indicated the feminine ending of adjectives (ex. **humà-ana** a. human, benevolent, humane).

Finally, the large number of different equivalences given in this dictionary should facilitate greater accuracy for the user than is normal with this type of dictionary.

ABBREVIATIONS USED
in this dictionary

a.	adjective	Lit.	Literature
Adm.	Administration	m.	masculine noun
adv.	adverb	Mat.	Mathematics
adv. phr.	adverbial phrase	Mec.	Mechanics
Aero.	Aeronautics	Med.	Medicine
Am.	American	Mil.	Military
Anat.	Anatomy	Mus.	Music
Arch.	Architecture	Naut.	Nautical
art.	article	Orn.	Ornithology
Bot.	Botany	Parl.	Parliament
Bri.	British	pers.	personal
Comm.	Commercial	pr. v.	pronominal verb
conj.	conjunction	Photog.	Photography
Crust.	Crustacean	phr.	phrase
Entom.	Entomology	pl.	plural
f.	femenine noun	Polit.	Politics
fam.	familiar	pos.	possessive
fig.	figurative	prep.	preposition
Geog.	Geography	prep. phr.	prepositional phrase
Geom.	Geometry	Print.	Printing
ger.	gerund	pron.	pronoun
Gram.	Grammar	s.	see
Gymn.	Gymnastics	sing.	singular
Icht.	Ichthyology	Theat.	Theatre
interj.	interjection	tr.	transitive
interrog.	interrogative	U.S.	United States
intr.	intransitive	v.	verb

DICCIONARI
CATALÀ - ANGLÈS

A

abadessa f. abbess.
abadia f. abbey.
a baix adv. down.
abaixador m. cloth-shearer.
abaltir-se pr. v. to send to sleep/to calm.
abandonar tr. to abandon, leave, forsake.
abans adv. before.
abaratir tr. to cheapen, reduce in price.
abarrotar tr. to bar, strengthen with bars / to overstock, cram / to tie, moor.
abast m. range, scope / grasp.
abastar tr. to supply reach, equip.
abat m. abbot.
abatiment m. depression.
abatre tr. to overwhelm.
abdomen m. abdomen.
abella f. bee.
abellir intr. to tempt, seduce / to desire, long for.
abeurar tr. to water.
abisme m. abyss.
abjurar tr. to forsake.
ablanir tr. to soften / to assuage.
abnegació f. self-denial.
abolir tr. to abolish, repeal.
abonament m. security / subscription / discount / manure.

abonyegament m. dent / bump / bruise.
abonyegar tr. to dent, batter.
abraçar tr. to embrace, hug, clasp / to include.
abreujament m. abbreviation.
abreujar tr. to shorten, abbreviate.
abreviació f. abbreviation.
abreviatura f. abbreviation.
abric m. overcoat.
abrigall m. blanket.
abril m. April.
abriüll m. thistle thorn / crowfoot.
abrivament m. boldness, audacity / fieriness.
abrivat -ada a. bold, audacious / fiery / restless.
abrupte -a a. steep / abrupt.
abrusar tr. to burn, parch.
absència f. absence.
absent a. absent / away.
absolt-a a. absolved, acquitted.
absolució f. absolution, pardon, remission.
abstemi -èmia a. abstemious, teetotaler.
abstenir-se pr. v. to abstain.
abstracte-a a. abstract.
absurd-a a. absurd.
abundància f. plenty, abundance, rifeness.
abús m. abuse.
abusar intr. to abuse.
acabalar tr. to hoard.

acabament m. ending, conclusion, end.

acabar tr. to finish, end, complete, do, terminate.

acadèmia f. academy.

acampar tr. - intr. to camp out.

acaronar tr. to caress, fondle.

accedir intr. to accede.

accelerar tr. to accelerate, quicken.

accent m. stress, accent.

acceptar tr. to accept.

accés m. access.

accessible a. accessible, obtainable.

accident m. accident.

acció f. action, deed.

accionista m. -f. shareholder, stockholder.

acer m. steel.

ací adv. here.

àcid-a a. acid.

aclamació f. cheer.

aclamar tr. to acclaim, cheer.

aclaparar tr. to overwhelm.

aclariment m. explanation.

aclarir tr. explain, clear up.

aclucar tr. to close the eyes.

acolliment m. reception, entertainment.

acoltellar tr. to stab, slash.

acomodador-a m. usher. f. usherette.

acompanyar tr. to accompany / to assist.

aconseguir tr. to get, reach.

aconsellar tr. to advise.

acord m. agreement, accordance, (mus.) chord.

acostar tr. to move towards, approach / to pass.

acostumar tr. - intr. to accustom.

acovardir tr. to frighten, daunt.

acovardir-se pr. v. to quail, flinch.

acte m. act.

actitud f. attitude.

actiu-iva a. active, brisk.

activitat f. activity.

actor m. actor.

actriu f. actress.

actualment adv. at present.

actuar intr. to act, perform / to operate.

acudir intr. to go to.

acudir-se pr. v. (idea) to occur to one.

acudit m. joke, jest.

acumulació f. accumulation.

acumulament m. accumulation.

acumular tr. to heap up, pile up, accumulate.

acurat-ada a. careful, mindful, painstaking.

acusació f. charge, accusation, impeachment (US).

acusador -a a. accuser / U.S. impeacher

acusar tr. to accuse, impeach.

adagi m. proverb.

adaptació f. adaptation.

adaptar tr. to adapt.

addicte-a a. devoted, faithful.

adelitar-se pr. v. to enjoy, delight in, take pleasure in.

adepte -a a. adept, initiated / adherent, follower.

adequat -ada a. appropiate, adequate.

adesiara adv. sometimes, from time to time.

adéu! interj. good-bye, farewell.

àdhuc adv. even, including.

adient a. ideal, suited, worthy.

administració f. management, administration.

administrador a.t.m. -f. administrator, steward.

administrar tr. to administer.

admiració f. admiration, wonder.

admirador -a a. admirer.

admirar tr. to admire.

admissió f. entrance, admittance.

adob m. manure / repair.

adobar tr. to mend, repair.

adolescència f. adolescence.

adonar-se pr. v. to realize, be aware of.

adoptar tr. to adopt.

adorar tr. to worship, adore.

adornar tr. to adorn.

adquirir tr. to acquire, get.

adquisició f. acquisition.

adreça f. address.

adreçar tr. to address, refer / to redress.

adreçar-se pr. v. to. address.

adroguer m. grocer.

adrogueria f. grocer's.

adulació f. flattery.

adular tr. to adulate, flatter.

adult -a a. adult, grown-up.

adulterar tr. to adulterate.

adulteri m. adultery.

adust -a a. unkind.

adverbi m. adverb.

advertiment m. warning / reminder.

advertir tr. to advise, warn, to admonish / to observe, notice.

advocat m. lawyer, barrister, advocate.

aeròdrom m. aerodrome.

aeroplà m. aeroplane, aircraft.

afaiçonar tr. to form, shape.

afaitar tr. to shave.

afalagar tr. to flatter.

afanar tr. to rob, steal / to thieve.

afany m. anxiety, eagerness / effort, toil.

afanyar tr. to hasten / to strive for.

afanyar-se pr. v. to toil.

afartar tr. to satiate, stuff (slang).

afavorir tr. to favour, help.

afeblir tr. to weaken, debilitate, enfeeble.

afecció f. interest, hobby, pastime.

afeccionat-ada a. amateur.

afectar tr. to affect.

afecte m. affection, fondness.

afectíssim-a a. affectionate.

afectuós -osa a. affectionate, fond.

afegir tr. to add.

afeixugar tr. to burden / to oppress.

afermar tr. to make fast, secure / to affirm, assert.

afillada f. goddaughter.

afillat m. godson, godchild.

afinador m. tuner.

afinament (de pes) m. balance.

afirmació f. affirmation, assertion.

afirmar tr. to affirm, assert.

afflicció f. affliction, grief, sorrow, distress.

afligir tr. to distress, afflict.

afligit -ida a. sorrowful, sorrowing, grieving, distressed.

afluixament m. looseness.

afluixar tr. to loosen.

afonar tr. to sink / to go deep, penetrate.

afortunat -ada a. lucky, fortunate.

afranquir tr. to free / to liberate.

afrau f. canyon / ravine.

afront m. affront, dishonour.

afrós -osa a. horrible, dreadful.

afuar tr. to whet, sharpen.

afusellar tr. to shoot / to execute by firing squad.

agafador m. knob, handle.

agafar tr. to hold, seize, grasp, catch.

agençament m. adornment, ornament.

agençar tr. to adorn / to beautify, ornament.

agenda f. diary, agenda.

agenollar-se pr. v. to kneel.

agent a. / m. -f. agent.

agermanar tr. to mate, match / to make compatible.

àgil a. agile, nimble.

agilitat f. agility, nimbleness / lightness.

agiotista m. / f. jobber.

agitar tr. to stir.

agombolar tr. to fondle, caress.

agonia f. agony.

agost m. August.

agradable a. nice, pleasant, agreeable.

agradar intr. to like, please, love.

agradós- osa a. agreeable, pleasing.

agraïment m. thankfulness, gratefulness, gratitude.

agrair tr. to thank.

agraït -ïda a. thankful, grateful.

agre -a a. sour, bitter, tart.

agregar tr. to aggregate.

agrejar intr. to sour, embitter.

agressió f. aggression

agrest -a a. wild.

agreujar tr. to aggravate.

agricultura f. agriculture.

aguait m. ambush, lying in wait, lurking / trap.

aguant m. endurance.

aguantar tr. to endure, suffer, stand, undergo / to hold.

agudament adv. sharply, keenly.

agudesa f. keenness.

àguila f. eagle.

agulla de cap f. pin.

agulla (de cosir) f. needle / (arch.) spire.

agullonar tr. to prick / to encourage, stimulate.

agusar tr. to sharpen.

agut -uda a. sharp, keen.

agutzil m. constable, peace officer.

ah! interj. oh!

ahir adv. yesterday.

ai! interj. ouch!, alas!

aigua f. water.

aigualit -ida a. watery, washy.

aiguamoll m. marsh, swamp, fen.

aiguardent m. brandy / liquor.

aiguat m. heavy shower, downpour.

aigüera f. scullery.

ai las interj. woe.

aïllar tr. to isolate / to insulate.

aire m. air.

airejar tr. to air / to take the air.

aixa f. adze.

aixada f. hoe.

aixafar tr. to crush.

aixecament m. rising.

aixecar tr. to rise, raise, lift, heave up.

aixecar-se pr. v. to get up, rise.

aixella f. armpit.

aixeta f. tap.

així adv. like this, like that, so.

això pron. that.

aixopluc m. refuge, shelter.

ajaçat -ada a. lying down, recumbent.

ajagut -uda a. lying down, recumbent.

ajeure's pr. v. to lie down.

ajornar tr. to delay, postpone.

ajuda, ajut f.-m. help, aid, assistance.

ajudant m. helper, assistant.

ajudar tr. to aid, help, assist.

ajuntament m. town hall, town council / joining.

ajuntar tr. to join.

ajupir tr. to stoop, squat.

ajupir-se pr. v. to crouch, stoop.

ajustar tr. to fit / to adjust.

ajut m. help, aid, assistance.

ala f. wing / side.
alarit m. shout, yell.
alarma f. alarm.
alba f. dawn.
albada f. dawn.
àlber m. poplar.
albercoc m. apricot.
alberg m. lodging, inn.
alberginia f. eggplant, aubergine.
albirar tr. to see from a distance, to perceive indistinctly / to conjecture, imagine.
alça f. advance, rise in price.
alçada f. height, tallness.
alcaldia f. town hall.
alcalde m. mayor.
alçaprem m. lever.
alçar tr. - intr. to raise, rise up.
alçària f. height.
alcohol m. alcohol.
al costat adv. beside.
aldarull m. disturbance, racket, riot, uproar.
alè m. breath / wind.
alegrar tr. to make merry, gladden / to rejoice / to get tipsy.
alegrar-se pr. v. to rejoice.
alegre a. happy, merry, cheerful.
alegria f. joy.
alemany -a a. German.
alenar intr. to breathe / to exhale.
aleshores adv. then.
aletejar tr. to flutter.
alfabet m. alphabet.
alforja f. saddlebag / knapsack.
algú -una pron. someone, somebody, anyone, anybody.
algun -a a. some, any.
algutzir m. sheriff.
aliança f. alliance.
aliat -ada m.-f. ally / a. allied.
aliè -ena a. alien.
aliment m. food, feed.
alimentar tr. to feed.

alinear tr. to line.
all m. garlic.
allà adv. there.
allargar tr. to lengthen, elongate.
al·legació f. plea, allegation / argument.
al·legar tr. to plead.
al·leluia f. hallelujah.
alletar tr. to suckle.
alleugerir tr. to lighten.
allí adv. there.
alliberament m. release.
alliberar tr. to free, liberate, release.
allistar tr. to enlist.
allistar-se pr. v. to enlist, join up.
allò pron. that.
allotjar tr. to lodge.
al·ludir intr. to hint, refer, allude.
allunyar tr. to remove to a distance / to separate.
almenys adv. at least.
almirall m. admiral.
almoina f. alms.
alosa f. lark.
alt -a a. tall / high, loud.
alt (en veu alta) adv. aloud.
altar m. altar.
altaveu m. loudspeaker.
alteració f. alteration.
alterar tr. to alter.
altitud f. altitude, height / loftiness.
altiplà m. table, tableland.
altrament adv. besides, otherwise, conj. or, or else, if not.
altre -a, altres a. other, another.
altura f. altitude.
alumini m. aluminium.
alumne m. pupil.
alzina f. evergreen oak.
amabilitat f. kindness, niceness.
amable a. kind, gentle, nice / lovable.

amablement adv. kindly.
amagar tr. to hide, conceal.
amagatall m. hiding-place / lair.
amanida f. salad.
amaniment m. relish.
amanir tr. to dress or season salads, etc.
amanyagar tr. to caress.
amar tr. to love.
amarar tr. to soak, saturate, drench.
amarg-a a. bitter.
amargor f. bitterness.
amassar tr. to amass / to mash.
amatent a. attentive, heedful / polite.
amb prep. with.
ambaixada f. embassy.
ambaixador m. ambassador.
ambdós -ambdues a. - pron. both / either.
ambició f. ambition.
ambient m. environment / atmosphere, ambient.
ambulància f. ambulance.
amè -ena a. pleasant / delightful.
amenaça f. menace, threat.
amenaçar tr. to menace, threaten.
americana (vestit) f. jacket.
a més adv. moreover, besides.
ametlla f. almond.
amic -iga m.-f. / a. friend.
amidador m. meter.
amígdales f. pl. tonsils.
amistançada f. mistress.
amistat f. friendship.
amo m. master, boss.
amoïnar tr. to bother, fuss, trouble, worry.
amoixar tr. to pat.
amonestació f. warning.
amonestar tr. to warn, advise, admonish.
amor m. love.

amorós -osa a. affectionate, kind / loving.
amplada f. width, breadth.
ample -a a. wide, broad.
ampli -àmplia a. wide, broad / loose / ample.
àmpliament adv. widely.
ampliar tr. to extend / to amplify.
amplitud f. extent.
ampolla f. bottle.
amunt adv. up, aloft.
amuntegar tr. to heap, to pile.
analfabet-a m.-f. / a. illiterate.
anàlisi f. analysis.
analitzar tr. to analyse / (gram.) to parse.
analogia f. analogy.
ananàs f. pineapple, ananas.
anar intr. to go, move, travel.
anarquia f. anarchy.
anar-se'n pr. v. leave, to depart.
anca f. haunch.
àncora f. anchor.
ancorar tr. to anchor.
andana f. sidewalk, pavement.
ànec m. duck.
ànega f. (female) duck.
anell m. ring / segment.
anella f. bangle.
àngel m. angel.
angle m. angle.
anglès -esa a. English.
angoixa f. anguish, woe, worry / agony.
anguniós -osa a. anxious.
anhel m. anxiety, eagerness.
anhelar tr. - intr. to long, yearn.
ànim m. courage, pluck / energy.
ànima f. soul.
animal m. / a. animal.
animar tr. to encourage.
animat -ada a. lively, spirited, brisk.
animós -osa a. plucky.
aniquilar tr. to annihilate.

anit adv. last night.
anivellador -a a. leveller.
anivellar tr. to level.
annex m. annexe.
anodí -ina a. harmless, innocuous.
anomenar tr. to name, term.
anotació f. note.
anotar tr. to make note / to comment.
ànsia f. anxiety.
antagonista a. / m.-f. antagonist, opponent.
antany adv. years past.
antena f. aerial / (entom.) antenna.
anterior a. former.
antesala f. waiting-room.
antic -iga a. old, ancient / senior.
anticipadament adv. beforehand.
anticipar tr. to anticipate, forestall, advance.
anticipat -ada a. premature, prospective, future.
antigament adv. formerly, once / in ancient times.
antiquat -ada a. antiquated, old-fashioned / obsolete.
antre m. cavern.
anual a. annual, yearly.
anualment adv. yearly.
anul·lar tr. to annul, nullify.
anunci m. announcement / advertisement / notice.
anunciar tr. to advertise, to announce.
any m. year.
anyell m. lamb.
apa! interj. gee-up!, get moving!
apagar tr. to turn off / to extinguish / to quench.
apaivagar tr. to calm, to quell.
apallissar tr. to thrash.
aparcar tr. to park.
aparèixer tr. to appear.

aparell m. appliance.
aparença f. appearance, seeming.
aparent a. apparent, seeming.
aparentment adv. apparently.
apartar tr. to separate / to remove / to withdraw.
apassionat -ada a. passionate.
àpat m. meal.
apedaçar tr. to patch, to patch up.
apel·lar intr. to appeal, to request.
a penes adv. hardly, scarcely.
apesarat -ada a. sorry.
apetit m. appetite.
apetitós -osa a. tasty, appetising.
api m. celery.
apilar tr. to heap up.
aplanar tr. to level, flatten / to remove obstacles / to strike down, prostrate.
aplaudiment m. applause, clapping.
aplaudir intr. to applaud, clap.
aplec m. jamboree.
aplegar tr. to meet, reunite, congregate / to join, meet.
aplicació f. application.
aplicat -ada a. industrious, diligent, hard-working.
apoderat m. manager.
aposta f. bet, wager.
apostar tr. to bet.
apòstol m. apostle.
apreciar tr. to appreciate / to value / to cherish.
apreciat -ada a. dear / appreciated, well thought of.
aprendre tr. to learn.
aprenent -a a. apprentice.
apressadament adv. hurriedly, hastily.
apressant a. urgent, pressing / eager.
apressar tr. to hurry, hasten / to urge, compel.
apressat -ada a. hasty.

aprimar tr. to thin, slim / to be exact.

aprofitar tr. profit, to make good use of, to take advantage of, to avail.

aprofitar-se pr. v. to benefit, profit, take advantage of.

apropar tr. to approach.

apropiar-se pr. v. to assume, appropriate.

apropiat -ada a. appropriate.

aprovació f. approval.

aprovar tr. to approve.

aproximat -ada a. approximate.

apte -a a. apt, suitable.

aptitud f. aptitude.

apuntar tr. to note, make note of / to suggest (ideas) / to prompt.

aquarel·la f. watercolour.

aqueix -a a. that.

aquell -a a. that.

aquest -a pron. this.

aquí adv. here.

aquós -osa a. watery.

ara adv. now.

àrab a. / m.-f. Arab, Arabian.

arada f. plough.

aram m. copper.

aranya f. spider.

àrbitre m. arbitrator, referee, umpire.

arbre m. tree.

arbust m. bush.

arc (de cercle) m. arc.

arc (de volta) m. arch.

arc de Sant Martí m. rainbow.

arca f. ark / chest.

ardit -ida a. bold, audacious.

ardor m.-f. ardour / great heat / fieriness.

ardu -àrdua a. laborious, arduous.

àrea f. area.

arena f. sand.

areng m. herring.

arengada f. herring.

argelaga f. gorse.

argent m. silver.

argenter m. silversmith.

argent viu m. mercury, quicksilver.

argila f. clay.

argot m. jargon / slang.

argüir intr. to argue.

argument m. argument / (lit). plot, story.

ariet m. ram.

aritmètica f. arithmetic.

arma f. weapon, arm.

armada f. navy.

armadura f. armour.

armar tr. to arm / to cause, provoke.

armari m. cupboard, wardrobe.

armilla f. waistcoat.

arnès m. harness.

aroma f. aroma.

arpa f. harp.

arpó m. harpoon.

arquebisbe m. archbishop.

arquejar tr. to arch.

arquer m. archer.

arquitecte m. architect.

arquitectura f. architecture.

arrabassar tr. to pull up by the roots / to eradicate, extirpate.

arracada f. earring.

arranjar tr. arrange / to repair / (mus.) to arrange.

arrapar-se pr. v. to cling.

arrasar tr. to demolish, raze to the ground.

arrecerar tr. to take cover.

arreglar tr. to organize, arrange.

arrel f. root.

arrelar tr. to root.

arrencada f. start, onset.

arrencar tr.-intr. to root out / to extirpate, wrest, pull out / to start.

arrendament m. lease.

arrendar tr. to lease, rent.

arrendatari -ària a. tenant, lessee.

arrenglerar tr. to range.

arrest m. arrest.

arreu adv. everywhere, throughout.

arreus m. harness, trappings / appurtenances.

arribada f. arrival.

arribar tr. to arrive, reach, get to.

arriscar tr. to hazard, venture, risk.

arriscat -ada a. risky, dangerous, hazardous.

arrissar tr. to curl, frizzle, crimp.

arromangar tr. to tuck up the sleeves or petticoats.

arròs m. rice.

arrossegar tr. to creep, drift, haul.

arruga f. wrinkle, corrugation, rumple, crease, line.

arrugar tr. to corrugate / to wrinkle.

arrugat -ada a. corrugated, wrinkled.

arruïnar tr. to ruin.

art m. art.

artell m. knuckle.

artèria f. artery.

artesà -ana m. -f. artisan, craftsman, m.

artesania f. handicraft, craftsmanship, skill.

article m. article.

articulació f. articulation.

artificial a. artificial.

artiller m. gunner.

artista m.-f., artist.

arxiu m. archives / file / register.

arxivar tr. to file.

ascendent a. / m.-f. upward, ascending.

ascendir intr. to rise, ascend.

ascens m. rise, ascent.

ascensor m. (Am.) elevator (Bri.), lift.

ase m. donkey.

asfixia f. asphyxia, suffocation.

aspecte m. aspect, bearing.

aspiració f. aspiration.

aspirar tr. to aspire to, to aim for to aim / inhale.

asprament adv. roughly, harshly.

aspre -a a. rough, harsh / sour.

assabentar tr. to inform, acquaint oneself with.

assaborir tr. to savour / to flavour.

assagista m.-f. essayist.

assaig m. essay / rehearsal / test.

assajar tr. to test / to rehearse / to try, attempt.

assalt m. assault.

assaonador m. tanner.

assassí m. murderer / assassin.

assassinar tr. to murder / to assassinate.

assecat -ada a. dry.

assedegat -ada a. thirsty.

assedegat -ada a. thirsty.

assegurança f. insurance.

assegurar tr. to assure, insure / to make sure.

assegut -uda a. seated, settled.

assemblar-se pr. v. to look like, resemble.

assemblea f. assembly, meeting.

assentiment m. assent.

assentir tr. to assent.

assenyadament adv. wisely.

assenyat -ada a. wise, sensible, judicious.

asseure's pr. v. to sit (oneself) down.

assiduïtat f. regularity.

assimilar tr. to assimilate.

assistència f. attendance.

associació f. association, guild.

associat m. member.

assolar tr. to raze, to lay waste.

assolir tr. to attain, obtain.

assortit m. set, stock / variety, assortment.

assossegat -ada a. restful, sedate.

assotar tr. to beat, whip, spank.

assumir tr. to assume.

assumpte m. subject, business, matter, affair.

ast m. spit.

astorar tr. to amaze.

astúcia f. cunning, astuteness.

astut -uta a. shrewd, cunning, astute.

atac m. attack.

atacar tr. to attack / to charge.

atemorir tr. to frighten, scare, daunt.

atenció f. attention.

atendre tr. pay attention to, attend, heed.

atent -a a. attentive.

atenuar tr. to attenuate.

aterrar intr. to land.

atipar (fam.) tr. to satiate, stuff.

atleta m.-f. athlete.

atmosfera f. atmosphere.

àtom m. atom.

atordir tr. to make dizzy / to perplex, stupefy.

atordit -ida a. dizzy / stupefied, perplexed.

atorgar tr. to grant.

atracció f. attraction.

atractiu -iva a. attractive, taking / absorbing.

atrafegar-se pr. v. to toil.

a través adv. across.

atresorar tr. to hoard.

atreure tr. to attract.

atreure (al parany) tr. to lure, decoy.

atreviment m. boldness, daring.

atrevir-se pr. v. to dare.

atrevit-ida a. daring.

atribuïble a. referable, attributable.

atribuir tr. to attribute, impute.

atrocitat f. atrocity.

atropellar tr. to trample underfoot / knock down / insult / to violate the law.

atuell m. vessel, pot.

atzar m. chance, hazard, luck.

atzucac m. blind alley, impasse.

au f. bird, fowl.

audaç a. bold, audacious.

auditori m. auditory / auditorium, hall.

augment m. gain, increase.

augmentar tr. to increase.

augurar tr. to forecast.

auguri m. omen.

aula f. classroom.

auster-a a. stern, austere.

austeritat f. austerity, sternness.

auto m. motor car.

autobús m. bus.

autodidacte-a a. self-educated.

automòbil a. / m. car, motorcar, automobile.

automobilista m.-f. motorist.

autonomia f. autonomy, self-government, home rule.

autopista f. motorway.

autor -a s. author, composer.

autoritat f. authority.

autorització f. warrant, authorization.

autoritzar tr. to. authorize, warrant, empower.

auxili m. aid, help, assistance.

avall adv. down, downwards.

avaluar tr. to evaluate, value, estimate.

avançar (de quatre grapes) tr. to creep along.

avançat -ada a. advanced.

avant adv. onward, forward.

avantatge m. advantage, vantage / odds.

avantbraç m. forearm.

avantguarda f. vanguard, avant-garde.

avantpassat m. ancestor, fore-bear.

avar -a a. avaricious, mean, nig-gardly, miserable.

avaria f. failure, breakdown, damage.

avellana f. hazelnut.

avellaner m. hazel.

aventura f. adventure, ventu

aventurar tr. to hazard, vent

aventurer -a a. adventurer, turer.

avergonyir tr. to shame, pu shame.

avergonyit -ida a. ashamed.

aversió f. distaste, disgust, loa-ting, aversion.

avesar tr. to habituate.

avi m. grandfather.

àvia f. grandmother.

aviació f. aviation.

aviador -a s. aviator.

aviat adv. early, soon.

aviciar tr. to pamper.

àvid -a a. avid, eager.

avidesa f. eagerness.

avinguda f. avenue.

avió m. aeroplane, aircraft.

aviram f. poultry, fowl.

avis m. pl. grandparents.

avís m. advice, counsel / notice, warning.

avisar tr. to advise / to warn.

avituallar tr. to provision, vic-tual.

avorrir tr. to hate, detest / to bore.

avorrit -ida a. dull, boring / hated.

avui adv. today.

B

babau s. silly, foolish / simple-ton

babord m. port.

bacallà m. cod.

bací m. shaving-dish / urinal, chamberpot.

badall m. yawn, yawning.

badallaire m. -f. yawner.

badallar intr. to yawn.

badallera f. yawn, yawning.

badia f. bay, harbour.

baf m. vapour / stale atmosphere / breath.

bagatel·la f. trifle.

balard m. stretcher, litter.

baix-a a. low, short / (pl.) ground floor, basement / bass.

baixa (per mort, captura, acci-dent, etc.) f. casualty.

baixada f. descent, sloping street.

baixar tr. - intr. to descend, go down / to lower.

baixesa f. meanness.

bajanada f. idiocy.

bala f. bale / bullet.

balada f. ballad.

baladrejar intr. to bawl, vocife-rate.

balanceig m. wobble.

balancejar tr.- intr. to wobble, to dangle.

balances f. pl. scales.

balancí m. rocking chair.

balandreig m. wobble.

balbucejant ger. falteringly.

balcó m. balcony.

balda f. latch / knocker.

balder -a a. loose, lax, easy / at leisure.

baldó m. latch.

baldufa f. whipping top.

balena f. whale.

balener -a a. whaler.

ball m. dance.

ballar intr. to dance / to slide, wobble.

balma f. small cave.

bàlsam m. balm, balsam / ointment.

baluard m. rampart.

banc m. bank / bench, seat / shoal.

banda f. band / gang, troop / sash / side.

bandada f. covey / flock of birds.

bandera f. flag, banner.

bandit m. bandit / outlaw.

bàndol m. faction.

banquer m. banker.

banquet m. dinner / banquet.

banús m. ebony.

bany m. bath.

banya f. horn.

banyar tr. to have a bath, to bathe / to swim.

banyar-se pr. v. to bathe.

banyera f. bath.

bar m. bar, public house.

baralla f. quarrel.

barallar-se pr. v. to quarrel.

barana f. handrail, railing.

barat-a a. cheap.

barba f. beard / chin.

bàrbar a. m. barbarian / barbarous.

barber m. barber, hairdresser.

barbotejar intr. to mumble.

barca f. boat.

bardissa f. hedge.

barnilla f. small rod / curtain rod / spindle / switch / rib of an umbrella.

baró m. baron / male, man.

baronessa f. baroness.

baronívol-a a. virile, manly / intrepid.

barquer m. boatman / ferryman.

barra f. bar / (fam.) cheek.

barraca f. hut, hovel.

barranc m. ravine.

barreja f. blend, mixture / medley.

barrejar tr. to mix, mingle / to jumble.

barrera f. fence, barrier.

barret m. hat.

barreter m. hatter.

barri m. district, ward / neighbourhood, quarter.

barriada f. neighbourhood.

barril m. barrel.

barrina f. drill.

barrinar tr. to bore, drill / to blast / (fig.) to ponder, muse upon.

barroc-a a. baroque.

barroer-a a. bungler, botcher.

basar m. bazaar.

base f. base, basis.

basament m. base and pedestal.

basarda f. fear, terror.

bàsic-a a. basic.

bassa f. pool, pond.

bassiol m. pool.

bast-a a. coarse, rough.

bastaix m. porter, carrier.

bastant a. - adv. quite / enough.

bastar intr. to suffice.

baster m. saddler.

bastida f. scaffold.

bastiment m. construction, building / frame, door-case / boat, vessel, ship.

bastó m. stick.

bata f. housecoat, dressing gown.

batalla f. battle, action.

batalló m. battalion.

batec m. beat, palpitation.

batedor m. whisk.

bategar intr. to beat, pulse, throb.

bateig m. baptism.

batejar tr. to christen / to baptise.

batlle m. mayor

batre tr. - intr. to beat / to break down.

batussa f. battle, fight / quarrel.

batuta f. stick, baton / wand.

batxiller -a m.- f. bachelor.

batxillerat m. baccalaureate / certificate of secondary education.

batzegada f. shake, shock.

baula f. link.

bava f. slobber.

bavejar intr. to slobber.

be m. sheep.

bé adv. well, fine, good, right.

bebè m. baby.

bec m. beak.

becaina f. nap.

bedoll m. birch tree.

befa f. jeering, mockery, scoffing.

beguda f. drink.

beina f. scabbard.

belar intr. to bleat / to crave.

bell -a a. beautiful.

bellesa f. beauty, loveliness

bèl·lic -a a. warlike.

bellugar tr. to move / to wag.

bellugar-se pr. v. to bustle / to fidget.

ben adv. well, perfectly.

benedicció f. blessing.

beneficència f. beneficence.

benefici m. benefit, profit, gain.

beneficiar tr. to benefit.

beneficiar-se pr. v. to benefit, profit.

beneir tr. to bless.

beneït -ida a. blessed / holy.

benestar m. comfort, ease, welfare.

benèvol -a a. kind, benevolent.

benifet m. benefit, profit / benefice, ecclesiastical living.

benigne -a a. benign / kind / mild / merciful.

benvinguda f. welcome.

benvingut -uda a. welcome.

benvolença f. goodness, benevolence.

benvolgut -uda a. dear.

benzina f. benzene.

berenar m. afternoon snack

bergant m. scoundrel, rascal.

berruga f. wart.

bes m. kiss.

besada f. kiss.

besar tr. to kiss.

besavi m. great-grandfather.

besàvia f. great-grandmother.

bescambra f. water closet, toilet.

bescantar tr. to defame / to denigrate.

bescuit m. biscuit.

besnét -a m. great-grandson / f. great-granddaughter.

bessó -ona m. -f. twin.

bèstia f. beast.

bestiar m. cattle.

beure tr. to drink.

bevedor -a a. drinker.

bíblia f. Bible.

biblioteca f. library / ... **circulant** lending library.

bicicleta f. bicycle.

bifurcació f. junction / fork.

biga f. beam, joist, rafter.

bigarrat -ada a. variegated.

bigoti m. mustache.

bilis f. gall.

biografia f. biography.

biologia f. biology.

bisbe m. bishop.

bisell m. bevel, bevel edge.

bisó m. bison.

bistec m. beefsteak.

bisturí m. scalpel

bitlla f. ninepin.

bitllet m. ticket / banknote.

blanc-a a. white.

blancor f. whiteness.
blanesa f. softness, gentleness, tenderness.
blanor f. softness, blandness, mildness, smoothness.
blanquejar intr. - tr. to whiten.
blanquer m. tanner.
blasfemar intr. - tr. to swear, blaspheme.
blasmar tr. to blame / to reproach.
blasme m. reproach.
blat m. wheat.
blat de moro m. corn, maize.
blau -ava a. blue.
ble m. wick.
bloc m. block.
blonda f. broad silk lace, blond lace.
bloquejar tr. to blockade.
bo -ona a. good.
bòbila f. tile-works.
boc m. he-goat, billy goat.
boca f. mouth.
bocaterrós -osa a. prone, prostrate.
boci m. mouthful, morsel / chip / scrap.
boda f. marriage, wedding.
bodega f. wine vault, cellar / storeroom / hold of a ship.
bogeria f. madness.
boig -oja a. mad.
boira f. fog, mist / smog.
boirós -osa a. foggy.
bolcar tr. to upset, overturn.
bolet m. mushroom, fungus / toadstool.
bolquer m. swaddling clothes / tail of a shirt.
bolquet m. wheelbarrow.
bomba f. bomb.
bombolla f. bubble.
bondat f. goodness, kindliness.
bonic -a a. pretty.
bony m. swelling, bump, lump / dent.
bonyegut -uda a. bulky, covered with bulges.
bord -a a. bastard, spurious, illegitimate.
bordar intr. to bark.
bordegàs -assa m.- f. lad.
borra f. wad.
borralló m. snowflake.
borrasca f. storm, tempest.
borratxo m. drunkard.
borsa f. stock exchange.
bosc m. forest, wood.
bossa f. purse / bag.
bota f. boot.
bóta f. cask.
botànic -a a. botanical / m.-f., botanist.
botànica f. botany.
botar intr. to leap, jump.
botella f. bottle.
boter m. cooper, hooper, barrel-maker.
botifarra f. black pudding / a Catalan pork sausage.
botiga f. shop.
botiguer m. shopkeeper, tradesman.
botó m. button.
botre intr. to cast, throw, fling, launch / to bound / to bounce.
bou m. ox, steer, bullock.
boxa f. boxing.
braç m. arm.
braçalet m. bangle, bracelet.
bram m. bray / bellow.
bramar intr. to bray.
bramul m. roar.
branca (d'arbre) f. branch, bough.
brandar (una campana) intr. to toll.
brau -brava a. brave, valiant, courageous.
brasa f. live coal, embers.
bressol m. cradle.

brètol m. swine, knave.
bretolada f. knavery.
breu a. brief, short.
brevetat f. brevity, shortness, conciseness.
brillant a. bright.
brillar intr. to shine, glisten.
brindar intr. to toast.
brindis m. toast.
brisa f. breeze.
brivall m. lad, youth.
broca f. reel for twist, or thread / drill for boring holes in iron / shoemaker's tack.
brodar tr. to embroider.
brollador m. fountain.
brollar m. to ooze.
bola f. ball.
broma f. joke.
bromera f. foam.
bromista a. joker.
bromós -osa a. foggy.
bronze m. bronze.
brossa f. brushwood, remains of leaves / thicket.
brot m. shoot / offspring.
brotar intr. to sprout.
brou m. broth.
bru -una a. brown, swarthy.
bruc m. heather.
bruixa f. sorceress, witch.
brúixola f. compass.
bruixot m. sorcerer, wizard, a male witch.
brunyir tr. to brighten, shine, polish.
brunzit m. buzz.
brusa f. blouse.
brusc -a a. rude / peevish / forward.
brut -a a. dirty.
brutícia f. dirt.
budell m. bowell.
bufada f. puff / blast.
bufanda f. scarf, muffler.
bufar tr. to blow.
bufetada f. slap.

bugadera f. washerwoman, launderess.
buidar tr. to empty.
buidor f. emptiness, void.
buit -buida a. empty, hollow, bare / m. vacuum.
bullir intr. to boil, simmer.
burg m. borough.
burgesia f. bourgeoisie.
burro m. ass, donkey.
bus m. diver.
buscar tr. to search, look for.
bústia f. letterbox.
butaca f. armchair / (theat.) stall.
butxaca f. pocket.

C

ca m. dog.
ca f., **cal** m., **can** m. variations of «casa» = house.
cabal m. wealth, capital / pl. money / abundance / flow.
cabana f. hut, cabin, shack / hovel.
cadbell m. ball of thread.
cabdill m. leader, chief.
cabdillatge m. leadership.
cabell m. hair.
cabellera f. hair, mane.
caber, cabre intr. to fit / to be natural, fitting.
cabina f. cabin (of a ship) / telephone box.
cable m. cable.
cabòria f. preoccupation.
cabra f. goat.
cabrer -a m.- f. goatherd, m / goatherdess, f.
cabreta f. kid.
cabridet m. yearling.
cabriolé m. cabriolet.
cabrit m. kid.

cabuda f. content, space, capacity.

cabussada f. plunge, ducking, dive.

cabussar tr. to plunge, dip, duck.

caça f. hunt, game, chase.

caçador -a m.- f. hunter.

caçar tr. to hunt.

cacau m. cocoa, cacao.

cacauet m. peanut.

cacera f. hunting.

cada a. each / pron. every.

cadafal m. scaffold, catafalque.

cadàver m. corpse.

cadell m. puppy, whelp.

cadena f. chain.

cadenat m. padlock.

cadernera f. goldfinch.

cadira f. chair.

cadiraire m. chairmaker.

caduc -a a. decrepit/deciduous.

caducar intr. to decay / to be worn out by service / to fall into disuse/ to lapse.

cafè m. coffee / (place) café.

cafetera f. coffee-pot.

cagalló m. excrement

caiguda f. fall.

caire m. intersection / sight, look, aspect.

caixa f. box / cashdesk.

caixa (moneda) f. cash.

caixer m. cashier.

caixó m. drawer.

calaix m. drawer.

calaixera f. chest of drawers.

calamarsa f. hail.

calamarsejar intr. to hail.

calamitat f. disaster, calamity.

calavera f. skull.

calb -a a. bald.

calç m. whitewash.

calçada f. roadway, highway, causeway.

calçat m. footwear.

calces f. pl. woman's panties.

calçotets m. pl. pants, underpants (US).

càlcul m. calculation.

calcular tr. to calculate.

caldera f. cauldron / boiler.

caldre tr. to be necessary.

caler tr. to be necessary

calefacció f. heating.

calendari m. calendar.

calent -a a. hot / warm.

calfred m. shiver, chill.

càlid -a a. warm.

caliu m. cinders, ashes.

callar intr. to keep quiet

cal·lígraf m. scribe.

calma f. calm.

calor f. warmth / heat.

calúmnia f. slander.

calumniar tr. to slander.

calvície f. baldness.

calze m. chalice / (bot.) calyx.

cama f. leg.

camàlic m. porter, carrier.

camamilla f. camomile.

camarada m. comrade.

cambra f. chamber, room.

cambra de bany f. bathroom.

cambrer m. waiter, steward.

cambrera f. waitress, stewardess.

camell -a m.- f. camel.

càmfora f. camphor.

camí m. path.

caminada f. walk, hike, tramp, walking trip.

caminant m. walker, hiker.

caminar intr. to walk, step, go.

camió m. lorry, truck.

camioneta f. van.

camisa f. shirt.

camp m. field.

campament m. camp.

campana f. bell.

campanar m. belfry.

camperol m. peasant, countryman, farmer.

campió -ona a. champion.

campionat m. championship.
camús -usa a. flat, flat-nosed.
canal m. channel, canal.
cancel·lar tr. to cancel / to invalidate / to annul.
canceller m. chancellor.
càncer m. cancer.
cançó f. song.
candela f. candle, taper.
càndid -a a. candid.
canell m. wrist.
canella f. water pipe.
canelobre m. candlestick.
canera f. kennel.
canó m. gun, cannon.
cànon m. canon, ecclesiastical rule or law.
canonada (conducció) f. wastepipe, water, drainpipe.
canonge m. canon, clerical dignitary.
cansalada f. bacon.
cansalader m. pork seller, porkbutcher.
cansament m. fatigue, tiredness.
cansar tr. to tire.
cansar-se pr. v. to tire, get tired.
cansat- ada a. tired, weary.
cant m. song, chant, singing.
cantaire a. m.-f. singer.
cantant s. singer.
cantar tr. – intr. to sing.
cantell m. brim / edge, border.
càntic m. chant.
cantimplora f. water bottle.
càntir m. pitcher, jug.
cantó m. corner.
cantonada f. corner.
canvi m. change, exchange.
canviable a. changeable, exchangeable.
canviar tr. to change, exchange.
canya f. reed.
canyella f. cinnamon.
canyella (cama) f. shinbone
caos m. chaos.
cap m. head / (geog.) cape.

capa f. cloak, mantle, cape / layer, cover / coat / stratum.
capaç m. capable.
capacitar tr. to enable.
capacitat f. capacity.
capatàs m. foreman.
capbussada f. ducking, dive, diving.
capcinejar intr. to nod.
capell m. hat.
capella f. chapel.
capellà m. chaplain, priest, clergyman, parson.
capgirar tr. to invert, turn upside down.
capgirat -ada a. upside down.
cap-gros m. tadpole, pollywog (Am.).
capir tr. to understand, comprehend.
capità m. captain, chieftain.
capital m. capital.
capitell m. capital of a column or pilaster / spire over the dome of a church.
capítol m. chapter.
capitost m. chief, leader.
capó m. castrated, gelded animal / chicken.
capoll m. (bot.) bud / pupa, chrysalis.
caprici m. fancy, whim, caprice.
capriciós -osa a. fanciful, whimsical, capricious.
capsa f. box.
captaire m. beggar.
captar tr. to beg.
capteniment m. behaviour.
captenir-se pr. v. to behave.
captiu -iva a. captive.
captivitat f. captivity.
captura f. capture.
capturar tr. to capture.
capvestre m. twilight, dusk, evening.

caqui a. khaki.
car -a. expensive, dear.
cara f. face.
caràcter m. character.
caramel m. sweet / caramel.
caravana f. caravan.
carbassa f. pumpkin, gourd.
carbó (mineral) m. coal / (vegetal) charcoal.
carboni m. carbon.
carcanada f. caparison, / skeleton.
carceller m. jailer, gaoler.
careta f. mask.
cargol m. snail / (mec.) screw, bolt.
cargolar tr. to screw, wind up.
caricatura f. cartoon, caricature.
carícia f. caress.
caritat f. charity.
carmesí -ina a. crimson.
carmí m. rouge
carn f. flesh, meat.
carnatge m. carnage.
carnet m. card / identity card.
carnisser -a s. butcher.
carnisseria f. slaughterhouse / butcher's shop / massacre.
carpeta f. file.
càrrec m. load / charge / office, position.
carregar tr. to charge / to burden, load.
càrrega f. cargo / charge / load, burden.
carrer m. street.
carrera f. race, course / racetrack / career, profession.
carreró m. narrow street, lane, alley.
carret m. trolley, tea trolley.
carreter m. wheelwright.
carretera f. road, highway.
carril m. rail / lane (on a motorway, etc.).

carro m. cart, wagon / (blindat) armoured car / chariot.
carta f. letter.
cartell m. poster.
carter m. postman.
cartera f. wallet / portfolio.
cartipàs m. memorandum book, notebook, writing book.
cartró m. cardboard.
carxofa f. artichoke.
cas m. case.
casa f. house.
casal m. mansion.
casament m. marriage.
casar tr. to marry, join, match.
casar-se pr. v. to marry.
casat -ada a. married.
cascada f. waterfall, fall, cataract, cascade.
caserna f. barrack.
casolà -ana a. home-loving / domestic / home-made.
caspa f. dandruff.
casquet m. helmet / skullcap, cap / cap, bonnet.
cassola f. pan, saucepan.
castany -a (color) a. chestnut, auburn, brown.
castanya f. chestnut.
castanyer m. chestnut tree.
castanyoles f. pl. castanets.
castedat f. chastity.
castell m. castle.
castellà -ana a. Castilian.
càstig m. punishment, penalty.
castigar tr. to punish.
castor m. beaver.
casual a. occasional / casual, unforseen.
casualitat f. chance, accident / coincidence.
casualment adv. by chance, accident or coincidence.
català -ana a. Catalan.
catàleg m. catalogue.
cataplasma f. poultice
catecisme m. catechism, instruc-

tion in the principles of Christianity.

càtedra f. seat or chair of a professor / professorship.

catedral f. cathedral.

categoria f. category, class, standing, status, grade.

catifa f. carpet.

catòlic -a a. Catholic.

catolicisme m. Catholicism.

catorze a. m. fourteen.

catorzè-ena a. m.- f. fourteenth.

cau m. lair.

caució f. pledge / caution.

caure intr. to fall, drop.

causa f. cause, reason, sake.

causar tr. to cause.

caut-a a. cautious, wary, prudent.

cautelós -osa a. wary, cautious.

cautelosament adv. cautiously, gingerly.

cautxú m. rubber.

cavalcada f. parade, pageant.

cavalcar intr. to ride, mount

cavall m. horse.

cavaller m. gentleman / horseman / knight.

cavalleria (institució) f. chivalry / (mil.) cavalry.

cavallets m. pl. merry-go-round.

cavar tr. to dig.

càvec m. hoe.

ceba f. onion.

cec -cega a. blind, sightless.

cedir tr. - intr. to hand over, give up / to give way.

cèdula f. certificate / order / warrant.

ceguesa f. blindness.

cel m. heaven, sky.

celebrar tr. to celebrate / to hold (a meeting, etc.).

cèlebre a. famous, celebrated, well-known.

celebritat f. fame / celebrity.

celestial a. celestial, heavenly.

cella f. eyebrow, brow.

cel·la f. cell.

celler m. cellar.

cementiri m. cementery, graveyard.

cendra f. cinders, ashes.

censura f. censorship / rebuke.

cent a. / m. hundred.

cent-ena a. / m.- f. hundredth

centelleig m. sparkle.

centellejar intr. to sparkle, twinkle.

centenar a. i m. hundred.

centèsim -a a. hundredth.

cèntim m. centime.

centímetre m. centimetre.

central a. central.

centre m. middle, centre, core / (US) center.

centúria f. century.

cenyidor m. girdle.

cenyir tr. to gird, bind round / to pull in, tighten / ... **el cinturó** (fig.) to tighten one's belt.

cep m. vine.

ceptre m. sceptre.

cera f. wax.

ceràmica f. ceramics, pottery.

cercar tr. to look for, search for.

cerclar tr. to enclose.

cercle m. circle.

cèrcol m. hoop.

cereal m. cereal.

cerilla f. match.

cerimònia f. ceremony.

cerimoniós -osa a. formal, ceremonious.

cert -a a. certain, sure, true.

certament adv. certainly, surely.

certificar tr. to certify / to register (a letter).

certificat m. certificate / **-ada** a. registered.

cervell m. brain.

cervesa f. beer.

cervesa (clara) f. ale.

cerveser m. brewer / beerseller.
cervo m. deer.
cérvol m. deer.
cérvola f. hind.
cicatriu f. scar.
ciència f. science.
científic-a a. scientific / m.-f. scientist.
cigar m. cigar.
cigarret -a m.- f. cigarette.
cigne m. swan.
cigonya f. stork.
cigró m. chickpea.
cilindre m. cylinder.
cim m. summit.
cimal m. peak, summit.
ciment m. cement.
cinc a. / m. five.
cinema m. cinema, pictures, movies (Am.).
cingle m. precipice.
cinquanta a. / m. fifty.
cinquantè-ena a. / m.-f. fiftieth.
cinquè-ena a. / m.-f. fifth.
cinta f. tape, ribbon / ...mètrica f. tape measure.
cintura f. waist.
cinturó m. belt.
cinyell m. belt / waist.
circ m. circus.
circuit m. circuit.
circulació f. circulation.
circular intr. circulate.
circumdant a. surrounding.
circumferència f. circumference.
circumstància f. circumstance.
cirera f. cherry.
cirugia f. surgery.
cirurgià m. surgeon.
cisellar tr. to carve.
cisma m. schism.
cistell m. basket.
cistella f. hamper.
cita f. appointment, rendez-vous / citation, quotation.
citació f. quotation, quote / summons.

citar tr. to cite, quote.
cítara f. zither.
ciutadà m. citizen.
ciutadans m. pl. citizens, townsfolk, townspeople.
ciutat f. city, town.
civada f. oats.
civilització f. civilization.
clam m. clamour, scream, plaint, knell.
clandestí -ina a. clandestine, underground, undercover.
clar -a a. clear / light (colour).
classe f. class.
classificar tr. to classify.
clatell m. nape.
clau f. key / cipher/nail.
clau (anglesa) f. wrench.
claustre m. cloister.
clavar tr. to hammer, nail.
claveguera f. sewer.
clavell m. carnation.
clavetaire m. nailer.
clemència f. forgiveness, clemency.
clericat m. clergy.
client -a m.- f. customer, client.
clima m. climate.
clímax m. climax.
clínica f. clinic, private hospital.
clofolla f. shell (of nuts).
clos m. hedge.
closca f. peel / shell.
clot m. pit, depression / grave / hole in ground for planting trees, etc.
cloure tr. to close, shut up, lock.
coagular tr. to coagulate.
cobdícia f. covetousness, cupidity.
cobejós -osa a. covetous, greedy.
cobert m. shed / hangar.
coberta f. cover.
coberta (d'un vaixell) f. deck.
cobertor m. wrap.

cobrador m. bus conductor, fare collector.

cobrar tr. to gain, obtain, earn, collect / to charge / to recover.

cobrellit m. quilt.

cobrir tr. to cover up, to coat, face / wrap up.

coca f. cake, sponge / tart.

codi m. code, digest.

codony m. quince.

codonyer m. quince tree.

coet m. rocket.

còfia f. white cap

cognom m. surname.

col m. hammock.

coincidir intr. to coincide, meet.

coïssor f. smart, sharp pain.

coix -a a. lame, limping.

coixejar intr. to limp, hobble.

coixesa f. lameness, limping.

coixí m. pillow, bolster / pad.

coixinet (mec.) m. bearing.

col f. cabbage.

còlera m. cholera / f. indignation, rage.

colgar tr. to cover, conceal / to inter, bury.

coll m. neck / throat.

coll (de la camisa, vestit) m. collar.

colla f. gang.

col·laborar intr. to collaborate.

collaret m. necklace.

col·lecció f. collection, set.

col·lega m.- f. colleague.

col·legi m. school / college.

col·lidir intr. to collide.

collir tr. to crop, harvest.

collita f. crop, harvest.

col·locació f. employment.

col·locar tr. to place, site / employ, dispose.

col·loqui m. colloquy, conversation, talk.

colom m. pigeon.

colomar m. pigeonhouse.

còlon (anat.) m. colon.

colònia f. colony.

colonitzador a. colonizing / m. colonist, pioneer, settler.

colonitzar tr. to colonize, settle.

color m. colour.

colpejar tr. to beat.

colpir tr. to beat, strike, hit, knock.

colrat -ada a. tannned

coltell m. knife.

columna f. column.

colze m. elbow.

com adv. how / as, like.

coma f. (gram.) comma / (med.) coma.

comanda f. order, command.

comarca f. region, area.

combat m. fight, combat / match.

combatre intr. to combat, fight.

combinació f. combination.

combinar tr. to combine.

combustible m. fuel, combustible.

comèdia f. comedy.

començament m. beginning, start.

començar tr. to begin, start.

comentar tr. to comment.

comerç m. commerce, trade.

comerciant m. merchant, trader.

comestible a. edible, eatable.

cometes f. pl. quotation marks, inverted commas.

comiat m. farewell, leave-taking.

còmic m. comedian / comic.

commoure tr. to move, effect / to disturb.

commovedor -a a. touching, moving / soulful.

còmode -a a. comfortable.

commutador m. switch

comoditat f. ease, comfort.

compacte -a a. compact, tight.

compadir-se pr. v. to pity.

company m. companion, fellow, mate, comrade.

companya f. mate, comrade.

companyia f. company.

companyonia f. companionship.

comparació f. comparison.

compartir tr. to share.

compassió f. compassion, pity.

compassiu -iva a, merciful, compassionate, a compassionate person.

compatriota m. -f. fellow-countryman, compatriot.

compendi m. compendium.

compensació f. compensation / offset / recompense.

compensar tr. to compensate / to repay, offset.

competència f. competence.

competent a. competent, capable.

competició f. competition.

complaure tr. to please.

complement m. complement.

complet -a a. whole, complete, utter, entire, thorough.

completament adv. completely, absolutely.

completar tr. to complete.

complex -a a. complex.

complicar tr. to complicate.

complidor -a a. diligent, observant.

complir tr. to accomplish / to honour (a debt, obligation, etc.).

compliment m. compliment, courtesy.

compondre tr. to compose, compound / to construct.

comporta f. sluice / hatch.

composició f. composition.

compost -a a. compound.

compra f. purchase.

comprador -a m. -f. purchaser, buyer.

comprar tr. to purchase, buy.

comprendre tr. to comprehend, understand / to include, embrace.

comprensió f. understanding, comprehension.

comprensiu -iva a. comprehensive / sympathetic.

comprometre tr. to compromise / engage.

compromís m. engagement.

comprovant m. receipt / voucher.

comptabilitat f. accountancy, book-keeping.

comptable m. accountant.

comptador m. meter / computer.

comptar tr. to count, reckon.

compte m. account.

computador m. computer.

comtat m. county / earldom.

comte m. earl, count.

comtessa f. countess.

comú -una m. common.

comunicació f. communication.

comunicar tr. to communicate.

comunió f. communion.

comunisme m. communism.

comunitat f. community.

concedir tr. to award / to grant, concede.

concentració f. concentration / rally.

concentrar tr. to concentrate.

concepte m. concept.

concernir tr. to concern.

concert m. concert.

concessió f. grant, concession.

concili m. council.

conciliar tr. to conciliate.

concloure tr. to conclude, finish.

concòrdia f. concord, peace.

concórrer intr. to concur / to coincide.

concret -a a. concrete.

concretar tr. to make concrete or precise.

concurs m. concurrence / collaboration / competition, tournament.

condeixeble-a a. schoolfellow, schoolmate.

condemnar tr. to condemm.

condensar tr. to condense.

condició f. condition.

condiment m. relish, condiment.

condimentar tr. to flavour.

condol m. condolence.

conducció f. conveyance, carriage, transportation / leading.

conductor m. driver.

conduir tr. to drive, steer / convey.

coneixença f. knowledge / acquaintance.

conferència f. lecture / conference.

conèixer tr. to know.

confecció f. ready-made.

conferenciant m. lecturer, speaker.

confessar tr. to confess.

confessió f. confession.

confiança f. trust / credit / confidence, reliance, familiarity.

confiar tr. to trust, rely, confide.

confidència f. confidence, secret.

confinar tr. to bound, limit.

confirmar tr. to confirm, ratify.

confitar tr. to candy / to preserve in syrup.

confitura f. jam.

conflagració f. conflagration, fire.

conflicte m. conflict.

confondre tr. to confuse.

conformitat f. agreement, conformity / resignation.

confusió f. confusion / misunderstanding.

congelar tr. to freeze.

congesta f. glaciar.

congost m. gap (between mountains).

congratulació f. congratulation.

congrés m. congress.

conhort m. comfort, consolation.

conhortar tr. to console, comfort.

conill m. rabbit.

conillera f. warren.

cònjuge s. partner, mate, spouse.

conjunció f. joining, junction / (gram.) conjunction.

conjunt m. group / whole.

connectar tr. to connect, swich on.

connexió f. connexion, liaison.

conqueridor -a a. conquering / m. conqueror.

conquerir tr. to conquer.

conquesta f. conquest.

conrear tr. to cultivate, till, farm.

conreu m. cultivation, tillage / culture of the mind.

consagrar tr. to hallow, consecrate.

consciència f. conscience.

conscient a. aware, conscious.

consegüent a. consequent.

consell m. counsel, advice / (adm.) council.

conseller m. adviser, consultant / counsellor.

consentir tr.-intr. to consent, agree / to tolerate, comply.

conseqüència f. consequence.

conserge m. porter / caretaker.

conserva f. jam, preserve.

conservació f. upkeep, maintenance, conservation.

conservar tr. to conserve, preserve.

consideració f. consideration, regard.

considerant conj. whereas.

considerar tr. to consider, reckon, regard / to look at.

consistir intr. to consist.

consoci -òcia m.- f. partner, associate.

consol m. consolation, comfort.

consolador -a a. consoler, comforter.

consolar tr. to console, comfort.

consolidar tr. to consolidate, strengthen.

consonant a. / f. consonant.

conspiració f. conspiracy, plot.

conspirador m. plotter, conspirator.

conspirar intr. to plot, conspire, contrive.

constant a. steady, constant.

consternació f. dismay, consternation.

constipat m. cold, catarrh.

constituir tr. to constitute.

constrènyer tr. to compel, urge.

construir tr. to build, construct.

consum m. consumption.

consumidor -a a. / m.-f. consumer / destroyer.

contagi m. contagion, infection.

contagiar tr. to infect.

contagiós -osa a. contagious, infectious.

contalla f. tale.

contaminar tr. to contaminate, pollute.

contar tr. to recount, tell.

conte m. story, tale.

contemplar tr. to behold, contemplate.

contemporitzar intr. to temporize.

contenir tr. to contain.

content -a a. glad, content, merry, joyful, happy.

contesa f. contest, contention, fight.

contesta f. answer, response.

contestació f. answer, response.

contestar tr. / intr. to answer, reply.

continent m. mainland, continent.

contingent m. quota, contingent.

continu -ínua a. continuous.

continuar tr. continue.

contra prep. against, opposite to / versus.

contraban m. smuggling, contraband.

contrabandista m. smuggler.

contractar tr. to engage.

contracte m. contract, agreement.

contrafort m. (Arch.) buttress / wadding.

contrapunt (mus.) m. counterpoint.

contrari -ària m. contrary, opposed, antagonistic / **al ...**, on the contrary.

contrarietat f. misfortune / annoyance.

contrast m. contrast / opposition.

contreure tr. to contract.

contribució f. contribution.

contribuir intr. to contribute.

control m. control.

convèncer tr. to convince.

conveni m. agreement, covenant.

conveniència f. convenience, fitness.

convenient a. convenient / appropriate, suitable, opportune.

convenir tr. to agree.
convent m. monastery / (de monges) convent, nunnery.
conversa f. chat, talk, conversation.
conversar intr. to chat, talk, converse.
convertir tr. to convert.
convidar tr: to invite.
convit m. invitation.
conyac m. brandy.
cooperar tr. to cooperate.
coordinar tr. to coordinate.
cop m. blow, stroke, hit, knock.
copa f. cup, goblet.
copalta m. top-hat.
copejar tr. to hit, beat, bash, batter.
còpia f. copy.
copiar tr. to copy.
coquineria f. cowardice / niggardliness, meaness
cor m. heart.
coratge m. courage, pluck, valour.
coratjós -osa a. courageous.
corb m. raven.
corba f. curve.
corbata f. tie, necktie.
corc m. woodworm.
corcar tr. to gnaw, corrode / to decay.
corda f. rope, cord / (mus.) string / spring (of watch).
cordar tr. to button up / to string.
cordial a. hearty, cordial.
cordialment adv. heartily, cordially.
cordill m. cord.
cordó m. cord, lace, string.
corn m. horn.
cornamusa f. cornemuse, bagpipe.
cornamusaire m. bagpiper.
cornella·f. rook.
corneta f. cornet.

corona f. crown.
coronel m. colonel.
corral m. farmyard, yard.
correctament adv. correctly.
correcte -a a. correct, right / accurate.
corredissa f. dispersal.
corredor -a m.-f. runner , m. corridor.
corregir tr. to correct / to mend.
corrent m. current, stream, drift.
córrer intr. to run / to travel over.
correspondència f. correspondence, mail.
correspondre intr. to correspond / to requite.
corresponsal m. correspondent.
corretja f. strap.
correu m. mail, post.
corriol m. path, lane.
corriola f. pulley.
corroborar tr. to corroborate.
corrompre tr. to corrupt.
corrua f. row, line.
corrupció f. corruption.
corsari m. corsair, pirate.
corsecar tr. to dry thoroughly.
cortès -esa a. polite, courteous.
cortesà -ana m. -f. courtier.
cortesia f. courtesy, politeness, graciousness.
cortina f. curtain.
cos m. body.
cosa f. thing.
cosí -ina m. i f. cousin.
cosir tr. to sew.
cost m. cost.
costa f. coast, seaboard.
costar tr. to cost.
costat m. side.
costella f. rib.
costós -osa a. expensive.
costum m. custom, habit, usage.

costura f. seam.
cotització f. quotation.
cotó m. cotton.
cotó fluix m. cotton-wool.
cotxe m. car.
cotxe (de cavalls) m. cab.
cotxer m. cabman.
coure m. copper.
coure tr. to cook / to smart.
coure (en el forn) tr. to bake.
cova f. cave.
coval m. small cave.
covar tr. to hatch, incubate.
covard-a a.t.m. -f. coward.
covardia f. cowardice.
cove m. bread basket.
cranc (de riu) m. crawfish, crayfish.
cranc (verd o de mar) m. crab.
crani m. skull.
creació f. creation.
creador m. creator, maker.
crear tr. to create.
crèdit m. credit / a ..., on loan.
crit m. shout, cry, scream, yell, shriek.
crit (d'ase) m. bellow.
creditor -a m. -f. creditor.
creença f. belief.
créixer tr. to grow, thrive.
crema f. cream, custard.
cremar intr. to burn.
crepuscle m. twilight, dusk.
cresta f. comb, crest, tuft / crest, top, summit.
creu f. cross.
creuar tr. to cross.
creuer m. cruise / (mil.) cruiser.
creure tr. to believe.
cria f. breeding.
criar tr. to breed, raise, rear.
criat m. servant.
criatura f. creature / baby, infant, child.
criatures f. pl. children / creatures.

cric m. (mec.) jack.
crida f. call.
cridar intr. to call, cry.
crim m. crime.
crinera f. mane.
cripta f. crypt, vault.
cristall m. crystal.
cristià -ana a. Christian.
crítica f. criticism.
criticar tr. to criticize.
croada f. crusade.
crònica f. chronicle.
croquis m. sketch.
crossa f. crutch / walking stick, staff.
crosta f. crust. / bark / peel, skin.
cru-crua a. raw.
crucifix m. crucifix, rood.
crucigrama m. crossword.
cruel a. cruel, merciless, ruthless.
crueltat f. cruelty, ruthlessness.
cruixir intr. to crunch / creak / rustle.
cruixit m. creack.
crustaci m. crustacean.
cua f. tail / queue.
cubell m. large earthen jar / vat, dyer's copper / tub.
cuc m. worm.
cucurull m. cornet.
cucurutxo m. cornet.
cucut m. cuckoo.
cugula f. weed.
cuina f. kitchen / cooker, stove.
cuinar intr. to cook.
cuiner -a m.-f. cook.
cuir m. leather, hide.
cuirassa f. armour.
cuixa f. thigh.
cullera f. spoon, tablespoon.
cullerada f. spoonful, ladleful.
cullereta f. teaspoon.
cullerot m. ladle.
culpa f. fault, blame, guilt.

culpabilitat f. guilt.
culpable a. guilty.
cultiu m. cultivated land.
cultivar tr. to cultivate.
cultura f. culture.
cunyat -ada m.-f. brother-in-law / sister-in-law.
cúpula f. dome.
cuquet m. mite.
cura f. care.
curar tr. to look after, treat, care for / to propose.
curiós -osa a. curiously.
curiosament adv. curiously
curosament adv. carefully
curs m. course, term / way, current.
cursa f. race, course, running.
curt -a a. short.
curull -a a. full, filled, heaped.
cúspide f. summit.
custodiar tr. to keep, guard.

D

dada f. datum, fact / admitted truth.
daga f. dagger.
dàlia f. dahlia.
dalla f. scythe.
dalt adv. up, on top.
damisel·la f. miss.
dama f. dame, lady, gentlewoman.
damnar tr. to damn / to defame.
damnat -ada m. -f. damned.
damunt prep. above, on, upon.
dansa f. dance.
dansaire m. -f. dancer.
dany m. damage, harm.
dard m. dart.
darrer -a a. last, latter / latest.

darrera adv. - prep. back / behind.
darrerament adv. lately.
dàrsena f. dock, wharf / basin.
data f. date.
dàtil m. date (fruit).
dau m. dice, die.
daurat -ada a. golden, gilt / f. (icht.) goldfish.
davall adv. - prep. beneath.
davallada f. descent.
davallar intr. to descend.
davant adv. in front, before.
davantal m. apron.
davanter -a a. forward.
de prep. of / from.
debanador -a a. / m. -f. winder, spool, quill, reel.
debanar tr. to reel, spool, wind.
debatre tr. to argue, discuss, debate.
dèbil a. weak, feeble, faint.
debilitar tr. to weaken.
debilitat f. frailty, weakness.
debut m. debut.
decadència f. decline, decay, decadence.
decaigut -uda a. haggard.
decantar tr. to decant / to incline, tilt.
decapitar tr. to behead.
decaure intr. to decay / decline / languish.
decència f. decency.
decent a. decent.
decepció f. disappointment.
decidir tr. to decide.
decidit -ida a. decided, determined, resolute.
decisió f. decision, determination.
decisiu -iva a. decisive.
declaració f. declaration.
declarar tr. to declare.
declinació f. decline / declension.
declinar tr. to decline.

declivi m. ramp, declivity.
decomís m. confiscation.
decoració f. decoration / scenery, set.
decorar tr. to decorate.
decret m. decree.
dèdal m. labyrinth, maze.
dedicar tr. to dedicate.
deduir tr. tó to deduce.
deessa f. goddess.
defalliment m. languor / dejection of mind / swoon.
defallir intr. to weaken.
defecte m. defect, fault, flaw / vice.
defectuós -osa a. defective.
defensa f. defence.
defensar tr. to defend, shield.
definició f. definition.
definir tr. to define.
definitiu -iva a. definitive.
deforme a. shapeless / deformed.
defugir tr. to shirk.
defunció f. decease.
degà m. dean, senior.
degotar intr. to drip, leak.
degudament adv. properly, duly.
degut -uda a. due.
deixalla f. scrap.
deixalles f. pl. refuse, rubbish, waste.
deixar tr. to leave / to lend.
deixatar tr. to dissolve.
deixeble m. disciple, follower.
deixies f. pl. litter.
dejú -una a. fasting.
dejunar intr. to fast.
delatar tr. to report (a crime) / to betray (a secret).
delectar tr. to delight.
deler m. desire, yearning, wish.
deliberar tr. to deliberate.
delicadesa f. delicacy.
delicat -ada a. delicate.
delícia f. delight.

delirar intr. to rave.
deliri m. delirium / nonsense.
delmar tr. to decimate.
demà adv. tomorrow / ...passat the day after tomorrow.
demanar tr. to ask for, beg, solicit / to crave.
demanda f. demand.
demandar tr. to demand, request.
democràcia f. democracy.
demolir tr. to demolish / to throw down.
demostració f. demonstration, display, show.
demostrar tr. to demonstrate.
dempeus adv. upright, standing.
denegació f. denial, refusal.
dens -a a. dense.
densitat f. density.
dent f. tooth / cog.
dentat -ada a. toothed, dentate.
dentició f. teething.
denúncia f. denunciation / accusation.
departament m. department, division.
dependent a. / m. dependent, subordinate / employee, clerk.
dependre intr. to depend.
deplorar tr. to lament, wail.
depressió f. depression.
deprimir tr. to depress.
derivar intr. to derive.
derogar tr. to repeal.
derrota f. defeat, rout.
desaflament m. challenge.
desafiar tr. to challenge, defy.
desagradable a. unpleasant.
desagraït -ïda a. ungrateful.
desallotjar tr. - intr. to dislodge / to move out.
desaparèixer intr. to vanish, disappear.
desarrelar tr. to uproot.
desastre m. disaster.

desatenció f. inattention, disregard.

desavantatge m. disadvantage, handicap.

desavinença f. misunderstanding.

descalç -a a. barefooted.

descans m. rest, break.

descansar tr. to rest, repose.

descaradura f. cheekiness, sauciness, insolence.

descarat -ada a. impudent, insolent, saucy.

descàrrec m. exoneration, discharge, acquittal.

descarregar tr. to discharge / unload.

descendència f. offspring, descent / descendants.

descendir tr. - intr. to descend.

descens m. fall, descent.

descobriment m. detection, discovery.

descobrir tr. to discover, detect / to reveal.

descofat -ada a. bareheaded.

descolorit -ida a. wan / discoloured, faded.

descompte m. discount.

desconcert m. bewilderment.

desconcertat tr. to baffle, bewilder.

desconeixedor-a a. unaware, ignorant.

desconèixer tr. to ignore.

desconfiança f. distrust, mistrust.

desconnectar tr. to disconnect, switch off.

descoratjar tr. to discourage, daunt, frighten.

descordar tr. to unclasp, unbutton.

descortès -esa a. impolite, rude.

descosir tr. to unpick.

descregut -uda a. godless, unbelieving.

descripció f. description.

descriure tr. to describe.

descuidar-se v. pr. to forget, leave behind.

descuit m. negligence / forgetfulness, carelessness.

descurat -ada a. careless, mindless.

des de prep. phr. since.

desdeny m. disdain, scorn.

desdenyós -osa a. scornful, disdainful, contemptuous.

desè -ena a / m. -f. tenth.

deseixir-se pr. v. to get rid of.

desembarcador m. quay, jetty.

desembarcar tr. to land, disembark.

desembocar intr. to flow into, meet, lead into.

desembre m. December.

desena f. group of ten.

desencís m. disenchantment, disillusionment.

desencolat -ada a. unglued, unstuck.

desenganxat -ada a. unglued, unstuck.

desenrotllar tr. to unroll, unwind.

desenterrar tr. to unearth, dig up.

desenvolupament m. development.

desenvolupar tr. to develop.

desert -a a. desert / deserted / void (prize, etc.).

desertar tr. to desert.

desesper m. despair.

desesperació f. despair.

desesperar tr. to despair.

desesperat -ada a. desperate, hopeless / despairing.

desfer tr. to undo, unmake.

desferra f. plunder / debris.

desfeta f. defeat.

desfici m. uneasiness

desfigurar tr. to disfigure, distort.

desfilada f. parade, pageant.

29

desfullar tr. to strip off the leaves.

desglaç m. thaw.

desglaçar tr. to thaw.

desgràcia f. misfortune, disaster / disgrace / distress.

desgraciat -ada a. unfortunate, unlucky / indigent, in need.

desgrat m. discontent, displeasure.

desguarnir tr. to strip down / to unharness / to remove the garrison from.

desguarnit-ida a. unguarded.

desguassar tr. - intr. to drain, empty / to flow.

deshonor m. shame, dishonour.

desídia f. indolence.

desig m. desire, wish, thirst.

designar tr. to designate.

designi m. design.

desigual a. unlike, unequal.

desil·lusió f. disillusion, want, wish.

desil·lusionar tr. to disillusion, disappoint, let down

desistir intr. to desist, stop.

desitjable a. desirable.

desitjar tr. to desire, want, wish / to long for.

deslletar tr. to wean.

deslligar tr. to loosen, undo.

deslliurar tr. to free, liberate.

deslluir tr. to tarnish, dull, discolour.

desmai m. faint, swoon.

desmesurat -ada a. untold, beyond measure.

desnatar tr. to skim (milk).

desnivell m. slope.

desobeir tr. to disobey.

desordenat -ada a. untidy / disorderly.

desordre m. disorder, confusion, turmoil.

despatx m. office / dispatch.

despatxar tr. to dismiss / to attend to / to dispatch.

despectiu -iva a. contemptuous, scornful, disdainful.

despendre tr. to use up / to spend.

despenjar tr. to take down.

despentinat -ada a. unkempt, dishevelled.

despertador m. alarm clock.

despertar tr. to awaken, wake up.

despesa f. expenditure, expense.

despietat -ada f. pitiless, merciless.

despit m. spite, rancour, indignation, irritation, annoyance.

desplaçar tr. to displace.

desplaçar-se pr. v. to move, shift.

desplaure intr. to displease.

desplegar tr. to display / to deploy, unfold.

desposseir tr. to dispossess, deprive.

despreocupat -ada a. unworried, happy-go-lucky.

després prep. after, adv. afterwards.

després -esa a. generous.

despullar tr. to strip, undress.

despullat -ada a. bare, naked.

dessobre adv. above, over / at the top / overhead / over and above / besides.

dessota adv. under, below.

destacar tr. to detach / to stand out.

destacat -ada a. outstanding.

destapar tr. to uncover.

destí m. fate, destiny / destination.

destil·lar tr. to distil.

destorb m. impediment, hindrance, obstruction / nuisance.

destorbar tr. to obstruct, hinder.

destral f. hatchet, axe.

destre -a a. dexterous, skilful.

destresa f. dexterity, skill, expertise.

destret m. jam, difficulty.

destrucció f. destruction, havoc.

destruir tr. to destroy, to undo.

desvalgut -uda a. helpless.

desvariejar intr. to rave.

desvergonyiment m. cheek, sauciness.

desvergonyit -ida a. impudent, saucy, cheeky.

desvestir tr. strip, undress.

desvetllar tr. to awake, wake / rouse, arouse.

desviar tr. to turn aside / to deflect, divert.

desxifrar tr. to decipher, make out.

detall m. detail.

detectiu m. detective.

detenció f. arrest / stop.

deterioració f. deterioration, decline.

determinació f. determination.

determinar tr. to determine, decide, settle, fix.

Déu m. God.

deu a. / m. ten.

deu f. fountain, source.

deure m. duty, obligation.

deure tr. to owe.

deures (treballs escolars) m. pl. homework.

deute m. debt.

deutor -a a. / m.-f. debtor.

devastar tr. to devastate, to lay waste.

devers prep. towards.

dia m. day.

diabetis f. diabetes.

diable m. devil.

diabòlic -a a. devilish, diabolical.

diaca m. cuate, deacon.

diagnòstic-a a. diagnostic / m. diagnosis.

diagnosticar tr. to diagnose.

diagram m. diagram / chart.

dialecte m. dialect.

diàleg m. dialogue.

diamant m. diamond.

diàmetre m. diameter.

diari m. newspaper, daily / journal.

dibuix m. drawing, design.

dibuixar tr. to draw.

dic m. dyke, dam / dock.

dictador m. dictator.

dictar tr. to dictate.

dictat m. dictation.

diccionari m. dictionary.

dida f. wet-nurse.

didal m. thimble.

dietari m. diary.

difamació f. defamation, calumny, slander.

difamar tr. to defame, vilify, backbite.

difamatori -òria a. defamatory.

diferència f. difference.

diferenciar-se pr. v. to differ.

diferent a. different.

diferir tr. to defer, postpone / to differ.

difícil a. difficult, hard.

dificultat f. hardship, difficulty.

difondre tr. to diffuse.

difusió f. diffusion, spread.

digerir tr. - intr. to digest.

digestió f. digestion.

dignament adv. worthily.

digne -a a. worthy, deserving.

dignitat f. dignity.

dijous m. Thursday.

dilació f. delay.

dilapidar tr. to dilapidate.

dilatar tr. to dilate.

dilatar-se pr. v. to expand, dilate, swell.

31

diligent a. hard-working, diligent, industrious.

dilluns m. Monday.

diluvi m. deluge, flood.

dimarts m. Tuesday.

dimecres m. Wednesday.

dimensió f. dimension, size.

dimissió f. resignation.

dimitir tr. to resign.

dimoni m. demon.

dinàmic -a a. dynamic.

dinar m. lunch.

dinar intr. to have lunch.

diner m. currency, coin, money / wealth, fortune.

dinou a. / m. nineteen.

dinovè -ena a / m -f. nineteenth.

dins prep. - adv. inside.

dintre prep. - adv. inside, in, within.

diplomàcia f. diplomacy.

dipòsit m. deposit / store, storehouse warehouse, depot / reservoir.

dir tr. to say / to tell.

direcció f. direction / lead / administration.

directe -a a. direct.

director -a m. -f. director / manager, manageress.

director (de col·legi, etc.) m. headmaster.

director (d'orquestra) m. conductor.

director (d'una publicació) m. editor.

directora (de col·legi, etc.) f. headmistress.

dirigir tr. to conduct, lead, direct.

dirigir-se pr. v. to go towards / to address.

disbarat m. stupidity / blunder.

disbauxa f. unruliness, licentiousness / orgy.

disc m. disk / gramophone record, / (de telèfon) dial.

discerniment m. discernment, insight.

disciplina f. discipline.

discòrdia f. discord, disagreement, variance.

discrepar tr. to differ, disagree.

discret -a a. discrete / discreet, tactful.

disculpa f. apology.

discurs m. speech.

discussió f. argument, disagreement, quarrel, row.

discutir tr. to argue / to discuss, reason.

dissertació f. dissertation.

disfressa f. disguise.

disfressar tr. to disguise.

disminució f. diminishing, lessening, decrease.

disminuir tr. to diminish.

disparador m. trigger.

disparar tr. to shoot, fire.

dispesera f. hostess.

disponible a. available / vacant.

disposar tr. to dispose, prepare.

disputar tr. to dispute.

dissabte m. Saturday.

dissentiment m. dissent, disagreement.

dissentir tr. to dissent, disagree.

disseny m. design, sketch.

dissertació f. lecture / dissertation.

disset a. / m. seventeen.

dissetè -ena a. / m.-f. seventeenth.

dissimular tr. to conceal, hide / to dissimulate, disguise.

dissolvent a. / m. solvent.

dissort f. misadventure, misfortune, disaster.

dissortat -ada a. unlucky, unfortunate.

distància f. distance.

distinció f. distinction, refinement.

distingir tr. to distinguish.

distingir-se pr. v. to distinguish / to differ.

distint -a a. distinct.

distreure tr. to distract.

distribució f. distribution.

distribuïdor-a a. com. distributor / dealer.

distribuir tr. to distribute, share out / to deal out.

districte m. district.

dit m. finger / toe.

dita f. saying.

diumenge m. Sunday.

divendres m. Friday.

divergir intr. to diverge, differ.

divers-a a. diverse / pl. several, various.

diversificar tr. to diversify.

divertiment m. amusement, fun.

divertir tr. to amuse, have fun.

divertit -ida a. entertaining, amusing, funny.

diví -ina a. divine, godlike.

dividir tr. to divide, part.

divisa f. emblem, device / pl. foreign exchange.

divisió f. division.

divorci m. divorce.

divuit a. / m. eighteen.

divuitè-ena a. / m.-f. eighteenth.

doblar tr. to double.

doble a. double.

doblec m. crease, fold.

doblegar tr. to fold / to bend.

dòcil a. meek, docile.

docilitat f. docility / flexibility.

docte -a a. lettered.

doctor m. doctor.

doctrina f. doctrine.

documentació f. documentation / papers, documents.

dofí m. dolphin.

dol m. mourning.

dolç -a a. sweet.

dolcesa f. sweetness.

doldre intr. to ache, pain.

dolença f. aching, ache / disease.

dolent -a a. bad.

dolenteria f. badness, evilness.

doll m. fountain / jet, torrent, flow.

dolor s. pain, ache / distress.

dolorit -ida a. painful, aching, sore, tender.

dolorós -osa a. painful.

domar tr. to tame / to break in / to subdue.

domèstic -a a. domestic, household.

domesticar tr. to tame, master, domesticate.

domesticat -ada a. tame / pet.

domicili m. abode, home address.

dominació f. dominion, domination / mastery.

dominar tr. to dominate, rule / to repress / to master.

domini m. dominion, power, sway / mastery, command.

domtar s. domar.

dona f. woman.

donació f. donation, grant.

donar tr. to give / to donate.

donar (a entendre) tr. to mean.

donar (feina, ocupació) tr. to engage.

donar (escorta) tr. to escort.

donar nom tr. to term.

doncs prep. so, then, in that case.

donzella f. maid, lass.

dormint ger. asleep.

dormir intr. to sleep.

dormisquejar intr. to snooze.

dormitori m. bedroom.

dos -dues a. / m. -f. two.

dosser m. canopy, dais.

dot m. dowry.

dotació f. endowment.

dotze a. / m. twelve.
dotzè -ena a. / m. -f. twelfth.
dotzena f. dozen.
draga f. dredger.
dragar tr. to drag / to dredge.
dramaturg m. dramatist, playwright.
drap m. cloth / rag.
drapaire m. ragman.
drassana f. arsenal / rack for lances /shipyard.
dret m. law, justice.
dret-a a. m. just, lawful / a. standing, upright.
dring m. tinkle, jingle.
dringadissa f. tinkle.
droga f. drug, medicine.
dropo -a a. idle.
duana f. customs.
dubtar tr. doubt, to hesitate.
dubte m. doubt, misgiving, indecision / suspense.
dubtós -osa a. doubtful.
duc m. duke.
duplicat -ada a. duplicate, double.
duquessa f. duchess.
dur tr. to bring, fetch / to wear.
dur -a a. hard, harsh, tough / rude / stiff.
durant prep. during / for.
durar intr. to last.
duresa f. hardness, toughness.
duro m. five-peseta coin.
dutxa f. shower.
dutxar -se pr. v. to have a shower.

E

eben m. ebony.
ebenista m. cabinetmaker, carpenter.
ebenisteria f. cabinetmaking, woodwork / carpenter's.

ebri -èbria a. drunk, tipsy.
eburni -úrnia a. eburneous.
eclipsi m. eclipse.
eco m. echo.
economia f. economy / thrift.
edat f. age.
edició f. edition.
edicte m. edict, proclamation.
edificar tr. to build, construct / to edify.
edifici m. building.
editar tr. to publish, to edit.
editor -a a. / m. -f. publisher.
editorial (casa) f. publishing house.
edredó m. eiderdown.
educació f. education / breeding, manners.
educar tr. to educate / to bring up.
efecte m. effect.
efectiu -iva a. actual / effective / in cash.
efeminat m. effeminate.
efectuar tr. to carry out.
eficaç a. efficacious, effective, telling.
eficàcia f. efficacy, efficiency.
eficient a. efficient.
efimer -a a. ephemeral.
efusiu -iva a. effusive.
efusivament adv. warmly, effusively.
egoisme m. selfishness, egoism, egotism.
egoista a. egotistic, egotistical, selfish / m. egoist.
egregi -ègia a. eminent, distinguished.
egua f. mare.
eh? interj. interrog. eh? pardon?
eina f. tool, implement.
eix m. axle / axis.
eixam m. swarm, cluster.
eixamplar tr. to widen, expand, broaden, extend.
eixamplament m. expansion,

extension, widening, broadening / stretch.

eixarreït -ïda a. dry, dried up / barren.

eixida f. exit.

eixir intr. to go out, depart / grow, spring up / come forth.

eixorc-a a. barren.

eixordador -a a. deafening.

eixordar tr. to deafen / to grow deaf.

eixorivir tr. to awake, enliven, excite.

eixugar tr. to wipe, to dry.

eixut -a a. dry, dried up.

el art. m. sing. the / pron. pers. him, it.

elàstic-a a. elastic.

elàstics m. pl. suspenders.

elecció f. election / choice.

elector m. voter.

elèctric -a a. electric.

electricista m. electrician.

electricitat f. electricity.

elefant m. elephant.

elegància f. elegance, gracefulness / neatness.

elegant a. elegant, smart / fashionable.

elegir tr. to elect.

elemental a. elementary, elemental.

elevació f. height / elevation.

elevador m. hoist / lever.

elevar tr. to elevate / to edify.

elevat -ada a. lofty, high, elevated.

eliminar tr. to eliminate.

ell pron. m. he, him.

ella pron. f. she, her.

ells -elles pron. pl. they, them.

elogi m. eulogy, praise.

eloqüència f. eloquence.

els art. m. pl. the / pron. them.

eludir tr. to avoid, to shirk, to elude.

embadaliment m. reverie.

embadalir tr. to charm / to fascinate.

embafar tr. to pall on, cloy / to bore / to upset, sicken.

embalum m. bundle / parcel, package.

embaràs m. obstruction, nuisance / pregnancy.

embarassada f. pregnant.

embarcar tr. to embark, ship.

embassament m. reservoir, pond.

embenar tr. to bandage.

embenat m. bandage.

emblanquinar tr. to whiten.

emblanquir tr. to whiten.

èmbol m. plunger / piston.

embolcall m. wrapping.

embolic m. bundle / predicament, mess, pickle.

embolicar tr. to wrap / to envelop, enfold / to confuse.

embotir tr. to pack, stuff, cram.

embotit -ida a. inlaid work, marquetry / sausage.

embriac m. drunkard.

embriaguesa f. drunkenness / rapture.

embrió m. embryo.

embrollar tr. to muddle, complicate.

embruixar tr. to bewitch.

embrutar tr. to soil, dirty.

embullar tr. to entangle.

embussar tr. to jam, obstruct, block.

embut m. funnel.

emergir intr. to emerge.

emetre tr. to emit / to broadcast / to issue.

emigració f. emigration.

emigrar intr. to migrate, emigrate.

eminent a. high, eminent.

emissari m. emissary.

emissió f. issue / emission / broadcasting.

emmagatzemar tr. to store.
emmalaltir intr. to sicken.
emmanillar tr. to manacle, handcuff.
emmetzinar tr. to poison, envenom.
emmidonar tr. to starch.
emmordassar tr. to gag.
emmotllar tr. to mould.
emoció f. emotion, thrill.
emocionant a. thrilling, exciting, moving.
empaitar tr. to pursue, persecute.
empanada f. meat or fish pie (from Galicia).
empaquetar tr. to pack.
emparentar tr. to relate.
empastar tr. to paste / to fill (a tooth).
empedrar tr. to pave.
empedrat m. pavement.
empelt m. graft, grafting.
empeltar tr. to graft.
empenta f. jog, push, impulse.
empentejar tr. to jog, push.
empenya f. vamp.
empènyer tr. to push.
empenyorar tr. to pledge, vow.
emperador m. emperor.
empipar tr. to vex, irritate, anger / to displease.
empitjorar tr. to get worse, deteriorate.
empleat m. employee.
emportar-se pr. v. to take away, carry off.
empolsegat -ada a. dusty.
empostissat m. parquetry, inlaid floor.
emprar tr. to use, employ.
empremta f. print, trace.
emprendre tr. to undertake.
empresa f. enterprise, firm, company.
empresari m. manager, contractor.

empresonar tr. to imprison.
empresonat m. prisoner.
emprèstit m. loan.
empunyadura f. hilt, handle.
en prep. in, into, on, upon, at.
enagos f. pl. petticoat.
enamorament m. state of being in love / infatuation.
enamorat -ada a. in love / lover.
enardir tr. to kindle, excite.
ençà adv. here, hither, this way / since.
encabir tr. to put, set / to meddle, intrude.
encadenar tr. to chain.
encaixada f. handshake.
encaixar tr. - intr. to fit / to shake hands / to pack in boxes.
encalçar tr. to chase, pursue.
encallar tr. to jam.
encant m. charm, enchantment.
encanyissat m. protective fence.
encapçalament m. heading.
encara adv. even, still, yet.
encarcarat -ada a. stiff.
encàrrec m. errand / order, commission / message.
encarregar tr. to entrust.
encarregat m. person in charge.
encegament m. blindness.
encegar tr. to grow blind / to blind.
encendre tr. to light, kindle, ignite.
encenedor m. lighter.
encerclar tr. to enclose, fence, hedge, surround.
encert m. good guess / good hit / ability.
encertar tr. to be right / to hit a target.
encetar tr. to initiate.
enciam m. lettuce.
enciclopèdia f. encyclopaedia.
encís m. charm, glamour.

encisador -a a. delightful, charming.
encisat -ada a. rapt.
encloure tr. to include / to involve.
enclusa f. anvil.
encobrir tr. to hide, conceal, cloak, mask.
encoixinar tr. to bolster.
encomanar tr. to commend, entrust.
encontorns m. pl. surroundings.
encontre m. encounter.
encoratjar tr. to encourage.
encreuament m. crossroads / junction.
encunyar tr. to mint.
endarrera adv. backwards.
endarrerir-se pr. v. to lag behind.
endavant adv. forwards, onward.
endegar tr. to manage, arrange.
endemà m. the day after.
endemés adv. besides, too, also.
enderrocar tr. to demolish, pull down, raze.
endevinalla f. riddle.
endevinar tr. to guess.
endins adv. inside.
endintre adv. inside.
endolcir tr. to sweeten.
endormiscar-se pr. v. to doze.
endós m. endorsement.
endossament m. endorsement.
endreç m. cleanliness, neatness, tidiness.
endreçar tr. to tidy.
endurir tr. to harden, toughen.
endurir-se pr. v. to harden, stiffen.
endur-se pr. v. to take away, carry off.
enemic -iga a. / m.-f. enemy, foe, adversary.
energia f. energy.
enèrgic -a a. energetic, active / bold, drastic / forceful.

enervar tr. to enervate.
enfadar tr. to irritate, annoy.
enfadat -ada a. angry.
enfangar tr. to cover with mud.
enfangat -ada a. muddy.
enfardellar tr. to bale up.
enfilar tr. to thread.
enfilar-se pr. v. to climb.
enfonsar tr. to plunge into the depths / to stick into / to break down / to cave in.
enfonsar-se pr. v. to sink, founder / to become demoralised.
enfora adv. out, outside /.
enfortir tr. to strengthen, fortify.
enfosquir-se pr. v. to darken, get dark.
engabiar tr. to cage.
enganxar tr. to hook, couple / to stick / to trick into a compromise.
enganxós -osa a. sticky.
engany m. deceit, trick / pl. wiles, tricks.
enganyar tr. to deceive, beguile, mislead.
engegar tr. to set in motion, start to work / to push away, remove.
engendrar tr. to beget, engender, breed.
enginy m. wit, smartness / inventive faculty.
enginyer m. engineer.
enginyós -osa a. ingenious, clever / witty.
engolir tr. to devour, gobble, gorge.
engrandiment m. enlarging, increase.
engrandir tr. to enlarge, increase.
engreixar tr. - intr. to fatten, get fat / to fertilize / to become rich.
engrillonar tr. to fetter.

engròs (a l') adv. phr. wholesale.

engruna f. crumb.

engrunar tr. to crumble.

enguany adv. the current year.

enguixar tr. to plaster.

enguixat -ada a. plastered.

enhorabona f. congratulations.

enigma m. enigma, riddle.

enjogassat -ada a. playful, frisky, wanton.

enlairar-se pr. v. to rise up, soar.

enlaire adv. in the air.

enllà adv. over there / beyond.

enllaç m. liaison / marriage.

enllaçar tr. to tie, link, connect.

enllestir tr. to finish, complete.

enllestit -ida a. ready.

enlloc adv. nowhere.

enlluernar intr. to glare / to dazzle.

enllumenar tr. to illuminate.

enmig adv. - prep. amid, mid.

ennegrir tr. to blacken.

ennuvolat-ada a. cloudy.

enorme a. enormous.

enormement adv. enormously.

enquadernar tr. to bind.

enquesta f. inquest / investigation, research.

enquitranar tr. to tar.

enquitranat -ada a. tarry, tarred.

enrabiada f. rage, fit of temper.

enrajolat m. brick floor, tiled floor.

enraonar tr. - intr. to chat, chatter / to discuss, examine.

enraonies f. pl. gabble, gossip.

enravenar tr. to stiffen.

enredaire m.-f. entangler / tattler, busybody.

enredar tr. to entangle.

enregistrar tr. to register, record.

enrenou m. bustle, noise, tumult, uproar.

enrera adv. backwards.

enriquir tr. to enrich.

enrogallat -ada a. hoarse.

enrogir tr. to redden.

enrojolament m. blush.

enrojolar-se pr. v. to blush.

enrolar tr. to recruit.

ens pron. us.

ensabonar tr. to soap, lather / to flatter.

ensacar tr. to put into a sack.

ensenya f. badge, ensign.

ensenyament m. teaching, discipline.

ensenyança f. teaching, discipline.

ensenyar tr. to instruct, teach.

ensinistrament m. training, coaching.

ensopegada f. stumble.

ensopegar tr. to stumble.

ensopit -ida a. torpid, lethargic, sluggish.

ensucrar tr. to sugar, sweeten.

ensumar tr. to smell, sniff.

entalladura f. carving.

entapissar tr. to hang with tapestry.

enteixinat a. / m. panelled, panelling.

entendre tr. - intr. to understand.

entendrir tr. to soften.

entenimentat -ada a. judicious.

enter-a a. entire, whole.

enterc -a a. obstinate, stubborn / rigid, stiff.

enterrament m. burial.

enterrar tr. to bury.

entès -esa a. knowledgeable, well-informed.

entonar tr. to intone.

entorn adv. around.

entrada f. entrance.

entranyable a. intimate.

entranyes f. pl. entrails, bowels, insides / (fig.) compassion.

entrar int. to enter, to go in.

entre prep. amongst, between.

entrebanc m. stumble, trip / obstacle / difficulty.

entremaliadura f. naughtiness.

entremaliat -ada a. naughty.

entremig adv. in the middle.

entrenador m. trainer.

entrenament m. training, coaching.

entrenar tr. to train.

entrepà m. sandwich.

entretant adv. meanwhile, in the meantime.

entretela f. wadding.

entreteniment m. pastime, entertainment.

entretenir tr. to amuse, entertain / to interrupt, keep someone back.

entrevista f. interview.

entristir tr. to sadden.

entroncament m. junction.

entusiasme m. enthusiasm.

enutjós -osa a. troublesome, annoying.

envair tr. to invade.

envàs m. packing, wrapping / bottling / canning.

enveja f. envy.

envejable a. enviable.

envejar tr. to envy / desire, covet.

envejós -osa a. envious, jealous.

envellir tr. - intr. to age, get old.

envernissador -a m.-f. varnisher.

envernissar tr. to varnish.

envers prep. to, towards.

enviar tr. to send, remit.

enyorança f. nostalgia / regret.

enyorament m. longing, yearning / homesickness, nostalgia.

enyorar tr. to miss, to long for / regret.

ep! interj. eh! here!

epidèmia f. epidemic.

epígraf m. epigraph / heading, title.

època f. age, era, time, epoch.

equilibri m. equilibrium, balance.

equip m. team / kit, equipment.

equipament m. equipment, kit.

equipar tr. to equip.

equipatge m. luggage.

equitatiu -iva a. fair, equitable.

equivocació f. error, mistake, confusion.

equivocar tr. to mistake, confuse.

equivocat -ada a. mistaken, wrong.

era f. era.

eriçó m. hedgehog / sea urchin.

erm-a a. barren.

ermita f. hermitage.

ermità m. hermit.

ermot m. moor.

error m. error, lapse, mistake.

erudició f. erudition, scholarship.

erudit -ita m. -f. lettered, erudite, learned / m. scholar.

eruga f. caterpillar.

esbalaïment m. spasm, convulsion / astonishment.

esbaldir tr. to rinse.

esbargiment m. recreation.

esbarzer m. blackberry bush.

esberlar tr. to cleave.

esborrador m. eraser, rubber.

esborrar tr. to cross out, rub out, erase.

esbrinar tr. to detect, to find out.

esbufec m. puff, puffing, wheeze, snort.

esbufegar tr. to puff, wheeze, snort.

escabetx m. liquid for pickling fish, composed of oil, vinegar, bay-leaves, paprika, and garlic.

escafandra f. diving suit.

escafandrer m. diver.

escaient a. fit, apt.
escala f. staircase.
escala portàtil f. ladder.
escaldada f. scald.
escaldar tr. to scald.
escalfador m. warming pan.
escalfallits m. warming pan.
escalfar tr. to heat, warm.
escalfar-se pr. v. to heat up, get warm.
escalfor f. warmth, heat, hotness.
escalinata f. outside staircase.
escamot m. gang.
escampar tr. to scatter, disperse, spread / to disseminate, extend.
escandinau -ava a. Scandinavian.
escàndol m. scandal / noisy disorder, tumult.
escanyar tr. to strangle.
escapar intr. to escape.
escapar-se pr. v. to escape, run away.
escarabat m. beetle.
escarceller m. gaoler, jailer, warder.
escarlata a. / f. scarlet.
escarlatina f. scarlet fever.
escarment m. lesson, warning, example.
escarni m. derision, mockery.
escarnir tr. to make fun of, mock.
escarpa f. slope.
escarpat -ada a. sheer, steep / craggy.
escarrassar-se pr. v. to toil.
escarxofa f. artichoke.
escàs -assa a. scant, scanty, scarce.
escassament adv. scarcely.
escassetat f. shortage.
escatainar intr. to cackle.
escatimar tr. to become scarce / scrimp.

escena f. scene.
escenari m. the stage, the boards.
escèptic -a a. / m.-f. sceptic.
esclatar intr. to explode, burst, blow up / to break out.
esclau- ava m. -f. slave.
esclavatge m. slavery.
esclavitud f. slavery.
esclofolla f. rind, peel / eggshell / bark.
esclops m. pl. clogs. sabots.
escó m. bench with a back / (Parl.) seat.
escon m. bench with a back / (Parl.) seat.
escocès-esa m.-f. Scots, Scottish.
escola f. school.
escollir tr. to choose, select, pick out.
escollit -ida a. chosen / choice, prime.
escoltar tr. to listen.
escombra f. broom.
escombrar tr. to sweep.
escombraries. f. pl. rubbish, refuse, sweepings.
escombriaire m. dustman / scavenger.
escomesa f., attack, assault.
escometre tr. to attack, assault / to undertake.
escopidora f. spittoon.
escopir intr. - tr. to spit.
escorça f. bark.
escorcollar tr. to search every corner.
escorxador -a m.-f. butcher / slaughterhouse.
escotilla f. hatch.
escriptor m. writer, author.
escriptora f. writer, authoress.
escriptura f. script, writing.
escriure tr. - intr. to write.
escrivent m. clerk.
escrúpol m. scruple, doubt.
escrutar tr. to scan, scrutinize:
escrutini m. scrutiny.

escudar tr. to shield.
escudella f. a stew made from rice or paste with vegetables / the earthenware pot in which the stew is made.
escuder m. shield bearer, squire, page.
escull m. reef, rock.
escullera f. breakwater.
esculpir tr. to carve, sculpt.
escultural a. sculptural / statuesque.
escultor m. sculptor.
escultura f. sculpture.
escuma f. spray, foam / skim, scum, lather, froth.
escumar tr. to skim off.
escumejar intr. to foam.
escurçar tr. to shorten.
escurçó m. viper, adder.
escut m. shield / coat of arms / a gold or silver coin.
esdevenidor m. future.
esdeveniment m. event, occurrence.
esdevenir intr. to become / happen.
esfera f. sphere.
esforç m. effort, endeavour, toil.
esforçar-se pr. v. to endeavour.
esfumar-se pr. v. to vanish.
esgarrapada f. long, deep scratch.
esgarrapar tr. to scratch.
esgarriar tr. to mislay.
esgarriat -ada a. lost.
esgarrifança f. shiver.
esgarrifar-se pr. v. to shiver.
esglai m. scare, start.
esglaiar tr. to scare.
esglaó m. step, rung.
església f. church.
esgotar tr. to exhaust / to go out of print.
esgroguèit -ïda a. sallow.
esguardar tr. to look.

eslau -ava a. m.-f. Slav / Slavonic.
esllavissada f. landslide.
esmalt m. enamel.
esmaragda f. emerald.
esmena f. amendment / modification.
esmenar tr. to amend / to modify.
esmerçar tr. to invest, / to employ, utilize.
esmolar tr. to sharpen.
esmorzar m. breakfast / intr. to have breakfast.
esmunyir-se pr. v. to slip, slide.
espacial a. spatial.
espai m. space / stretch, gap, interval.
espaiós -osa a. spacious, capacious, roomy.
espant m. fright.
espantall m. scarecrow.
espantar tr. to scare.
espantós -osa a. frightful, dreadful, ghastly.
espanyol -a m. -f. Spaniard / a. Spanish.
espaordiment m. awe, dread.
esparadrap m. sticking plaster / adhesive tape.
espardenya f. a rope-soled sandal.
espargir tr. to spread, scatter, sow.
esparracat -ada a. ragged.
espàrrec m. asparagus.
esparver m. hawk.
espasa f. sword.
espatlla f. shoulder.
espatllar tr. to break / to ruin.
espavilat -ada a. lively, brisk / clever.
espècia f. spice.
especial a. special.
especificar tr. to specify.
espècimen m. specimen.
espectacle m. spectacle, sight, show.

espectador -a m. -f. spectator, onlooker.

espectre m. ghost, spectre / spectrum.

espelma f. candle, candlestick.

espera f. waiting.

esperança f. hope.

esperar tr. to wait, await / to expect / to hope.

esperit m. spirit.

Esperit Sant m. Holy Ghost.

espès -essa a. thick / stupid, dense.

espesseir tr. to thicken.

espessor m. thickness.

espia m.-f. spy.

espiar tr. to spy on / to lie in wait.

espigat -ada a. tall, grown.

espigol m. lavender.

espill m. mirror, looking-glass.

espina f. thorn / fishbone.

espinada f. backbone.

espiral f. spiral, curl.

espitllera f. loophole.

espoliar tr. to despoil, plunder.

esponja f. sponge.

espontani -ània a. spontaneous.

esporgar tr. to prune, lop.

esport m. sport.

esportista a. / m. sportsman.

esportiu -iva a. sports, sporting.

espòs m. husband.

esposa f. wife.

esposalles f. pl. betrothal.

esprémer tr. to squeeze (fruit).

esprint m. sprint.

espurna f. spark, sparkle.

esput m. spit, spittle / sputum.

esquadra f. fleet / squadron.

esquelet m. skeleton.

esquema m. scheme.

esquena f. back.

esquerda f. crack.

esquerdar tr. to crack.

esquerp -a a. shy / intractable, aloof, distant.

esquerra f. left.

esquerre -a a. left.

esquí m. ski.

esquiar intr. to ski.

esquifit-ida a. small.

esquilador m. shearer.

esquilar tr. to fleece, shear.

esquinçar tr. to rend, tear / to claw.

esquitx m. splash, spatter.

esquitxada f. sprinkle.

esquivar tr. to dodge, shirk.

essència f. essence.

essencial a. essential.

ésser m. being.

ésser v. to be.

est m. east.

estable a. steady, stable.

establiment m. establishment / settlement.

establir tr. to establish, set up / to settle.

establir-se pr. v. to settle down.

estabornir tr. to daze.

estaca f. stake / stick.

estació f. station / season.

estacionari -ària a. stationary.

estadant m. lodger.

estadista m. statesman.

estafa f. swindle, fraud.

estafada f. swindle, fraud.

estafador -a m. -f. fraud, swindler, cheater.

estafar tr. to swindle, defraud, deceive.

estalvi m. saving, economy.

estalviador -a a. thrifty, saving / economizer, saver.

estalviar tr. to save, spare.

estampa f. print / figure, stamp / engraving.

estanc m. shop where state monopoly goods (tobacco, stamps) are sold.

estança f. residence; (Lit.) stanza.

estanquer -a m. -f. tobacconist.

estany m. pond, small lake / tin.
estar v. to be.
estar (a punt de) v. to be ready to.
estat m. state.
estàtua f. statue.
estatuari -ària a. statuesque.
estatut m. statute.
estatutari -ària. a. statutary.
estel m. kite / star.
estellar tr. to chip, splinter / to chop up.
estendard m. standard, banner.
estendre tr. to extend, expand, widen.
esternut m. sneeze.
estès -esa a. widespread, extended.
estiba f. stowage.
estibador m. docker.
estil m. style.
estilogràfica f. fountain pen.
estimable a. reputable.
estimar tr. to love / to estimate, calculate.
estimat -ada a. darling.
estímul m. stimulus, incentive.
estimular tr. to stimulate.
estirar tr. - intr. to stretch / to pull up (socks, etc.).
estiu m. Summer.
estofar tr. to stew.
estofat m. stew.
estoig m. case, box.
estol m. squad / fleet.
estómac m. stomach.
estona f. time, while, spell, period, moment.
estovalles f. pl. tablecloth.
estovar tr. to melt.
estrada f. stand.
estrafer tr. to copy, imitate / to mock / to disguise.
estrall m. havoc, ravage.
estranger a. foreign / stranger / m.-f. foreigner.
estrangular tr. to strangle.

estrany -a a. strange, odd, weird / m. -f. stranger.
estrat m. layer / stratum.
estrebada f. haul.
estrella f. star.
estrella de mar f. starfish.
estremiment m. shiver, quiver.
estremir-se pr. v. to tremble.
estrènyer tr. to narrow / to squeeze / to bunch together / to press hard (enemy).
estrèpit m. loud, noise, bang.
estret -a a. narrow, tight / m. strait, channel.
estretesa f. narrowness / tightness, lack of money.
estretor f. hardship, scantiness.
estribord m. starboard.
estricte -a a. strict.
estripar tr. to disembowel / to tear.
estruç m. ostrich.
estructura f. structure.
estudi m. study.
estudiant m.-f. student.
estudiar tr. to study.
estufa f. stove, heater.
estúpid -a a. stupid, silly.
esvanir-se pr. v. to decrease.
esvelt- a a. slender, slim.
esverament m. perturbation / alarm, fright / shock.
esvoranc m. hole / slight wound.
etcètera phr. etcetera.
etern -a a. eternal.
eternitat f. eternity, lifetime.
etiqueta f. label, tag / ceremony, etiquette.
euga f. mare.
europeu -ea a. European.
evangeli m. gospel.
evident a. evident, obvious, undisputed.
evitar tr. to avoid.
evolució f. development, evolution.

exactament adv. exactly.
exacte-a a. exact.
exageració f. exaggeration.
exagerar tr. to exaggerate.
examen m. examination, test / survey.
examinar tr. to examine, test, probe, scan.
exànime a. lifeless.
excedir tr. to exceed, surpass.
excel·lent a. excellent / sterling.
excèntric-a a. eccentric.
excentricitat f. eccentricity.
excepció f. exception.
exceptuar tr. to except.
excessiu -iva a. excessive, exceeding, inordinate.
excitar tr. to excite.
exclamació f. exclamation.
exclamar tr. to exclaim.
excursió f. trip, excursion, tour / picnic.
excusa f. apology / excuse.
excusar-se pr. v. to apologize.
execució f. carrying out / performance / execution.
executar tr. to execute.
exemple m. example.
exercici m. exercise.
exèrcit m. army.
exhaurir tr. to exhaust.
exhaurir-se pr. v. to give out, become exhausted / to go out of print.
exhibició f. display, show, exhibition.
exhibir tr. to display, show, exhibit.
exhumar tr. to unearth.
exigir tr. to demand, require.
exili m. banishment, exile.
eximir tr. to exempt, free from.
existència f. existence, being.
existències f. pl. stock.
existir intr. to exist.
èxit m. success.

expatriar tr. to expatriate, put into exile.
experiència f. experience.
experiment m. experiment, test.
expert -a a. expert, skilled.
expiar tr. to atone.
expirar tr. to expire, die / to exhale.
explicar tr. to explain, expound.
explorador-a m. -f. explorer / scout.
explorar tr. to explore, reconnoitre.
explosió f. explosion.
explotar tr. - intr. to exploit / to explode.
exposar tr. to expose, exhibit / to risk.
exposat -ada a. exhibited.
exposició f. exhibition.
expositor -a a. / m.-f. exhibitor.
expressar tr. to express.
exquisit -ida a. exquisite, delicious.
èxtasi m. ecstasy, rapture / trance.
extens -a a. wide, broad, extensive / capacious.
extensió f. stretch, span / extension.
extensor -a a. protractor.
exterior a. external, outside.
extern -a a. external, outside.
extingir tr. to quench, extinguish.
extractar tr. to extract.
extraordinari -ària a. extraordinary.
extravagància f. oddity / extravagance.
extravagant a. odd, queer, wild, extravagant, nonsensical.
extraviar tr. to lead astray, go astray.
extrem m. extreme.
extremitat f. limb, extremity.
extremitud f. shaking, shudder.

extreure tr. to pull, draw out, extract.

exuberant a. luxuriant.

F

fàbrica f. factory / construction.

fabricació f. manufacture.

fabricant m. manufacturer / builder.

fabricar tr. to manufacture, make.

faç f. face.

façana f. front, façade.

facció f. faction / pl. features.

facècia f. fun, jest.

faceciós -osa a. funny / jester.

fàcil a. easy / facile.

facilitar tr. to facilitate, provide.

facilitat f. easiness, facility.

fàcilment adv. easily.

facinerós -osa a. wicked, / outlaw, malefactor.

factible a. feasible, workable.

factoria f. factory / fabric.

factura f. bill, invoice.

facultar tr. to empower.

facultat f. faculty.

fada f. fairy.

fadrí -ina m.- f. young, youthful / m. bachelor, f. spinster / workman.

faisà m. pheasant.

faixa f. band, girdle, sash.

falç f. sickle.

falca f. wedge, quoin.

falcar tr. to wedge, quoin.

falciot m. swift (orn.).

falcó m. hawk.

falda f. lap / skirt.

faldilles f. pl. skirt.

falguera f. fern.

fallar tr. to fail / to miss.

fal·lera f. whim.

fallida f. bankruptcy.

fals -a a. false, treacherous / sham.

falsedat f. falsehood, untruth.

falsificar tr. to falsify, forge, fake.

falsificació f. forgery, fake.

falta f. shortage, lack / mistake / fault, infraction.

faltar tr. to lack /.to fail to appear / to show disrespect for.

fam f. hunger, famine.

fama f. fame, glory.

famejar intr. to famish.

família f. family, household.

famolenc -a a. hungry, famished, ravenous.

famós -osa a. famous, renowned.

fanal m. lantern / headlight.

fanatisme m. fanaticism.

fanfarró-ona a. / m.-f. boaster, swaggerer, blusterer.

fanfarronejar tr. to bluster, swagger, boast.

fang m. clay, mud.

fantasia f. fancy, fantasy.

fantasiejar intr. to daydream.

fantasista m. -f. fanciful.

fantasma m. phantom, ghost.

far m. beacon / lighthouse.

farcell m. bundle.

farciment m. filling, stuffing.

farcir tr. to pad, stuff.

fardell m. bale, package.

farga f. forge, smithy.

farigola f. thyme.

farina f. flour.

farinetes f. pl. porridge.

faringe f. pharynx.

faristol m. music stand.

farmàcia f. pharmacy / chemist's.

farratge m. forage.

farsant a. m.-f. player / deceiver.

fart-a a. satiated, / fed up.

fascinació f. fascination.

fascinar tr. to fascinate.
fase f. phase.
fàstic m. disgust, nausea, loathing / despicable thing, abomination.
fastiguejar tr. to tire, bore, bother, vex.
fat m. fate, destiny.
fatalitat f. fatality.
fatigós -osa a. tiring, exhausting.
fatxenda f. vanity, presumptuousness / snobbery.
faula f. fable, tale, story.
faune m. faun.
fava f. broadbean.
favor m. favour.
favorit -a a. favourite.
fe f. faith.
feble a. feeble, weak.
febre f. fever.
febrer m. February.
febrós -osa a. feverish.
fecundació f. fertilization.
fecunditat f. fecundity.
federació f. federation.
federar tr. to federate.
feina f. job, work, task.
feix m. sheaf.
fel f. gall.
felí-ina (jove) a. kitten.
feliç a. happy / fortunate.
felicitació f. congratulation / written greeting.
felicitar tr. to congratulate / to offer one's best wishes.
felicitat f. happiness, felicity.
fem m. manure, fertilizer.
femella f. female.
femení -ina a. feminine.
femer m. dunghill.
fems m. .pl. dung, excrement / fertilizer.
fenc m. hay.
fenomen m. phenomenon.
fer tr. to do, make.
fer saber tr. to let know.

fer -a a. fierce / f. wild beast.
fèretre m. coffin, bier.
ferida f. hurt, injury, wound.
ferir tr. to hurt, injure, wound.
ferm -a a. firm, fast, steady.
fermentació f. fermentation.
fermesa (corporal) f. fitness.
fermesa f. firmness, stability, steadiness / resoluteness, endurance.
ferotge a. fierce.
ferradura f. horseshoe.
ferrer m. blacksmith.
ferro m. iron.
ferrocarril m. railway.
fèrtil a. fertile.
fertilitat f. fertility, fruitfulnees.
fervent a. fervent, ardent.
fervor a. fervour, ardour.
fervorós -osa a. fervent, ardent.
fesol m. French bean.
festa f. holiday / entertainment / festival.
festejar tr. to woo, make love / to feast, celebrate.
festes f. pl. festivities, festivals / Christmas or Easter holidays.
festí m. feast, banquet.
festiu -iva a. festive, merry, gay.
festivitat f. holiday, festivity.
fet m. deed, act, fact.
fetge m. liver.
fetor f. stench, stink.
fi m. end / purpose, sake.
fi -ina a. fine / refined / sharp / slim.
fiador m. guarantor.
fiança f. bail.
fibra f. (Am) fiber, fibre (Bri).
fibrós -osa a. fibrous / sinewy.
ficar-se pr. v. to get into.
ficció f. fiction.
fidel a. faithful, true / truthful.
fidelitat f. fidelity, loyalty, faithfulness.
fidelment adv. faithfully, closely.

fideu m. vermicelli, noodle.
figa f. fig.
figura f. shape, form / figure / image.
fil m. thread, yarn / cutting-edge, blade.
fila f. queue, file, line / facial appearance.
filaberquí m. drill.
filar tr. to spin.
filat m. spinning, yarn / net, netting / wire netting, wire screen, wire cover.
filera f. row.
filferro m. wire.
filigrana f. filigree.
fill m. son.
filla f. daughter.
fillastra f. stepdaughter.
fillastre m. stepson.
fillol m. godson, godchild.
fillola f. goddaughter.
filòsof m. sage, philosopher.
final a. last / m. final / m. end.
finalitat f. goal, finality.
financer -a a financial / m. financier.
finar intr. to die / to finish.
finca f. estate, land / farm / house.
finestra f. window.
finestreta f. wicket, ticket window.
finestró m. shutter.
fingiment m. sham.
fingir tr. to feign, sham, pretend.
finir tr. to terminate, end, finish.
finor f. fineness / courtesy / refinement.
fins prep. until, till.
fira f. fair.
firaire m.-f. trader at fairs.
firma f. signature.
firmament m. heaven, sky, firmament.
firmar tr. to sign.

físic -a a. physical / m.-f. physicist.
física f. physics.
fisonomia f. physiognomy, face, features
fita f. milestone / boundary.
fitó m. target.
fitxa f. chip, counter, marker / index-card.
fix -a a. fixed.
fixament adv. firmly, steadily / fixedly.
fixar tr. to fix, secure / to affix / to settle.
flabiol m. flageolet / small flute.
flac -a a. thin, lank, lean / frail.
flagell m. whip / spanking / plague, calamity, affliction.
flagel·lar tr. to lash, whip.
flairar tr. to smell.
flaire f. odour, scent.
flairós -osa a. odorous.
flama f. flame / blaze.
flamarada f. blaze.
flascó m. vial.
flema f. phlegm.
flemàtic -a a. phlegmatic.
flequer -a m.-f. baker.
fletxa f. arrow, dart, shaft.
flor f. flower.
florida f. blossom.
floridura f. must, mustiness.
florir intr. to blossom / flourish.
florista s. florist.
flota f. fleet.
flotant a. afloat, floating.
flotar intr. to float.
fluir intr. to flow.
fluix -a a. loose, slack, limp.
fluixedat f. weakness.
foc m. fire.
foca f. seal.
focus m. focus.
fogassa f. loaf.
fogó m. stove, kitchen range / (of gun) vent.
foguera f. bonfire.

folgat -ada a. loose, lax, easy / at leisure.
foll -a a. mad, insane.
folrar tr. to pad.
fomentar tr. to foment / to warm / to excite.
fonament m. basis, foundation.
fonamental a. fundamental.
fonamentar tr. to base, found.
fonda f. hotel, inn.
fondalada f. ravine.
frondre tr. to melt, fuse.
fonedor -a a. smelter, founder.
fonoll m. fennel.
fons m. fund, finance, resources / bottom.
font f. fountain / source.
fontada f. picnic.
fora adv. out.
fora (a l'estranger) adv. abroad.
foradada f. tunnel.
foradar tr. to drill, hole, pierce.
foragitar tr. to expel.
foragitat -ada a. outcast.
foraster-a a. / m.-f. stranger.
forat m. hole.
forca f. fork.
forca (patíbul) f. gallows.
força f. power, force.
forçar tr. to force, strain.
foresta f. wood.
forfet m. misdeed, crime.
forja f. forge, smithy.
forjador m. smith.
forjar tr. to forge.
forjat -ada a. wrought.
forma f. form, shape.
formal a. formal / serious, earnest.
formar tr. to form, make up.
formatge m. cheese.
formiga f. ant.
formigó m. concrete.
formós -osa a. beautiful.
fórmula f. formula.
forn m. oven, furnace, kiln.
fornada f. batch.

fornal f. forge.
forner -a m.-f. baker.
fornir tr. to equip.
forquilla f. fork.
forrellat m. lock, bolt.
fort -a a. strong / loud.
fortificació f. fort, fortification.
fortificar tr. to fortify, strengthen.
fortuna f. fortune, chance / fortune, wealth.
fosc -a a. dark, obscure, gloomy / f. darkness.
foscor f. darkness, dimness.
foscúria f. darkness / obscurity.
fosquedat f. darkness, dark.
fossa f. grave, pit.
fossar m. cementery, churchyard.
fossat m. trench, ditch.
fotografia f. photograph / photography.
fotografiar tr. to photograph.
frac m. dress-coat, tails.
fracàs m. failure.
fracassar intr. to fail.
fracció f. fraction.
fragant a. fragrant.
fràgil a. fragile, frail.
franc -a a. Frank / free / frank.
francès -esa a. French / Frenchman, Frenchwoman.
francmaçó m. freemason, mason.
franel·la f. flannel.
franja f. fringe, border, strip.
franqueig m. postage.
frare m. friar.
frase f. phrase / sentence.
frasejar tr. - intr. to phrase.
frau m. fraud, swindle.
fre m. brake.
fred -a a. cold / bleak.
fredament adv. coldly.
fredolic -a a. sensitive to cold.
fredor f. cold.
fregall m. mop.

fregar tr. to scrub, rub, scour.
fregir tr. to fry.
fregit -ida a. fried.
frenar tr. to brake.
frenètic -a a. frantic.
freqüència f. frequency.
freqüent a. frequent, regular.
freqüentar tr. to haunt, frequent.
freqüentment adv. frequently, often.
fresc -a a. cool / fresh / f. coolness.
frescor f. cool, coolness.
fressa f. noise, clamour, crash.
fretura f. want, lack, deprivation.
freu m. strait, channel.
frigorífic m. refrigerator.
frisança f. shiver.
front m. forehead.
frontera f. frontier, border, boundary.
fronterer -a a. frontier, border.
frontis m. façade.
frontispici m. frontispiece.
frontissa f. knuckle / hinge.
fruir tr. to enjoy.
fruit -a m. -f. fruit.
frustració f. failure / frustration.
frustrar tr. to frustrate, thwart, fail.
fuet m. whip / dried and spiced pork sausage.
fuga f. flight, escape.
fugir intr. to flee, escape.
fugitiu -iva a. fugitive / fleeting.
fulgor m. brilliance, glow.
full m. leaf.
fulla f. leaf.
fullaraca f. trash, rubbish.
fullatge m. foliage.
fullejar tr. to look over, look through.
fum m. smoke.
fumar tr. to smoke.

fumat -ada a. smoky, reeky / smoked (salmon, etc.).
funció f. function / religious ceremony / show, performance.
funcionar intr. to function.
fundació f. foundation.
fundador -a a. founder.
fundar tr. to. found.
funeral a. / m. funeral.
furgar tr. - intr. to stir / to poke.
furgoneta f. van.
furiós-osa a. furious.
furor m. fury, madness, rage.
furtar tr. to steal, thieve.
fusell m. gun, rifle.
fusió f. fusion, melting.
fusta f. wood, timber, lumber.
fuster m. carpenter.
fustigar tr. to thrash, whip.
futbol m. football.
futilesa f. futility.
futur -a a. future / m. future.

G

gàbia f. cage.
gabinet m. cabinet.
gafet m. clasp, catch.
gaig (ocell) m. jay.
gaire adv. much, many / (with neg.) hardly, scarcely any.
gairebé adv. almost, nearly.
gaita f. flageolet, bagpipe, hornpipe.
gaiter m. piper.
galania f. gentility, gallantry.
galant (love) a. gallant.
galera f. galley.
galès -esa a. i. m.-f. Welsh / Welshman, Welshwoman.
galeta f. ship's-biscuit, hardtack / biscuit, wafer.
galió m. galleon.

galiot m. galley slave.
gall m. rooster, cock.
gallard -a a. gallant, dashing.
galleda f. bucket, pail.
gallet m. trigger / weather vane.
gallina f. hen.
galop m. gallop.
galta f. cheek, jowl.
gamba m. prawn.
gambada f. long stride.
gana f. hunger / wish, desire.
gandul -a a. idle / layabout.
gandula (moble) f. lounge chair.
gandulejar intr. to idle.
ganduleria f. idleness.
ganivet m. knife.
ganiveta f. big knife.
ganxo m. hook, crook / catch.
ganyota f. grimace, face.
garantia f. guarantee, warranty.
garantir tr. to guarantee.
garatge m. garage.
garba f. sheaf.
garbell m. sieve.
garbellar tr. to sift.
gargamella f. throat.
gàrgola f. gargoyle.
garlanda f. garland, wreath.
garrell -a a. bow-legged.
garrofer m. carob tree.
garsa f. magpie.
gas m. gas.
gasela f. gazelle.
gasiu -iva a. miserly / niggardly.
gasolina f. (Bri) petrol, (Am.) gasoline.
gasós -osa a. gaseous, gassy.
gastar tr. to spend, use up, wear out.
gat m. cat.
gatet m. kitten.
gatzara f. revelry, merrymaking.
gaubança f. mirth, hilarity.
gaudi m. enjoyment.
gaudir tr. to enjoy / to rejoice.
gavina f. seagull.

gec m. jacket.
gegant m. giant.
gegantí -ina a. giant.
gel m. ice.
gelar tr. to freeze, ice.
gelat (retresc) m. ice cream.
gelat -ada a. freezing, icy.
gelatina f. gelatine, jelly.
gelea f. jelly.
gelera f. glacier.
gelós -osa. a. jealous.
gelosia f. jealousy / lattice (window).
gemat -ada a. lush, luxuriant / sprightly, lively.
gemec m. moan, groan / wail, whine.
gemegar intr. to moan.
gemma f. gem, jewel.
gendre m. son-in-law.
gener m. January.
generació f. generation.
general a. / m. general.
generar tr. to generate.
gènere m. kind, sort.
generós-osa a. generous.
genet m. horseman, rider.
geni m. temper, mood / spirit, genie / genius.
genialitat f. genius.
genoll m. knee.
gens adv. a little / (with neg.) not in the least / absolutely not.
gent f. pleople, folk.
gentada f. crowd, throng.
gentil a. courteous, considerate / m. gentile.
gentussa f. mob, rabble.
geografia f. geography.
gep -a m. - f. hump.
geperut -uda a. crooked, humpbacked / hunchback.
gerani m. geranium.
gerència f. management.
gerga f. jargon / slang.
germà m. brother.
germana f. sister.

germanastra f. stepsister.
germanastre m. stepbrother.
germànic -a a. German, Germanic.
gemanor f. fraternity, brotherhood.
germen m. germ / germ, seed / source, origin.
germinar intr. to germinate, sprout.
gerra f. jar.
gerro m. vase.
gerundi m. gerund.
gespa f. grass, lawn, turf.
gest m. gesture.
gibrell m. earthenware washing-bowl.
gibrelleta f. chamberpot, urinal.
gimnàs m. gymnasium.
ginebra f. gin.
ginebre m. juniper.
gira f. reverse side.
gira-sol m. sunflower.
girar tr. to turn.
giratori -òria a. revolving, rotatory.
giravolt m. whirl.
giravoltar intr. to twirl, whirl, revolve.
girell m. weather vane, weather cock.
gitano -a. m. - f. gypsy.
gla f. acorn.
glaçada f. frost.
glaçar tr. to freeze.
glacial a. icy.
glàndula f. gland.
globus m. globe, balloon.
glop m. sip.
glòria f. glory, bliss.
gnom m. gnome, dwarf.
goig m. joy, pleasure, satisfaction.
gola f. throat, gullet / canyon / ravine / gluttony.
goleta f. schooner.
golfes f. pl. loft.

goma f. rubber.
gorja f. throat.
gorra f. cap, bonnet.
gos m. dog.
gosar intr. to dare.
gossa f. bitch.
gossera f. kennel.
got m. glass.
gota f. drop, bead, blob.
gota (malaltia) f. gout.
gotejar intr. to drip, leak.
gotera f. drip, leak.
govern m. government.
governador m. governor.
governar tr. to govern / guide / manage.
gra m. grain / pimple / bead.
gràcia f. grace / wit, charm / jest.
gràcies f. pl. thanks, thank you.
graciós -osa a. graceful, pleasing / gracious, funny.
gradualment adv. gradually.
graduar tr. to graduate.
gralla (ocell) f. jackdaw.
gram m. gramme.
gramàtica f. grammar.
gran a. big, large, great.
grandària f. size, bigness, magnitude.
grandesa f. greatness.
grandiós -osa a. impressive, magnificent, grandiose.
graner m. barn.
granger -a m.-f. farmer.
granit m. granite.
granja f. farm, farmhouse / dairy.
granota f. frog.
graó m. stair, step.
grapa f. claw.
grapat m. handful.
gras -assa a. fatty / fat, obese.
grat -a a. grateful / pleasant.
gratar tr. to scratch / to scrape.
gratificar tr. to gratify.
gratitud f. gratitude.

grau m. degree / grade, rank.
graula f. rook.
gravar tr. to engrave / to carve / to levy a tax.
gravat m. engraving.
gravetat f. gravity.
grec -grega a. Greek.
greix m. fat.
greixar tr. to grease, oil.
greixós -osa a. greasy, oily.
gremi m. guild, trade union, corporation.
gresca f. revelry, merrymaking / uproar.
greu a. serious, grave / (mus.) bass.
greuge m. grievance, wrong.
greument adv. gravely, dangerously.
grèvol (boix) m. holly.
grilló m. fetter.
grillons m. pl. fetters, shackles.
grinyol m. screech.
gripau m. toad.
gris -a a. grey.
groc-groga a. yellow / pale.
grogós -osa a. yellowish.
groller -a a. ill-bred, illmannered, rude, impolite.
gronxador m. seesaw / swing.
gronxar-se pr. v. swing, dangle.
gropa f. crupper / rump of a horse.
gros -ossa a. big, large / gross, fat / thick.
grua f. crane, hoist.
gruix m. thickness.
gruixut -uda a. thick / weighty, full of meaning.
grunyir intr. to snarl, growl.
grup m. group.
gualtar tr. - intr. to observe, look.
gual m. ford / entrance-exit in front of which parking is forbidden.
guant m. glove.

guany m. gain, profit, winning.
guanyador -a a. winner.
guanyar tr. to earn / to win / to acquire, get, gain.
guanys m. pl. income.
guarda m. guard, watch.
guardabosc m. ranger.
guardar tr. to guard, protect / to keep / to reserve / to avoid doign something.
guardar-se pr. v. to beware.
guarderia f. kindergarten, nursery school.
guàrdia m. constable, policeman / watch.
guardià m. keeper, guard.
guardiola f. moneybox.
guariment m. cure, healing.
guarir intr. to cure, heal.
guarniment m. harness / pl. fittings.
guatlla f. quail.
guenyo -a a. squint-eyed.
guerra f. war.
guerrer -a a. warlike / m. warrior.
guerxo -a a. squint-eyed.
guia s. guide, leader.
guiar tr. to guide, lead.
guineu f. fox.
guió m. (gram.) hyphen, dash.
guix m. plaster / chalk.
guspira f. spark, sparkle.
gust m. taste, flavour.
gustosament adv. willingly, with pleasure.

H

hàbil a. able, skilful, clever.
habilitat f. ability, skill.
hàbit m. habit / habitude / custom.
habitació f. room / habitation.

habitant m.-f. inhabitant.
habitar tr. to inhabit, dwell.
habitud f. habit.
habituar tr. to accustom.
hac f. letter H.
haca f. pony.
ham m. hook.
hamaca f. hammock.
hangar m. hangar.
harmonia f. harmony / music.
haver tr. - intr. to have.
hepàtic -a a. hepatic.
herald m. herald.
herba f. grass / herb.
herbei m. grass, lawn, green.
herbolari -ària m.-f. herbalist.
herència f. inheritance, heritage.
heretar tr. -intr. to inherit.
heretatge m. heritage, inheritance.
heretge m. heretic.
heretgia f. heresy.
hereu m. heir.
hereva f. heiress.
hermètic -a a. hermetic, sealed.
heroi m. hero, champion.
heroic -a a. heroic.
heroïna f. heroine.
heura f. ivy.
higiene f. hygiene.
himne m. hymm, anthem.
hípic -a a. equine.
hipnotisme m. hypnotism.
hipoteca f. mortgage.
hisendat m. squire, landowner.
hissar tr. to hoist.
història f. history / story.
hivern m. Winter.
hola! interj. hallo, hello.
home m. man.
homenatge m. homage, tribute.
homogeni -ènia a. homogeneous.
hongarès -esa a. Hungarian.
honor m. honour.
honoraris m. pl. fees, wages.

honradesa f. fairness.
honrat -ada a. honest, honourable.
hoquei m. hockey.
hora f. hour / time.
horari m. timetable.
horrible a. horrible, dreadful, ghastly, hideous.
horror m. horror / fright.
hort m. orchard / kitchen garden.
horta f. orchard / vegetable garden.
hospital m. hospital.
hostaler m. innkeeper, landlord, host.
hostalera f. landlady.
hoste m. boarder, lodger.
hostessa (de l'aire) f. air hostess, stewardess.
hòstia f. Host.
hotel m. hotel.
humà -ana a. human / benevolent, humane.
humanitari -ària a. humanitarian, humane.
humanitat f. humanity, mankind.
humil a. humble.
humiliar tr. to humble, humiliate.
humit -ida a. wet, damp, moist, humid.
humitat f. humidity, damp, dampress, moisture.
humor m. temper, humour, mood.
huracà m. hurricane.

I

i conj. and.
iaia f. (fam.) grandma, granny.
ianqui a. / m.-f. Yankee.

iarda f. yard.
ibèric -a a. Iberian.
iceberg m. iceberg.
icona f. icon.
ics f. name of the letter X.
ictèric -a a. jaundiced.
ictericia f. jaundice.
idea f. idea.
ideal a. / m.-f. ideal.
idear tr. to conceive, create, hatch an idea.
idèntic -a a. identical.
identificar tr. to identity.
identitat f. identify.
idil·li m. idyll.
idioma m. language / idiom.
idiota a. idiot.
idiotesa f. idiocy.
idòlatra a. idolater.
idolatria f. idolatry.
ignició f. ignition.
ignomínia f. shame, opprobium, ignominy.
ignorant a. ignorant, unaware.
ignorar tr. to ignore.
igual a. equal, even, alike.
igualar tr. to equalize / to (make, become) equal to.
igualtat f. equality.
illa f. island.
il·legal a. illegal.
illenc -a a. islander.
il·lès -esa a. unhurt, uninjured, unharmed.
il·limitat -ada a. boundless, unlimited.
il·luminar tr. to illuminate, light / to enlighten.
il·lús -usa a. deluded, deceived.
il·lusió f. illusion.
il·lusionat -ada a. hopeful / excited, eager.
il·lustració f. illustration / enlightenment.
il·lustrar tr. to illustrate / to enlighten.
imaginar tr. to imagine.

imant m. magnet, lodestone.
imatge f. image.
imbècil a. imbecile, blockhead.
imitació f. imitation, fake.
imitar tr. to imitate.
immediatament adv. immediately, at once.
immens -a a. immense.
immòbil a. motionless / immovable, immobile.
immoble a. immovable / m. building.
immoral a. immoral.
immortal a. immortal.
immund -a a. filthy, unclean.
impacient a. impatient, eager.
imparcialitat f. impartiality, fairness.
imparcialment adv. impartially, fairly.
impassible a. impassible, cold, unmoved.
impàvid -a a. undaunted, fearless.
impecable a. impeccable, faultless.
impediment m. impediment, hindrance.
impedir tr. to impede, hinder.
impel·lir tr. to impel.
imperi m. empire / dominion.
imperdible m. safety-pin.
imperfecció f. imperfection, flaw, fault.
impermeable a. impermeable, waterproof / m. raincoat, mackintosh.
impertinència f. impertinence.
impetuós -osa a. impetuous.
impiadós -osa a. irreverent, impious, ungodly.
impiu -ia a. irreverent, impious, ungodly.
implicar tr. to imply.
implorar tr. to implore.
implume a. featherless.

import m. amount, sum / cost, charge, price.
importació f. import.
importància f. importance.
important a. important / great, large.
importar tr. to import.
imposar tr. to impose.
impositor -a m.-f. depositor.
impossible a. impossible.
impost m. tax, duty, levy / income tax.
impotent a. impotent.
imprecisió f. imprecision.
impremta f. printing / printing-works, printer's.
impressionant a. impressive, striking.
impressionar tr. to impress, strike / to affect.
impressor m. printer.
imprevisor -a a. happy-go-lucky.
imprimir tr. to print, imprint.
impropi -impròpia a. improper inappropiate, unsuitable.
improvisar tr. to improvise.
imprudent a. imprudent, rash.
impuls m. impulse.
imputació f. impeachment.
imputar tr. to impute.
inacabable a. unending.
inacabat -ada a. undone, unfinished.
inacceptable a. unacceptable.
inalterable a. unalterable, constant / unmoving.
inamovible a. immovable.
inanició f. starvation.
inanimat -ada a. inanimate, lifeless.
inaugurar tr. to inaugurate.
incansable a. tireless.
incapaç a. unable, incapable.
incapacitat f. inability, incapacity.
incaut -a a. incautious, unwary.
incendi m. fire.

incendiari m. fire-raiser.
incentiu m. incentive.
incert-a a. uncertain.
incertesa f. uncertainty.
inclinació f. inclination.
inclinar tr. to incline, slope, tilt.
inclinar-se pr. v. to bow / to be inclined to.
incloure tr. to include, embody / to enclose.
inclús -usa a. including.
incòmode -a a. uncomfortable, uneasy.
incompetència f. incompetence.
incompliment m. default.
incomunicar tr. to isolate.
inconegut- uda a. unknown.
inconscient a. unconscious / unaware.
inconvenient a. inconvenient / m. disadvantage.
incorporar tr. to embody.
incrèdul -a a. unbeliever, incredulous.
increment m. increase.
incrementar tr. to increase.
increpar tr. to rebuke.
incubar tr. to incubate.
inculte -a a. untutored, uncultivated.
incursió f. raid.
indagació f. inquiry, inquest.
indecís -isa a. undecided, hesitating.
indecisió f. hesitation.
indefens -a a. unguarded.
indegut -úda a. undue, improper, illicit.
independent a. independent.
indesitjable a. undesirable.
índex m. index, catalogue / ratio, rate / (finger) forefinger.
indicar tr. to indicate.
indici m. clue, indication.
indiferent a. indifferent.
indígena a. / m.-f. native.
indignació f. indignation.

indigne -a a. ignoble, mean, unworthy.

individu -ídua m.-f. individual, person.

individual a. single, individual.

indivis -isa a. undivided.

indolent a. indolent, indisposed to activity / (Med.) not painful.

indret m. place, spot, site.

indubtable a. doubtless.

induir tr. to induce / to tempt, instigate.

indulgència f. indulgence, forgiveness / pardon.

indult m. pardon.

indústria f. industry, manufacture / hard work.

industriós -osa a. industrious.

ineptitud f. ineptitude, incompetence.

inesperadament adv. unexpectedly / suddenly.

inexplicable a. unaccountable.

inèrcia f. inertia.

inevitable a. inevitable, unavoidable.

infància f. infancy.

infantament m. parturition, giving birth.

infanteria f. infantry.

infantesa f. childhood, infancy.

infantó m. baby.

infatigable a. indefatigable, tireless, untiring.

infecció f. infection.

infectar tr. to infect.

infeliç a. unhappy, unfortunate, wretched / m. -f. wretch.

inferior a. inferior, lower, subordinate.

infermer -a m.-f. nurse.

infern m. hell.

infinit -a a. infinite, endless. / m. infinite.

inflamar tr. to ignite, blaze.

inflamat -ada a. inflamed, sore.

inflar tr. to inflate, fill, swell.

inflexible a. inflexible, unbending.

inflor f. swelling.

influir intr. to influence.

informació f. information.

informar tr. to inform, report.

informe m. report.

infracció f. trespass, infraction.

infringir tr. to infringe, trespass.

ingressos m. pl. income, revenue / receipt.

inicial a. initial.

iniciar tr. to initiate.

iniquitat f. iniquity.

injecció f. injection.

injectar tr. to inject.

injúria f. insult, affront, offense.

injuriat -ada a. offended, insulted.

innoble a. ignoble.

innocent -a a. innocent.

innocu-òcua a. innocuous, harmless.

innominat -ada a. nameless.

inocular tr. to inoculate, vaccinate.

inodor -a a. odourless / m. lavatory, toilet.

inofensiu-iva a. inoffensive, harmless.

inoxidable a. stainless.

inquiet -a a. restless, uneasy.

inquietud f. uneasiness.

inquilí -ina m.- f. tenant, lodger, inmate.

inquirir tr. to ask, inquire.

insà -ana a. insane, mad / unhealthy.

insània f. insanity.

inscriure tr. to register / to record.

insecte m. insect.

insegur -a a. insecure / unsafe / (weather) changeable.

insensible a. insensitive / unnoticeable, imperceptible.

inserir tr. to insert.
insígnia f. badge, insignia.
insignificant a. insignificant, tri-fling.
insípid -a a. insipid, flavourless.
insistència f. insistence.
insistir intr. to insist.
insolació f. sunstroke.
insolent a. insolent.
insomni m. insomnia.
inspecció f. inspection.
inspeccionar tr. to inspect.
inspector -a m.-f. inspector.
inspirar tr. to inspire / to breathe in, inhale.
instal·lació f. installation.
instal·lar tr. to install.
instància f. request / petition, application form.
instant m. instant.
instantània f. (photog.) snapshot.
instigar tr. to instigate, incite.
instint m. instinct.
institut m. institute.
institutriu f. governess.
instruir tr. to instruct, teach.
instruït -ïda a. knowledgeable, versed.
instrument m. instrument.
insuficiència f. shortage, lack / insufficiency, inadequacy.
insuficient a. insufficient, scanty.
insular a. insular / m.-f. islander.
insult m. insult.
insultar tr. to insult.
insuportable a. unbearable, intolerable.
insurrecció f. insurrection, rising, revolt.
intacte -a a. intact, unbroken, whole.
íntegre -a a. integral, whole.
intel·ligència f. intelligence.
intel·ligent a. intelligent, clever.

intens -a a. intense, hard.
intensitat f. intensity / power, strength.
intent m. attempt, try.
intentar tr. to try / to propose, intend, attempt.
intercalació f. insertion.
intercalar tr. to insert.
interès m. interest.
interessant a. interesting.
interessar tr. to interest, care.
interí -ina a. provisional, temporary / f. charwoman.
interior a. interior, inner, inside, inward.
intern -a a. interior, inward / intern.
internat m. boarding school, boarder.
intèrpret m. -f. interpreter / performer.
interpretació f. interpretation / performance.
interpretar tr. to interpret / to translate / to perform.
interrogació f. interrogation, questioning.
interrogant m. query, question.
interrogar tr. to interrogate, question.
interrompre tr. to interrupt.
interruptor m. switch.
interval m. interval.
intervenir tr. to intervene / (comm.) to audit.
interviu m. interview.
intestí m. intestine, gut.
íntim -a a. intimate, inmost.
intrèpid -a a. intrepid, fearless, dauntless.
intrepidesa f. intrepidness, fearlessness, dauntlessness, boldness.
intriga f. intrigue / plot.
intrigar intr. to plot.
introduir tr. to introduce.
intrús -usa a. intruder.

intuïció f. intuition, insight.
inundació f. flood.
inútil a. useless, needless.
invasió f. invasion / attack.
invasor -a a. / m.-f. invader.
invenció f. invention.
invendible a. unsaleable.
inventar tr. to invent, devise, make up.
inversemblant a. unlikely.
inversió f. inversion, reversal / investment.
invertir tr. to invert / to invest.
investigació f. research, investigation, inquiry.
investigar tr. to research, investigate.
invisible a. invisible, unseen.
invitar tr. to invite.
invitat -ada a. guest.
iogurt m. yoghourt.
iol m. (naut.) yawl.
iot m. yacht.
ira f. anger, rage, wrath, ire.
irlandès -esa a. Irish / m.-f. Irishman, Irishwoman.
ironia f. irony.
irradiar tr. to radiate.
irreflexió f. rashness.
irrigar tr. to irrigate.
irrompre intr. to raid.
isard m. chamois / a. wild.
isolar tr. to isolate / to insulate.
istme m. isthmus.
italià -ana a. / m.-f. Italian.
itàlic -a a. italics.
ítem adv. also.
iuca f. yucca.
ivori m. ivory.
ixent a. (sun) rising.

J

ja adv. already.
jaç m. bed / litter.
jacent a. lying flat.
jacint m. hyacinth.
jade m. jade.
jamai adv. never.
japonès -esa. a. / m.-f. Japanese.
jaqueta f. coat, jacket.
jardí m. garden.
jardiner m. gardener.
jaspi m. jasper.
javelina f. javelin.
jerarquia f. hierarchy.
jeràrquic -a a. hierarchical.
jersei m. jersey.
Jesucrist m. Jesus Christ.
jeure intr. to lie (down).
jo pron. pers. I.
joc m. game, play.
joglar m. court entertainer, jongleur, minstrel, zany.
joguina f. toy.
joia f. jewel, gem.
joiell m. jewel.
joier m. jeweler.
joiós -osa a. joyful, happy.
jònec -ega m.-f. young bull or steer / yearling calf.
joquei m. jockey.
jorn m. day.
jornal m. working day / daily wage.
jota f. name of the letter J / Aragonese folk dance.
jou m. yoke.
jove a. young, youthful / m. youth, young person, youngster.
jovençà -ana a. youthful.
joveneta f. lass, lassie.
jovenívol -a a. youthful, juvenile.
joventut f. youth.
jovialitat f. gaiety.

jubilar-se pr. v. to retire.
jubileu m. jubilee.
judaic -a a. Jewish.
judici m. judgement / trial.
jueu m. Jew.
jueva f. Jewess.
jugador -a a /m.-f. player.
juganer -a a. playful, frolicsome.
jugar tr. to play.
jugular f. jugular.
juliol m. July.
julivert m. parsley.
jungla f. jungle.
junta f. board.
juntura f. joint.
juny m. June.
junyir tr. to yoke.
jurament m. oath.
jurar tr. to swear.
jurat m. jury.
jurista m. jurist.
just -a a. just, fair, right / righteous.
justament adv. fairly, justly / exactly, precisely.
justícia f. justice.
justicier -a a. just.
justificació f. justification.
justificant m. warrant, proof.
justificar tr. to justify.
justificatiu -iva a. justificative.
jutge m. judge.
jutjar tr. to judge.
jutjat m. tribunal, court of justice / judicature.
juvenil a. juvenile, youthful.

L

laberint m. labyrinth, maze.
labor f. labour, work / needlework / embroidery.
laboratori m. laboratory.

laboriós -osa a. laborious.
laca f. lacquer.
lacai m. lackey.
laceració f. rip, laceration.
lacònic-a a. laconic.
laconisme m. laconic style.
lacre m. sealing wax.
lactació f. lactation.
laic -a a. lay, not clerical.
lamentable a. regrettable, lamentable.
lamentació f. lamentation, sorrow.
lamentar tr. to mourn, lament.
làmina f. plate, sheet,
lampista m. plumber.
lànguid -a a. languid, slothful.
làpida f. stone, tablet / (sepulcral) gravestone.
lapidari -ària a. lapidary.
lapsus m. lapse.
laringe f. larynx.
larinx f. larynx.
larva f. larva, grub.
lasciu -iva a. lascivious.
lassar tr. to tire, fatigue.
lassitud f. lassitude.
latitud f. latitude.
latrina f. latrine.
laudable a. praiseworthy, laudable.
lavabo m. lavatory / washstand, washbasin.
laxant m. laxative.
laxar tr. to purge / to relax.
lector -a m.-f. reader.
lectura f. reading.
legal a. lawful, legal.
legalitat f. legality, lawfulness.
legió f. legion.
legislació f. legislation.
legítim -a a. legitimate, legal, lawful.
legitimar tr. to legitimate.
lema f. theme / slogan / device.
lent -a a. slow, tardy.
lentitud f. slowness.

lepra f. leprosy.
leprós -osa a. leprous / leper.
les art. f. pl. the / pron. f. pl. them.
lesió f. lesion, injury.
levita f. frock coat / m. Levite.
li pron. to him, to her, to it.
libel m. libel.
libel-lista a. libeller.
liberal a. liberal, generous / (polit.) liberal.
liberalitat f. liberality.
lícit -a a. lícit, lawful, legal.
licor m. liquor, liqueur.
lila f. lilac.
límit m. límit, bound.
limitar tr. to bound, limit.
línia f. line.
líquid -a a. liquid.
liquidar tr. to liquidate / to wind up (business).
lira f. lyre.
literalment adv. literally / verbatim.
literari -ària a. literary.
literatura f. literature.
litigar tr. to dispute at law, litigate, contend.
litigi m. litigation, lawsuit, legal action / (fig.) dispute.
litoral m. littoral, seaboard.
litre m. litre.
lívid -a a. pale.
llac m. lake.
llaç m. bow, knot.
llacuna f. lagoon.
lladrar int. to bark.
lladre m. robber, thief.
llagosta f.(insect) locust / (crust.) lobster.
llagostí m. prawn, crayfish.
llagoteria f. flattery.
llàgrima f. tear.
llambregada f. peep, glimpse.
llambregar tr. to. peep, glimpse.
llaminadura f. tidbit / delicacy.
llamp m. lightning.

llampec m. lightning, flash.
llampegar intr. to flash.
llampeguejar intr. to flash (lightning).
llana f. wool.
llança f. lance.
llançadora f. shuttle.
llançar tr. to throw, hurl.
llancer m. lancer.
llanceta f. lancet.
llangardaix m. lizard.
llangor f. languor.
llangorós -osa a. languid, faint.
llanguir intr. to languish, pine away.
llanós -osa a. woolly.
llanterna f. lantern.
llàntia f. lamp.
llanut -uda a. woolly, woollen / ignorant, numskull.
llapis m. pencil.
llar f. home, household / ... de foc f. fireplace, hearth.
llard m. lard.
llarg -a a. long.
llargada f. length, longitude.
llast m. ballast.
llàstima f. pity, compassion.
llatí -ina a. Latin.
llatzeret m. quarantine hospital.
llàtzer m. lazarus.
llauna f. tinplate / tin, can.
llauner m. tinker.
llaurador m. ploughman.
llaüt m. lute.
llautó m. brass.
llavi m. lip.
llavor f. seed.
llavors adv. then, afterwards.
llebre f. hare.
llebrer m. greyhound.
llebrós -osa a. leper, leprous.
llec -ega a. lay / m. ignorant, laic.
llefiscós -osa a. viscous, sticky.
lleganya f. rheum.
llegenda f. legend.
llegidor -a a. m.-f. reader.

llegir tr. to read.
llegua f. league.
llegum m. vegetable.
llei f. law, rule, precept.
lleial a. loyal, faithful.
lleialtat f. loyalty.
lleig -lletja a. ugly.
lleixiu m. bleach, lye.
llenç m. linen, canvas.
llençar tr. to throw / to throw away.
llençol m. sheet.
llengua f. tongue / language.
llengüeta f. small tongue / (mus.) reed / needle (of a scale, balance.
llentilla f. lentil.
llenya f. firewood.
llenyataire m. woodman, wood-cutter.
lleó m. lion.
lleona f. lioness.
llepar tr. to lick, lap.
llesca f. slice.
llesamí m. jasmine.
llest -a a. clever / ready.
llet f. milk.
lletania f. litany.
lleteria f. dairy.
lletjor f. ugliness.
lletra f. letter.
lletrejar tr. to spell.
lletrat -ada a. learned / m. law-yer.
lletuga f. lettuce.
lleuger -a a. light, slight / nimble.
lleugerament adv. lightly / slightly.
lleugeresa f. levity, lightness.
lleure m. leisure.
llevadora f. midwife.
llevant m. Levant.
llevar tr. to remove, take away / to get up / to produce fruit.
llevat m. yeast.
lli m. flax / linen.
liberal a. liberal / free.

llibertat f. liberty, freedom.
llibre m. book.
llibreria f. bookstore, bookshop / bookcase.
llibreta f. notebook, copybook / bank book.
llicència f. license.
llicenciat -ada a. bachelor, having a university degree.
lliçó f. lesson.
lliga f. league.
lligacama f. garter.
lligar tr. to tie, bind, lace, fasten, knot.
llim m. ooze.
llima f. file.
llimac m. slug.
llimar tr. to file.
llimona f. lemon.
llindar m. threshold, sill.
lliri m. lily.
llis -a a. even, smooth, level.
lliscar intr. to slip, slide.
llista f. list.
llit m. bed.
llitera f. litter / stretcher / bunk.
lliura f. pound (weight).
lliura esterlina f. pound ster-ling.
lliurament m. delivey / warrant.
lliurar tr. to deliver, hand over / to give, give in, hand in.
lliure a. free.
lloable a. praiseworthy.
lloança f. praise.
lloar tr. to praise.
llòbrec -ega a. dismal, gloomy.
lloc m. place, post, stand, site, spot.
llogar tr. to rent, hire.
llogarret m. village.
llogater -a m. -f. tenant, lessee.
lloguer m. hire, rent.
llombrígol m. navel.
llonganissa f. pork sausage.
llonguet m. roll.

llop m. wolf.
llorejat -ada a. laureate.
llorejar tr. to crown with laurel / to honour.
llorer m. laurel, bay
lloro m. parrot.
llosa f. flagstone.
llot m. mire, mud.
llotja f. market / exchange / grocer's shop.
lluç m. hake.
lluent a. brillant, bright, shining.
lluir intr. to shine, glow.
lluita f. struggle, fight, conflict.
lluitador m. fighter, wrestler.
lluitar intr. to fight, struggle, contend.
llum m. lamp.
llum f. light, clarity.
llumí m. match, wax match, paper match.
lluna f. moon.
lluny adv. far, far away, far off.
llunyà -ana a. far off, distant, remote.
llúpia f. cyst, wen.
llur a. sing. his, her, its / pos. pron. his, hers, its.
llurs a. pl. their / pos. pron. theirs.
localitat f. locality.
locomotora f. locomotive.
locomotriu a. f. locomotive.
locutor m. speaker.
locutori m. parlour.
lògica f. logic.
longitud f. length.
lot m. lot, portion, share.
loteria f. lottery.
lúgubre a. sad, mournful.
lupa f. lens, magnifying glass.
luxe m. luxury.
luxós -osa a. luxurious.

M

ma my, femenine of possessive adjective «mon».
mà f. hand.
mà foradada a. phr. spendthrift.
maça f. mace.
macar tr. to bruise.
macarrons m. pl. macaroni.
maceració f. maceration, steeping.
màcula f. stain, spot, blemish.
madrastra f. stepmother.
madeixa f. hank, coil, skein.
maduixa f. strawberry.
madur -a a. ripe / mature / mellow.
madurar intr. to mature, ripen.
maduresa f. maturity, ripeness.
magall m. pickaxe.
magatzem m. warehouse, store, depository.
magatzematge m. storage.
màgia f. magic.
màgic -a a. magical / m. - f. magician.
magistral a. magisterial.
magistrat m. magistrate.
magnànim -a a. magnanimous.
magnanimitat f. magnanimity.
magnet m. magnet.
magnetòfon m. tape recorder.
magnífic -a a. magnificent.
magnificar tr. to magnify.
magnificència f. magnificence, glory.
magrana f. pomegranate.
magre -a a. meagre, lean.
mai adv. never.
maig m. May.
mainadera f. governess.
maionesa f. mayonnaise.
majestat f. majesty, royalty.
majestuós -osa a. majestic.
majordom m. butler, steward.

majordona f. housekeeper, mistress.
majoria f. majority.
majoritat f. majority.
majúscula f. capital letter.
mal adj. bad / m. evil / m. illness / m. damage / adv. badly.
malabarisme m. juggling.
malabarista m.-f. juggler.
malagradós -osa a. sullen, morose, grim.
malalt -a a. ill, sick.
malaltia f. illness, sickness.
malaltís -issa a. ill, sick, unwell.
malament adv. badly.
malastrugança f. misfortune, calamity / misery.
malaurança f. misadventure, misfortune.
malaurat -ada a. unhappy, unfortunate.
malbé (fer malbé) v. phr. to break, damage.
maldar intr. to strengthen, invigorate.
maldat f. badness, wickedness.
malediccíó f. damn, damnation.
maleir tr. to damn.
maleït -ïda a. damned.
malendreç m. shabbiness.
malendreçat -ada a. shabby.
malentès m. misunderstanding.
malesa f. mischievousness / overgrowth of weeds.
malestar m. uneasiness, discomfort.
maleta f. suitcase, case, valise.
malefactor m. malefactor, evildoer, criminal.
malfiança f. mistrust.
malfiar tr. to mistrust.
malgastador -a a. wasteful, spendthrift.
malgastar tr. to waste.
malgrat conj. although, despite.
malícia f. mischievousness / malice / shrewdness.

malifeta f. misdeed.
maligne -a a. malignant.
mall m. mallet.
malla f. mesh, network.
mallorquí -ina a. / m.-f. Majorcan.
malnom m. nickname.
malsà -ana a. unhealthy.
malson m. nightmare.
maltractar tr. to mistreat.
maluc m. hip.
malva f. mallow.
malvat -ada a. evil, wicked, villainous / m. villain.
mamà f. mummy, mum / mammy (Am.).
mamífer -a a. mammal.
mampara f. screen, partition.
mamut m. mammoth.
manar tr. to command, order.
manat m. handful.
manc -a a. one handed.
manca f. lack, shortage.
mancança f. lack, shortage.
mancar intr. to lack.
mandarina f. tangerine.
mandíbula f. jaw.
mandra f. laziness, sloth.
mandrejar intr. to laze.
mandrós -osa a. lazy / m.-f. idler, layabout.
mànec m. haft, handle.
mànega f. sleeve / hose.
manejable a. manageable / wieldy.
manejar tr. to operate, handle / to move, move about.
manera f. manner, mode.
manifestar tr. to state, declare / to demonstrate.
màniga f. sleeve.
manilles f. pl. manacles, handcuffs.
manipulació f. manipulation.
manipular tr. to manipulate.
maniquí s. mannequin / model / tailor's dummy.

manllevar tr. to borrow / to steal.

manobre m. builder's assistant, building worker.

manotada f. smack.

mansoi a. mild and affectionate.

mansuetud f. mildness, meekness.

manta f. blanket /

mantega f. butter.

mantell m. mantle, cloak.

manteniment m. upkeep, maintenance.

mantenir tr. to keep, maintain.

manufactura f. manufacture.

manuscrit m. manuscript.

manxa f. bellows.

manyà m. smith.

manyós -osa a. skilful, dexterous / ingenious.

maó m. brick.

mapa m. map.

maquillar -se pr. v. to make up.

maquillatge m. make-up.

màquina f. machine.

maquinària f. machinery.

mar m. sea.

maragda f. emerald.

marbre m. marble.

marc m. frame / door case. Deutsche mark.

marca f. mark / make.

març m. March.

marcador m. scorer / scoreboard.

marcar tr. to mark / to score / to dial.

marcial a. warlike.

marcir-se pr. v. to decay, fade, wither.

marcit -ida a. dead, withered, faded, sere.

mare f. mother.

mareig m. seasickness.

marejar tr. to be travelsick or seasick.

marejat -ada a. seasick.

màrfega f. paillasse, straw mattress.

margarida f. daisy.

marge m. border, margin, edge / verge.

marginar tr. to leave margins on.

marí -ina a. marine.

marina f. navy.

mariner m. mariner, sailor.

mariscal m. marshal.

marit m. husband.

marítim -a a. maritime / marine, sea.

marmessor m. executor.

marmori -òria a. marble.

marquès m. marquis.

marquesa f. marchioness.

marrar tr. - intr. to miss / to go astray

marrec m. lad, youth.

marró m. brown /maroon.

marruix m. knave.

marruixa f. knave.

marta f. marten.

martell m. hammer.

martinet m. ram.

màrtir m.-f. martyr.

martiri m. martyrdom.

martiritzar tr. to martyrize.

marxa f. march.

marxapeu m. sill.

marxar intr. to march / to go / to function, work.

mas m. farmhouse.

màscara f. mask / mummer.

mascle m. male.

masculí -ina a. masculine.

masia f. farmhouse.

masover -a a. resident farm overseer or caretaker.

massa adv. too, too much / f. mass / crowd.

massatge m. massage.

massís-issa a. massive / m. massif.

mastegar tr. to chew.

mastí m. mastiff.

mata f. bush.

matador m. killer / matador.
matalàs m. mattress.
matalasser -a m.-f. quilter.
matança f. slaughter, massacre.
matar tr. to kill.
mateix -a a. same / self / very.
matemàtiques f. pl. mathematics.
matèria f. matter, material / subject, theme.
material m. material.
matí m. morning.
matinada f. dawn, early morning.
matís m. shade, hue, tint, tone / nuance.
matisar tr. to tinge, tint.
matrimoni m. marriage / married couple.
matrimonial a. matrimonial.
matriu f. womb, uterus / mould, die, matrix.
matrona f. matron.
màxim m. maximum.
meandre m. meander.
mecànic m. mechanic.
mecànica f. mechanics.
mecanògraf -a m.-f. typist.
medalla f. medal.
medecina f. medicine.
medicament m. medecine, medicament.
mèdul·la f. marrow, pith.
medusa f. (icht.) jellyfish.
meitat f. half, middle.
mel f. honey.
melangia f. melancholy.
melic m. navel.
melmelada f. marmalade, jam.
meló m. melon.
melodia f. melody.
membrana f. membrane.
membre m. limb / member.
memòria f. memory / report, memoir.

mena f. sort, type / ore.
menció f. mention, quote, reference.
mencionar tr. to mention, quote.
menjada f. meal.
menjador m. dining room.
menjadora f. manger.
menjar tr. to eat.
menor a. lesser, less, smaller / junior, minor.
ment f. mint.
mentida f. lie, falsehood, fib.
mentider -a a. / m.-f. liar, fibber, deceitful person.
mentir intr. to lie.
mentre conj. while, whilst, as.
mentrestant adv. meanwhile, meantime.
menut -uda a. small / petty, trivial / m.- f. little boy, girl.
menuts (d'un animal) m. pl. innards, entrails.
menys adv. less.
menyspreable a. worthless, trashy / despicable.
menyspreu m. scorn, contempt, disdain.
merament adv. merely.
meravella f. marvel, wonder.
meravellar -se pr. v. to marvel, wonder.
meravellós -osa a. marvellous, wonderful.
mercadejar tr. to deal, trade.
mercaderies f. pl. goods, merchandise, wares.
mercat m. market.
mercè f. grace.
mercuri m. mercury, quicksilver.
mereixedor -a a. deserving, worthy.
mereixer tr. to deserve.
meridional a. southern / m.f. southerner.
mèrit m. merit, worth, credit.

meritori -òria a. meritorious, worthy, praiseworthy.

mes m. month.

més adv. more.

mescla f. mix, blend, mixture / medley.

mesclar tr. to mix.

mesquí -ina a. paltry / miserable / tiny / mean, avaricious.

mesquinesa f. meaness.

mesquita f. mosque.

messies m. Messiah.

mestra f. teacher, schoolmistress.

mestratge m. mastery / teacher-training.

mestre m. master, teacher.

mestressa f. landlaly, mistress.

mestria f. mastery, skill, expertise.

mesura f. measure.

mesurar tr. to measure.

meta f. goal.

metall m. metal.

metamorfosi f. metamorphosis.

metge m. doctor, physician.

mètode m. method.

metòdic -a a. methodical.

metre m. meter (Am.), metre (Bri.).

metro m. underground, tube, (Am.) subway.

metzina f. poison, venom.

meu -meva a. sing. my / pron. pos. mine.

meus -meves a. pl. my / pron. pos. mine.

mi pron. me / m. mi (mus.).

mica f. bit, jot, small quantity.

mida f. measure / size.

midó m. starch.

mig -mitja a. half, middle.

migdia m. noon, midday.

migdiada f. nap.

migranya f. migraine.

migrat -ada a. short, sparing, insufficient.

mil a. thousand.

mile -ena a./ m.-f. thousandth.

milió m. million.

militant a. militant.

militar a. military / m. serviceman, military man / v. intr. to serve in the army / to militate.

milla f. mile.

millor a. better.

millora f. improvement.

millorar tr. - intr. to improve, get better, make better.

mina f. mine (both senses).

minaire m. miner.

mineral m. mineral, ore.

mineria f. mining.

minestra f. vegetable soup, stew.

mínim -a a. / m. minimum, smallest.

ministeri m. ministry.

ministre m. minister.

minoria f. minority.

minoritat f. minority.

minut m. minute.

minva f. decrease, decline, wane.

minvant a. decreasing / (lluna) waning.

minvar intr. - tr. to wane, decrease.

minyó m. lad, boy.

miop a. short-sighted, near-sighted / m.-f. short-sighted person.

miracle m. miracle.

miraculós -ósa a. miraculous.

mirada f. look, glance, gaze.

mirador m. belvedere.

mirall m. mirror, looking-glass.

mirar tr. to look at, watch, gaze at, glance.

miratge m. mirage.

mirra f. myrrh.

miserable a. miserable.

misèria f. need, misery, want.

misericòrdia f. compassion, mercy, pity.
misericordiós -osa a. merciful, compassionate.
missa f. mass.
missatge m. message.
missatger -a a. / m.-f. messenger, herald.
missió f. mission.
misteri m. mystery, secret.
mite m. myth.
mitigar tr. to mitigate.
mitja f. stocking.
mitjà -ana a. middle, medium.
mitjana f. average / chop.
mitjançant prep. by means of.
mitjania f. mediocrity.
mitjanit f. midnight.
mitjans m. pl. means.
mitjons m. pl. socks.
mixt -a a. mixed, mingled.
mobiliari m. furniture.
moble m. piece of furniture / a. movable.
mocador m. handkerchief.
moda f. fashion, mode.
mode m. mode.
model m. model.
modelar tr. to model.
moderació f. moderation, temperance.
moderat -ada a. moderate, temperate.
modern -a a. modern, present-day, up-to-date.
modest a a. humble, modest.
modificar tr. to modify.
modista f. dressmaker.
mofa f. mockery, jeer.
mofar-se pr. v. to deride.
moixaina f. pat.
moldre tr. to mill, grind.
molestar tr. to annoy, pester, bother, trouble.
molèstia f. annoyance, nuisance, trouble.

molestós -osa a. troublesome, annoying.
molí m. mill.
moliner m. miller.
molinet m. windmill.
moll m. dock, wharf, quay, pier / (icht.) red mullet.
molló m. milestone / boundary.
molt adv. very, greatly, much.
molt -a a. much, plenty.
moltíssim adv. badly.
moltíssims -imés a. great many.
moltó m. mutton, sheep.
moment m. moment.
mòmia f. mummy.
món m. world / people.
mona f. ape, monkey.
monarca m. monarch.
monarquia f. monarchy.
moneda f. coin, money.
monestir m. monastery.
mongeta f. kidney bean, French bean.
monitor -a m.-f. monitor.
monja f. nun.
monjo m. monk.
monotonia f. monotony.
monsó m. monsoon.
monstre m. monster.
mostruós -osa a. monstruous.
mont m. mount.
móra f. blackberry.
moral a. moral.
moralment adv. morally.
mordassa f. gag.
morè -ena a. dark, dusky, swarthy.
moreno -a a. dark / sunburned, tanned.
moresc m. corn, maize.
moribund -a a. dying.
morir int. to decease, die.
moro -a m.-f. Moorish.
morro m. muzzle, snout.
morsa f. walrus.
mort -a a. dead

mortal a. deadly / mortal.
mortaldat f. slaugther.
mosca f. fly.
moscatell m. muscatel.
mosquit m. mosquito.
mossada f. morsel.
mossegada f. bite.
mossegar tr. to bite.
mosso m. stableboy / porter / waiter.
most m. must.
mostassa f. mustard.
mostela f. weasel.
mostra f. sample.
mot m. word.
motí m. mutiny, revolt, rising, riot, disturbance.
motiu m. motive, cause, reason, sake.
motivar tr. to motivate.
motlle m. mould.
motocicleta f. motocycle.
motonau f. motorboat.
motor m. motor, engine.
motxilla f. rucksack, knapsack, pack.
moure tr. to move.
moviment m. movement, motion.
mudar tr. to move house / to change clothes / to moult (animals, birds).
mul -a m.- f. mule.
mullar tr. to wet.
muller f. wife.
múltiple a. multiple, manifold.
multiplicar tr. to multiply.
multitud f. multitude / crowd.
mundial a. worl-wide, universal.
municipalitat f. municipality / town council.
municipi m. municipality / town council.
munió f. herd, multitude.
munt m. heap, pile.
muntanya f. mountain.

muntanyós -osa a. hilly, mountainous.
muntar tr. to mount, get on, ride.
munyir tr. to milk.
mur m. wall.
murmuri m. murmur, mutter / whisper / ripple.
murri -múrria a. sly, crafty / knavish.
muscle m. shoulder.
musclo m. mussel.
múscul m. muscle.
musell m. muzzle, snout.
museu m. museum.
músic m. musician / a. musical.
música f. music.
mussol m. red owl.
mut -muda a. mute, dumb.
mutu -mútua a. mutual.
mutual a. mutual.

N

nació f. nation.
nacional a. national.
nacionalitat f. nationality.
nacre m. nacre.
Nadal m. Christmas.
nadala f. carol / Christmas carol.
nadiu -a a. indigenous / native, natal.
nadó m. baby.
nafra f. wound / ulcer / sore.
nàiade f. naiad.
naixement m. birth.
nan -a a. dwarf, midget.
nansa f. handle, haft.
nap m. turnip.
narcis m. narcissus, daffodil.
narius f. pl. nostrils.
narració f. narration.

narrar tr. to relate, narrate, recount, tell.

nas m. nose.

natació f. swimming.

natalici m. birthday.

natges f. pl. buttocks.

natura f. nature.

natural a. natural.

naturalesa f. nature.

naturalment adv. naturally, of course.

nau f. ship, sailing vessel / (arch.) nave.

naufragar tr. to be wrecked, sink.

naufragi m. wreck, shipwreck.

nàusea f. nausea, queasiness.

nauseabund -a a. repugnant.

navalla f. razor.

navegació f. navigation.

navegar intr. to navigate / to sail.

neboda f. niece.

nebot m. nephew.

necessari -ària a. necessary.

necessitar tr. to need, want.

necessitat f. necessity, need, want.

neci -nècia a. silly / fool.

nedar intr. to swim.

nedador -a a. / m.-f. swimmer.

negar tr. to deny, refuse / to flood, drown.

negatiu -iva a. negative.

negativa f. denial, refusal.

negligència f. negligence, neglect.

negligir tr. to neglect.

negoci m. business.

negre -a a. black / m.-f. negro, negress.

neguitós -osa a. restless.

nèixer intr. to be born.

nen -a m. -f. child.

nenúfar m. water lily.

nervi m. nerve / vitality, energy.

nerviós -osa a. nervous.

nerviüt -üda a. nervous.

net -a a. clean, tidy, neat.

nét m. grandson.

néta f. granddaughter.

netedat f. neatness, tidiness.

netejar tr. to clean, tidy.

neu f. snow.

neutralitat f. neutrality.

neutre -a a. neutral / neuter.

neutró m. neutron.

nevada f. snowstorm, snowfall.

nevar intr. to snow.

nevera f. refrigerator, icebox.

ni conj. nor.

niada f. little birds in the nest.

niciesa f. nonsense, silliness.

nimfa f. nymph.

nina f. doll / pupil (of the eye).

ningú pron. nobody, none.

ninot m. puppet / scarecrow / cartoon character.

níquel m. nickel.

nit f. night.

nitrat m. nitrate.

niu m. nest.

nivell m. level.

no adv. no, not, nay.

noble a. noble.

noblement adv. nobly.

noblesa f. nobility.

noces f. pl. wedding.

noció f. notion.

nociu -iva a. harmful, noxious.

nocturn -a a. nightly, nocturnal.

nodrir tr. to nourish, feed.

nodrissó m. suckling.

nogensmenys adv. nevertheless.

noguera f. wallnut tree.

noi m. boy.

noia f. girl.

nom m. name.

nom (de pila) m. first name, Christian name.

nòmada a. nomad.

nombre m. number.

nombrós -osa a. numerous.

nomenament m. appointment.
nomenar tr. to name, nominate, appoint.
només adv. only.
nora f. daughter-in-law.
noranta a. / m.-f. ninety.
norantè -ena a. / m.-f. ninetieth.
nord m. North.
nòrdic -a a. Norse.
norma f. standard.
normalment adv. normally.
normand -a a. / m.f. Norman.
noruec -ega a. Norwegian.
nosa f. hindrance, obstacle, obstruction.
nosaltres pron. we, us, ourselves.
nosaltres mateixos pron. ourselves.
nostàlgia f. nostalgia, homesickness, longing.
nostre -a, nostres a. / pron. pos. our, ours.
nota f. note.
notable a. noteworthy.
notar tr. to note.
notari m. notary public.
notícies f. pl. news, tidings.
notificar tr. to notify.
notori -òria a. well-known.
notorietat f. fame.
nou a. / m. nine. •
nou -nova a. new, fresh.
nou f. walnut, nut.
novament adv. once again.
novè -ena m.-f. ninth.
novel·la f. novel, romance, fiction.
novembre m. November.
novençà a. beginner, rookie (jargon).
novetat f. novelty.
novici -icia a. novice.
nu -nua a. bare, nude, naked.
nuar tr. to knot.
nuca f. nape, scruff.
nucli m. nucleus.

nuesa f. nudity.
nul-nul·la a. void / useless.
numerar tr. to number.
número m. number.
nunci m. messenger / Papal nuncio / herald.
nuós -osa a. knurled / gnarled.
nupcial a. nuptial, bridal.
nus m. knot.
nutritiu -iva a. nourishing, nutritious.
nuvi m. bridegroom.
núvia f. bride.
nuvial a. nuptial, bridal
núvol m. cloud.
nyam m. yam.

O

o conj. or.
oasi m. oasis.
obac -obaga a. shady / f. shady place, grove.
obcecar tr. to blind; obfuscate.
obediència f. obedience.
obedient a. obedient.
obeir tr. to obey.
obelisc m. obelisk.
obert -a a. open.
obertura f. opening / (mus.) overture.
obès -esa a. obese, fat.
obesitat f. obesity.
objectar tr. to object.
objecte m. object, purpose, cause, sake.
objectiu -iva a. objective / m. objective, target / m. lens.
oblidadís -issa a. forgetful.
oblidar tr. to forget.
obligació f. obligation, duty.

obligar tr. to oblige.
oblit m. oblivion.
obra f. work.
obrador m. workshop.
obrar tr. - intr. to work, operate, act.
obrer -a a. / m.-f. worker, workman.
obrir tr. to open, unlock.
obscur -a a. obscure, gloomy, dusky, dark.
obscuritat f. obscurity, gloom, darkness.
obsequiar tr. to entertain, to lavish attentions on.
observador -a a. / m.-f. observant / observer.
observança f. observance.
observant a. observant.
observar tr. to observe, watch, notice / to heed, comply with.
obstacle m. obstacle, hindrance, barrier.
obstaculitzar tr. to obstruct, hinder.
obstinació f. obstinacy.
obstinat -ada a. obstinate, stubborn, heady.
obstrucció f. obstruction.
obstruir tr. obstruct, to block.
obvi - òbvia a. obvious.
obtenir tr. to obtain, get, secure.
oca f. goose.
ocàs m. sunset, setting / occident, west / decadence.
ocasió f. chance, occasion.
ocasional a. occasional.
ocasionalment adv. occasionally.
ocasionar tr. to occasion, bring about.
occident m. the West.
occidental a. western.
occir tr. to kill, murder, slay.
oceà m. ocean.

ocell m. bird.
oci m. leisure, idleness.
ociosament adv. idly.
ocórrer intr. to happen / occur / to take place / to strike one / occur to one.
octubre m. October.
oculista a. oculist.
ocult -a a. occult, hidden.
ocupació f. employment, job, occupation, profession.
ocupar tr. to employ / to occupy.
ocupat -ada a. busy.
odi m. hate.
odiar tr. to hate.
odiós -osa a. odious, hateful.
oest m. West.
ofegar tr. to smother, suffocate / drown.
ofegar -se pr. v. to drown.
ofendre tr. to offend.
ofensa f. offence, injury.
ofensiu -iva a. offensive.
oferiment m. offer.
oferir tr. to give, offer.
oferta f. offer.
ofici m. profession, occupation / service.
oficial a. official.
oficialment adv. officially.
oficiar tr. to officiate.
oficina f. bureau, office.
ofrena f. offering.
ofuscar tr. to daze.
oh! interj. oh!.
oi? interj. isn't that so?.
oïda f. hearing, ear.
oient a. listener, hearer.
oir tr. to hear.
oli m. oil.
òliba f. owl.
oligarquia f. oligarchy.
olimpíada f. olympiad.
oliós -osa a. oily.
oliva f. olive.
olivera f. olive tree.

olla f. pot / stew.
olor f. odour, scent.
olorar tr. to smell.
olorós -osa a. odorous.
om m. elm tree.
ombra f. shade, shadow.
ombrel·la f. parasol, sunshade.
ombriu -iva a. shady, sombre.
ometre tr. to miss, omit / to shirk.
omissió f. omission, oversight.
omplir tr. to fill.
on adv. where, whereabouts.
ona f. wave, billow.
oncle m. uncle.
ondular tr. - intr. to undulate.
onejar intr. to wave.
onze a. i m. eleven.
onzè -ena a. / m.-f. eleventh.
opac -a a. opaque.
opacitat f. opacity.
opció f. option.
òpera f. opera.
operació f. operation.
operar tr. to operate.
opi m. opium.
opinar tr. to think, give an opinion.
opinió f. opinion, view.
oportunitat f. opportunity, chance.
oposant a. opponent.
oposar tr. to pit A against B.
oposició f. opposition / competition / public entrance exam.
opressiu -iva a. oppressive.
oprimir tr. to oppress / squeeze, press.
oprobi m. opprobrium.
optimista a. optimistic.
opulència f. opulence.
or m. gold.
oració f. prayer / (gram.) sentence.
orador -a m.-f. orator, speaker.
oral a. oral.

orar intr. to pray / to make a speech.
oratori m. oratory.
oratòria f. oratory.
orb -a a. sightless, blind.
orde m. religious order.
ordenar tr. to order.
ordenat - ada a. orderly.
ordi m. barley.
ordinari -ària a. ordinary / vulgar.
ordre f. order.
ordre (de detenció) m. warrant.
oreig m. breeze, light wind.
orella f. ear.
orfe -òrfena a. / m.-f. orphan.
orfeó m. choir.
òrgan m. organ.
organització f. organization.
organitzar tr. to organize.
orgue m. organ.
orgull m. pride.
orgullós -osa a. proud, haughty.
origen m. origin.
originalitat f. originality.
originar tr. to originate, give rise to.
orina/ f. urine.
orinador m. urinary.
orinal m. chamberpot, urinal.
orins m. pl. urine.
oripell m. tinsel.
orla f. border, fringe, selvage.
ornament m. ornament.
ornamentar tr. to ornament.
ortografia f. orthography, spelling.
os m. bone.
ós m. bear.
osca f. notch, nick / groove, slot, score.
oscat -ada a. jagged.
oscil·lació f. oscillation, swing.
oscil·lar intr. to oscillate, swing, sway, waver.
ossa t. she-bear.
ostatge m. hostage.
ostra f. oyster.

ostracisme m. ostracism.
ou m. egg.
ovella f. ewe, sheep.
oxigen m. oxygen.

P

pa m. bread.
paciència f. patience.
pacient a. patient.
pacífic -a a. peaceful, pacific.
pacificació f. pacification.
pacificar tr. to pacify.
pacifisme m. pacifism.
pacte m. pact, bargain, agreement.
padrastre m. stepfather.
padrí f. godfather.
padrina f. godmother.
paella f. frying pan. Valencian rice dish made with chicken, shellfish, etc., and the shallow metal pan in which it is prepared.
paga f. payment, salary.
pagà -ana a. heathen, pagan.
pagament m. payment.
paganisme m. paganism.
pagar tr. - intr. to pay.
pagès -esa m. -f. peasant, farmer, countryman.
pàgina f. page.
paginar tr. to page, paginate.
païdor m. stomach.
pair tr. to digest.
país m. country, land.
paisatge m. landscape.
paixà m. pasha.
pal m. pole / mast / staff, stick.
pala f. spade / paddle.
paladar m. palate.
paladí m. champion, chivalresque hero, paladin.

palanca f. lever / crossbeam / crowbar.
palangana f. basin.
palatí -ina a. palatial.
palau m. palace.
palès -esa a. patent.
palesar tr. to make evident, obvious.
palet m. small boulder / cobblestone.
paleta m. bricklayer / mason.
palla f. straw.
pallassada f. clownish joke or action.
paller m. haystack.
pallera f. hayloft.
pàl·lid -a a. pale, wan, pallid.
pal·lidesa f. paleness.
pallissa f. barn / beating.
palma f. palm.
palmell m. palm (hand).
palmera f. palm.
palpable a. palpable, tactile, perceptible, obvious.
palpar tr. to touch, feel.
pamflet m. pamphlet.
pàmpol m. young vine-branch.
panera f. bread-basket / hamper.
panet m. roll.
panorama m. view, panorama, prospect.
pansa f. raisin.
pansir tr. to wither, fade.
pansit -ida a. dried up.
pantà m. moor, marsh, swamp / reservoir.
pantalla f. screen / shade / lampshade.
pantalons m. pl. trousers / (Am.) pants.
pantanós -osa a. marshy, boggy.
panteix m. pant, wheezing.
panteixar intr. to pant, wheeze.
pantera f. panther.
panxa f. paunch, belly.
pany m. lock.

papa m. pope.
papà (fam.) m. dad, daddy / (Am.) pop, poppa.
papagai m. parrot.
papallona f. butterfly.
papat m. papacy.
paper m. paper.
paperer m. stationer.
papereria f. stationer's.
paperina f. cornet (ice-cream, paper, etc.).
paquet m. package, packet.
paquetaire a. packer.
par m. peer (title).
paràbola f. parable / (geom.) parabola.
paracaigudes m. parachute.
paracaigudista m.-f. paratrooper, parachutist.
parada f. stand / stop, halt.
paradís m. paradise.
paràgraf m. paragraph.
paraiguas m. umbrella.
paràlisi f. palsy, paralysis.
paralític -a a. paralytic.
paralitzat -ada a. paralysed.
paral·lel -a a. parallel.
parany m. trap, snare / decoy.
parar tr. to halt, pause.
paràsit -a a. / m.-f. parasite.
para-sol m. sunshade.
paraula f. word, term.
parc m. park.
parcial m. partial.
parcel·la f. plot of land.
parcel·lar tr. to divide into plots of land.
pardal m. sparrow.
pare m. father.
parell m. couple, pair.
parell -a. a. even, equal, like / pair, couple.
parella f. couple / partner.
Parenostre m. Lord's prayer.
parent -a m. -f. relative.
parèntesi m. parenthesis, brackets.

parentiu m. kindred.
parer m. opinion, advice.
paret f. wall.
parir tr. to give birth / to breed.
parlador -a a. / m.-f. talkative, chatty, voluble / gabbler.
parlament m. parliament.
parlamentari -ària a. parliamentary.
parlar intr. to speak.
parleries f. pl. gabble.
parpella f. eyelid, lid.
parpelleig m. wink.
parpellejar intr. to blink, wink / (star) to twinkle.
parra f. grapevine.
parrac m. rag.
parròquia f. parish.
part m. parturition, childbirth.
part f. part, share, allotment.
partença f. departure.
partera f. parturient, woman who has just given birth.
participant a. participant, partaker.
participar tr. to participate, take part / to share, partake.
participi m. participle.
partícula f. particle.
particular a. private / particular.
partidari -ària a. supporter, partisan.
partir tr. to halve, part, split / intr. to depart.
partió f. partition / boundary.
partit m. match, game / (political) party.
pas m. pace, step / passage / tread.
Pasqua de Resurrecció f. Easter.
passa f. pace, step / epidemic.
passadís m. corridor, lobby.
passamà m. rail.
passaport m. passport.

passar tr. to pass / to hand over, give.

passat m. past / past tense.

passat -ada a. past, last.

passatemps m. pastime, hobby.

passatge m. passage.

passatger -a m.-f. passenger.

passeig m. stroll, walk.

passejada f. walk, sally, excursion.

passejant m.-f. walker.

passejar tr. to walk, ramble.

passi m. pass.

passió f. passion.

pasta f. paste / pastry.

pastada f. mash.

pastanaga f. carrot.

pastar tr. to knead.

pastel m. crayon / dibuixar al..., tr. to crayon.

pastilla f. tablet.

pastís m. cake.

pastisseria f. pastrycook's, confectioner's, cake shop.

pastor m. shepherd.

pastora f. shepherdess.

pastós -osa a. pasty.

patata f. potato.

patent a. patent.

patentar tr. to patent.

patentitzar tr. to show, demonstrate, make evident.

patètic -a a. pathetic, moving, touching.

patge m. page.

pati m. court, courtyard.

pati m. skate.

patíbul m. gallows.

patilles f. pl. side whiskers.

patinador -a a. / m.-f. skater.

patinar intr. to skate / to skid, slip.

patir tr. - intr. to suffer.

pàtria f. fatherland, native land, homeland, country.

patriota m.-f. patriot.

patró m. boss, employer / patron.

patrocinador -a a. / m.-f. sponsor.

patrulla f. patrol.

patrullar intr. to patrol.

pau f. peace.

pausa f. pause, interval / rest.

pavelló m. bell tent / pavilion.

paviment m. pavement.

pavimentar tr. to pave.

peatge m. toll.

pebre m. pepper.

pebre vermell m. paprika.

pebrot m. pepper.

peça f. piece, part.

pecador -a a. / m.-f. sinner / sinful.

pecaminós -osa a. sinful.

pecar intr. to sin.

pecat m. sin.

pedaç m. patch.

pedal m. pedal, treadle.

pedestal m. stand.

pedra f. stone.

pedrera f. quarry.

pega f. glue, paste.

pegar tr. to stick.

peix m. fish.

peixatera f. fishwife.

peix espasa m. swordfish.

pèl m. hair, fibre.

pela f. peel / (slang) peseta.

pelar tr. to peel.

pelegrí -ina m.-f. pilgrim.

pell f. skin, fur / leather / peel.

pel·lícula f. film.

pellofa f. hull / skin.

pelós -osa a. hairy.

pelut -uda a. hairy, shaggy.

pena f. suffering, misery, anguish / punishment, sentence.

pendent a. pendent, unsettled / m. slope, declivity.

pèndol m. pendulum.

penediment m. regret.

penedir-se pr. v. to repent.

penell m. weather vane.
penic m. penny.
penicil·lina f. penicillin.
peninsula f. peninsula.
penjador m. hanger.
penjar tr. to hang.
penós -osa a. painful.
pensador -a a. / m.-f. thinker.
pensament m. thought, idea, thinking.
pensar intr. to think, imagine, consider.
pensarós -osa a. thoughtful, pensive.
pensió (casa de dispeses) f. boarding house.
pensionat m. boarding school / pensioner.
Pentecosta f. Whitsun, Whitsuntide, Pentecost.
pentinar tr. to comb.
pentinat m. hairdressing, hairstyle.
penyal m. rock.
penyora f. pledge, token.
peó m. pedestrian / day labourer / footsoldier / pawn.
peoner -a m. -f. pioneer.
per prep. for, by.
per a prep. for, to, in order to.
pera f. pear.
percala f. calico.
percebre tr. to perceive.
perdiu f. partridge.
perdó m. pardon, forgiveness.
perdonar tr. to forgive, pardon.
perdoni interj. I am sorry.
perdre tr. to lose, mislay / to miss.
pèrdua f. loss.
perdut -uda a. lost, stray, astray.
peresa f. laziness, idleness.
peresós -osa a. lazy, indolent.
perfecte -a a. perfect.
perfil m. profile, outline, silhouette.
perforar tr. to pierce, perforate.

perfum m. perfume.
perfumar tr. to perfume.
pergamí m. parchment.
perícia f. skill, dexterity.
perill m. peril, danger, risk.
perillós -osa a. dangerous, perillous, risky.
període m. period, term, stage.
periòdic m. journal, newspaper.
periodista m. -f. journalist.
perir intr. to perish, die, expire.
perjudici m. detriment, harm.
perjudicial a. harmful.
perjuri m. perjury, false oath.
perla f. pearl.
perllongar tr. to elongate / to prolong.
permanència f. permanence.
permetre tr. to allow, let, pemit.
permís m. permission, permit.
permutar tr. to permute.
pernil m. ham.
però conj. but, however.
perol m. pan.
perola f. pan.
perpal m. lever.
perquè conj. because.
per què? conj. why
perquè no conj. lest, for fear that.
perruca f. wig.
perruquer m. hairdresser.
persecució f. persecution.
perseguir tr. chase, to pursue / to persecute.
persistir intr. to persist.
persona f. person.
perspectiva f. perspective / view, prospect.
perspicaç a. perspicacious.
perspicàcia f. perspicacity, insight.
persuadir tr. to persuade.
persuasió f. persuasion.
per tant adv. therefore, consequently, so.

pertànyer intr. to belong.
pertinaç a. obstinate, persistent.
pertorbador -a a. troubler, disturbing.
pertorbar tr. to disturb, harass.
pervers -a a. perverse, wicked, depraved.
pes m. weight, heaviness / load, burden.
pesar tr. - intr. to weigh / to weigh down upon.
pesat -ada a. heavy / nuisance.
pesca f. fishing, the fishing industry / catch.
pescador a. / m. fisherman.
pescar tr. to fish.
pèsol m. pea.
pesseta f. peseta.
pessic m. pinch, nip / small bit.
pessigar tr. to pinch, nip.
pessigollejar tr. to tickle.
pessigolles f. pl. tickling.
pestanya f. eyelash.
pestell m. latch.
petició f. petition, request.
petit -a a. small, little.
petja f. track, footstep / impression.
petjada f. tread, treading
petó m. kiss.
petri -pètria a. stony, rocky.
petricó m. pint.
petroli m. petroleum, crude oil.
peu m. foot / paw, trotter / stand.
pi m. pine, pine tree.
piadós -osa a. pious, devout.
piano m. piano, pianoforte.
pic m. pick / peak / knock / time.
pica f. pike, lance / stone trough, basin / font.
picada f. sting
picapedrer m. stonecutter, quarryman.
picaporta m. knocker.
picar tr. to prick / to peck / to

bite (insects) / to pick / to sting.
picar (pedra) tr. to hew.
picardia f. roguery.
picor f. itch.
pietat f. mercy, pity / devotion, piety.
pietós -osa a. pious, devout.
pijama m. pyjamas.
pila f. heap.
pilar m. pillar, post.
pillet m. knave, rogue, urchin.
pilós -osa a. hairy.
pilot m. pile.
pilot (conductor) m. pilot.
pilota f. ball.
pilotejar tr. to pilot.
pinça f. clip.
pinces f. pl. tweezers, tongs, pincers / claws.
pinta f. comb.
pintar tr. to depict, paint.
pintor -a m. -f. painter.
pintoresc -a a. picturesque.
pintura f. painting / paint.
pinya f. pinecone / pineapple.
pinyó m. pinion (mec.) / pine kernel.
pinyol m. pip (of fruit) / sustained high-pitched note.
pinzell m. artist's brush.
pipa f. pipe.
pirata m. pirate.
piratejar intr. to practise piracy.
pis m. apartment, flat, storey.
piscina f. swimming pool.
pissarra f. slate / blackboard.
pista f. track.
pistó m. piston.
pistoler m. gunman.
pit m. breast, chest.
pitjor adv. worse.
pitxer m. vase.
piuladissa f. twitter, chirp, chirping.
piular intr. to twitter, chirp.
pla m. plan.

pla -ana a. plain, flat.
plaça f. square / seat / market / ...forta, fortress.
plaent a. lovely.
plaer m. pleasure, enjoyment.
plantejar tr. to devise.
plaga f. wound / ulcer / sore / plague.
planar intr. to glide (aero.).
planer -a a. level / smooth, easy / unaffected.
plànol m. plan.
planta f. plant / floor, storey / plan.
plantar tr. to plant / to abandon someone.
planúria f. plain.
planxa f. plate / iron.
planxar tr. to iron.
plany m. complaint, plaint.
plàstic m. plastic.
plat -a m. -f. dish.
plata f. silver.
plàtan m. banana / plane tree.
plàtera f. salver.
platet (volador) m. flying saucer.
platí m. platinum.
platja f. beach.
plaure intr. to please.
ple -ena a. full.
plebeu -ea a. plebeian.
plec m. fold, crease / sheet of paper.
pledejar tr. - intr. to plead.
plegar tr. to fold / to finish work.
plet m. lawsuit, case.
plom m. lead / boring person.
ploma f. feather, quill / pen / ...estilogràfica f. fountain pen.
plomall m. plume / feather duster.
plomar tr. to pluck.
plomat -ada a. feathered.
plomatge m. plumage, feathers.

plor m. crying, flood of tears.
plorar tr. - intr. to cry, weep.
plorós -osa a. tearful.
ploure intr. to rain.
plovisquejar intr. to drizzle, mizzle.
pluja f. rain.
plujós -osa a. rainy, showery, wet.
plural a. / m. -f. plural.
plusquamperfet m. pluperfect.
poagre m. gout.
poagrós -osa a. gouty.
poal m. pitcher / bucket.
població f. population, borough, village.
poblament m. population.
poble m. village / people, folk.
pobre -a a. poor.
poc -a a. little.
poc a poc adv. slowly.
pocs-poques m. -f. pl. few.
poder m. power, might.
poder tr. to be able to, can / may.
poderós -osa a. powerful, forceful, mighty.
podridura f. pus, rot, rottenness.
podriment m. rotting, rot, putrefaction.
podrir tr. to rot, decompose.
podrit -ida a. rotten.
poema m. poem.
poesia f. poetry.
poeta m. poet.
poetessa f. poetess.
pol m. pole.
policia m. policeman.
policia f. police.
polifacètic -a a. many-sided, versatile.
poliment m. polish.
polir tr. to polish, brighten.
polissó -ona m. -f. stowaway.

polit -ida a. neat, tidy, trim, smart / polite.
polític -a m.-f. politician / a. political.
política f. politics / policy.
politja f. pulley.
poll m. chick / louse.
pollastre m. chicken / rooster.
pollet m. chick.
polpa f. pulp, flesh.
pols m. pulse / f. dust.
polsinós -osa a. dusty.
poltrona f. easy-chair.
pòlvora f. gunpowder.
polvoritzador m. spray, sprayer.
polzada f. inch.
polze m. thumb.
pom m. knob / bouquet.
poma f. apple.
pomada f. ointment.
poncell -a a. adolescent, young / f. maid, virgin, maiden, lass / flower bud.
pondre tr. to lay eggs.
pont m. bridge.
pontífex m. pontiff.
pontificat m. papacy.
pop m. octopus.
popa f. poop, stern.
por f. dread, fear.
porc m. pig.
porcellana f. porcelain, chinaware.
porció f. portion, lot, share.
porfídia f. obstinacy.
porpra f. purple, / purple shell.
porqueria f. filth.
port m. haven / harbour, port / **(de muntanya)** mountain pass.
porta f. door / gate.
porta (principal) f. front door.
portada f. frontispiece, title page. / gateway.
portalada f. porch, vestibule / town gate.

portamonedes m. purse.
portar tr. to bring / to carry / to wear.
portell m. gap.
porter m. caretaker, concierge / goalkeeper.
pòrtic m. porch.
porus m. pore.
porxo m. porch / arcade, gallery.
posada f. lodging house.
posar tr. to put, set, lay.
posar-se pr. v. to settle.
posició f. position / standing, status.
positiu -iva a. positive.
posseir tr. to possess, have, own.
possessions f. pl. possessions / estate.
possible a. possible.
possiblement adv. possibly.
posta de sol f. sunset, dusk.
postal (targeta) f. postcard.
posteritat f. posterity.
postís m. false / pad.
postres f. pl. dessert.
postura f. posture, position / bid, wager.
pot m. jug, pot, jar.
pota f. leg (of animal or furniture).
potable a. drinkable.
potada f. kick.
potatge m. stew.
potser adv. perhaps, maybe.
pou m. well / shaft, pit.
pràctic -a a. practical.
pràctica f. practice.
practicant a. practitioner / a. practising.
practicar tr. to practise / to play.
prada f. prairie / meadow.
prat m. meadow / lawn.
prec m. request / prayer.
precedent a. former.

precedir tr. to precede.
precinte m. seal / strap, bind.
precipici m. precipice, cliff.
precipitació f. rush.
precís -isa a. precise, accurate.
precoç a. precocious.
precursor -a a. / m.-f. forerunner.
predicador -a a./ m.-f. preacher.
predicar tr. to preach.
predir tr. to predict, foretell, forecast.
prefaci m. preface, foreword.
preferir tr. to prefer.
pregar tr. to pray.
pregon -a a. deep, profound.
pregunta f. question, inquiry.
preguntar tr. to ask, inquire, question.
prejudici m. prejudgement / prejudice.
prémer tr. to press.
premi m. award, prize.
premsa f. press.
premsar tr. to press.
prendre tr. to take / accept / acquire.
preocupació f. worry, fret, preoccupation.
preocupar tr. to worry, bother, concern, trouble.
preocupat -ada a. worried, concerned, anxious / preoccupied.
preparar tr. to prepare.
pres -a a. / m.-f. prisoner.
presa f. capture / prey / dike, dam.
present a. present / m. the present moment / m. present, gift.
presentar tr. to present.
preservar tr. to preserve, protect.
president m. president / chairman.
presó f. prison, jail, gaol.

presoner -a m.-f. prisoner.
pressa f. hurry, haste, speed, urgency.
préssec m. peach.
pressió f. pressure, stress.
pressupost m. budget / quotation, estimate.
prest -a a. quick, prompt / ready / disposed.
prestador -a a. pawnbroker, lender.
prestar tr. to lend.
prestatge m. shelf, rack, stand, ledge.
préstec m. loan, lending, borrowing.
prestigi m. prestige.
pretendent -a m.-f. pretender, candidate / suitor.
preu m. price, fare, worth.
prevalent a. prevailing, prevalent.
prevenció f. prevention / prejudice.
prevenir tr. to prevent, alert / to prepare, warn.
preveure tr. to foresee.
previ -prèvia a. previous.
previsió f. foresight.
prim -a a. thin, slim, slender, slight.
prima f. premium, subsidy.
prima (d'assegurança) f. premium.
primal -a m.-f. yearling.
primavera f. spring.
primer -a m.-f. first, former / prime.
primicer -era a. prime.
primitiu -iva a. primitive / primary.
primmirat -ada a. scrupulous, cautious.
príncep m. prince.
princesa f. princess.
principal a. main, chief, principal.

principalment adv. principally, chiefly, mainly.

principi m. beginning, start, origin / principle.

principiant a. / m.-f. beginner.

privar tr. to deprive.

privat -ada a. private.

privilegi m. privilege.

proa f. prow, fore.

probable a. probable, likely.

probabilitat f. probability.

problema m. problem.

procaç a. impudent.

procediment m. procedure, proceedings.

procés m. process / trial, prosecution, action.

procurador m. attorney.

pròdig -a a. to lavish.

prodigalitat f. prodigality, wastefulness.

prodigar tr. to lavish.

prodigi m. prodigy / miracle, wonder.

producció f. production.

producte m. product.

productor -a a. / m.-f. producer.

produir tr. to produce.

profecia f. prophecy.

professar tr. to profess, declare.

professió f. profession / career.

professor -a m.-f. teacher, instructor / professor.

profetitzar tr. to foretell.

profit m. profit.

profund -a a. deep, profound.

profunditat f. depth, profundity.

profunditzar tr. to deepen / to study in depth / to fathom, get to the bottom of.

programa m. programme.

progrés m. progress.

progressar intr. to progress, come on, improve.

progressiu -iva a. progressive.

prohibir tr. to forbid, prohibit.

proïsme m. fellow being.

projectar tr. to project.

projecte m. project, plan.

projectil m. projectile, missile.

pròleg m. prologue / preface.

prolongar tr. to prolong / to elongate.

promesa f. promise.

prometatge m. courtship / engagement.

prometença f. vow.

prometre tr. - intr. to promise, pledge / to betroth.

promoure tr. to promote, further.

prompte adv. soon.

pronom m. pronoun.

pronosticar tr. to forecast, foresee, divine.

pronunciació f. pronunciation, utterance.

prop adv. near.

propagació f. propagation, spread.

propaganda f. propaganda / publicity, advertisement.

propagar tr. to propagate, spread.

proper -a a. next, near, close.

propi-pròpia a. proper, correct / own / self.

propietat f. property, possession, estate / properness / propriety.

propina f. tip, gratuity.

proposar tr. to propose.

proposició f. proposal, proposition.

propòsit m. purpose, aim.

propulsar tr. to propel, drive / to promote.

propvinent a. forthcoming.

prorrogar tr. to adjourn / to extend (period).

prosaic -a a. prosaic, commonplace.

pròsper -a a. prosperous, thriving.

prosperar tr. - intr. to prosper.
prosperitat f. prosperity.
protecció f. protection.
protector -a a. /m.-f. protector, patron.
protegir tr. to protect, defend, shield.
protestar tr. - intr. to protest / to profess.
prou a. - adv. enough / quite.
prova f. test, trial / proof / sample.
provar tr. to prove, show, demostrate / to try, try on.
proveïment m. equipment.
proveir tr. to provide, supply, furnish.
provençal a. Provençal.
proverbi m. proverb.
província f. province.
provisionalment adv. provisionally / tentatively.
pròxim -a a. next.
prudent a. prudent, careful.
pruna f. plum.
pruna (seca) f. prune.
pruner -a m.-f. plum tree.
psicologia f. psychology.
pubilla f. heiress.
públic -a a. / m. public.
publicar tr. to publish, issue.
puça f. flea.
pudent a. fetid, stinking.
pudor m. modesty / f. pestilence.
pueril a. childish.
puig m. peak.
pujada f. rise, climb.
pujar tr. ascend, go up / to get into / to grow.
pulcre -a a. neat, smart, tidy.
pulcritud f. neatness, tidiness.
pulmó m. lung.
púlpit m. pulpit.
pulsació f. pulse.
punt m. point, dot / full stop.
punta f. point.

puntejar tr. to dot.
puntuar tr. to punctuate / to score points.
punxa f. prick, thorn.
punxada f. puncture, prick, jab / twinge.
punxar tr. to puncture, pierce, prick, punch.
punxegut -uda a. sharp.
punxó m. punch, burin, engraving tool, bodkin.
puny (de la camisa, vestit) m. cuff.
pupil -il·la a. pupil / f. pupil (of the eye).
pupitre m. desk.
pur -a a. pure / simple, sheer.
puresa f. purity.
purga f. purge.
purgant a. / m. purgative.
purgar tr. to purge.
purgatori m. purgatory.
purificar tr. to purify.
purità -ana a. Puritan.
purpurat m. cardinal.
putxinel·li m. puppet / pl. Punch and Judy show.

Q

quadern m. writing book, exercise book.
quadra f. stable / block of houses / ward.
quadrat m. square.
quadrat -ada a. quadrate, square.
quadre m. painting, picture / square / (theat.) scene / (mil.) chiefs of staff / administrative board.
quadrícula f. squares, criss-cross pattern.
qual a. pron. which, who, whom.

qualificació f. qualification.
qualificar tr. to qualify.
qualitat f. quality.
qualsevol pron. anybody, anyone.
qualsevol a. whichever.
qualsevulla a. whichever.
quan adv. when.
quant -a a. - pron. how much, how many / pl. all those that / adv. how.
quantitat f. quantity, deal.
quants a. - pron. how many?.
quàquer -a a. Quaker.
quaranta a. m. forty.
quarantè -ena a. / m.-f. fourtieth.
quarentena f. quarantine / a collection of forty.
Quaresma f. Lent.
quart -a a. / m.-f. fourth / m. quarter.
quarter (general) m. headquarters.
quasi adv. nearly.
quatre a. m. four.
que pron. that / who, whom / which / while / because, since / how.
què pron. what / which.
quec -a a. stuttering / m. -f. stutterer, stammerer.
quedar intr. to remain, stay.
quefer m. job, task.
queixa f. complaint.
queixal m. molar, grinder.
queixar -se pr. v. to complain.
quelcom pron. anything, something / adv. rather, somewhat.
quequejant ger. faltering.
quequejar intr. stammer, stutter.
querella f. contention, lawsuit.
qüestió f. question.
qüestionar intr. to question / to debate.
queviures m. pl. provisions.

qui pron. who / whom.
quiet -a a. calm. still, tranquil.
quietud f. quietude, stillness.
quilogram m. kilogram.
quilòmetre m. kilometer.
quilla f. keel.
químic m. chemist / a. chemical.
química f. chemistry.
quin -a a. which, what.
quins a. which.
quinze a. / m. fifteen.
quinzè -ena a. / m.-f. fifteenth.
quinzena f. fortnight.
quiosc m. kiosk.
quiti -quítia a. quit.
quocient m. quotient.
quota f. quota, share / fee.
quotidià -ana a. everyday, daily.

R

rabadà m. shepherd.
rabassot m. stub.
rabejar-se pr. v. to irritate, enrage / to wallow, walter.
rabent a. rapid, impetuous.
ràbia f. rage, wrath / rabies.
rabiós -osa a. raging, rabid.
raça f. race, breed.
ració f. ration / portion.
racional a. rational.
racionar tr. to ration.
racó m. corner.
radi (metall) m. radium.
radi (geom.) m. radius.
radiador m. radiator.
radiar tr. to radiate.
radicació f. radication.
ràdio f. radio.
ràdio-receptor m. radio set.
ràfaga f. blast of wind, squall, gust.
rai m. raft.
raig m. ray, jet.

raig (de llum) m. beam.
rail m. rail.
raïm m. grape.
raima f. ream.
rajada f. ray / jet / stream.
rajar intr. to pour out from.
rajola f. tile.
rajoler m. tilemaker, tiler.
rajolí m. trickle.
ram m. bouquet.
ramada f. herd, drove.
ramal m. strand (of rope) / branch (of a road, railway).
ramat m. flock, drove.
rambla f. sandy or dry ravine / avenue.
ramell m. bouquet.
ramificació f. ramification.
rampa f. ramp.
rampell m. impulse / paroxysm, rage / rapture.
rampellada f. impulse / paroxysm, rage / rapture.
rampoina f. residue, waste, rubbish.
rancor m. rancour.
rancorós -osa a. spiteful.
randa f. lace.
ranera f. rattle in the throat / death rattle.
rang m. rank / social position or status.
ranura f. groove, slot.
raó f. reason.
raonablement adv. reasonably / wisely.
raonar intr. to reason.
rapaç a. rapacious / grasping, greedy.
rapacitat f. rapacity.
ràpid -a a. rapid, fast, quick, swift, speedy, nimble.
ràpidament adv. rapidly, fast, quickly.
rapidesa f. speed.
rapinya f. rapine, plundering, plunder.

raqueta f. racket, racquet.
raquític-a a. rickety.
raquitisme m. rickets.
rar -a a. rare, scarce, uncommon / strange / rarified.
rarament adv. rarely, seldom.
raresa f. queerness / rarity.
rasa f. trench, intrenchment / ditch.
rasant a. levelling / grazing.
rascar tr. to scratch / to scrape.
rasclet m. rake.
raspall m. brush.
raspallar tr. to brush.
rastre m. trace.
rata f. rat.
ratificació f. ratification.
ratificar tr. to ratify.
ratlla f. line, stripe, streak.
ratllar tr. to line.
ratolí m. mouse.
raucar intr. to croak.
raure tr. - intr. to wind up, take root / to have dealings with.
rauxa f. rashness.
ravals m. pl. outskirts.
rave m. radish.
reacció f. reaction.
reaccionar intr. to react.
reajustar tr. to readjust.
real a. real.
realitat f. reality / fact.
realització f. achievement, realization / carrying out.
realitzar tr. to achieve, realize.
realment adv. really.
reanimar tr. to revive.
reaparèixer intr. reappear.
reassegurança f. reinsurance.
rebaixa f. diminution / rebate, reduction, discount.
rebaixar tr. to lower / to detract / to humiliate.
rebedor m. hall.
rebel a. / m.-f. rebel.
rebel·lar-se pr. v. to rebel.
rebel·lió f. rebellion.

rebentar intr. to burst / to splash / to vex, annoy.
reblar tr. to rivet.
rebló m. rivet.
rebost m. pantry, larder / store-room.
reboster-a m. -f. larderer.
rebosteria f. pastry.
rebot m. rebound.
rebotre tr. to rebound.
rebre tr. to welcome, receive, greet.
rebregar tr. to wrinkle, crumple.
rebregat-ada a. wrinkled, crumpled.
rebuig m. rebuff, refusal.
rebut m. receipt.
rebutjar tr. to reject.
rec m. canal, drain.
recambra f. dressing room / breech of a gun.
recança f. sentiment / feeling / regret.
recaptador -a a. / m.-f. collector.
recàrrec m. surcharge.
recaure intr. to relapse.
recel m. suspicion.
recelós -osa a. suspicious, mistrustful.
recent a. recent, fresh.
recepció f. reception.
recepcionista m. -f. receptionist.
recepta f. recipe / prescription.
receptor-a a. / m.-f. receiver.
recerca f. quest, search / research.
recés m. privacy.
recinte m. enclosure.
reciprocitat f. reciprocity.
recitar tr. to recite.
recitar (per a memoritzar) tr. to rehearse.
reclamació f. claim, demand, reclamation.
reclamar tr. to claim, demand.

reclinar tr. to recline.
recloure tr. to seclude / to imprison, to shut away.
recluta m. recruit.
reclutar tr. to recruit.
recol·lectar tr. to harvest.
recollir tr. to gather, collect / to concentrate / to give shelter to / to seek refuge.
recolzar tr. to lean / to back, support.
recomanació f. recommendation.
recomanar tr. to recommend.
recompensa f. reward, recompense.
recompensar tr. to reward, recompense / to requite.
recomptar tr. to recount.
reconciliació f. reconciliation.
reconciliar tr. to reconcile.
reconeixement m. aknowledgement / recognition.
reconèixer tr. to acknowledge / to recognize / to reconnoitre.
recopilació f. digest, compilation.
record m. recollection, remembrance, memory.
recordar tr. to remember, remind, recollect.
recordatori m. reminder, memento, souvenir.
records m. pl. regards / memories.
recórrer tr. - intr. to turn to, appeal to / to cover distance.
recte -a a. straight / just, moral, right.
rectificació f. rectification.
rectitud f. rectitude, uprightness, integrity.
rector m. parson / rector.
recular intr. to quail, recoil.
recuperació f. recovery.
recuperar tr. to recover.
recurs m. recourse, resort.

redactar tr. to write, draft / to edit.

redemptor -a m. -f. redeemer.

redimir tr. to redeem.

rèdits m. pl. income.

reducció f. decrease, reduction.

reduir tr. to reduce / to overpower.

reeiximent m. achievement, success.

reeixir intr. to succeed.

reembossar tr. to reimburse.

reemplaçar tr. to replace.

refer tr. to remake.

referència f. reference.

referir tr. to refer / to relate.

reflar-se pr. v. to rely.

reflat -ada a. happy-go-lucky.

refilar tr. to trill.

refilet m. trill, chirp.

refinament m. refinement.

refinar tr. to refine.

refineria f. refinery.

reflectir tr. to reflect.

reforç m. reinforcement.

reforçar tr. to reinforce.

reforma f. reformation, reform / alteration.

reformar tr. to reform.

refrany m. proverb / (publicity) slogan.

refredar tr. to cool, cool down, cool off / to chill.

refredat m. cold, chill.

refrenar tr. to refrain / to restrain.

refresc m. refreshment.

refrescar tr. to cool, refresh.

refrigerador m. refrigerator.

refrigeri m. coolness / snack.

refugi m. refuge, haven, shelter.

refusar tr. to refuse, reject, decline / to deny.

refutar tr. to rebut, refute.

regadora f. watering can, sprinkler.

regal m. gift.

regalar tr. to give away / make a present of.

regalim m. trickle.

regany m. snarl, growl / grumble.

regar tr. to irrigate, water.

regatejar tr. - intr. to haggle / (sport) to dribble.

regatge m. watering, irrigation.

regenerar tr. to regenerate.

regenerat -ada a. regenerate.

regi -règia a. regal.

règim m. régime / diet.

regió f. region.

regir tr. to rule, govern.

registrador m. recorder.

registre m. register, record.

regla f. rule / ruler.

reglament m. regulations, rules, by-laws.

regna f. rein.

regnar intr. to reign.

regnat m. reign.

regne m. kingdom.

regraciament m. thanksgiving.

regraciar tr. to thank.

regulació f. regulation.

regular a. regular / tr. to regulate.

regularitzar tr. to regularize, put in order.

rei m. king.

reial a. kinglike, royal, regal.

reialesa f. royalty.

reialme m. kingdom, realm.

reina f. queen.

reincidir intr. to relapse.

reintegrar tr. to refund.

reixa f. iron railing.

relació f. narration / report, statement / relationship.

relatar tr. to relate.

realtiu -iva a. relative.

relaxar tr. to relax.

religió f. religion.

religiós -osa a. / m. -f. religious.

relíquia f. relic.

rella f. plough.
relleu m. relief, raised work / importance.
rellevar tr. to relieve.
relliscada f. slip, slide, skid.
relliscar intr. to slip, slide, skid.
rellotge m. clock / watch.
rellotge de butxaca m. watch.
rellotge de sol m. sundial.
rellotger m. watchmaker, clockmaker.
rem m. oar.
remar intr. to row.
remarca f. remark.
remarcar tr. to remark.
remei m. redress, remedy.
remeiar tr. to redress, remedy.
remenar tr. to shake / stir, whisk / to wag / (cards) to shuffle.
remer m. oarsman.
remesa f. delivery, remittance.
remetre tr. to deliver.
remitent m. - f. sender.
remolatxa f. beetroot.
remolcar tr. to tow.
remolí m. swirl, eddy, whirlpool.
remor m. rumble.
remordiment m. remorse, regret.
remoure tr. to remove / to shake, stir.
remugant a. ruminant.
remull m. steeping, soaking.
remullada f. soaking, drenching.
remullar tr. to steep, soak, drench.
renda f. income, revenue / rent.
renaixement m. revival, rebirth / renaissance.
Renaixença f. modern Catalan Renaissance.
rendiment m. profit, yield / income rent.
rendir tr. to render / to yield, surrender.
rendir-se pr. v. to surrender.

renec m. execration, blasphemy.
renegaire a. / m.-f. blasphemer.
renglera f. line / queue, row.
renill m. neigh, whinny.
renillar intr. to neigh, whinny.
renom m. renown, fame.
renovació f. renewal, renovation.
renovar tr. to renew.
renovellar tr. to refresh.
rentador m. laundry.
rentadora f. washing machine / washerwoman.
rentar tr. to wash, clean, launder.
renunciar tr. - intr. to waive, resign, renounce, give up.
renyar tr. to reprove, reprehend, chide, scold.
reorganitzar tr. to reorganize.
reparació f. repair.
reparar tr. to mend, repair.
repartiment m. partition, distribution, sharing out, apportionment.
repel·lent a. repellent, repugnant.
repartir tr. to distribute, share.
repel·lir tr. to repel.
repercussió f. rebound / repercussion.
repercutir intr. to rebound / to have repercussions on.
repetició f. recurrence, repeat, repetition.
repetir tr. to repeat.
rèplica f. reply / replica.
repòrter m. reporter.
repòs m. rest, repose, calm.
reposar tr. to rest, repose.
reposició f. replacement / revival / replay.
reprendre tr. to resume / to reprehend, admonish, tell off.
represàlia f. reprisal.
representant m. representative.

representar tr. to represent.
representatiu -iva a. representative.
repressió f. repression.
reprimir tr. to rebuke / to quell, repress.
reproduir tr. to reproduce.
reprovació f. reproval.
reprovar intr. to reprove, reprehend.
reptador -a m.-f. challenger.
reptar tr. to defy, challenge.
rèptil a. / m. reptile.
república f. republic.
repudiar tr. to repudiate.
repugnant a. repugnant, disgusting.
repulsió f. repulsion.
reputació f. reputation, renown.
requeriment m. requirement, requisite, requisition.
requerir tr. to require / to send for.
requesta f. request.
res, no res pron. nothing, none.
rés m. prayer.
resar tr. to pray.
rescat m. ransom, rescue.
rescatar tr. to rescue, ransom.
resclosa f. lock, sluice, floodgate.
reserva f. reserve.
reservar tr. to reserve.
reservat -ada a. private, reserved.
residència f. residence, abode.
residir intr. to reside.
residu m. residue, remnant, rest.
resignació f. resignation.
resina f. resin.
resistència f. resistance, toughness / stand, resistence.
resistir tr. - intr. to resist, withstand / to endure.
resoldre tr. to solve, resolve, to decide.

resolució f. resolution, resolve.
respecte m. respect.
respir m. breath.
respiració f. respiration, breathing.
respirar intr. to breathe, inhale.
resplendent a. shining.
resplendir intr. to shine, gleam, glow.
resplendor m. radiance, gleam, glow.
respondre tr. to respond, answer.
responsabilitat f. responsibility, liability.
responsable a. responsible.
resposta f. answer, reply.
ressagar-se pr. v. to lag behind.
ressecar tr. to parch.
ressentiment m. resentment.
ressentir-se pr. v. to resent.
ressò m. resonance, echo.
ressonar intr. to echo.
resta f. remainder, rest / subtraction / residue / remnant.
restabliment m. revival.
restar tr. to subtract, to deduct / intr. to remain, to stay.
restaurant m. restaurant.
restaurar tr. to restore.
restituir tr. to return, give back, repay / to recover.
restrenyiment m. constipation.
restringir tr. to restrict, limit.
resultar intr. to turn out (to be).
resultat m. result, effect, outcome.
resum m. summary, résumé.
resumir tr. to summarize.
resurrecció f. resurrection.
retall m. piece, remnant.
retallar tr. to cut off, cut out.
retard m. delay / slowness.
retardar tr. to delay / to slow down / (watch) to be slow.
retaule m. reredos.
retenir tr. to withhold, retain / to keep.

retícula f. network.
retirada f. likeness, resemblance / withdrawal, retreat.
retirar tr. - intr. to retire, recall, withdraw.
retoc m. retouching.
retocar tr. to amend / to touch up, retouch.
rètol m. signpost / label.
retolar tr. to label.
retòrcer tr. to twist, wring.
retorn m. return, coming back / home trip, homecoming.
retornar tr. - intr. to return.
retractar tr. to retract, take back.
retransmetre tr. to relay, retransmit.
retrat m. portrait.
retratar tr. to portray, to draw or paint a portrait.
retret m. reproach.
retribució f. pay.
retribuir tr. to remunerate, reward.
retrocedir tr. to move back / to retire / to recoil / to withdraw.
retrocés m. recoil, withdrawal.
reu-rea a. / m.-f. culprit / convict.
reunió f. meeting, reunion / party, rally.
reunir tr. to assemble, call, turn out (to be) / to join / (qualities) to possess.
reunir-se pr. v. to flock, gather.
revelació f. revelation.
revelat (photog.) m. developing.
revelar tr. to reveal / to develop (photo).
revenedor -a a. / m.-f. retailer.
reverenciar tr. to revere.
reverenciós -osa a. respectful.
revers m. back.
revés m. reverse.
reveure tr. to see again.
revifar tr. to revive.

revisar tr. to revise.
revisió f. review.
revista f. magazine / review / revue / (mil.) parade.
revocació f. revocation.
revolta f. rebellion, revolt.
rialla f. laughter.
rialleta f. smile.
riba f. shore.
ribera f. shore, strand, beach.
ric -a a. rich, wealthy.
ridícul -a a. ridiculous / m. ridicule.
riera f. stream, brook.
rifa f. raffle.
rifar tr. to raffle.
rígid -a a. rigid, stiff.
rigidesa f. rigidity.
rima f. rhyme.
rínxol m. curl, lock.
riota f. derision, jeer.
riquesa f. richness, wealth, riches.
risc m. risk, perill, danger.
ritus m. rite.
riu m. river.
riure m. laughter, laugh.
riure intr. to laugh.
riure's pr. v. to deride, laugh at.
rival a. / m.-f. rival.
rivalitat f. rivalry.
roba f. cloth / clothes, clothing.
robar tr. to rob, steal.
robatori m. robbery, theft.
robí m. ruby.
robust -a a. stout, robust.
roca f. rock.
rocós -osa a. rocky.
roda f. wheel.
rodalies f. pl. outskirts, surroundings, hinterland.
rodamón m. wanderer.
rodanxó -ona a. plump.
rodar intr. - tr. to wheel.
rodejar tr. to surround.
rodera f. rut.
rodet m. bobbin, reel.

rodó -ona a. round.
rodolar intr. to roll / to wheel.
roig -roja a. red.
roïnesa f. shabbiness.
roleu m. roller.
rom -a a. blunt / m. rum.
romana (balança) f. steelyard.
romandre intr. to remain.
romanent m. remnant / remainder, rest.
romaní m. rosemary.
ronc -a a. hoarse.
roncar intr. to snore.
rondalla f. tale, story.
rondar intr. to patrol / to wander, ramble.
rondinar intr. to snarl, growl.
ronya f. scab.
ronyó m. kidney.
ros -ossa a. blond.
rosa f. rose.
rosari m. rosary.
rosca f. nut and bolt / screw thread.
rosec m. gnawing / inquietude / remorse.
rosella f. poppy.
roser m. rosebush, rose tree.
ròssec m. balance.
rossinyol m. nightingale.
rostidor m. spit.
rostir tr. to roast, broil.
rostit -ida a. roast.
rostoll m. stubble.
rostre m. human face.
rotatiu -iva a. rotary, revolving.
rotllana f. hoop, roll.
rotlle m. coil, roll.
roure m. oak.
rovell m. rust.
rovell (d'ou) m. yolk.
rovellar tr. to rust.
rovellat -ada a. rusty.
rubor m. blush.
ruboritzar-se pr. v. to blush.
ruc m. donkey.

rude a. simple, uncultured, rough.
rúfol -a a. stormy, boisterous.
rugit m. roar.
ruïna f. ruin / ruins, remains.
ruïnes f. pl. ruins, remains.
ruixada f. spray, sprinkle.
ruixar tr. to sprinkle.
rull m. curl, frizzle.
rumb m. course, route.
ruminant m. ruminant.
ruptura f. rupture.
rusc m. beehive, hive.
ruta f. route.

S

sa -ana a. healthy, sound, wholesome.
saba f. sap.
sabata f. shoe.
sabater m. shoemaker.
sabedor -a a. informed, knowledgeable.
saber tr. to know.
sabó m. soap.
sabonera f. lather.
sabor m. flavour, taste, savour.
saborós -osa a. tasty, flavoursome, savoury.
sabre m. sabre, saber (Am.)
sac m. bag, sack.
sacerdot m. priest.
saciat -ada a. satiated, saturated.
sacrifici m. sacrifice.
sacristia f. vestry, sacristy.
sacsejar tr. to agitate / to shake, jerk, beat.
sadollar tr. to satiate, saturate, glut.
safareig m. washing place, laundry.
safata f. salver.

safir m. sapphire.
safrà m. saffron.
sagaç a. sagacious.
sageta f. arrow, dart, shaft.
sagí m. grease or fat.
sagnar tr. to bleed.
sagnia f. bleeding.
Sagrades Escriptures f. pl. Holy Scriptures.
sagrat -ada a. holy, sacred.
sainet m. sketch.
sal f. salt.
sala f. drawing room, hall, room.
salamandra f. salamander.
salar tr. to salt.
salari m. earnings, salary, wages, income.
saldo (comm.) m. balance.
saliva f. saliva, spit, spittle.
salmó m. salmon.
salmòdia f. chant.
salmorra f. pickle / brine.
saló m. drawing room, salon, lounge.
salsa f. sauce.
salsitxa f. sausage.
salt m. jump, hop, leap / (of water) waterfall.
saltar intr. to jump, leap, bound.
saltiró m. leap.
saludable a. healthy, wholesome.
saludar tr. to greet, salute, hail.
salut f. health / interj. cheers!
salutació f. salutation.
salutifer -a a. healthy, wholesome.
salvació f. salvation.
salvador -a a. / m.-f. rescuer / saviour.
salvaguarda f. safeguard.
salvament m. rescue, rescuing / salvage.
salvar tr. to save, rescue, deliver / to except, exclude / (obstacle) to overcome.
salvatge a. wild / m.-f. savage.

sàlvia f. sage, salvia.
salze m. willow.
samarreta f. vest, undershirt, T-shirt.
sanció f. sanction.
sandàlia f. sandal.
sang f. blood.
sanglotar intr. to sob.
sangonera f. leech.
sanitat f. health.
sanitós -osa a. healthy, wholesome, salutary.
sant -a a. / m.-f. saint.
santedat f. holiness, sanctity.
santificar tr. to sanctify, hallow.
santuari m. sanctuary, shrine.
saó f. maturity, ripeness, season / opportunity.
sapa f. sap.
saqueig m. ravage, sack.
saquejar tr. to ravage, harry.
sardana f. national dance of Catalonia.
sardina f. sardine.
sargir tr. to darn.
sarraí -ïna a. Saracen, Moor.
sàrria f. pannier.
sarró m. shepherd's pouch / gamebag / leather bag.
sastreria f. tailoring.
sastre m. tailor.
satisfacció f. satisfaction.
satisfer tr. to satisfy.
satisfet -a a. satisfied.
saturat -ada a. saturated.
saüc m. elder or eldertree.
savi -sàvia a. / m.-f. wise, sage.
saviesa f. wisdom, knowledge.
sebollir tr. to bury, inter.
sec -a a. dry / lean, skinny / hard, insensitive.
séc m. crease.
seca (fàbr. moneda) f. mint.
secció f. section.
secret -a a. / m. secret.
secretament adv. privately, secretly.

91   secretament

secretari -ària m.-f. secretary.
secretaria f. secretary's office / secretaryship.
sector m. sector, section.
seda f. silk.
sedàs m. sieve.
seducció f. seduction.
seduir tr. to seduce.
sega f. harvest, reaping / mowing.
segador -a a. / m.-f. reaper.
segar tr. to mow, reap.
segell m. seal.
segell (post) m. stamp.
seglar a. / m.-f. lay, secular.
segle m. century.
segó m. bran.
sègol m. rye.
segon m. second.
segon -a a. / m. -f. second.
segons prep. according to.
segrest m. kidnapping / confiscation, sequestration.
segrestador-a a. / m.-f. kidnapper.
segrestar tr. to confiscate / kidnap.
següent a. following, next.
seguici m. suite, cortège, train, followers.
seguidament adv. forthwith.
seguidor -a a. / m.-f. follower.
seguir tr. to follow.
segur -a a. safe, secure / steady.
segurament adv. surely.
seguretat f. assurance, safety, surety.
seient m. seat.
seixanta a. / m. sixty.
seixantè -ena a. / m.-f. sixtieth.
seleccionar tr. to select.
selecte -a a. select.
sella f. saddle.
selva f. forest, jungle.
semàfor m. semaphore / traffic lights.
semblança f. likeness, resemblance.

semblant a. similar, like / m. face.
semblantment adv. similarly.
semblar intr. to seem, appear, look like, resemble.
sembrar tr. to sow.
semença f. seed.
semitic -a a. Semite, Semitic.
sempre adv. forever, always.
senalla f. two-handled frail or rush basket.
senar a. odd, uneven.
senat m. senate.
sencer -a a. whole, entire, complete.
senectut f. old age / senility.
senglar m. boar.
sensació f. feeling, sensation.
sensat -a a. judicious, prudent, sensible, wise.
sense prep. without.
sensible a. sensitive.
sentència f. sentence / saying.
sentiment m. sense, feeling, sentiment.
sentinella m. sentinel, sentry.
sentir tr. to hear.
sentit m. meaning, sense / wit / way, direction.
sentor f. smell, odour, scent / stink.
seny m. common sense, judgement, reason.
senyal m. token, indication, signal / sign.
senyera f. banner, standard.
senyor m. gentleman, lord, sir, mister / Lord.
senyora f. lady, madam, mistress, wife / Lady, gentlewoman.
senyoreta f. miss.
senyoriu m. domain, dominion / manor.
senzill -a a. single, plain / simple, easy.
senzillesa f. simplicity.
separació f. separation, parting.

separadament adv. apart, aside.
separar tr. to separate, sunder, isolate.
separar-se pr. v. to secede.
sepulcre m. sepulchre.
seqüela f. sequel.
sèquia f. irrigation channel.
serafí m. seraph.
serè -ena a. serene / cloudless.
serenata f. serenade.
serf m. serf.
sergent m. sergeant.
sèrie f. series, sequence, succession / range, set.
seriós -osa a. serious, solemn, grave.
sermó m. sermon.
serp f. snake / serpent.
serpejar intr. to wriggle / to creep, meander.
serpent m. i f. snake / serpent.
serpentejar intr. to wriggle, creep, meander.
serra f. saw / mountain range.
serradures f. pl. sawdust.
serralada f. range, ridge.
serrar tr. to saw.
servar tr. - intr. to keep, guard / to observe.
servei m. service.
servent m. servant, valet.
serventa f. maid.
servicial a. helpful, obliging, willing.
servidor -a a. serviceable / m.-f. servant / yours truly.
servil a. servile / slavish.
servir intr. to serve.
servitud f. servitude.
sessió f. session.
set f. thirst.
set a. / m. seven.
setanta a. / m. seventy.
setantè -ena a. / m.-f. seventieth.
setè -ena a. / m.-f. seventh.
setembre m. September.

setí m. sateen, satin.
setmana f. week.
Setmana Santa f. Holy Week, Easter.
setrill m. oil jar.
setze a. / m. sixteen.
setzè -ena a. / m.-f. sixteenth.
seu -seva a. pos. m.-f. sing. your, his, her, its, their / pron. pos., yours, his, hers, its, theirs.
seure intr. to sit, seat.
seus -seves a. pos. m.-f. pl. your, his, her, its, their / pron. pos. pl. yours, his, hers, its, theirs.
sever -a a. severe, stern, strict.
severitat f. severity, sternness.
sexe m. sex.
sí adv. yes.
si conj. if.
sidra f. cider.
signar tr. to sign.
signatura f. signature.
signe m. sign.
significar tr. to mean, signify / to stand for.
significat m. meaning, signification.
silenci m. silence, quiet.
silenciós -osa a. quiet, silent.
sil·laba f. syllable.
símbol m. symbol.
simfonia f. symphony.
simi m. monkey, ape.
similar a. like, similar.
similitud f. likeness, similarity.
simpatia f. sympathy.
simpàtic -a a. nice, likeable, genial, pleasant / sympathetic.
simple a. simple.
simplificar tr. to simplify.
símptoma m. symptom.
simular tr. to simulate, feign, sham.
sina f. bosom / lap of a woman / breast.
sincer -a a. sincere.

sinceritat f. sincerity.
sincronitzar tr. to synchronize.
sindicat m. syndicate, trade union / union member.
síndria f. watermelon.
singlot m. hiccough.
singular a. singular / unique / strange, weird.
sínia f. waterwheel.
sinistre -a a. left / sinister / m. accident, calamity.
sinó conj. but / only / on the contrary.
sintaxi f. syntax.
síntesi f. synthesis.
sípia f. cuttlefish / sepia.
sis a. / m. six.
sisè -ena a. / m.-f. sixth.
sistema m. system.
situació f. situation.
so m. sound.
sobirà -ana a. / m.-f. sovereign.
soborn m. bribe, / hush money.
sobrant a. spare, remaining, surplus.
sobre m. envelope.
sobre prep. about, on, upon.
sobrecoberta f. wrap.
sobreeixir intr. to overflow.
sobrenatural a. supernatural, unearthly, weird.
sobresortir intr. to jut out.
sobretot adv. above all.
sobreviure intr. to survive.
sobrietat f. thrift, moderation, sobriety.
sobte (de) adv. phr. suddenly.
soc m. sabot / clog.
soca f. trunk, stump / vine stock / origin of a family.
socarrimar tr. to scorch.
soci -sòcia m. -f. partner / associate, fellow / member.
social a. social.
societat f. society.
sòcol m. stand / skirting board.

socórrer tr. to succour, aid, help.
soda f. soda, soda water.
sofà m. couch, sofa, settee.
sofert -a a. patient.
sofre m. sulphur.
sofriment m. endurance.
sofrir tr. to suffer.
sogre m. father-in-law.
soja f. soya.
sol m. sun.
sòl m. soil, ground.
sol -a a. only, alone, lone, single.
sola f. sole / sole-leather.
solament adv. only, merely, solely.
solapa f. lapel / flap.
solar m. plot.
solc m. furrow, line / wrinkle.
soldadura f. welding, soldering.
soldar tr. to weld, solder.
soldat m. soldier.
soledat f. loneliness, solitude / wilderness.
solellós -osa a. sunny.
solidificar tr. to solidify.
solista (mus.) m. -f. soloist.
sòlid -a a. solid / m. solid.
solitari -ària a. lonely, solitary.
sollar tr. to stain, soil, sully, foul / to defile.
sol·licitar tr. to request, apply for.
sols adv. only, merely.
solt -a free, untied.
solter -a a. single, unmarried / m. bachelor / f. spinster.
soltera f. single woman, spinster.
solució f. solution.
solvent a. solvent.
somiar intr. to dream.
somier m. spring mattress.
somni m. dream.
somrís m. smile.
somriure intr. to smile.

son f. sleep / sleepiness.
sonar intr. to sound.
sondejar tr. to fathom.
sonet m. sonnet.
sopa f. soup.
sopar m. dinner, supper.
sopar intr. to dine, have dinner.
sopera f. soup tureen.
soprano f. soprano, treble.
sord -a a. deaf.
sordesa f. deafness.
sorgir intr. to arise, emerge, spring up.
sorneguer -a a. cunning, sly, crafty.
soroll m. noise.
sorollós -osa a. loud, noisy.
sorpresa f. surprise.
sorra f. sand.
sorrut -uda a. surly.
sort f. luck / destiny, fate.
sortejar tr. to draw lots for, raffle / to get round.
sortida f. exit, issue, excursion / (theatre) entrance.
sortida de sol f. sunrise.
sortir intr. to go out, leave / to issue / (bird) to hatch.
sortós -osa a. lucky.
sortosament adv. luckily.
sosa f. (Bicarbonate of) soda / ...càustica f. caustic soda.
sospir m. sigh.
sospitar tr. to suspect.
sospitós -osa a. suspicious, suspect.
sosteniment m. sustenance, maintenance / support.
sostre m. ceiling.
sostreure tr. to subtract.
sota adv. under, underneath, below.
sotabosc m. underwood.
sotana f. cassock.
sotasignar tr. to undersign.
sotasignat -ada a. undersigned.
soterrani m. basement.

sotmetre tr. to submit / to subdue.
sotrac m. jerk.
sotragar tr. to toss.
sotragueig m. jolt.
sou m. wages, pay, salary.
sovint adv. frequently, often.
suar intr. to sweat, ooze.
suau a. smooth / soft.
suaument adv. smoothly / softly.
subhasta f. auction.
subjecte m. subject.
subjugar tr. to subdue, subjugate.
submergir tr. to submerge, dip.
submergir-se pr. v. to dive.
submís -isa a. submissive, meek, obedient.
subornar tr. to bribe.
subratllar tr. to underline.
substància f. substance.
substantiu -iva a. substantival / m. noun.
substituir tr. to substitute.
substracció f. subtraction.
subterrani -ània a. underground, subterranean.
subtil a. subtle.
suburbi m. suburb / slum quarter.
suc (fruit) m. juice, squash.
succeir intr. to happen, take place.
succés m. event.
sucós -osa a. juicy.
sucre m. sugar.
Suècia f. Sweden.
sud m. South.
suèter m. sweater.
suficient a. sufficient.
sufix -a a. added / m. suffix.
sufragi m. suffrage.
suggeriment m. suggestion, hint.
suggerir tr. to suggest / to hint.
suís -ïssa a. Swiss.

suma f. sum, amount.
sumar tr. to add.
sumari m. digest, summary.
sumptuós -osa a. luxurious, sumptuous.
suor f. sweat.
superar tr. to surmount, surpass.
superbiós -osa a. self-important / haughty.
superfície f. surface.
superior a. top, upper, uppermost, top, higher / m. superior.
superioritat f. superiority.
supervivent a. survivor.
suplicar tr. to entreat, beg.
suport m. support / bracket.
suportar tr. to stand, bear, endure.
suposar tr. to suppose, imagine, deem.
suprimir tr. to suppress.
surar intr. to float.
suro m. cork.
susceptible a. susceptible, sensitive, touchy.
suspendre tr. to suspend / to fail (examinations).
suspicàcia f. suspicion.
sustentar tr. to sustain.
sutura f. seam.

T

tabac m. tobacco.
tabaquer -a m.-f. tobacconist.
tabola f. mirth, jollity.
taca f. stain, blot.
tacar tr. to stain, blot.
taciturn -a a. taciturn, silent, sullen.

tacte m. feel, feeling, touching, touch / tact.
tàctica f. tactics.
tafanejar tr. - intr. to pry into other's affairs / to pry, peep.
tal a. - pron. such / like.
talaia f. watchtower / guard.
talar tr. to create havoc / to raze to the ground / to cut down.
talc m. talc, talcum powder.
tall m. cutting, cut.
talla f. height, size, stature / cut / carving (in wood, etc.).
tallada f. slice.
tallant m. chopper.
tallar tr. to cut / chop / slash.
taller m. workshop, works, mill, shop.
taló m. heel.
talment adv. how, as, like, in such a way.
talp m. mole / cyst, wen.
també adv. also, as well, too, besides.
tambor m. drum.
tambora f. bass drum.
tamboret m. stool.
tampó m. pad.
tampoc adv. neither, either
tan adv. as, so, such.
tanc m. tank.
tanca f. fence, hedge / latch.
tancar tr. to close, bolt.
tancat m. enclosure.
tanda f. shift, relay, turn.
tanmateix adv. however, nevertheless, notwithstanding.
tant -a a. / pron. / adv. as much as many.
tantost adv. forthwith.
tany m. stem.
tap m. stopper, cork / difficulty.
tapaboques m. scarf.
tapadora f. lid.
tapar tr. to stop up, cork, put the lid on / to cover over.
tapís m. tapestry.

tapisseria f. tapestry.
taquilla f. booking office.
tard adv. late.
tarda f. afternoon, evening.
tardà -ana a. late, tardy.
tardança f. delay, slowness, tardiness.
tardar intr. to delay, arrive late.
tardor f. autumn (Bri.), fall (Am.).
targeta f. card.
tarifa f. tariff, rate.
taronger m. orange tree.
taronja f. orange.
tasca f. task.
tascó m. wedge / plug.
tassa f. cup, bowl.
tast m. taste.
tastar tr. to taste.
tastet m. taste.
taula f. table / notice board / contents, index.
taulell m. counter / board, panel.
tauló m. table.
tauró m. shark.
tava m. horsefly.
tavella f. fold, crease.
taverna f. pub, tavern.
taxador -a a. / m.-f. valuer.
taxi m. taxi, cab.
te m. tea.
teatre m. theatre.
tebi -tèbia a. tepid.
tecla f. key.
teclat m. keyboard.
tècnic -a a. technical / m.-f. technician, expert.
tècnica f. technique, method.
tela f. torch, firebrand.
teix m. yew.
teixidor m. weaver.
teixir tr. to weave.
teixit m. textile, fabric, tissue.
tela f. cloth, web, stuff.
telèfon m. telephone.
telefonar tr. to telephone.

telègraf m. telegraph.
telegrafiar tr. -intr. to telegraph, wire.
telegrama m. telegram.
teler m. loom.
telescopi m. telescope.
televisió f. television.
tema m. theme, topic, subject / (mus.) theme, piece.
temença f. dread, fear.
témer tr. to fear, dread.
temerari -ària a. rash, reckless.
temeritat f. temerity, recklessness.
temor m. fear, dread.
temorenc -a a. afraid.
temperança f. temperance.
temperat -ada a. temperate.
temperatura f. temperature.
tempesta f. tempest, storm.
temple m. temple.
temporada f. season.
temporer -a a. temporary.
temps m. time / tense / weather.
temptació f. temptation.
temptador -a a. tempting / m. tempter.
temptar tr. tempt, tantalize.
temptativa r. attempt.
tenaç a. tenacious / stubborn.
tenalles f. pl. tongs.
tenda f. tent / shop.
tendència f. trend, tendency, drift.
tendenciós -osa a. tendentious, biased.
tendir tr. to tend.
tendó m. tendon, sinew.
tendre -a a. tender, kind, delicate.
tendresa f. tenderness.
tenebra f. darkness, gloom.
tenebrós -osa a. gloomy.
tenir tr. to have.
tens -a a. tense, taut.
tensió f. strain, stress, tension / voltage.

tentinejar intr. to toddle.
tenue a. tenuous / thin, faint.
tenyir tr. to dye.
teologia f. theology.
teorema m. theorem.
teoria f. theory.
teòric -a a. theoretical / m.-f. theorist.
teòricament adv. theoretically.
teranyina f. cobweb, web.
terapèutica f. therapeutics.
tèrbol -a a. muddy, turbid / obscure.
terbolí m. whirlwind, dustcloud / whirl.
tercer -a a. m.-f. third.
terciari-ària a. tertiary.
tergiversació f. distortion, prevarication.
tergiversar tr. to distort.
terme m. bound, limit, term.
tèrmit m. termite.
termòmetre m. thermometer.
terra f. land, earth.
terraplè m. embankment / terrace / rampart.
Terra Santa f. Holy Land.
terrat m. terrace / flat roof.
terratrèmol m. earthquake.
terrenal a. earthly.
terreny m. ground, soil, land, plot.
terrestre a. overland / terrestrial / earthy.
terrible a. terrible, awful.
terriblement adv. terribly.
terrisseria f. pottery.
territori m. territory.
terror m. terror.
tertúlia f. social gathering.
tesi f. thesis.
test -a a. rigid, stiff / m. flowerpot.
testa f. head.
testificar tr. to testify.
testimoni m. testimony / witness.

testimoniar tr. to witness, vouch.
tetera f. teapot / kettle.
teu, teva, teus, teves pron. pos. your, thine / pl. yours.
teula f. roof tile.
teulada f. roof.
tèxtil a. textile.
tia f. aunt.
tibant a. tight, taut, tensed.
tibar tr. to tighten
tifó m. typhoon.
tigre m. tiger.
tija f. stem.
til·la f. infusion of lime flowers.
til·ler m. lime tree, linden.
timbal m. drum, tambour.
timbre m. fiscal stamp / bell / timbre / mark of honour.
tímid -a a. bashful, timid, shy.
timó m. helm, rudder.
timoner m. helmsman, steersman, wheelman.
tinent m. lieutenant.
tint m. tint, dye.
tinta f. ink.
tinter m. inkstand, inkwell.
tió m. brand, firebrand.
típic -a a. typical.
tiple f. soprano, treble.
tipografia f. typography.
tir m. shot, shooting / round of ammunition / team of oxen, etc.
tirà m. tyrant.
tirabuixó m. corkscrew.
tirada f. cast, throw / distance / (print.) edition, issue.
tirador m. shooter.
tirania f. tyranny.
tiranitzar tr. to tyrannize.
tirar tr. to pull, shoot / to reproduce, copy / to go, proceed / to last.
tirar-se (de cap) pr. v. to plunge, dive.
tisores f. pl. scissors.

tísic -a a. consumptive.
titella m. puppet, marionette.
titil·lar intr. to twinkle.
títol m. title, heading, charter.
títol (honorífic) a Anglaterra m. sir.
titular tr. to title, entitle.
titulars m. pl. headlines.
tocadiscs m. record player, phonograph.
tocador m. dressing table.
tocar tr. to feel, touch, handle / to play.
tòfona f. truffle.
toga f. toga / gown, robe.
toix -a a. obtuse, blunt / flatnosed.
tolerància f. tolerance.
tolerar tr. to allow, tolerate, indulge.
tomàquet m. tomato.
tomb m. turn.
tomba f. tomb.
tombar tr. to turn, turn over.
ton, ta a. pos. sing. your.
tona f. ton.
tonada f. tune, air.
tonalitat f. tonality, tone, hue.
tonatge m. tonnage.
tondre tr. to shear.
tonyina f. tuna, tunny.
topada f. bump / casual encounter.
topar intr. to collide, bump / to come across, to run into.
topazi m. topaz.
tòrax m. thorax, chest.
torbar tr. to disturb / to upset.
torçar tr. to bend.
tòrcer tr. to bend, twist, flex.
torn m. winch, drum / shift, turn / lathe.
tornado m. tornado.
tornar tr. - intr. to return, go back, come back.
torneig m. tourney, tournament.

toro m. bull.
torrada f. toast.
torrar tr. to parch, toast.
torre f. tower.
torrent m. torrent, rushing stream.
torsió f. twist, torsion.
tort -a a. twisted / m. damage.
tórtora f. turtledove.
tortuga f. tortoise.
tortuga de mar f. turtle.
torturar tr. to torture.
torxa f. torch.
tos f. cough.
tossir intr. to cough.
tot m. everything.
tot -a pron. all, every, whole.
total a. whole, utter, entire, total.
totalitari -ària a. totalitarian.
totalitat f. whole, totality, wholeness.
totalment adv. totally, absolutely.
tothom pron. everybody.
tot just adv. phr. hardly.
tot seguit adv. phr. at once.
totxo m. a brick with a thickness of 5 cms.
tou -tova a. soft, gentle, mild.
tovalles f. pl. tablecloth.
tovalló m. napkin.
tovallola f. towel.
trabucar tr. to upset, tip over / (words) to jumble up, misplace.
traç m. mark, trace.
tracció f. traction.
tractament m. treatment.
tractar tr. to deal with, treat / to have relations with / to try, attempt.
tractat m. treaty.
tracte m. dealings, intercourse, relationship / agreement, deal.
tractor m. tractor.

tracut -uda a. handy, skilful.
tradició f. tradition.
traducció f. translation.
traductor -a m.-f. translator.
traduir tr. to translate.
tràfic m. traffic / trade, business.
traficar intr. to trade, deal / (drugs) to peddle.
traficant m.-f. dealer, trader / peddler, pusher (drugs).
tragèdia f. tragedy.
traguet m. drink.
traïció f. treason, treachery, betrayal.
traïdor -a a. / m.-f. traitor.
trair tr. to betray.
tralla f. whip, lash.
trama f. weft, woof / connection, link / plot, scheme.
tramesa f. remittance.
trametre tr. to remit, send.
trampa f. trap, snare / decoy / act of cheating, trick.
tramvia m. tram, tramway.
tranquil -il·la a. quiet, calm.
tranquil·litat f. peace, quiet.
transbordador m. ferry.
transeünt a. transient, transitory / m.-f. passer-by, pedestrian.
transferència f. transfer.
transferir tr. to transfer.
trànsit m. transit.
transmetre tr. to transmit.
transmissió f. shafting.
transpirar intr. to perspire, sweat.
transport m. transport.
transportar tr. to transport.
transsubstanciació f. transubstantiation.
transvasar tr. to decant.
tranversal a. transverse, transversal, crosswise.
trapelleria f. mischief.
trapezi (gymn.) m. trapeze / (mat.) trapezium.

tràquea f. trachea.
trasbals m. upset, upheaval / move / decanting.
trasllat m. removal.
traspassar tr. to cross over / to run through, to transfer, make over.
traspuar tr. to ooze.
trau m. buttonhole.
travar tr. to join, fetter.
travessar tr. to cross, traverse.
travessia f. passage, voyage, traverse.
treball m. work, labour, job.
treballador -a a. hard-working / m. worker, labourer .
treballar intr. - tr. to work, labour.
tremolar intr. to tremble, shake, shiver, quake.
tremolor m. quake, trembling, thrill.
tremolós -osa a. trembling, shivering.
trempaplomes m. penknife.
tren m. train.
trena f. plait.
trenar tr. to plait.
trenca-closques m. puzzle, riddle.
trencadís -issa a. brittle, fragile.
trencall m. short cut / convenience.
trencanous m. nutcracker.
trencar tr. to break, crack.
trenta a. / m. thirty.
trentè·-ena a. / m. -f. thirtieth.
trepanar tr. to trepan.
trepig m. tread.
trepitjar tr. to tread.
tres a. / m. three.
tresor m. treasure, thesaurus.
tresorer -a m.-f. treasurer.
tresoreria f. treasury.
trespeus m. tripod.
tret (caràcter) m. trait.
tretze a. / m. thirteen.

tretzè-ena a. / m. -f. thirteenth.

treure tr. to take out, get out, pull out / to extract.

treva f. break, rest, respite / truce.

triangle m. triangle.

triar tr. to choose, elect.

tribu f. tribe.

tribú m. tribune.

tribuna f. tribune, platform, rostrum / grandstand.

tribunal m. court, jury.

tribut m. tribute, tax, impost.

tributació f. taxation.

tricicle m. tricycle.

trillió m. trillion.

trimestral a. quarterly.

trimestralment adv. quarterly.

trimestre m. trimester (Am.), term (Bri.).

trineu m. sledge, sleigh.

trinxant m. carving knife.

trinxar tr. to chop, cut up.

trinxera f. trench / ditch.

triomf m. triumph / success.

triomfar intr. to triumph, win.

tripa f. intestine, gut.

triple a. treble.

triplicar tr. to treble.

tripulació f. crew.

tripular tr. to man.

trist -a a. dreary, sad, sorry.

tristesa f. sadness.

tritlleig m. tinkle, jingle.

triturar tr. to triturate, grind, crush.

tro m. thunder.

trobada f. encounter.

trobador m. troubadour, minstrel.

troballa f. discovery, finding.

trobar tr. to find.

troca f. hank.

trofeu m. trophy, cup.

tròlei m. trolley.

troleibús m. trolley bus.

trombosi f. thrombosis.

trompada f. bang, bump.

trompeta f. trumpet.

tron m. throne.

tronada f. thunderstorm.

tronar intr. to thunder.

tronc (de cavalls) m. team.

trontoll m. jolt.

trontollar intr. to totter.

tropa f. troop.

tròpics m. pl. tropics.

tros m. piece.

truà a. jester, buffoon / rogue.

truc m. knock, ring / trick, stratagem.

trucador m. knocker.

trucar (per telèfon) intr. to call, ring up / (doorbell) to knock, to ring.

trufa f. truffle.

truita f. omelette, (icht.) trout.

truja f. sow.

tsar m. tzar.

tu pron. per. you / thou.

tub m. tube, pipe.

tubercle m. tuber.

tubèrcul m. tuber.

U

u m. one.

udol m. howl.

udolar intr. to howl.

ufana f. pride, conceit / gaiety.

ufanós -osa a. proud, haughty / gay.

uixer m. usher.

úlcera f. ulcer.

ull m. eye.

ullada f. glimpse, glance.

ullal m. eyetooth, canine tooth / fang.

ullar tr. to glimpse.

ulleres f. pl. glasses, spectacles.

últim -a a. last, later / latest, most recent.

últimament adv. lately.
ultratge m. grievance, offence.
ulular intr. to ululate, hoot, screech.
un art. m. a, an.
un -a a. one.
unànime a. unanimous.
unció f. unction, anointing.
ungla f. nail.
ungüent m. ointment.
únic -a a. unique / only, single.
uniforme a. uniform, constant, steady / m. uniform.
unió f. union, junction, joint.
unir tr. to unite, join, connect associate.
unir-se pr. v. to join, join together, convene.
unitat f. unity.
universal a. universal, worldwide.
universitat f. university.
untar tr. to anoint, oil, salve.
untura f. ointment, anointment.
urani m. uranium.
urbà -ana a. urban.
urbanitat f. courtesy, politeness / urbanity, refinement.
urc m. pride, haughtiness, arrogance.
urgència f. hurry, urgency.
urgent a. urgent.
urgir intr. to be urgent.
urinari m. lavatory, urinary.
urpa f. claw, fang, paw.
ús m. use.
usar tr. to use, to wear.
usual a. usual, customary.
usura f. usury.
usurpació f. usurpation.
usurpar tr. to usurp.
úter m. uterus, womb.
útil a. useful, helpful / m. tool.
utilitat f. utility.
utilitzar tr. to utilize.

V

va -ana a. vain.
vaca f. cow.
vacances f. pl. holidays (Bri.), vacation (Àm.).
vacant a. vacant.
vacil·lació f. hesitation, vacillation.
vacil·lar tr. to hesitate, vacillate.
vacu -vàcua a. empty.
vacuïtat f. vacuity.
vacuna f. vaccine.
vacunar tr. to vaccinate.
vaga f. rest, leisure / strike.
vagabund m. vagabond, tramp, wanderer, waif.
vagar intr. to idle, wander, roam, rove / to lounge.
vagó m. coach, carriage, car, wagon.
vagó (restaurant) m. dining car.
vague -vaga a. vague.
vaguetat f. vagueness.
vaguista m.-f. striker.
vallet m. boy.
vainilla f. vanilla.
vaixell m. vessel, ship, boat.
vaixell (de guerra) m. man-of-war.
vaixella f. crockery.
valedor -a m.-f. protector.
valent -a a. brave, fearless, bold, valiant.
valer intr. to be worth / to be effective / to use, take advantage of.
vàlid -a a. valid.
validesa f. validity.
vall f. valley.
valor a. value, worth / efficiency / courage, valour, pluck.
vals m. waltz.
vàlua f. value.
valuós -osa a. valuable.
vàlvula f. valve.

vampir m. vampire.
vanament adv. vainly.
vanitat f. vanity.
vanitós -osa a. vain, conceited.
vapor m. vapour / steam / steam boat.
vaporós -osa a. vaporous.
vara f. rod / pole, staff / stick / wand, emblem of authority / yard / shaft.
vareta f. wand / twig.
vari -vària a. varied / various.
variable a. variable.
variablement adv. variably.
variació f. variation.
variar tr. - intr. to vary.
variat -ada a. varied, manifold.
varietat f. variety.
vas m. glass, vessel, receptacle.
vaselina f. vaseline.
vassall m. vassal.
vast -a a. vast, broad, wide.
vastitud f. vastness.
vat m. watt.
vedat m. game preserve.
vedell-a m.-f. calf, heifer / veal.
vegada f. time, occasion.
vegetació f. vegetation.
vegetal a. vegetable.
vegetar intr. to vegetate.
vegetarià -ana a. vegetarian.
vehemència f. vehemence.
vehicle m. vehicle.
veí -ïna a. / m.-f. neighbour.
veïnatge m. neighbourhood, vicinity.
vel m. veil.
vela f. sail.
veler m. sailing ship / sail maker.
vell -a a. old.
vel·leïtat f. fickleness / whim.
vellesa f. old age.
velló m. fleece, sheepskin.
vellositat f. pubescence.
vellut m. velvet.
vellutat -ada a. velvety.

veloç a. quick, fast, rapid, swift.
velocitat f. speed, velocity.
vena f. vein.
venalitat f. venality.
vencedor -a a. winner, vanquisher, victor / conqueror.
vèncer tr. - intr. to win, overcome, vanquish.
venda f. sale.
vendible a. saleable.
vendre tr. to sell.
venedor -a a. / m.-f. seller, salesman, saleswoman.
verenós -osa a. poisonous.
veneració f. veneration, worship.
venerar tr. to worship, venerate.
vènia f. licence.
venidor -a a. forthcoming.
venir intr. to come.
venjança f. vengeance, revenge.
venjar tr. to revenge, avenge.
venjatiu -iva a. vengeful.
vent m. wind, air.
ventall m. fan.
ventar tr. to fan.
ventijol m. breeze.
ventilació f. ventilation.
ventilador m. ventilator, electric fan.
ventilar tr. to fan, ventilate.
ventre m. belly.
venturós -osa a. fortunate, lucky.
veracitat f. veracity, truthfulness.
veranda f. verandah.
verb m. verb.
verbalment adv. verbally.
verd -a a. green.
verdet m. rust.
verdor f. greenness / verdure, lushness.
verdura f. greenness / verdure / boiled vegetables.
veredicte m. verdict.
verema f. vintage.

103

verge f. virgin.
vergonya f. shame.
vergonyós -osa a. shameful.
veri m. venom, poison.
verídic -a a. true, truthful, veracious.
verificació f. verification.
verificar tr. to verify.
verinós -osa a. venomous, virous.
veritable a. veritable, true, real, veracious.
veritablement adv. truly.
veritat f. verity, truth.
vermell -a a. red.
vermellor f. redness.
vermellós -osa a. reddish.
vermina f. vermin.
vermut m. vermouth.
vernal a. spring, vernal.
vernís m. varnish, polish.
verola f. smallpox, variola.
vers m. (poetry) line.
vers prep. towards, to.
versat -ada a. versed.
versàtil a. changeable / versatile.
versicle m. verse.
versificar tr. to versify.
versió f. version.
vertebrat -ada a. vertebrate.
vertical a. vertical, upright.
verticalment adv. vertically.
vertigen m. giddiness, dizziness / sudden impulse.
vertiginós -osa a. dizzy, vertiginous.
vesània f. insanity.
vescomte -essa m. - f. viscount, viscountess.
vespa f. wasp / hornet.
vesprada f. evening.
vespre m. evening.
vespres m. pl. vespers.
vessar tr. to spill, pour / to leak.
vestíbul m. hall.
vestir tr. to clothe, dress.
vestit m. costume, dress.

vestits m. pl. clothing.
vestuari m. clothes, wardrobe.
veta f. ribbon / vein.
veterà -ana a. veteran.
veterinari -ària a. / m. - f. veterinary / veterinary surgeon, vet.
vetlla f. vigil / vespers, evensong.
veu f. voice.
veure tr. to see.
vexar tr. to vex.
vexatori -òria a. vexatious, bothersome.
vi m. wine.
via f. way.
viaducte m. viaduct.
vianant m. traveller / passenger / passer-by.
viandes f. pl. supplies, food.
viarany m. path.
viatge m. journey, trip, tour, travel.
viatger m. traveller, voyager.
viatjar intr. to travel, journey, tour.
vibració f. vibration.
vibrar intr. to vibrate, quiver, throb.
vicari m. curate, vicar.
vicaria f. vicarage.
vici m. vice, defect.
vicissitud f. vicissitude, change of fortune.
viciós -osa a. vicious, depraved, dissolute.
víctima f. victim.
victor m. hurrah.
victòria f. victory.
victoriós -osa a. victorious.
vida f. life.
vident m. - f. seer, prophet.
vidre m. glass.
vidriera f. glass window.
vidriós -osa a. vitreous.
vidu m. widower.
vidua f. widow.

vigilància f. vigilance.
vigilant a. watchful, vigilant / m. watchman, caretaker.
vigilar tr. to watch, guard, be wary.
vigília f. vigil / vespers.
vigor m. vigour.
vigorós -osa a. strong, sinewy / vigorous.
vil a. vile, mean.
vila f. town, municipality.
vilesa f. vileness, baseness.
vil·la f. villa.
vímet m. wicker.
vinagre m. vinegar.
vinater -a a. vintner.
vincladís -issa a. flexible, ductile.
vincle m. tie / entail.
vindicar tr. to vindicate.
vinguda f. arrival, coming.
vint a. / m. twenty.
vintè -ena a. / m. -f. twentieth.
vinya f. vine, vineyard.
viola (mus.) f. viola.
violar tr. to violate / to rape.
violència f. violence.
violeta a. violet.
violí m. violin, fiddle.
violinista a. / m. -f. violinist, fiddler.
violoncel m. cello.
virilitat f. virility, manhood.
virrei m. viceroy.
virtuós -osa a. virtuous.
virtuós (mus.) m. virtuoso.
virtut f. virtue.
visat m. visa.
viscós -osa a. viscous, sticky.
visca! interj. hurrah! / Long live!
visera f. visor.
visible a. visible.
visibilitat f. visibility.
visita f. visit, call / visitor.
visitant a. visiting / m. visitor, caller.
visitar tr. to visit, call.

vista f. view / eyesight.
vitalment adv. vitally.
vitalitat f. vitality.
vitamina f. vitamin.
vitamínic -a a. vitamin.
vitrificar tr. vitrify.
vitualles f. pl. victuals, provisions.
vituperi m. vituperation.
viu -viva a. alive, live.
viure intr. to live.
vivament adv. in lively fashion, briskly.
vivent a. live.
vocabulari m. vocabulary.
vocal f. vowel / a. vocal.
vocació f. vocation.
vocatiu m. vocative.
vociferar tr. to yell.
vogar intr. to row.
vol m. flight.
volador -a a. flying.
volar intr. to fly.
volcà m. volcano.
volenterós -osa a. willing / wilful.
voler tr. to will, want, wish.
voler (dir) tr. to mean.
volició f. volition.
volt m. turn.
volta (arch.) f. vault.
voltadits m. whitlow.
voltants m. pl. surroundings, outskirts, environs.
voltar tr. - intr. to surround / to make a diversion, go around.
voltatge m. voltage.
voltor m. vulture.
volum m. volume.
voluntari -ària a. voluntary / m. volunteer.
voluntat f. will, volition, purpose / desire, pleasure.
volva f. small bundle of cotton, hemp, flax, or silk / snowflake.
vora f. edge, border.

voraç a. voracious.
vorada f. kerb.
voravia f. kerb.
vorera f. wayside, sidewalk.
vori m. ivory.
vòrtex m. vortex.
vós pron. per. you, thou / you, thee.
vosaltres pron. pl. you.
vostè pron. you (polite form).
vostre -a a. sing. your / pron. pos. yours.
vostres a. pl. your / pron. pos. yours.
vot m. vote / vow.
votació f. voting, vote, poll.
votant a. / m.-f. voter.
votar tr. intr. to vote.
votiu -iva a. votive.
vuit a. / m. eight.
vuitanta a. / m. eighty.
vuitantè -ena a. / m. -f. eightieth.
vuitè -ena a. / m. -f. eighth.
vulgaritat f. vulgarity.

W

wàter m. toilet, water closet, lavatory.
whisky m. whisky.

X

xa m. sha.
xabec m. xebec.
xacal m. jackal.
xafarderia f. gossip.
xàfec m. rainfall, squall.
xai -a m. -f. lamb.

xalet m. chalet, villa, cottage.
xamós -osa a. pretty.
xàntic a. xanthic.
xapa f. plate.
xaragall m. channel made by rainfall / catchwater, conduit.
xarop m. syrup.
xarpa f. paw.
xarrup m. sip.
xarrupada f. sip, sup.
xarrupar tr. to sip, sup.
xaruc -uga a. worn out / senile, decrepit / perishable.
xarxa f. net, mesh / railway system.
xassís m. chassis.
xavalla f. small change.
xec (taló bancari) m. (Am.) check, (Bri.) cheque / **(escacs)** interj. check.
xemeneia f. chimney.
xeringa f. syringe.
xeringar tr. to syringe, inject.
xerinola f. fun, merriment, revelry.
xeroftalmia f. xerophthalmia.
xerrada f. chatter, small talk, gossip.
xerraire a. / m. -f. talkative.
xerrameca f. jabber.
xerrar intr. to chatter, chat, gossip.
xic -a a. little.
xiclet m. chewing gum.
xicot -a m. -f. lad, fellow, chap.
xifra f. figure / cipher, number / abbreviation.
xiling m. shilling.
xilofon m. xylophone.
xilografia f. xilography.
ximpanzé m. chimpanzee.
ximple a. simpleton.
ximpleria f. nonsense.
xinès -esa a. Chinese / m. Chinese language.
xinxa f. bug.
xinxeta f. drawing pin / tack.

xisclar intr. to scream, shriek, squeal.

xiscle m. scream, screech, squeal, shriek.

xiulador -a a. whistler.

xiular intr. i tr. to whistle.

xiulet m. whistle, siren, hooter.

xiuxiueig m. whisper, rustle.

xiuxiuejar intr. to whisper, hiss.

xivarri m. noise, fuss, clatter, shout / crowd.

xoc m. collision, bump, clash.

xocar intr. to collide / to shock, surprise.

xocolata f. chocolate.

xollar tr. to shear.

xop -a a. soaked, drenched / m. black poplar-tree.

xuclar tr. to suck.

xurma f. rabble.

xurriaques f. pl. whip.

xut m. kick.

Z

zebra f. zebra.

zebú m. zebu.

zèfir m. zephyr.

zel m. zeal.

zenc m. zinc.

zenit m. zenith.

zero m. nought, zero, nil.

ziga-zaga f. zigzag.

zigzaguejar intr. to zigzag.

zodíac m. zodiac.

zona f. zone.

zoologia f. zoology.

zoològic -a a. zoological.

zumzejar intr. to vibrate / to brandish.

DICCIONARI
ANGLÈS - CATALÀ

ADVERTIMENT ÚTIL
per al maneig del diccionari

Els articles van entrats amb lletra **negreta** i les equivalències amb lletra corrent (ex.: **admonish (to)** v. amonestar, reprendre / avisar).

Per tal d'assenyalar en quina vocal o grup de vocals recau l'accent tònic (fent excepció dels monosíl·labs), en el mot d'entrada en **negreta** hi hem representat la vocal forta –o grup de vocals si així s'escau– en lletra corrent; i en les equivalències en lletra corrent hi hem representat la vocal en la qual recau l'accent, en lletra **negreta**, per a orientació fonètica de l'usuari.

Pel que fa als mots d'entrada en anglès, hem de fer les següents puntualitzacions: els monosíl·labs anglesos en què apareixen dues vocals, si aquestes corresponen a un sol so, aniran en **negreta**, (ex.: **raw**), però si les dues vocals corresponen a dos sons diferents, com en el cas dels dígrafs, indicarem la vocal tònica en lletra corrent (ex.: **rear** o **bough**). Això ho fem extensiu als mots d'entrada polisil·làbics (ex.: **sea-son** o **accountant**).

D'altra banda, hem tractat monosíl·labs anglesos com «hide» o «make» com si tinguessin dues síl·labes; així apareixeran com **hide** i **make** en els mots d'entrada.

En els casos de paraules polisil·làbiques que tenen dues síl·labes tòniques, així ho fem constar (ex.: **sixteen** o **readjust**).

De la mateixa manera; a les paraules compostes, indiquem la vocal o vocals tòniques. Dos exemples serien **top hat** o **test tube**. Això és així encara que les paraules individuals es puguin comportar d'una altra manera. Dit d'una altra forma, quan veiem entrades monosil·làbiques en què la vocal està en lletra **negreta**, l'explicació és que formen part d'una paraula composta.

Volem també fer constar que a les entrades en anglès només indiquem l'accent primari del mot.

Quant a les equivalències catalanes dels mots entrats en anglès, hem indicat el gènere dels substantius; al final, si totes les equivalències pertanyen al mateix gènere, i si alguna no hi pertany ho indiquem a continuació immediata de la que està en aquest cas, entenent-se que totes les altres són del gènere indicat al final (ex.: **hat** s. barret, capell, m.; **hedge** s. clos, m., bardissa, cleda, f.).

També, i això és una qualitat excepcional del nostre diccionari, tinguin l'extensió que tinguin altres diccionaris, que a les equivalències catalanes dels adjectius indiquem la terminació femenina (si els escau de tenir-la diferent de la del respectiu masculí) (ex.: **heavenly** a. celestial, m. f., divi-ina).

ABREVIATURES EMPRADES
en aquest diccionari

a.	adjectiu	loc. adv.	locució adverbial
Aero.	Aeronàutica	loc. verb.	locució verbal
Adm.	Administració	loc. prep.	locució preposicional
adv.	adverbi	m.	substantiu masculí
Am.	Americà	m. -f.	substantiu masculí o femení
Anat.	Anatomia	m. pl.	substantiu masculí plural
Arq.	Arquitectura	Mat.	Matemàtiques
art.	article	Mec.	Mecànica
Astr.	Astronomia	Med.	Medicina
Bot.	Botànica	Meteor.	Meteorologia
Brit.	Britànic	Mil.	Militar
Com.	Comercial	Mús.	Música
conj.	conjunció	Nàut.	Nàutica
Crust.	Crustaci	Orn.	Ornitologia
Elec.	Electricitat	Ortog.	Ortografia
f.	substantiu femení	p.p.	participi passat
f. pl.	substantiu femení plural	pers.	personal
fam.	familiar	pl.	plural
fig.	figurat	Polít.	Política
Fotog.	Fotografia	pos.	possessiu
Gal.	Gal·licisme	prep.	preposició
Geogr.	Geografia	pron.	pronom
Geom.	Geometria	Quím.	Química
ger.	gerundi	Rel.	Religió
Gimn.	Gimnàstica	s.	substantiu
Gram.	Gramàtica	Teat.	Teatre
Ict.	Ictiologia	Tipog.	Tipografia
Insec.	Insecte	tr.	transitiu
interj.	interjecció	v.	verb
intr.	intransitiu	v. pr.	verb pronominal
Lit.	Literatura	vulg.	vulgarment
loc.	locució	Zool.	Zoologia

A

about prep. sobre, tocant a, aproximadament
above prep. damunt
abroad adv. a fora, a l'estranger
absence s. absència, f.
absent a. absent, m.-f.
abstain (to) v. abstenir-se,
estar-se de
absurd a. absurd -a.
abuse s. abús, m. / ultratge, m.
to... v. abusar / ultratjar
abyss s. abisme, m., abís, m.
academy s. acadèmia, f.
accede (to) v. accedir
accelerate (to) v. accelerar
accelerator s. accelerador,m.
accept (to) v. acceptar, admetre
access s. accés m. / atac, m.
accident s. accident, m.
acclaim (to) v. aclamar
accompany (to) v. acompanyar
accomplish (to) v. acomplir,
⁀ complir / dur a terme
accordance s. acord, m.
according to loc. prep. segons,
d'acord amb
account s. compte, m., relació, f.
informe, m.
accountant s. comptable, m.
accumulate (to) v. acumular
accumulation s. acumulació, f.
accurate a. exacte -a precís -isa
accusation s. acusació, f., càrrec,
m.

accuse (to) v. acusar
accused a. i s. acusat- ada
ace s. as, m.
ache s. dolor m. f. mal, m.
achieve (to) v. realitzar / reeixir,
aconseguir.
achievement s. execució, f. /
proesa, f., reeiximent, èxit, m.
acid a. i s. àcid -a / àcid, m.
acknowledge (to) v. reconèixer /
acusar recepció
acknowledgement s. reconeixement, m. / agraïment, m.
acorn s. aglà, m. f., gla, f.
acquaintance s. conegut, m.
coneixença, f.
acquire (to) v. adquirir
acquisition s. adquisició, f.
across adv. i prep. a través
act s. acte, m. / to... actuar,
representar, interpretar
action s. acció, actuació, f. / procés, m.
active a. actiu -iva
activity s. activitat, f.
actor s. actor, m.
actress s. actriu, f.
actual a. actual, m.-f./ efectiu
-iva, real, m.- f.
actually adv. de fet, en efecte, m.,
en realitat, f./ en aquest
moment, en aquest punt, m.
acute a. agut -uda, penetrant, m.-f.
adapt (to) v. adaptar
adaptation s. adaptació, f.
add (to) v. afegir, sumar
adder s. escurçó, m.

addition s. suma, addició, f., afegit, m.

address s. adreça, f./ to... v. adreçar, / adreçar-se, dirigir-se

adequate a. adequat -ada, escaient, m.-f.

adjective s. adjectiu.

adjust (to) v. ajustar, aplicar

adjustment s. ajust, m.

administer (to) v. administrar

admiral s. almirall, m.

admiration s. admiració, f.

admire (to) v. admirar

admonish (to) v. amonestar, reprendre / avisar

adolescence s. adolescència, f.

adopt (to) v. adoptar

adorn (to) v. adornar. ornar, guarir

adulate (to) v. adular, llagotejar

adult a. i s. adult -a

adulterate (to) v. adulterar

adultery s. adulteri, m.

advance (to) v. avençar, prestar

advantage s. avantatge, benefici, m.

adventure s. aventura, f.

adverb s. adverbi, m.

advertise (to) v. anunciar / avisar

advertisement s. anunci / avís, m.

advise s. consell / avís, advertiment, m.

advise (to) v. avisar, aconsellar, advertir

adviser s. conseller, assessor, m.

adviser s. conseller, assessor, m.

aerial a. aeri -aèria / s. antena, f.

aerodrome s. aeròdrom, m.

aeroplane s. avió, aeroplà, m.

afaffair s. assumpte, afer, m.

affect (to) v. afectar, impressionar

affection s. afecte, m. afecció f.

affectionate a. afectísim -a

affirm (to) v. afirmar, afermar

affirmation s. afirmació, f.

afford (to) v. proveir, subministrar, fornir

afloat a. flotant, surant / a flor d'aigua

afraid a. i m. -f. temorenc -a, temorós -osa

african a. africà -ana

after adv.i prep. després / darrera

afternoon s. tarda, f.

afterwards adv. després, tot seguit / doncs

again adv. de nou, novament, altre cop

against prep. contra

age s. edat, f. / època, era f.

agent s. agent, m.

aggravate (to) v. agreujar, agreujar-se / empitjorar

aggregate (to) v. agregar, afegir

aggression s. agressió, f.

ago adv. passat (temps), fa

agony s. agonia, f.

agree (to) v. convenir, estar d'acord

agreeable a. agradable, plaent

agreement s. acord, conveni, m contracte, m.

agriculture s. agricultura, f.

ahead adv. endavant, al davant

aid s. ajut m. / auxili, m. / to... v. ajudar

aim s. objectiu, designi, m / punteria, f. / to... v. aspirar, intentar / apuntar / encarar

air s. aire, m. / tonada, f. / semblant, m.

alarm s. alarma, f.

alas interj. ai!

alcohol s. alcohol, m.

ale s. cervesa anglesa forta, f.

alien a. aliè-ena, foraster-a, estranger-a.

alike a. igual, m.-f. / adv. igualment

alive a. viu -viva

all a. m. -f. sing i pl. tot -a, tots-totes

alley s. passatge / carreró m.

alliance s. aliança, f.

allow (to) v. permetre, concedir, tolerar

ally s. aliat / acostat, m.

almond s. ametlla, f.

almost prep. gairebé, quasi

alms s. almoina, f.

aloft adv. amunt enlaire

alone a. sol

along adv. i prep. al llarg

aloud adv. en veu alta, alt.

alphabet s. alfabet, m.

already adv. ja.

also adv. també

altar s. altar, m.

alter (to) v. alterar, modificar / canviar

alteration s. alteració, f.

although conj. encara que, malgrat

altitude s. altitud, altura, f.

altogether adv. en conjunt, tot junt, tot plegat / completament, totalment, del tot.

aluminium s. alumini, m.

always adv. sempre

amateur s. aficionat -ada

amaze (to) v. astorar, meravellar, sorprendre

ambassador s. ambaixador, m.

ambition s. ambició, f.

ambulance s. ambulància, f.

american a. americà -ana / nord-americà -ana.

amid prep. enmig

amiss a. impropi - impròpia / adv. fora de lloc

among prep. entre

amongst prep. entre, enmig de, entremig de

amount s. suma, f. / import, m.

ample a. ampli-àmplia, suficient, m.- f.

amplifier s. amplificador -a

amplify (to) v. ampliar, amplificar

amuse (to) divertir, entretenir, distreure

amusement s. divertiment, m. diversió, f.

an art. un, una

analogy s. analogia, f.

analysis s. anàlisi, f.

ananas s. ananàs, pinya d'Amèrica, f.

anarchy s. anarquia, f.

ancestor s. avantpassat, m.

anchor s. àncora, f. / to... v. ancorar

ancient a. antic -iga

and conj. i

angel s. àngel, m.

anger s. ira, f., enuig, m.

angle s. angle, m.

angler s. pescador de canya m.

angry a. enfadat -ada, enutjat

animal a. i s. animal

ankle s. turmell, m.

annihilate (to) v. aniquilar

announce (to) v. anunciar, revelar.

announcer s. anunciador -a, locutor -a

annoy (to) v. molestar, amoïnar

annoyance s. disgust, m., molèstia, f. empipament, m.

annual a. anual, anyal, m.-f.

annul (to) v. anul·lar

anoint (to) v. ungir / untar

anointment s. unció, f., ungiment, m., untura, f.

another a. un altre, m. una altra, f.

answer s. resposta, contestació, f. / to... v. contestar, respondre

ant s. formiga, f.

antelope s. antílop, m.

antenna s. antena, f.

anvil s. enclusa, f.

anxiety s. inquietud, ànsia, f. / anhel, m.

anxious a. desitjós -osa, inquiet -a, anguniós -osa

any a. algun -a, uns, unes / qualsevol, m. -f.

anybody pron. algú qualsevol, pl. qualssevol / ningú.

anyone pron. algú / qualsevol / ningú

anything pron. quelcom, alguna cosa / tot allò que, qualsevol cosa

anyway adv. de totes maneres, de qualsevol manera / no obstant

apart adv. a part / separadament

apartment s. pis, m. / estança f. / domicili, m., residència, f.

ape s. mona, f., simi, m.

apex s. àpex, cim, m.

apologize (to) v. excusar-se, disculpar-se

apology s. excusa, disculpa, f.

apostle s. apòstol, m.

apparatus s. aparell, m.

apparent a. clar, evident / aparent, m.-f.

apparently adv. clarament, evidentment / aparentment

appeal a. crida, f. / to... v. apel·lar, recórrer / cridar l'atenció.

appear (to) v. aparèixer, comparèixer

appetite s. apetit, m., gana, f.

applaud (to) v. aplaudir

applause s. aplaudiment, m.

apple s. poma, f.

appliance s. aparell, m.

application s. aplicació / sol·licitud, petició, f.

apply (to) v. dirigirse / sol·licitar.

appoint (to) v. nomenar, senyalar.

appointment s. cita, f., nomenament, m.

appreciate (to) v. estimar; calcular / augmentar

apprehend (to) v. témer, sospitar

apprentice s. aprenent -a

apprenticeship s. aprenentatge

approach (to) v. acostar, apropar

appropriate a. apropiat -ada, adequat -ada, convenient, m.-f.

approval s. aprovació, f.

approve (to) aprovar, sancionar, assentir

approximate a. aproximat -ada

apricot s. albercoc, m.

April s. abril, m.

apron s. davantal, m.

apt a. apte -a

aptitude s. aptitud, f.

arbitrator s. àrbitre, m.

arc s. arc (de cercle), m.

arch s. arc, m., volta, f./ to... v. arquejar

archbishop s. arquebisbe, m.

architect s. arquitecte, m.

architecture s. arquitectura, f.

area s. àrea, f.

argue (to) v. discutir, argüir, raonar

argument s. raó, f., demostració, f./ debat, m. / argument, tema, m.

arise (to) v. aixecar-se, elevar-se / sorgir, aparèixer.

arithmetic s. aritmètica, f.

ark s. arca, f.

arm s. braç, m. / arma, f. / to... v. armar

armchair s. butaca, f.

armour s. armadura, cuirassa, f. / carro blindat, m.

armpit s. aixella, f.

army s. exèrcit, m.

aroma s. fragància, f.

around adv.i prep. entorn, al voltant

arouse (to) v. desvetllar, despertar

arrange (to) v. arranjar, ordenar

arrest s. arrest, m., detenció, f.

arrival s. arribada, f.

arrive (to) v. arribar

arrow s. sageta, f. fletxa, f.

art s. art, m.

artery s. artèria, f.

article s. article, m.

articulation s. articulació, f.

artificial a. artificial, m.- f.

artisan s. artesà -ana, artífex, m.-f.

artist s. artista, m. -f.

as conj. tan, com, per tal com

ascend (to) v. ascendir, pujar, muntar

ash v. cendra, f. / freixe, m.

ashamed a. avergonyit -ida, confós -osa

asiatic a. asiàtic -a

ashtray s. cendrer, m.

aside adv. a un costat, de banda, a part / apart, m.

ask (to) preguntar, interrogar, inquirir

ask for (to) v. demanar, sol·licitar, inquirir

asleep a. adormit -ida

asparagus s. espàrrec, m.

aspect s. aspecte, m.

asphyxia s. asfíxia, f.

aspiration s. aspiració, f.

ass s. ase, ruc, m.

assault s. assalt, m. / to... v. assaltar

assay s. assaig, m.

assembly s. assemblea, reunió, f.

assent s. assentiment, m. / to... v. assentir

assert (to) v. afirmar, asseverar

assertion s. afirmació, f.

assimilate (to) v. assimilar

assist (to) v. ajudar, socórrer / assistir

assistant s. ajudant, assistent / a. auxiliar, m.- f.

association s. associació, f.

assume (to) v. assumir / suposar, imaginar-se, presumir / prendre, adoptar (una actitud) / apropiar-se.

assurance s. seguretat, certesa, f.

assure (to) v. assegurar, garantir, afirmar.

astray a. esgarriat -ada, desviat -ada

astronaut s. astronauta, m. -f.

at prep. a, en, prop de, sobre

atheism s. ateisme, m.

atheist s. ateu, m.

athlete s. atleta, m.

at least adv. almenys

atmosphere s. atmosfera, f.

atom s. àtom, m.

atone (to) v. expiar / reparar

at present adv. actualment

attack (to) v. atacar

attain (to) v. obtenir, merèixer

attempt s. prova, temptativa, f., assaig, m. / to... v. intentar / atemptar

attend (to) v. atendre / assistir, concórrer

attendance s. assistència, f.

attendant s. servent, acompanyant, m.

attention s. atenció, f.

attentive a. atent -a

attenuate (to) v. atenuar.

attitude s. actitud, f.

attorney s. procurador, m.

attraction s. atracció, f.

attribute (to) v. atribuir

auction s. subhasta, f.

audience s. públic, auditori, m. / audiència, f.

auditory a. auditiu-iva.

august s. agost, m.

aunt s. tia, f.
author s. autor, m.
authoress s. autora, f.
authority s. autoritat, f.
authorization s. autorització, f.
authorize (to) v. autoritzar
automatic a. automàtic -a
automobil s. automòbil, m.
autonomy s. autonomia, f.
autumn s. tardor, f.
avail (to) v. aprofitar, disposar
available a. disponible / aprofitable, m.- f.
avenue s. avinguda, f., passeig, m., via, f., vial, m.
average s. mitjana, f. / a. normal, corrent, m. -f.
aviation s. aviació, f.
aviator s. aviador -a
avoid (to) v. evitar, eludir
await (to) v. esperar
awake a. despert-a / conscient, m.- f. / to... v. desvetllar / v. pr. despertar-se
award s. premi, guardó, m. / sentència, f. / adjudicació, f. / to... v. concedir, atorgar
aware s. sabedor -a, coneixedor -a, assabentat -ada / conscient, m.-f., caut -a
away adv. fora / absent
awe s. por, f., terror reverenciós, espaordiment, m.
awful a. terrible, m.-f., paorós -osa / gran, enorme, m.-f.
awfully adv. enormement, terriblement, granment
awkward a. maldestre-a, estúpid-a, matusser-a / difícil, m.-f., perillós-osa.
awl s. alena, f.
axe s. destral, f.
axle s. eix, centre, m. / fusell, arbre (d'una roda)
axis s. eix, m.

B

babe s. criatura, f.
baboon s. (zool.) mandril, m.
baby s. infantó, bebè, nodrissó, m.
bachelor s. solter / llicenciat, m.
back s. esquena, f., revers, m. / adv. darrera
backbite (to) v. difamar
backbone s. espinada, f.
backwards adv. enrera, endaŕ rera / cap endarrera d'esquena
bacon s. cansalada, f.
bad a. dolent -a, nociu - iva.
badge s. distintiu, m., insígnia, f.
badly adv. malament / (fam.) moltíssim
badness s. maldat, dolenteria, vilesa, f.
baffle (to) v. desconcertar, frustrar
bag s. sac, m., bossa, f.
baggage s. equipatge, m. / bagassa, f.
bail s. fiança f.
bait s. esquer, m.
bake (to) torrar, coure (en el forn)
baker s. flequer -a, forner -a
balance s. balanç, m. / afinament (de pes) m., (com.) saldo m.
balcony s. balcó, m.
bald a. calb -a
baldness s. calvície, f.
bale s. fardell, m., bala, f. / to... v. embalar, enfardellar
ball s. bola, pilota, f.
balloon s. globus, m.
banana s. banana, f., plàtan, m.
band s. banda / faixa, f.
bandage s. embenat, m. / to... v. embenar
bang s. cop. estrèpit, terrabastall, m. / detonació, f.

bangle s. braçalet, m. / anella, f.

banishment s. exili, desterrament, bandejament, ostracisme, m.

banister s. barana, f.

bank s. banc, m. / ... **note** s. bitllet, m.

banker s. banquer, m.

banner s. senyera, bandera, f. estendart, m.

baptize (to) v. batejar

bar s. bar, m., barra, f.

barbarian a. i s. bàrbar, m.

barber s. barber, m.

bare a. nu-nua, despullat-ada / buit-ida.

barefoot a. descalç -a

bareheaded a. descofat -ada, descobert -a, sense capell

bargain s. pacte, acord, tracte, m. / ganga, f. / negoci, m. / regateig, m. / **to...** v. negociar, tractar, regatejar / intercanviar

barge s. barcassa, f.

bark s. escorça, f. / lladruc, m.

barley s. ordi, m.

barmaid s. cambrera de bar, f.

barman s. cambrer de bar, m.

barn s. graner, m. / pallissa. f.

baron s. baró, m.

barrack s. caserna, f.

barrel s. bóta, f., barril, m

barren a. eixorc-a, erm.

barrier s. obstacle, límit, m., barrera, f.

barrister s. advocat, m.

base s. fonament, m. base, f. / a. comú, vil, roí / **to...** v. fonamentar, basar

baseball s. beisbol, m.

basement s. soterrani, m.

bashful a. tímid-a, vergonyós-o-sa.

basin s. palangana, f., rentamans, m.

basis s. base, f. / fonament / principi bàsic, m.

basket s. cistell, paner, m., panera, f.

basketball s. basquetbol, m.

bass s. (mús.) baix, m.

bat s. rat-penat, m. rata-pinyada, f.

batch s. fornada f. / col·lecció, f. grup, m., sèrie de coses produïdes d'un seguit

bath s. bany, m. / banyera, f.

bathe (to) v. pr. banyar-se

bathroom s. cambra de bany, f.

baton s. batuta, f.

battalion s. batalló, m.

batter (to) v. copejar, batre/ deixatar / apallissar

battery s. bateria, f.

battle s. batalla, f.

bay s. badia, f.

bayonet s. baioneta, f.

bazaar s. basar, magatzem d'articles variats, m.

be (to) v. ésser, ser, estar.

be able (to) v. poder.

beach s. platja, f.

beacon s. alimara, f. / far, m.

beak s. bec, m.

beam s. raig (de llum), m. / biga, f.

bean s. fava/mongeta, f., fesol, m.

bear s. ós, m. / **she ...** óssa, f.

bear (to) v. portar, suportar

beard s. barba, f.

bearing s. aspecte, capteniment, m. / (mec.) coixinet, m.

beast s. animal, m., bèstia, f.

beat (to) v. copejar, colpejar / batre / picar

beautiful a. bell -a, formós, -osa

beauty s. bellesa, f.

beaver s. castor, m.

be born (to) v. néixer.

because conj. perquè.

become (to) v. esdevenir, ocórrer.

bed s. llit, m.

bedroom s. dormitori, m.
bee s. abella, f.
beefsteak s. bistec, m.
beehive s. rusc, m., arna, ~rnera, f.
beer s. cervesa, f.
beetle s. escarabat, m.
beetroot s. remolatxa, f.
before adv. i prep. davant, abans
beforehand adv. anticipadament, a la bestreta
befriend (to) v. protegir, afavorir
beg (to) demanar, captar
beggar s. captaire, mendicant, m.
begin (to) v. començar, iniciar
beginner s. principiant, debutant, m.
beginning s. començament, m. iniciació, f.
beguile (to) v. enganyar, seduir
behalf s. en nom de / de part de / a causa de
behave (to) v. pr. captenir-se, comportar-se
behaviour s. conducta, f., capteniment, m.
behead (to) v. decapitar, escapçar
behind adv. i prep. darrera
behold (to) v. contemplar, esguardar
being s. ésser, ens, m., essència, f. / persona, f. / existència, f.
Belgian a. belga, m. -f.
belief s. creença, fe, f.
believe (to) v. creure
bell s. campana, f.
bellow s. bram, crit (d'ase)
bellows s. manxa, f.
belly s. ventre, m.
belong (to) v. pertànver
belongings s. pl. propietats, possessions, pertinences, f. pl.
below adv.i prep. sota, dessota
belt s. cinturó, cinyell, m.

bench s. banc, seient, m.
bend (to) v. doblegar, torçar
beneath adv. i prep. davall, més avall
beneficence s. beneficència, f.
benefit s. benefici, profit, m., utilitat, f. / to... v. aprofitar, aprofitar-se, beneficiar
bent s. curvatura, f. / a. corb -a.
berry s. baia, f.
beside prep. al costat, prop.
besides adv. altrament, endemés, a més
bet s. aposta, juguesca, f. / to... v. apostar
betray (to) v. trair, revelar / delatar / vendre
betrayal s. traïció, f. / abús de confiança, m.
better a. millor, m.- f.
between prep. i adv. entre, entremig
beware (to) guardar-se, malfiarse.
bewilder (to) v. extraviar, perdre / atordir
beyond adv. més lluny, més enllà / prep. després de
Bible s. bíblia, f.
bicycle s. bicicleta, f.
big a. gros-ossa, gran, m.- f.
bigness s. obesitat, grassor, f.
bill s. factura, nota, f.
billow s. ona, onada, f.
bin s. arca, f.
bind (to) v. lligar / relligar, enquadernar
biography s. biografia, f.
biology s. biologia, f.
bird s. ocell, m. au, f.
birth s. naixement, m.
birthday s. natalici, aniversari, m.
biscuit s. bescuit m., galeta, f.
bishop s. bisbe, m.
bit s. trepant, / tros, m.
bitch s. gossa / prostituta, f.

bite (to) v. mossegar
bitter a. amarg-a, amargós-osa.
bitterness s. amargor, f.
black a. i s. negre -a.
blackberry s. móra, f. / esbarzer, m.
blackboard s. pissarra, f.
blacken (to) v. ennegrir / enfosquir
blacksmith s. ferrer, forjador, m.
blade s. fulla de ganivet / espasa, f.
bladder s. veixiga, bufeta, butllofa, f.
blame (to) v. blasmar, reprendre, culpar
blanket s. manta, f., abrigall, m.
blast s. ràfega, ratxa, ventada, f., bufarut, m.
blaze s. flamarada, f. / to... v. inflamar, flamejar, cremar
bleak a. fred-a, desolat-ada, trist-a / a. pàl·lid-a
bleed (to) v. sagnar
bleeding s. sagnia, f.
bless (to) v. beneir
blessed a. beneït-ïda, benaurat-ada / sant-a
blessing s. benedicció, f.
blind a. cec -cega, orb -a.
blindness s. ceguesa, ceguetat, f. / encegament, m.
blink (to) v. parpellejar.
blinkers s. aclucalls, m. pl.
bliss s. glòria, felicitat, f.
block s. bloc, m. llamborda, f. / obstacle, destorb, m. / to... v. obstruir, bloquejar
blockhead s. imbècil, m.- f. / estaquirot, m.
blond a. ros -rossa
blood s. sang, f.
bloom (to) v. florir
blossom s. flor, f., botó, capoll, m. / to... v. florir, florejar, brotar

blot s. taca, esmena, f. / to... v. tacar
blotter s. esborrany / paper assecant, m.
blouse s. brusa, f.
blow s. cop, buf, m., bufada, alenada, f. / to... v. bufar, alenar / panteixar / esclatar
blue a. blau -blava.
blunt a. esmussat -ada, / to... v. esmussar
blush s. rubor, vermellor, enrojolament / to... v. enrojolar-se, envermellir, ruboritzar-se
boar s. senglar, m.
board s. post, f., tauler, m. / junta directiva, f.
boarder s. dispeser, hoste, m.
boarding house s. pensió, casa de dispeses, f.
boarding school s. pensionat, internat, m.
boat s. barca, f., bot, m.
bobbin s. rodet, m.
bodkin s. punxó, m.
body s. cos, m.
boil (to) v. bullir
boiler s. caldera, f.
boiling a. bullent, m. -f.
bold a. valent -a, ardit -ida
boldness s. atreviment, m., intrepidesa, f.
bolster s. coixí, m.
bolster (to) v. encoixinar
bolt s. pany, forrellat, m. / to... v. tancar.
bomb s. bomba, f.
bomber a. bombarder, m.
bondage s. esclavatge, m. captivitat, f.
bone s. os, m. / espina, f.
bonfire s. foguera, fogatera, f.
bonnet s. bonet, m., gorra, f.
book s. llibre, m.
bookcase s. llibreria, prestatgeria per a llibres, f.
booking office s. taquilla, f.

121

book-keeping s. comptabilitat, tenidoria de llibres, f.
bookseller s. llibrer, m.
bookshop s. llibreria, f.
boot s. bota, f.
border s. frontera, vora, f., caire, límit, m.
bore (to) v. foradar, trepanar / avorrir-se
borough s. vila, població, f.
borrow (to) v. manllevar
boss s. patró, encarregat, cap, m.
botany s. botànica, f.
both a. i pron. ambdós - ambdues, tots dos - totes dues
bother (to) v. molestar, enutjar, fastiguejar
bottle s. ampolla, botella, f.
bottom s. fons / fonament, m.
bough s. branca (d'arbre), f.
bound s. límit, m. / fita, f. / molló, m. / salt, m.
bound (to) v. limitar, partionar, confinar / botre, botar, saltar
boundary s. partió, f., límit, m. / frontera, fita, f.
bouquet s. ram, ramell, m.
bow s. arc, m. / to... v. arquejar / saludar
bow (to) v. inclinar-se, reverenciar / sotmetre's
bowels s. intestins, budells, m. pl.
bowl s. bol, m. / escudella, f.
box s. caixa, capsa, f.
boxer s. boxejador, m.
boxing s. boxa, f.
boy s. noi, vailet, nen, m.
brace s. abraçadora, f., fermall, m. / to... v. lligar, amarrar
bracelet s. braçalet, m.
bracket s. suport, puntal, m. / pl. parèntesis, claudàtors, m.
brake (to) v. alentir, frenar
brain s. cervell, m.

brake s. fre / matoll, m.
bran s. segó, m.
branch s. ram / ramal, m.
brandy s. conyac, m.
brass s. llautó, m.
brave a. estrenu-ènua, brau-ava
bray s. bram, m. / to... v. bramar
bread s. pa., m.
breadth s. amplada, amplària, extensió, f. / (nàut.) mànega, f.
break (to) v. trencar, interrompre, interceptar, rompre / violar, infringir, crebantar
breakfast s. esmorzar, m.
breakwater s. escullera, f.
breast s. pit m., pitrera, f. / sina, f.
breastbone s. estèrnum, m.
breath s. alè, m.
breathe (to) v. alenar, respirar, exhalar
breathing s. respiració, f.
breed s. raça, casta, f. / to... v. criar, nodrir
breeding s. cria, f. / criança, educació, f.
breeze s. brisa, f., oreig, m., aura, f., ventijol, m.
bribe (to) v. subornar, seduir
brick s. rajola, f., cairó, maó, m.
bricklayer s. paleta, mestre de cases, m.
bridal a. nuvial, nupcial, m.- f.
bride s. núvia, f.
bridegroom s. nuvi, m.
bridge s. pont, m.
bridle s. brida, f.
brief a. breu, m. -f.
brigade s. brigada, f.
bright a. brillant, m.-f. lluminós-osa.
brighten (to) v. polir, enllustrar, brunyir / desemboirar-se / animar-se
brilliant a. refulgent, resplendent, m.- f.

brim s. cantell, caire, m., vora, f. (d'una copa, d'un vas, etc.) / ala, (f.) d'un capell m.

bring (to) v. portar o emportar-se, dur o endur-se / tornar, retornar.

bring up (to) v. educar

brisk a. viu-viva, ràpid-a, animat-ada

brittle a. trencadís-issa, fràgil, m.- f.

broad a. ample-a / extens-a

broad-bean s. fava, f.

broadcast (to) a. emetre per ràdio / sembrar a bolei

broil (to) v. rostir

broken a. trencat-ada / separat-ada / interromput-uda

bronze s. bronze, m.

brooch s. fermall, m.

broom s. (bot.) ginesta, f. / escombra, f.

broth s. brou, m.

brother s. germà, m. / ... in law s. cunyat, m.

brow s. cella, f. / front, m.

brown a. marró, m.- f., castany-a

brush s. raspall, m. / to... v. raspallar

brush (to) v. raspallar / netejar, fregar

bubble s. bombolla, f.

bucket s. galleda, f.

buckle s. sivella, f.

bud s. capoll, m.

budget s. pressupost, m.

buffalo s. (zool.) búfal, m.

buffer s. molla esmorteïdora, f., topall, m.

bug s. xinxa, f., cuc, verm, m.

build (to) v. construir, edificar

builder s. constructor, m.

building s. edifici, m.

bulb s. bulb, m. / bombeta, f.

bull s. toro, brau, m.

bullet s. bala, f.

bump s. topada, f., xoc, m. / to... v. topar, xocar.

bumper s. para-xocs, m.

bunch s. ram / grapat / gotim, m.

bundle s. farcell, lligall, m.

bungalow s. xalet, m.

buoy s. boia, f.

burden s. càrrega, f., pes, m. / to... v. carregar

bury (to) v. enterrar, inhumar, sebollir

burial s. enterrament, m.

burn s. cremada, f. / to... v. cremar

burst (to) v. rebentar, esclatar

bus s. autobús, òmnibus, m.

bush s. mata, f. / arbust / matoll, m.

business s. negoci, ocupació, assumpte / treball, afer, m.

bustle (to) v. pr. bellugar-se, moure's, afanyar-se.

busy a. ocupat -ada

but conj. però

butcher s. carnisser -a

butler s. majordom, m.

butter s. mantega, f.

butterfly s. papallona, f.

buttock s. natja, anca, f.

button s. botó, m.

buttonhole s. trau, m.

buy (to) v. comprar

buyer s. comprador -a

buzz s. brunzit, m.

by prep. per.

by-laws s. reglament, m.

C

cab s. fiacre, (gal.), cotxe, / taxi, m.

cabbage s. col. f.

cabin s. cabina, cabana, f..

cabinet s. gabinet, m.

cable s. cable, m.

cabman s. cotxer, / taxista m.

cabriolet s. cabriolé, (gal.), m.

cacao s. cacau, m.

cackle (to) v. escatainar

cactus s. cactus, m.

cage s. gàbia, f. / to... v. enga-biar

cake s. pastís, m.

calculate (to) v. calcular

calculation s. càlcul, m.

calculator s. calculador, m.

calendar s. calendari, m.

calf s. vedell -a

calico s. percala, f.

call s. crida, f. / crit, m. / to... v. cridar, avisar, despertar, visi-tar / v. pr. personar-se / ano-menar-se / dir-se

calm s. calma, tranquil·litat, f. / a. calmós -osa, tranquil -il·la, serè -ena, m.

calyx s. (bot.) calze, m.

camel s. camell -a

camera s. cambra obscura, f. / màquina fotogràfica, f.

camomile s. camamilla, f.

camp s. campament, m.

camp out (to) v. acampar

camping s. càmping, m., acam-pada, f.

canal s. canal, m.

canary s. (zool.) canari, m.

cancel (to) v. cancel·lar, supri-mir

cancer s. càncer, m.

candid a. ingenu-ènua, càndid-a

candidate s. candidat, aspirant, m.

candle s. espelma, candela, f.

candlestick s. canelobre, cande-ler, m.

candy s. sucre candi, m. /to... v. confitar

cane s. canya, f.

canon s. cànon, m. / canonge, m.

canine tooth s. ullal, m.

cannon s. canó, m. / regla, f.

canoe s. canoa, f., canot, m.

canteen s. cantina / cantimplora f.

canvas s. lona, f. / canemàs, m.

cap s. gorra, f., casquet, m. / tap, m.

capable a. capaç, competent, m.-f. apte-a

capacity s. capacitat, f.

cape s. cap. (geog.), m.

capital s. capital, f. / majúscula, f. / a. capital, fonamental, m.-f. / s. capital, cabal, m.

capsule s. càpsula, f.

captain s. capità -ana.

captive a. i s. captiu -iva

capture s. captura, f. / to... v. capturar

car s. cotxe, automòbil, auto, m.

caravan s. caravana / (gal.) rou-lotte, f.

carbon s. carboni, m.

card s. tarja, targeta, f.

cardboard s. cartó, cartró m.

care s. compte, m., cura, sol·lici-tud, f. / ... of, a l'atenció de / to... v. interessar, importar / to... for, tenir cura.

career s. carrera, professió, f., to... v. córrer a tota velocitat

careful a. acurat -ada, curós -osa / cautelós -osa, prudent -a / estalviador-a

carefully adv. curosament

careless a. descurat -ada, negli-gent, m.-f. / irreflexiu -iva, indolent, m.- f.

caress (to) v. acariciar, acaro-nar, amanyagar

cargo s. càrrega, f., carregament, m. / ...boat s. vaixell de càrrega

carnation s. clavell, m.

carol s. nadala, cançó de Nadal, f.

carpenter s. fuster, m.

carpet s. catifa, f.

carriage s. carruatge, cotxe / carreteig, tragí, m.

carrot s. pastanaga, f.

carry (to) v. portar, dur

cart s. carro, carretó, m.

carton s. envàs, m. capsa (f.) de cartró, m.

cartoon s. caricatura, f. ninot, m.

cartridge s. cartutx, m.

carve (to) v. esculpir, cisellar / partir, trinxar (viandes)

carving s. escultura / entalladura, talla, f.

carving knife s. trinxant, m., ganivet de trinxar

case s. cas, assumpte, m. / caixa, maleta, f.

cash s. caixa, f. / diner efectiu, m.

cashier s. caixer, m.

cask s. bóta, f.

cast (to) v. llançar, engegar / fondre

castanets s. castanyoles, f. pl.

castiron s. ferro colat, ferro fos, m.

castle s. castell, m.

casually adv. per casualitat, casualment

casualty s. desastre / sinistre, m. / (mil.) baixa, f. (per mort, captura, accident, etc.)

cat s. gat, m.

Catalan a. i s. català -ana

catalogue s. catàleg, m.

cataract s. cascada, f., salt d'aigua, saltant, m.

catch (to) v. agafar, prendre

catechism s. catecisme, m.

category s. categoria, f.

caterpillar s. eruga, f.

cathedral s. catedral, seu, f.

catholicism s. catolicisme, m.

cattle s. bestiar boví, m.

cauldron s. caldera, perola, f.

cauliflower s. col-i-flor, f.

cause s. causa, raó, f. / motiu, m. / to... v. causar / motivar.

caution s. caució, prevenció, f. / advertència, amonestació, f.

cautious a. caut-a, prudent, m.- f.

cavalry s. cavalleria, f.

cave s. caverna, cova, f.

cease (to) v. cessar, parar.

cedar s. cedre, m.

ceiling s. sostre, m.

celebrate (to) v. celebrar

celebrated a. cèlebre, m.-f.

celery s. api, m.

cell s. cel-la / cèl-lula, f. / nínxol, m.

cello s. violoncel, m.

cellar s. celler, m.

cement s. ciment, m.

cementery s. cementiri, m.

center s. centre, m.

centimetre s. centímetre, m.

centipede s. centpeus, m.

central a. central, m.- f.

centre s. centre, m.

century s. segle, m., centúria, f.

ceramics s. ceràmica, f.

cereal a. i s. cereal, m.

ceremony s. cerimònia, f.

certain a. cert-a, segur-a del tot

certainly adv. certament, segur

certificate s. certificat, m.

certify (to) v. certificar

chain (to) s. cadena, f. / to... v. encadenar

chair s. cadira / càtedra, f.

chairman s. president, m.

chalice s. calze, m.

chalk s. guix, m.

challenge (to) v. reptar, provocar, desafiar

challenger s. provocador -a, reptador -a

chamber s. cambra, f.

chamberpot s. orinal, m.

champion a. campió -ona / s.

paladí, m. / to... v. defensar, recolzar

chance s. ocasió, oportunitat / casualitat, f.

chancellor s. canceller, m.

change s. canvi, m. / to... v. canviar

changeable a. variable, canviable, inconstant, m.-f.

channel s. estret, canal, m. / estria, ranura, f.

chant s. càntic / salmòdia, f.

chaos s. caos, desordre, m.

chap s. xicot, minyó / individu, m.

chapel s. capella, f.

chapter s. capítol, m.

character s. caràcter, m.

charcoal s. carbó vegetal, m.

charge s. càrrec, m. / càrrega / despesa / acusació, f. / to... v. carregar / atacar

charity s. caritat, f.

charm s. encanteri, encantament, encís, m.

chart s. quadre, esquema gràfic, m. / (nàut.) carta de navegació, f.

charter s. cèdula, escriptura, f. / to... v. noliejar

chase s. caça, persecució, f.

chassis s. xassís, m.

chastity s. castedat, f.

chat s. conversa, xerrada, f.

chatter s. xerrada, garlada, f. / to... v. xerrar, garlar

cheap a. barat -a

cheat s. engany, m. trampa, f. / frau, m. / to... v. estafar

check s. repressió, f., obstacle, m. / xec bancari / (escacs), interj. escac al rei / taló, m. / to... v. reprimir, deturar, moderar.

cheek s. galta, f. / barra, f., desvergonyment, m.

cheer s. aplaudiment, m., aclamació, f. / to... v. aplaudir, animar

cheese s. formatge, m.

chemical a. químic-a

chemist s. farmacèutic, químic, m.

chemistry s. química, f.

cheque s. xec, taló bancari, m.

cherish (to) v. apreciar / acaronar / protegir / basar una il·lusió, una esperança

cherry s. cirera, f.

chess s. escacs, m. pl.

chest s. pit, tòrax, m. / caixa, arca, f.

chest of drawers s. calaixera, f.

chestnut s. castanyer, m. / castanya, f.

chew (to) v. mastegar, masticar

chewing gum s. xiclet, m., goma de mastegar, f.

chick s. pollet, pollastret, m.

chicken s. pollastre, m.

chickpea s. cigró, m.

chief a. i s. cap, director / capitost, m.

chiefly adv. sobretot, principalment.

chieftain s. cap, cacic, m. / capità, m.

child s. nen-nena, infant, m., criatura, f.

childhood s. infantesa, infància, f.

childish a. acriaturat-ada, animat-ada, pueril, trivial, m.- f.

children s. pl. nens, m., criatures, f.

chill a. fred -a, rúfol-a / s. fred, calfred, m. / to... v. refredar.

chilly a. fredolic -a / fred.

chimney s. xemeneia, f.

chimpanzee s. ximpanzé, m.

chin s. barba, f.

china s. porcellana xinesa, f. / servei de porcellana, m.

china cabinet s. vitrina. f.

chinese a. xinès -esa.

chip s. bri, bocí, m., mica, estella, f.

chips s. patates fregides, f. pl.

chisel s. cisell, m. / **to...** v. cisellar

chivalry s. cavalleria (institució) / cavallerositat, f.

chloroform s. cloroform, m.

chocolate s. xocolata, f.

choice s. elecció, tria, f.

choir s. cor, m., coral, f., orfeó, m.

choke (to) v. escanyar, ofegar, sufocar / obstruir

choose (to) v. escollir, triar

chop s. costella, f. / **to...** v. tallar, partir, trinxar

chopper s. tallant, m.

chorus s. cor (mús.) / tornada (cançó), f.

christen (to) v. batejar

Christian a. cristià -ana

Christmas s. Nadal, m.

chronicle s. crònica, f.

church s. església, f.

churchyard s. cementiri parroquial, m.

cider s. sidra, f.

cigar, m. cigar, m.

cigarette s. cigarret, m., cigarreta, f.

cinder s. carbonet, m. / cendra, f. / caliu, m.

cinema s. cinema, m.

cinnamon s. canyella, f.

cipher s. zero, m. / xifra / clau, f.

cipher (to) v. xifrar

circle s. cercle, m.

circuit s. circuit, m.

circulate (to) v. circular

circulation s. circulació, f.

circumference s. circumferència, f.

circumstance s. circumstància, f.

circus s. circ, m.

cite (to) v. citar.

citizen s. ciutadà, m.

city s. ciutat, f.

civilization s. civilització, f.

claim s. demanda, reclamació, pretensió, f. / **to...** v. demandar, reclamar, reivindicar

clap s. aplaudiment, m. / **to...** v. aplaudir

clarinet s. clarinet, m.

class s. classe / categoria, f.

classify (to) v. classificar

classroom s. aula, classe, f.

clatter s. xivarri, m., gatzara, f., brogit, m.

claw s. urpa, f., garfi, m.

clay s. argila, f.

clean a. net -a / aclarit -ida / **to..** v. netejar, aclarir.

clear a. clar a

cleave (to) v. partir, esberlar

clergy s. clericat, m.

clergyman s. sacerdot, clergue, m.

clerk s. escrivent, dependent m.

clever a. intel·ligent, hàbil, m.- f.

client s. client, m.

cliff s. cingle, talús, m., escarpa, f.

climate s. clima, m.

climax s. clímax, apogeu, súmmum, m.

climb (to) v. grimpar, enfilar-se

cling (to) v. arrapar-se, adherir-se, agafar-se

clinic s. clínica, f., dispensari, m.

clip s. clip, m. / grapa, f.

clock s. rellotge (de paret), m.

clockmaker s. rellotger, m.

clockwork s. màquina de rellotgeria.

clogs s. esclops, socs, m. pl. / trava, impediment

cloister s. claustre, m.

close (to) v. tancar.

closed a. tancat -ada

closely adv. fidelment, exactament, atentament

clothe (to) v. vestir, cobrir, revestir

clothes s. roba, f., vestits, m. pl. / vestuari, m.

cloth s. tela, roba, f., teixit, drap, m.

clothing s. roba, f., vestuari, m., vestits, m. pl.

cloud s. núvol, m.

cloudy a. ennuvolat-ada

clown s. pallasso, m.

club s. cercle, club, m. / porra, f., garrot, m.

clue s. guia, pista, f., rastre, indici, m.

cluster s. raïm, gotim / manat, eixam, m.

clutch (to) v. engrapar, agafar

coach s. cotxe, m.

coal s. carbó mineral, m., hulla, f.

coalpit s. mina de carbó, f.

coarse a. bast-a, groller-a

coast s. costa, f.

coat s. jaqueta, americana, f.

cobweb s. teranyina, f.

cock s. gall, m.

cockerel s. pollastre, m.

cockpit s. carlinga, cabina, f.

cockroach s. escarabat, m.

cockscomb s. cresta, f.

cocktail s. còctel, m.

cocoa s. cacau, m.

coconut s. coco, m.

cocoon s. capoll (del cuc de seda), m.

cod s. bacallà, m.

code s. codi, m.

coffee s. cafè, m.

coffeepot s. cafetera, f.

coffin s. taüt, fèretre, m.

coil s. espiral, rotlle, serpentí, m.

coin s. moneda, f.

coincide (to) v. coincidir

colander s. colador / sedàs, m.

cold a. i s. fred -a / congelat -ada / indiferent, m.-f.

collaborate (to) v. col·laborar

collar s. coll (de la camisa, vestit), m.

colleage s. col·lega, m.-f.

collect (to) v. recollir, aplegar

collection s. col·lecció, f.

collector s. recaptador, m.

college s. col·legi, m., universitat, f.

collide (to) v. col·lidir, xocar, topar

collier s. miner, minaire, m.

collision s. topada, col·lisió, f.

colon s. còlon (anat.), m. / (gram.) dos punts, m. pl.

colonel s. coronel, m.

colonize (to) v. colonitzar

colony s. colònia, f.

colour s. color, m.

column s. columna, f.

comb s. pinta, f.

combination s. combinació f.

combine (to) v. combinar / unir, unir-se

come (to) v. venir / arribar / esdevenir-se

come on (to) v. avançar, créixer, progressar

comedy s. comèdia, f.

comet s. cometa, m.

comfort s. confort, m., comoditat, f.

comfortable a. còmode -a, confortable, m.-f.

comforter a. consolador -a / s. bufanda (de llana) / Esperit Sant m.

comic s. còmic, m. / publicació infantil, f.

comma s. (gram.) coma, f. / cometes, f. pl.

command (to) v. manar, comandar

commence (to) v. començar

commend (to) v. lloar, alabar / encomanar, pregar per / recomanar comment s. comentari, m., observació, f. / to... v. comentar, glossar

commerce s. comerç, m.

commission s. encàrrec, m. / comanda, f.

committee s. comitè, m.

common a. comú -una, ordinari -ària / corrent, vulgar, m.-f.

communicate (to) v. comunicar / fer saber, notificar / combregar

communication s. comunicació, f.

communion s. comunió, f.

communism s. comunisme, m.

community s. comunitat, f.

compact s. acord, m. / a. compacte-a, breu, m.- f.

companion s. company, m.

companionship s. companyonia, f.

company s. companyia, f.

comparison s. comparació, comparança, f.

compartment s. compartiment, m.

compass s. circuit, límit, m. / brúixola, f. / to... v. aconseguir, idear, conseguir.

compassion s. compassió, f.

competence s. competència, f.

competent a. competent m.- f.

competition s. competició, f.

complaint s. queixa, f. / plany, m.

complement s. complement, m.

complete a. complet -a. / to... v. completar

complex a. complex -a

complicate (to) v. complicar

compliment s. compliment, m. / galanteria, f. / salutació, f.

comply (to) v. complir / acomplir

compose (to) v. compondre

composition s. composició, f.

compositor s. caixista / componedor, m.

compound a. compost -a, complicat -ada

comprehend (to) v. comprendre

comprehensive v. comprensiu -iva

compromise (to) v. comprometre

computer s. computador, m., calculadora, f.

comrade s. company -a, camarada, m.

conceal (to) v. amagar, dissimular, encobrir, ocultar

conceit s. opinió, idea / vanitat, f.

concentrate (to) v. concentrar

concept s. concepte, m.

concern (to) v. concernir, incumbir, preocupar

concert s. concert / acord, conveni, m.

concession s. concessió, f.

conciliate (to) v. conciliar.

concrete a. concret -a / s. formigó / to... v. revestir de formigó.

concur (to) v. concórrer

condemn (to) v. condemnar

condense (to) condensar

condition s. condició, f.

condolence s. condol, m.

conductor s. guia / conductor i/o cobrador (en un vehicle) / director d'orquestra, m.

cone s. con, m.

confess (to) v. confessar / confessar-se

confession s. confessió, f.

confidence s. confidència / confiança, f.

confirm (to) v. confirmar

conflagration s. conflagració, f. / incendi, m.

conflict s. conflicte, m.
confuse (to) v. confondre
confusion s. confusió, f.
congratulate (to) v. felicitar, congratular
congratulation s. enhorabona, congratulació, f.
congress s. congrés, m.
conjunction s. conjunció, f.
connect (to) v. connectar / unir, relacionar
connection s. connexió, f.
conquer (to) v. conquerir, conquistar
conqueror s. conqueridor -a, conquistador -a
conquest s. conquesta, f.
conscience s. consciència, f.
concious a. conscient, m.-f.
consecrate (to) v. consagrar
consent s. consentiment, permís, m.
consequence s. conseqüència / importància, f.
consequent a. conseqüent m.- f.
conserve (to) v. conservar
consider (to) v. considerar
consideration s. consideració, f.
consist (to) v. consistir
consolation s. consol, conhort, m.
console (to) v. consolar, conhortar.
consonant a. consonant, m.-f. / s. consonant, f.
constable s. guàrdia, policia, m.
constellation s. constel·lació, f.
constipate (to) v. restrènyer, produir restrenyiment
constipation s. restrenyiment, m.
constitute (to) v. constituir
construct (to) v. construir
consult (to) v. consultar
consupmtion s. consum, m. / tisi, f.
consumptive a. tísic-a

contagion s. contagi, m.
contagious a. contagiós -osa, encomanadís, -issa
contain (to) v. contenir
container s. contenidor, m.
contaminate (to) v. contaminar
contemptible a. menyspreable, vil, m.- f.
contemptuous a. desdenyós -osa, despectiu -iva
contend (to) v. lluitar, combatre / sostenir
content a. a. content-a, satisfet-a.
contention s. disputa, baralla, querella
continent a. i s. continent, m.
continuance s. continuació, f.
continue (to) v. continuar
continuous a. continu -ínua
contract s. contracte, pacte, conveni, m.
contract (to) v. contractar/ contreure, reduir, estrènyer
contrary s. contrari / **on the...**, al contrari
contrast (to) v. contrastar
contribute (to) v. contribuir
contribution s. contribució, f.
contrive (to) v. inventar, idear, acudir-se / tramar / conspirar
control s. control, m. inspecció, f.
controller s. controlador, inspector, interventor, m.
convene (to) v. convocar / unir-se
convent s. convent (de monges), m.
conversation s. conversació, conversa, f.
convert (to) v. convertir / convertir-se
convertible a. convertible, m.-f. / s. (auto) descapotable, m.
convey (to) v. conduir, transportar / transmetre
convince (to) v. convèncer

convoy (to) v. acomboiar

cook s. cuiner -a / **to...** v. coure, cuinar

cookery s. art de cuinar, m.

cooking-stove s. cuina econòmica, f.

cool a. fresc -a, tranquil·il·la / **to...** v. refrescar.

coolness s. frescor, fresca, f. / fredor, f.

cooperate (to) v. cooperar

coordinate (to) v. coordinar

copper s. coure, aram, m. / xavalla, moneda de coure, f.

copy s. còpia, f. / exemplar, m. / **to...** v. copiar

copybook s. llibreta, f., quadern, m.

copyright s. propietat literària, f., drets d'autor, m. pl.

coral s. corall, m.

cord s. cordill, cordó, m.

core s. nucli, centre, m.

cork s. suro / tap de suro, m./ ... **screw** s. tirabuixó, m.

corn s. moresc, blat de moro, m.

corned beef s. carn (f.) de bou (m.) en conserva f.

corner s. cantó, m., cantonada, f. / racó, m.

cornet s. corneta, f.-m. / paperina, f. / cucurull, cucurutxo, m.

corps s. col·lectivitat, f., conjunt, m.

corpse s. cadàver, m.

correct a. correcte -a / **to...** v. corregir.

correctly adv. correctament

correspond (to) v. correspondre

correspondence s. correspondència, f.

correspondent s. corresponsal, m.

corroborate (to) corroborar

corrugate (to) v. arrugar, rebregar

corrugated a. arrugat -ada, rebregat -ada / ondulat -ada

corrupt (to) v. corrompre

corruption s. corrupció, f.

corsair s. corsari, m.

cost s. cost, import, m. / **to...** v. costar, valer

costume s. vestit, m.

cot s. bressol, catre, m.

cottage s. xalet, m. / cabana, f.

cotton s. cotó, m.

cotton wool s. cotó fluix, m.

couch (to) v. ajeure's

cough s. tos, f.

council s. concili, m. / consell, m., junta, f.

counsel s. parer, consell, m., advertència, f. / conseller, assessor, m.

count (to) v. comptar

counter s. taulell, m.

counterfeit s. falsificació, imitació, f.

counterpoint s. contrapunt, m.

countess s. comtessa, f.

country s. país, m., pàtria, f. / camp, m.

countryman s. compatrici -ícia, compatriota, m.-f. / camperol, pagès, m.

county s. comtat, districte, m.

coupe s. cupé, m. berlina, f.

couple s. parella, f.

courageous a. coratjós, -osa, valent -a

course s. curs, m. / rumb, m.

court s. tribunal / seguici, m.

courtesy s. cortesia, atenció, gentilesa, f. / reverència, f. / favor, m.

courtier s. cortesà -ana

courtship s. festeig, prometatge, galanteig, m.

courtyard s. pati, m.

cousin s. cosí -ina.

covenant s. contracte, conveni, m., aliança, f.

cover s. coberta / tapadora, f. / to... v. cobrir, amagar, protegir

covetous a. cobejós -osa, cobdiciós -osa

cow s. vaca, f.

coward a. i s. covard, m.

cowshed s. establa, f.

crab s. cranc verd o de mar, m.

crack s. esquerda, f. cruixit, m. / to... v. esquerdar, cruixir / esquerdar-se

cradle s. bressol, m.

craft s. artesania, f. ofici, gremi, m. / astúcia, f., artifici, m.

craftsman s. artifex, artesà, m.

crafty a. astut-a, murri-úrria.

crane s. grua, f.

crash s. estrèpit, m. / fracàs, m., fallida, f.

crate s. cove, m. / gàbia, f.

crawfish s. cranc de riu

crawl (to) v. arrossegar-se, serpentejar

crayfish s. cranc de riu

crayon s. llapis de color, pastel m. / to... v. dibuixar al pastel

crazy s. alienat-ada, dement m.-f., esbojarrat-ada

cream s. crema / nata, f.

crease s. plec, doblec, m., arruga, f. / to... v. plegar, doblegar

create (to) v. crear.

creation s. creació, f.

creature s. criatura, f.

credit s. crèdit, m.

creditor s. creditor -a

creed s. credo, m., doctrina, f.

creep (to) v. arrossegar / arrossegar-se, avançar de quatre grapes

creeper s. el qui s'arrossega, m. / enfiladissa, f. (planta)

crescent a. creixent, m.-f. / s. mitja lluna, f.

crest s. cresta f., plomall, m.

crew s. tripulació, f.

cricket s. grill, m. / joc de... m.

crime s. delicte, crim, m.

crimson a. carmesí -ina / s. carmí, m.

cripple s. esguerrat -ada, paralític -a

criticism s. crítica, f.

criticize (to) v. criticar

croak (to) v. raucar

crocodile s. cocodril, m.

crook s. curvatura, f. / ganxo, m. / (rel.) crossa, f. / meandre, m.

crooked a. corb -a / tort -a, guerxo -a / pervertit -ida

crop s. collita, f. / to... v. collir, recol·lectar

cross s. creu, f. / to... v. creuar, travessar / vexar, frustar / ...out v. anul·lar, esborrar, passar ratlla

crossing s. pas de vianants, m. / gual, m.

crossword s. mots encreuats, m.

crouch (to) v. pr. ajupir-se

crow s. corb, m., cornella, f.

crowd s. multitud, munió, f. / to... v. amuntegar, estrènyer, atapeir.

crown s. corona, f.

crucifix s. crucifix, m.

crude a. cru-crua / rude, m.- f, tosc-a, grosser-a.

cruel a. cruel, m.-f.

cruise s. creuer, viatge per mar, m. / to... v. navegar, prendre part en un creuer

cruiser a. navegant. / creuer, m.

crum s. molla de pa, engruna, f.

crumble (to) v. esmicolar-se, engrunar / enderrocar-se, esfondrar-se

crunch (to) v. cruixir

crush (to) v. aixafar, moldre, esprémer, esmicolar

crusade s. croada, f.

crust s. crosta, f.
crustaceous s. crustaci, m.
crutch s. crossa, f.
cry s. crit / plor, m. / to... v. cri-
    dar / plorar
crystal s. cristall, m.
cub s. cadell, m.
cube s. cub, m.
cuckoo s. cucut, m.
cuff s. puny (de la camisa, vestit),
    m.
culprit s. culpable / reu, delin-
    qüent, m.
cultivate (to) v. conrear / culti-
    var
culture s. cultura, f.
cunning s. astúcia, f.
cup s. copa, tassa, f.
cupboard s. armari de paret, m.
curate s. capellà, diaca, m.
cure (to) v. curar, guarir / salar
curious a. curiós -a, tafaner -a
curl s. rull, rínxol, bucle, m. /
    espiral, f.
currency s. moneda corrent, de
    curs normal, f.
current, a. corrent, usual, m.-f. /
    s. corrent, m.
curtain s. cortina, f. teló, m.
curve s. corba, f.
cushion s. coixí, m.
custard s. crema, f., flam, m.
custom s. costum, hàbit, m. /
    clientela, f.
customer s. client -a.
customs house s. duana, f.
customs s. drets de duana, m.
cut (to) v. tallar, retallar / ...
    short (to) v. fer drecera /
    tallar en sec
cycle s. cicle, període, m. / bici-
    cle, m.
cylinder s. cilindre, m.
cymbal s. címbal, m.
cypress s. xiprer, m.

D

dad, daddy, s. papà, m.
daffodil s. narcís, m.
dagger s. daga, f., punyal, m.
dahlia s. dàlia, f.
daily a. diari, m. / adv. diària-
    ment
dainty a. elegant, m.- f., exquisit-
    ida
dairy s. lleteria, vaqueria, f.
daisy s. margarida, f.
dam s. dic, m., presa, resclosa, f.
damage s. dany, perjudici, m. /
    avaria, pana, f.
dame s. dama, senyora, f.
damm s. maledicció, f. / to... v.
    maleir, damnar
damp a. humit -ida / to... v.
    humitejar
dampness s. humitat, f.
dance s. ball, m., dansa, f. / to...
    v. ballar, dansar
danger s. perill, m.
dangerous a. perillós -osa
dangle (to) v. balancejar / intr.
    gronxar-se
dare (to) tr. fer front / intr.
    gosar, atrevir-se
daring a. atrevit -ida, agosarat
    -ada / s. atreviment, m.
dark a. fosc -a
darken (to) v. enfosquir / enfos-
    quir-se, fer-se fosc / entristir
darkness s. foscor, fosquedat, f.
darling a. estimat -ada, car -cara,
    dilecte -a
darn (to) v. sargir
dart s. dard m., sageta, fletxa, f. /
    to... v. disparar, llançar /
    tirar-se de cap
dash s. escomesa, f., embat, m. /
    guió, m.
date s. data, f. / dàtil, m.
daughter s. filla, f.
daughter-in-law s. nora, f.

133

daunt (to) v. acovardir, descoratjar

dauntless a. intrèpid -a

dawn s. alba, albada, matinada, f.

day s. dia, jorn, m.

daze s. enlluernament, m. / to... v. ofuscar, estabornir, atordir

dazzle (to) v. enlluernar.

dead a. mort-a / marcit-ida, pansit-ida.

deaden (to) s. esmorteir.

deadly a. mortal, m.-f. destructiu -iva

deaf a. sord-sorda.

deafening a. eixordador -a

deafness s. sordera

deal s. quantitat, part, f. / tracte, m. / to... v. comerciar, tractar / distribuir

dealer s. traficant, comerciant, m. / distribuïdor, m.

dean s. degà, m.

dear a. benvolgut -uda, apreciat -ada / car -a, costós -osa.

death s. mort, la mort, f.

deathless a. immortal, m.- f.

debate (to) v. debatre, discutir, qüestionar

debouch (to) v. desembocar

debt s. deute, m.

debtor s. deutor -a

debut s. debut, m., presentació, f.

decadence s. decadència, f.

decant (to) v. decantar / abocar / transvasar

decay (to) v. decaure, decandir-se / corcar-se

decease s. defunció, f., decés, m. / to... v. morir, expirar

deceit s. engany, m. / estafa, estafada, f.

deceitful a. mentider-a, fals-a.

deceive (to) v. estafar, enganyar

December s. desembre, m.

decency s. decència, f.

decent a. decent, m.-f.

deception s. engany, frau, m.

decide (to) v. decidir, determinar

decided a. decidit-ida / definit-ida.

decimal a. decimal, m.-f.

decimate (to) v. delmar

decision s. decisió, f.

decisive a. decisiu -iva

deck s. coberta (d'un vaixell), f.

declaration s. declaració, f.

declare (to) v. declarar

decline s. pendent, declivi, m. / deterioració / disminució / decadència, f. / to... v. lliscar / refusar / declinar

decorate (to) v. decorar / condecorar

decoration s. decoració, f.

decoy s. reclam, parany, m., trampa, f.

decrease s. minvada, minva, / reducció, f. / to... v. minvar, reduir / esvair-se

decree s. decret, m.

decry (to) v. desacreditar

dedicate (to) v. dedicar

deduce (to) v. deduir

deed s. acció, gesta, f., fet, m.

deem (to) v. suposar, jutjar

deep a. profund-a, pregon-a

deer s. cérvol, m. / cervo, m.

defamation s. difamació, f.

defamatory a. difamatori -òria

defame (to) v. difamar

default s. omissió, f. incompliment, m.

defeat s. derrota, desfeta, f.

defect s. defecte, m.

defence s. defensa, f.

defend (to) v. defensar

defendant s. demandat-ada, acusat-ada.

defender s. defensor -a

defer (to) v. retardar, ajornar, diferir

define (to) v. definir

definition s. definició, f.

definitive a. definitiu -iva
deflate (to) v. desinflar
defy (to) v. desafiar, reptar
degree s. grau, m. / títol, m.
delay s. retard, ajornament, m., dilació, f. / to... v. retardar, ajornar
deliberate (to) v. deliberar
delicacy s. delicadesa, finor, f.
delicate a. delicat-ada, fi-fïna. m.
delicatessen s. rebosteria, f. / venda de menges exòtiques i delicades
delight s. delícia, f., plaer, m. / to... v. delectar, plaure
deliver (to) v. lliurar, remetre / alliberar
delivery s. lliurament, m., remesa, f. / alliberament, m.
delta s. delta, m.
deluge s. diluvi, aiguat, m.
demand s. demanda f., prec, m. / to... v. demandar, requerir
democracy s. democràcia, f.
demolish (to) v. enderrocar / arrasar
demon s. dimoni, m.
demonstrate (to) v. demostrar
demonstration s. demostració, f. / manifestació, f.
den s. cova, f., coval, m., balma, f. / cau, amagatall, m.
dense a. dens-densa
density s. densitat, f.
dent s. abonyegament, bony, m. osca, f.
dentist s. dentista, odontòleg, m.
denude (to) v. despullar, denudar
denunciation s. denúncia, f.
deny (to) v. negar, refusar
depart (to) v. partir / anar-se'n
department s. departament, m.
depend (to) v. dependre
dependent s. familiar, m.- f., dependent, m.

depict (to) v. pintar, descriure
depot s. dipòsit, magatzem, m.
depress (to) v. deprimir
depression s. depressió, f.
deprive (to) v. privar / desposseir
depth s. fons, m. profunditat, f.
deputy s. diputat / delegat, m.
derange (to) v. espatllar, desarranjar
deride (to) v. riure's, mofar-se
derision s. escarni, m., riota, f.
derive (to) v. derivar, deduir
derrick s. grua, càbria, f.
descend (to) v. descendir, devallar, baixar.
descent s. descens, m., devallada, f. / descendència, f., llinatge, m.
describe (to) v. descriure
description s. descripció, f.
desert a. desert-a / s. desert, m. / to... v. desertar
deserve (to) v. merèixer
deserving a. mereixedor -a
design s. dibuix, disseny / designi, m.
designate (to) v. designar
designer s. dibuixant, dissenyador, m.
desirable a. desitjable, m. -f.
desire s. desig, m. / to... v. desitjar
desist (to) v. desistir
desk s. pupitre, escriptori, m.
desolate a. desolat -ada, desert -a
despair s. desesperació, f., desesper, m. / to... v. desesperar
despicable a. menyspreable, m.-f., roï-ïna.
despise (to) v. menysprear
despite s. despit, m. rancúnia, f. / prep. malgrat que, a desgrat de
dessert s. postres, f. pl.
destiny s. destí, fat, m.

destroy (to) v. destruir, destrossar

destroyer s. destructor, m.

destruction s. destrucció, f.

detach (to) v. destacar, separar

detail s. detall, m.

detain (to) v. detenir

detect (to) v. descobrir, esbrinar, detectar

detection s. descobriment, esbrinament, m.

detective s. detectiu, m.

deter (to) v. dissuadir

determinate (to) v. determinar, decidir

determination s. determinació, decisió, f.

determine (to) v. determinar, fixar, definir

determined a. determinat-ada, resolut-uda, decidit-ida.

detest (to) v. detestar

detriment s. perjudici, m.

develop (to) v. desenvolupar, desenrotllar / esdevenir / revelar (fotog.).

development s. desenvolupament, m., evolució, f. / revelat, m. (fotog.).

deviate (to) v. desviar

deviation s. desviació, f.

device s. artifici, dispositiu, aparell, m. / lema, m., divisa, f.

devil s. diable, m.

devilish a. diabòlic -a

devise (to) v. inventar, plantejar, idear

devoted a. fidel, lleial, m. - f. / dedicat-ada, consagrat-ada.

devour (to) v. engolir, devorar.

devout a. devot -a

dew s. rosada, f.

diabetes s. diabetis, f.

diagnose (to) v. diagnosticar

diagnostic a. i s. diagnòstic, m.

diagonal a. i s. diagonal, m.

dial s. esfera (de rellotge, comp-

tador, etc.) f., quadrant, m. / disc (de telèfon) m. / to... marcar, trucar (per telèfon)

dialect s. dialecte, m.

dialogue s. diàleg, m.

diameter s. diàmetre, m.

diamond s. diamant, m.

diary s. dietari, m. agenda, f.

dictate (to) v. dictar

dictation s. dictat, m.

dictator s. dictador, m.

dictionary s. diccionari, m.

die s. dau, m. / **to...** v. morir

differ (to) v. diferenciar-se, distingir-se / discrepar

difference s. diferència, f.

different a. diferent, m.-f.

difficult a. difícil, m. -f.

difficulty s. dificultat, f.

diffuse (to) v. difondre

dig (to) v. cavar, excavar / ...out, up, desenterrar

digest s. compendi, sumari, m., recopilació, f. / **to...** v. pair, digerir / meditar / assimilar

digestion s. digestió, f.

dignify (to) v. dignificar

dike s. dic, m.

dignity s. dignitat, f.

dilate (to) v. dilatar, dilatar-se / ampliar

diligent a. diligent m.- f., aplicat -ada

dim a. fosc -fosca, vague-aga, opac-aca

dimension s. dimensió, f.

diminish (to) v. disminuir

dimness s. foscor, fosquedat, obscuritat, f. / ofuscament, m.

dine (to) v. sopar

dining room s. menjador, m.

dinner s. àpat principal (del dia) / banquet, m.

dip (to) v. submergir / submergir-se, capbussar-se / inclinar-se

diplomacy s. diplomàcia, f.
direct a. directe -a / to... v. dirigir, guiar, governar
direction s. direcció / instrucció, f.
director s. director -a
directory s. directori / anuari, m. guia telefònica, f.
dirt s. brutícia, f.
dirty a. brut -a, empolsegat -ada / to... v. embrutar, tacar, empolsegar
disagree (to) v. dissentir, discrepar, diferir, discordar
disagreement s. desacord, dissentiment, m. dissensió, desavinença f.
disappear (to) v. desaparèixer
disappoint (to) v. decebre, desil·lusionar, defraudar
disappointment s. contrarietat, decepció, f.
disaster s. desastre, m., desgràcia, calamitat, dissort, f.
discharge (to) v. descarregar / disparar / destituir / alliberar
disciple s. deixeble, m.
discipline s. disciplina, f.
discount s. descompte, m.
discourse s. discurs, m. dissertació f. / conversa, f.
discover (to) v. descobrir
discovery s. descobriment, m., troballa, f.
discreet a. discret -a
discrete a. discret-eta / distint-a, desigual, m.-f.
discriminate (to) v. discriminar / distingir, discernir
discuss (to) v. discutir
discussion s. discussió, f.
disease s. malaltia, f. / mal, malestar, m.
disgrace s. desgràcia, f.
disguise s. disfressa, f. / to... v. disfressar
disgust s. repugnància, f. / to... v. disgustar

disgusting a. repugnant, m.-f., fastigós -osa.
dish s. plat-a.
dishonest a. trampós-osa, caragirat-ada.
disk s. disc, m.
dislike (to) v. desplaure, detestar / desaprovar
dismay s. consternació f. / basca, f. / desmai, m.
dismiss (to) v. destituir / acomiadar, despatxar
disobey (to) v. desobeir
disorder s. desordre. m.
display s. exhibició, demostració, ostentació, jactància, f., desplegament, m. / to... v. exhibir, manifestar, exposar
displease (to) v. enutjar, desplaure
dispose of (to) v. disposar de, desfer-se de / vendre / alienar
dispute (to) discutir, disputar
disregard s. indiferència, desatenció, f., menyspreu, m.
distance s. distància, f.
distant a. llunyà -ana, apartat -ada
distaste s. fastigueig, m., repugnància, aversió, f.
distil (to) v. destil·lar
distinct a. distint -a, definit -ida
distinction s. distinció, f.
distinguish (to) v. distingir
distort (to) v. retorçar, desfigurar / tergiversar
distract (to) v. distreure
distress s. dolor, m. f., aflicció, f. / to... v. afligir
distribute (to) v. distribuir
distribution s. distribució, f.
district s. districte, m.
distrust s. desconfiança, f., recel, m., descrèdit, m.
disturb (to) v. destorbar, pertorbar, desordenar

ditch s. trinxera, fossa, rasa, f.
dive s. capbussada, f. / to...v. capbussar-se, llançar-se a l'aigua
dive (to) v. pr. submergir-se
diver s. bus, escafandrer, m.
diverge (to) v. divergir
diverse a. divers-a, diferent,
m.-f.
diversify (to) v. diversificar
divide (to) v. dividir
divine a. diví -ina / to... v. endevinar, vaticinar, pronosticar
division s. divisió, f. / departament (com.)
divorce s. divorci, m. / to... v.
divorciar, separar
dizziness s. vertigen, m.
dizzy a. marejat -ada, atordit-ida
/ to... v. marejar, atordir
dock s. dic, m. dàrsena, f. moll m.
docker s. estibador, m.
doctor s. metge, doctor, m.
dodge (to) v. esquivar, defugir
dog s. gos, m.
doll s. nina, f.
dollar s. dòlar, m.
dolphin s. dofí, m.
domain s. domini, m.
dome s. cúpula, f.
dominate (to) v. dominar
domination s. dominació, f.
dominion s. domini, m., dominació, f. / senyoriu, m. / domini
(Polit.), m.
donkey s. ase, ruc, m.
doom s. fat, m.
door s. porta, f., portal, m.
doorway s. porta d'entrada, f.
dose s. dosi, f.
dot s. punt, pic, m. / to... v. puntejar
double s. doble, duplicat, m. /
to... v. doblar, duplicar
double a. doble m.-f. /ambigu -a
/ duplicat -ada
doubt s. dubte, m., incertesa, f. /
to... v. dubtar

doubtful a. dubtós-osa.
doubtless a. sens dubte, indubtable, m.-f.
dove s. colom, m.
down adv. avall, cap avall, a
baix
doze (to) v. dormisquejar /
endormiscar-se
dozen s. dotzena, f.
draft s. projecte, tiratge, esborrany, m.
drag s. draga, f. / rèmora, f., llast,
m. / to... v. dragar
dragon s. drac, m.
dragonfly s. libèl·lula, f.
drain (to) v. drenar, desguassar,
filtrar
drainage s. drenatge, m.
dramatist s. dramaturg. m.
draw (to) v. dibuixar / estirar /
desembeinar, sostreure
drawer s. caixó, calaix, m.
drawing s. dibuix, m.
drawing pin s. xinxeta, f.
drawing room s. sala, f., saló, m.
dread s. por, f., temor, m. / to...
v. témer
dream s. sommi, m. / to... v.
somiar
dreary a. trist -a, malenconiós
-osa, lúgubre, m. -f.
dress s. vestit, m. / to... v. vestir
/ agençar, empolainar
dress coat s. frac, m.
dressmaker s. modista / cosi-
dora, f.
drift s. corrent, m. / tendència f.
/allò que ve corrent o el vent
arrossega / to... v. arrossegar,
derivar
drill s. barrina, f. filaberquí, m. /
to... v. barrinar, foradar
drinker s. bevedor -a
drip s. gotera, f. / to... v. degotar,
gotejar
drive (to) v. conduir, guiar
driver s. conductor, xofer, m.

drizzle (to) v. plovisquejar
drop s. gota, f. / mica, f. / pastilla, f. / baixada, f. / rebaixa, f. / to... v. degotar, gotejar / descendir
drove s. ramat, m., ramada, f.
drown (to) v. ofegar / ofegar -se, negar -se
drug s. droga, f., medicament, narcòtic, m.
drum s. timbal, tambor, bombo, m. / timpà de l'orella, m.
dry a. sec -a, àrid -a / assecat-ada / avorrit -ida / to... v. assecar, eixugar
drunk s. borratxo, embriac, ebri, m.
duchess s. duquessa, f.
duck s. ànec, m. ànega, f.
duckling s. aneguet, m.
due a. degut -uda
duke s. duc, m.
dull a. avorrit-ida, estúpid-a, ensopit-ida.
duly adv. degudament
dumb a. mut -muda
dummy a. fingit -ida, falsejat -ada
dung s. fems, m. pl. / excrement, m.
dunghill s. femer, m.
during prep. durant, mentre
dusk s. capvespre, crepuscle, m.
dusky a. obscur -a, fosc -a / morè -ena
dust s. pols / escombraries, f.
duster s. plomall / guardapols, m.
dustman s. escombriaire, m.
dusty a. polsós-osa, polsinós-osa, empolsegat-ada.
duty s. deure, m., obligació, f.
dwarf s. nan, gnom, pigmeu, m.
dwell (to) v. viure, residir, habitar
dwelling s. residència, vivenda, f., domicili, m.

dye s. tint, color, m. / to... v. tenyir
dying a. moribund, m.
dynamic a. dinàmic-a / enèrgic-a, actiu-iva, eficient, m.- f.

E

each a. cada / cada / cada un, una, cadascum-una / pron. cada u, cadascú.
eager a. àvid -a, impacient, m.-f., desitjós -osa / ambiciós -a.
eagerness s. avidesa, f., anhel, m. osa / vehemència, f.
eagle s. àliga, àguila, f.
ear s. orella / oïda, f.
earl s. comte, m.
earldom s. comtat, m.
early adv. aviat, d'hora / a. primitiu -iva
earn (to) v. percebre, guanyar, cobrar /adquirir, obtenir / merèixer
earnings s. pl. jornal, salari, m. / guanys, m. pl.
earnest a. formal, m.-f. seriós -osa
earring s. arracada, f.
earth s. terra, f.
earthquake s. terratrèmol, m.
ease s. benestar, m. comoditat, f.
easel s. cavallet (de pintor), m.
easily adv. fàcilment.
easiness s. facilitat, f.
East s. est, orient, llevant, m.
Easter s. Pasqua de Resurrecció, f.
easy a. fàcil, m.-f.
easy chair s. butaca, f.
eat (to) v. menjar
eatable a. comestible, m.-f.
ebony s. banús, eben, m.
eccentric a. excèntric-a
echo s. eco, ressò, m. / to... v. ressonar, repetir
eclipse s. eclipsi, m.

economy s. economia, f., estalvi, m.

edge s. vora, f., marge, m.

edify (to) v. edificar / instruir / elevar moralment.

edit (to) v. redactar, dirigir)una obra literària) fins a punt d'impressió.

editio s. edició, f.

editor s. redactor -a, director -a (s. f.).

educate (to) v. educar

education s. educació, f.

eel s. anguila, f.

effect s. efecte, m.

efficacy s. eficàcia, f.

effort s. esforç, m.

effect s. efecte, m., conseqüència, f.

efficacious a. eficaç, m.-f.

effusive a. efusiu -iva

egg s. ou, m.

egg plant s. albergínia, f.

elderdown s. edredó, m.

eight a. i s. vuit, m.

eighteen a. i s. divuit, m.

eighth a. i m.- f. vuitè -ena

eighty a. i s. vuitanta, m.

either a. pron. l'un o l'altre / ambdós, m.

elastic a. elàstic -a

elbow s. colze, m.

elder a. de més edat, més gran

eldest a. el més gran, el primogènit

elect (to) v. elegir, triar, escollir

election s. elecció, f.

electric a. elèctric -a

electric fan s. ventilador, m.

electrician s. electricista, m.

electricity s. electricitat, f.

elegant a. elegant, m.- f.

elementary a. elemental, m.- f. / rudimentari-ària

elephant s. elefant, m.

elevator s. ascensor, elevador, m. / escala mecànica, f.

eleven a. i s. onze, m.

eleventh a. i m.- f. onzè-onzena

elide (to) v. elidir, frustrar

eliminate (to) v. eliminar

ellipse s. el·lipse, f.

elm s. om, m.

elongate (to) v. allargar, prolongar

else a. altre-a / adv. quelcom més, / altrament

elsewhere adv. en altra banda, a una altra banda

embark (to) v. embarcar

embarrass (to) v. destorbar embarassar, torbar, desconcertar.

embassy s. ambaixada, f.

embers s. pl. brasa, f., caliu, m.

ember days s. témpores, f. / dies de dejuni

emblem s. emblema, m.

embody (to) v. incloure, incorporar

embrace (to) v. abraçar, cenyir, incloure

embroider (to) v. brodar

embryo s. embrió, m.

emerald s. maragda, esmaragda, f.

emerge (to) v. sorgir / emergir

emergency s. emergència, f., destret, m. / urgència, f.

emery s. esmeril, m.

emigration s. emigració, f.

emit (to) v. emetre

emotion s. emoció, f.

emperor s. emperador, m.

empire s. imperi, m.

employ (to) v. ocupar, col·locar. donar feina

employee s. empleat, dependent, obrer, m.

employer s. patró, amo, m.

employment s. col·locació, ocupació, f.

empower (to) v. autoritzar / donar poders

empress s. emperadriu, f.

empty a. buit -ida / to... v. buidar

enable (to) v. capacitar, facilitar, permetre.

enamel s. esmalt, m. / to... v. esmaltar

enclose (to) v. cerclar, encerclar, tancar / adjuntar, incloure

enclosure s. tancat, recinte / annex, m.

encourage (to) v. encoratjar, animar

encounter s. encontre, m. trobada, f.

encyclopaedia s. enciclopèdia, f.

end s. fi, f., final, acabament, m. / to... v. acabar, finir

endeavour (to) v. intentar, provar, tractar de / esforçar-se

ending s. acabament, m. conclusió, f.

endless a. infinit-ita, inacabable, m.-f.

endorse (to) v. endossar.

endorsement s. endossament, endós, m.

endow (to) v. dotar

endowment s. dotació / fundació, f.

endurance s. sofriment, m. / fermesa, resistència, f.

endure v. aguantar, resistir

enemy e. i s. enemic-iga

energetic a. enèrgic-a

energy s. energia, f.

enervate (to) v. enervar, afeblir, debilitar

engage (to) v. contractar, donar feina, ocupació / comprometre, empenyorar.

engagement s. compromís, prometatge, m. cita, f.

engine s. motor, m. màquina, f.

engineer s. enginyer / cap de màquines, m.

english a. anglès -esa

engrave (to) v. gravar, cisellar.

engraving s. gravat, m. / làmina, f.

enjoin (to) v. prescriure, ordenar

enjoy (to) v. gaudir, fruir

enjoyment s. gaudi, plaer, m.

enlarge (to) v. ampliar, engrandir, augmentar.

enlighten (to) v. il·luminar, il·lustrar

enlist (to) v. allistar.

enliven (to) v. animar, vivificar

enmity s. enemistat, f.

enormous a. enorme, m.-f.

enough a. i adv. suficient, bastant / prou.

enrage (to) v. enrabiar, enfurir, irritar.

enrich (to) v. enriquir, adornar.

ensemble s. conjunt, m.

entangle (to) v. embolicar, enredar, embullar

enter (to) v. entrar / allistar-se, ingressar

enterprise s. empresa, f., intent, m.

entertain (to) v. obsequiar, afalagar.

entertaining a. divertit -ida, entretingut -uda

entertainment s. festa, f., convit, acolliment, m.

enthusiasm s. entusiasme, m.

entire a. enter-a, sencer-a

entrance s. entrada, f. / admissió, f.

entreat (to) v. suplicar, pregar

entrust (to) v. encarregar, encomanar / confiar.

entry s. vestíbul, m. / partida, f., assentament, m.

envelop (to) v. embolicar, empaquetar / cabdellar

envelope s. sobre, m., coberta, f., embolcall, m.

envenom (to) v. emmetzinar, enverinar
enviable a. enveiable, m.- f.
envious a. envejós -osa.
environment s. ambient, m., proximitat, rodalia, f.
environs s. pl. voltants, m. pl., rodalies, f. pl.
envy (to) v. envejar, cobejar
envy s. enveja, f.
epidemic s. epidèmia, f.
epoch s. època, era, f.
equal a. i s. igual, m.-f.
equality s. igualtat, f.
equalize (to) v. igualar.
equator s. equador, m.
equilibrium s. equilibri, m.
equip (to) v. equipar, fornir.
equipment s. equip, proveïment, m.
equity s. equitat, f.
equivocal a. equívoc-a, ambigu-a
era s. era, època, f.
erase (to) v. esborrar, ratllar.
eraser s. goma d'esborrar, f., esborrador, m.
erect (to) v. erigir, aixecar.
ermine s. ermini, m.
err (to) v. errar, equivocar
errand s. comanda, f., encàrrec, m. / missió, diligència, f.
error s. error, m., equivocació, f.
escalator s. escala mecànica, f.
escape (to) v. escapar, fugir.
escort (to) v. donar escorta / acompanyar.
especially adv. especialment.
Esq. (abreviatura de **esquire**) títol, tractament col·locat darrera del cognom.
esquire s. cavaller, el qui acompanya una dama, m.
essay s. assaig, m., prova, f.
essayist s. assagista, m-f.
essence s. essència, f.
essential a. essencial, m.-f.
establish (to) v. establir.

establishment s. establiment, m. institució f.
estate s. propietat, finca, f. / rang, m. / estat, m., condició, f.
estimate s. avaluació, valoració, f., càlcul, m. / **to...** v. avaluar, valorar, estimar.
estuary s. estuari, m.
eternal a. etern -a, eternal, m.-f.
ether s. èter, m.
ethics s. ètica, f.
eve s. vigília, f.
evaluate (to) v. avaluar, taxar, valorar.
even a. llis-llisa, pla -plana / igual, uniforme, regular m.-f. / **... if** adv. encara que, malgrat que / **...though** adv. encara, no obstant, malgrat que.
evening s. vespre, capvespre, m., vesprada, f.
event s. esdeveniment, succés, m.
ever adv. sempre, a vegades, mai
evermore adv. sempre, per sempre més, eternament.
every pron. cada, tot, tots.
everybody pron. tothom.
everywhere adv. arreu, pertot arreu.
evidence s. evidència, f.
evil a. dolent-a, pervers-a / perversitat, malvestat, f.
evoke (to) v. evocar.
ewe s. ovella, f.
exact a. exacte -a
exactly adv. exactament / (fam.) justa la fusta
exaggerate (to) v. exagerar.
exaggeration s. exageració, f.
examination s. examen, m. / exàmens, m. pl.
examine (to) v. examinar, inspeccionar
example s. exemple, m.
excavator s. excavadora, f.

exceed (to) v. excedir, sobresortir, excel·lir.

exceeding a. excessiu -iva, excedent, m.- f.

excellent a. excel·lent, m.- f.

except (to) v. exceptuar, fer excepció de / eximir

exception s. excepció, f.

excess s. excés, excedent, m.

exchange s. canvi, m., barata, f. / to... v. canviar, baratar

exchequer s. fisc, m. / hisenda. f. / tresoreria, f.

excite (to) v. excitar

excitement s. excitació, f., estímul, m.

exclaim (to) v. exclamar

exclamation s. exclamació, f. / ... mark s. punt d'admiració (ortog.)

exclude (to) v. excloure.

excuse (to) v. excusar, disculpar

execute (to) v. executar, acomplir.

executor s. marmessor, m.

exercise s. exercici, m.

exert (to) v. exercir

exhaust (to) v. esgotar, exhaurir

exhibit s. exposició, f., objecte exposat, m. / to... v. exhibir, exposar

exhibition s. exposició, exhibició, f.

exhibitor s. expositor, exhibidor, m.

exile s. exili, m., expatriació, f.

exist (to) v. existir

existence s. existència, f.

exit s. sortida, eixida / partença, f.

expand (to) v. eixamplar, estendre.

expansion s. expansió, eixamplament, f.

expatriate (to) v. expatriar, expatriar-se, emigrar

expect (to) v. esperar, confiar

expectation s. esperança, expectativa, f.

expel (to) v. expel·lir, expulsar

expend (to) v. despendre, desembossar.

expense s. despesa, f., cost, import, m.

expensive a. car -cara, costós -osa

experience s. experiència, f.

expert a. expert -a

explain (to) v. explicar, aclarir.

explanation s. aclariment, m., explicació, f.

explore (to) v. explorar, esbrinar

explorer s. explorador, m.

explosion s. explosió, f.

expose (to) v. exposar / demostrar, descobrir / arriscar-se

expound (to) v. explicar, exposar

express (to) v. expressar / esprémer.

extend s. amplitud, extensió f. / to... v. estendre, escampar, eixamplar

extent s. extensió, f., abast, m., magnitud, f.

external a. exterior, m.-f. extern-a

extinguish (to) v. apagar, extingir

extinguisher s. extintor (d'incendis), m.

extract (to) v. treure, extractar, arrencar.

extraordinary a. extraordinari -ària, rara.

extreme a. extrem-a, / darrer-a, últim-a / s. extrem, m.

eye s. ull, m. vista, f.

eyebrow s. cella, f.

eyeglasses s. pl. ulleres, f. pl.

eyelash s. pestanya, f.

eyelid s. parpella, f.

eye tooth s. ullal, m.

F

fable s. faula, f.
fabric s. teixit, m.
fabricate (to) v. fabricar
fabrication s. fabricació, f.
face s. cara, faç / façana, f.
facile a. fàcil, m.-f.
facilitate (to) v. facilitar.
facility s. facilitat, f.
fact s. fet, m. realitat, f.
factory s. factoria, fàbrica, f.
faculty s. facultat, f.
fail (to) v. fallar, fracassar / defa-
    llir
failing s. falta, f., defecte, m.
failure s. fracàs, m. fallida, f.
faint a. lànguid -a, abatut -uda,
    dèbil, m.- f., llangorós -osa / s.
    desmai, m.
faint (to) v. defallir, desmaiar-se /
    debilitar-se, afeblir-se
fair a. clar -a, perfecte, bell -a /
    just -a, honrat -ada / s. fira, f.,
    mercat, m.
fairly adv. justament, rectament,
    raonablement / bastant
fairy s. fada, f.
faith s. fe, fidelitat, f.
faithful a. fidel, m.- f., recte -a
faithfulness s. fidelitat, lleialtat,
    f.
fall s. caiguda, f. / descens, m. /
    baixada / cascada, f. / to... v.
    caure /descendir / to... in love
    v. enamorar-se.
false a. fals -a, postís -issa
falsehood s. falsedat, f.
falsify (to) v. falsificar, falsejar.
fame s. fama, celebritat, f.
    renom, m.
family s. família, f.
famine s. fam. f.
famous a. famós -osa
fan s. ventall, ventilador, m.

fancy s. fantasia f. / caprici,
    m.
far adv. lluny / a. llunyà-ana, dis-
    tant, m.-f.
farewell interj. adéu / s. comiat,
    m.
farm (to) s. cultivar la terra /
    arrendar-la
fascination s. fascinació, f.,
    encís, m.
fashion s. moda, f., costum,
    m.
fast (to) v. dejunar
fat a. i s. gros-ossa, gras-assa,
    obès-esa.
fatality s. fatalitat, f.
father s. pare, m.
father-in-law s. sogre, m.
fatherland s. pàtria, f.
fatty a. gras-assa / greixós-osa.
fault s. defecte, m., imperfecció,
    f. / falta, culpa, f.
faultless a. impecable, irre-
    protxable, m.-f.
faun s. faune, m.
favour s. favor, m. / to... v. afavo-
    rir
favourite a. i s. favorit -a, predi-
    lecte -a
fear s. por, f. / to... v. témer, tenir
    por
fearless a. intrèpid -a, audaciós-
    osa, audaç, m.- f.
feast s. festa, f. / banquet, tiberi,
    m.
feather s. ploma, f. / plomatge,
    m.
February s. febrer, m.
fecundation s. fecundació, f.
fecundity s. fecunditat, f.
fee s. honoraris, emoluments /
    drets a pagar, m. pl. / quota,
    f.
feed (to) v. nodrir, alimentar
feel (to) v. tocar, palpar / sentir,
    experimentar / tenir la sensa-
    ció del tacte

felicitate (to) v. felicitar

felicity s. felicitat, f.

fellow being s. proïsme, m.

fellow s. company / associat / proïsme. m.

female s. femella, f.

feminine a. femení -ina

fence s. clos, tancat, m. / defensa, f.

fennel s. fonoll, m.

fermentation s. fermentació, f.

fern s. falguera, f.

ferry s. transbordador / rai, m.

ferryboat s. transbordador per a vehicles.

fertileness s. fertilitat, fecunditat, f.

fervent a. fervent, m.-f., fervorós -osa

fetters s. grillons, m. pl.

fever s. febre, f.

feverish a. febrós -osa, febril m.-f.

fib s. mentida, f., engany, m. / to... v. mentir

fibber s. mentider -a m.-f.

fiction s. ficció, invenció, f / fàbula, novel·la, f.

fiddle s. violí, m.

fiddler s. violinista, m.-f.

field s. camp, m.

fierce a. ferotge, m.- f. / despietat -ada

fifteen a. i s. quinze, m.

fifteenth a. i m.- f. quinzè-ena

fiftieth a. i m.- f. cinquantè-ena

fifth a. i m.- f. cinquè -cinquena

fifty a. i s. cinquanta, m.

fig s. figa, figuera, f.

fight (to) v. lluitar, combatre.

figure s. figura, forma, f. / xifra, f., número, m.

file s. llima, f. / arxiu, m. / renglera, f. / to... v. llimar / arxivar.

filigree s. filigrana, f.

fill (to) v. omplir

filling s. farciment, m.

film s. pel·lícula, f.

filthy a. immund-a, fastigós-osa, brut-bruta.

financial a. financer-a.

find (to) v. trobar / ...out v. esbrinar

fine a. fi -fina / s. multa, f.

finger s. dit, m.

fingerprint s. empremta digital, f.

finish (to) v. finir, concloure acabar.

fir s. avet / pi, m.

fire s. incendi, foc, m.

firm a. ferm -ferma, sòlid -a / s. raó social, f.

first a. i m.- f. primer -a / ...name, nom de pila.

fish s. peix, m. / to... v. pescar

fisherman s. pescador, m.

fishing s. pesca, f.

fishwife s. peixatera, f.

fist s. puny, m.

fit a. escaient m.- f., adequat -ada, apte -a / en bones condicions físiques / to... v. adequar, ajustar / convenir, correspondre.

fitness s. conveniència, aptitud, f. / fermesa corporal f.

fittings s. pl. accessoris, atuells, m. pl.

five a. i s. cinc, m.

fix s. destret, estretor, m. / to... v. fixar, assegurar, ajustar.

fixed a. fix -fixa.

flag s. bandera / senyera, f.

flame s. flama, f.

flamingo s. (zool). flamenc, m.

flannel s. franel·la, f.

flap s. tapeta de la butxaca, faldilla, cartera d'un vestit, f. / full plegable d'una taula, m. / ala del capell, f. / tapa d'un sobre

145

flash s. llampec, resplendor, m. /
to... v. llampegar, fulgurar
flask s. flascó, m.
flat a. pla-ana.
flatter (to) v. adular, afalagar.
flattery s. adulació, llagoteria, f.
flavour s. sabor, gust, m. / salsa,
f. / to... v. condimentar, assaborir
flavourless a. fat -ada, insípid -a
flaw s. imperfecció, tara, f.,
defecte, m. / esquerda, f.
flea s. puça, f.
flee (to) v. fugir
fleece s. velló, toís, m., llana, f. /
to... v. esquilar
fleet s. flota, esquadra, f.
flesh s. carn, m. / polpa (de la
fruita), f.
flex (to) v. doblegar, vinclar /
vinclar-se
flight s. vol, m.
flipper s. aleta, f.
float (to) v. surar, flotar
flock s. ramat, m. ramada, f. /
to... v. reunir-se, aplegar-se.
flood s. inundació, riuada, f.,
diluvi, m.
floor s. paviment, m.
florist s. florista / florera f.
flour s. farina, f.
flourish (to) v. florir / prosperar
flow (to) v. fluir
flower s. flor, f.
flute s. flauta / estria, f. / to... v.
estriar, acanalar
flutter (to) v. espolsar, aletejar,
bategar
fly s. mosca, f. / to... v. volar
foam s. escuma, bromera, f. /
to... v. escumejar
focus s. focus, m.
foe s. enemic, m., adversari, m.
fog s. boira, f.
foggy a. boirós -osa, bromós
-osa

fold s. plec, doblec, m.
foliage s. fullatge, fullam, m.
folk s. gent, f., poble, m.
follow (to) v. seguir
follower s. seguidor, deixeble,
m.
following a. següent, m.-f.
fond a. afectuós -osa, afeccionat
-ada / fervorós -osa
food s. aliment, m.
fool a. i s. beneit-a, neci-nècia.
foolish a. ximple, m.- f. neci -nè-
cia
foot s. peu, m. / pota, f.
football s. futbol, m.
footwear s. calçat, m.
for prep. per, per a.
forbid (to) v. prohibir, impedir.
force s. força, f. / to... v. forçar
forceful a. vigorós -osa, fort -a /
enèrgic -ica
ford s. gual, m.
fore adv. avant, davant / s. proa,
f.
forearm s. avantbraç, m.
forecast (to) v. predir, augurar.
forefinger s. índex (dit), m.
forehead s. front, m.
foreign a. estranger-a, exòtic -a.
foreigner s. estranger -a
foreman s. capataç, majoral,
m.
forename s. nom, nom de pila,
m.
forerunner s. precursor -a
foresee (to) v. preveure.
foresight s. previsió / presciència,
f.
forest s. selva, f., bosc, m.
foretell (to) v. predir, profetitzar.
forever adv. sempre, per sempre.
foreword s. prefaci, pròleg, m.
forge s. forja, f. / to... v. forjar.
forget (to) v. oblidar.
forgive (to) v. perdonar.

forgiveness s. perdó, m., indulgència, f.

fork s. forquilla, forca, f. / bifurcació, f.

form s. forma, f., model, m. / to... v. formar.

former a. anterior, precedent, m.- f.

formerly adv. abans, antigament

formula s. fórmula, f.

forsake (to) v. abandonar / abjurar.

fort s. fortalesa, f., fortí, fort, m., fortificació, f.

forth adv. en endavant, davant / successivament.

forthcoming a. venidor-a, prop-vinent m.-f.

forthwith adv. immediatament, seguidament.

fortieth a. i m.- f. quarantè-quarantena

fortify (to) v. fortificar / envigorir, enfortir

fortnight s. quinzena, f.

fortress s. fortalesa, / plaça forta, f.

fortune s. sort, fortuna, f. / béns, cabals, m. pl.

forty a. i s. quaranta, m.

forward adv. avant, endavant / a. davanter -a

foster (to) v. nodrir, criar / encoratjar

found (to) v. fundar, fonamentar

foundation s. fundació, f. / fonament, m.

founder s. fundador-a / fonedor-a / to... v. enfonsar-se / fracassar.

fountain s. font, f., doll, m. deu, f. / brollador, m.

four a. i s. quatre, m.

fourteenth a. i m.-f. catorzè-catorzena

fourth a. i m.- f. quart-a

fowl s. aviram, f.

fox s. guineu, guilla, rabosa, f.

fraction s. fracció, f.

fragile a. fràgil, m.-f.

frail a. fràgil, m.- f., trencadís -issa / dèbil, m.- f., delicat -ada

frame s. marc, m. / to... v. idear, tramar, dreçar / emmarcar

frantic a. frenètic -a, enfurit -ida.

fraud s. frau, engany, m.

free a. lliure / lliberal, m.- f. / gratuït -ïta / to... v. alliberar, deslliurar / eximir.

freedom s. llibertat, f.

freeze (to) v. congelar, gelar, glaçar

french a. i s. francès -esa

french bean s. mongeta, f.

frequency s. freqüència, f.

frequent a. freqüent, m. -f.

frequently adv. freqüentment, sovint

fresh a. fresca, nou-nova, recent, m.-f.

friday s. divendres, m.

fridge s. refrigerador, m.

fried a. fregit -ida / ...egg ou ferrat, m

friend s. amic -iga

friendship s. amistat, f.

fright s. espant, ensurt, m.

frighten (to) v. espantar, sobresaltar.

frightful a. espantós -osa, horrible, m.- f., horrorós -osa

frill s. enciam, m.

frock s. vestit de dona, m. / bata, f., batí, m.

frock coat s. levita, f.

frog s. granota, f.

frolicsome a. juganer -a, enjogassat -ada, entremaliat -ada

from prep. de.

frond s. fronda, f.

front s. davant / front, m. / façana, f. / ...door porta principal.

frontier a. fronterer -a / s. frontera, f.

frontispice s. frontispici, m.

frost s. glaçada, gebrada, f.

frown (to) v. arrufar (el front o les celles)

fruit s. fruit, m. fruita, f.

frustate (to) v. frustrar, defraudar

fry (to) v. fregir.

frying pan s. paella, f.

fuel s. combustible, m.

fuel oil s. oli combustible, m.

fugitive a. fugitiu -iva, fugaç, m.-f.

full a. ple-ena, complet-a

fun s. facècia, broma, f. acudit, m.

function (to) v. funcionar

fund s. fons, capital, m., reserva, f. / fons públics, m. pl.

fundamental a. fonamental, essencial, m.- f. / principi bàsic, m.

funeral a. funeral, fúnebre, m.- f. / s. funeral.

fungus s. bolet, m.

funnel s. embut / túnel, m.

funny a. graciós -osa, divertit -ida / curiós -osa, estrany -a

fur s. pell, f. / tosca, f. / ...coat, abric de pells, m.

furious a. furiós -a, frenètic -a

furnace s. forn, m.

furnish (to) v. subministrar, proveir.

furniture s. mobiliari, m.

furrow s. solc, reguerot, m.

further adv. més lluny, més enllà

fuselage s. fusellatge, m.

fusion s. fusió / foneria, f.

future a. futur -a / s. futur, esdevenidor.

futurity s. el futur, l'esdevenidor, m.

G

gabble s. parleries, enraonies, f. pl.

gabbler a. parlador, xerraire, garlaire, m.

gag s. mordassa, f. / to...v. emmordassar.

gage s. penyora, caució, f.

gaiety s. jovialitat, alegria, exultació, f.

gain s. guany, benefici, m. / to... v. guanyar / millorar, aconseguir

galaxy s. galàxia, f.

gall s. fel, m., bilis, f.

gallant a. gallard-a, valent-a, coratjós-osa / galant, m. f., cortès-esa.

galleon s. galió, m.

gallery s. galeria, f.

galley s. galera (nàut. i tipog.), f.

galley slave s. galiot, m.

gallon s. galó (mesura de capacitat), m.

gallop s. galop, m.

gallows s. forca, f., cadafal, patíbul, m.

game s. joc, m., caça, f.

gang s. colla, f. escamot, m.

gaol s. presó, f.

gaoler s. escarceller, m.

gap s. pas, portell, congost / espai, interval, m. / bretxa, f.

garage s. garatge, m.

garden s. jardí, m.

gardener s. jardiner, m.

gargoyle s. gàrgola, f.

garlic s. all, m.

garment s. peça de vestir, f.

garter s. lligacama, f.

gas s. gas, m.

gassy s. gasós -osa

gate s. porta / barrera, f.

gather (to) v. reunir, acumular.

gauge (to) v. mesurar, aforar, calibrar.
gay a. joiós-osa, alegre, m.- f.
gazelle s. gasela, f.
gem s. gemma, f. / joiell, m.
general a. i s. general, m.
generate (to) v. generar, produir, ocasionar.
generation s. generació, f.
generous a. generós -osa.
genial a. simpàtic -a, afable, cordial, m.- f.
genius s. geni. m., genialitat. f.
gentile s. gentil, pagà, m.
gentleman s. cavaller, senyor, m. / persona d'alt rang, f.
geranium s. gerani, m.
gentle woman s. dama, senyora.
gently adv. amablement, delicadament, gentilment.
geography s. geografia, f.
germ s. germen, bacil, microbi, m.
German a. i s. alemany -a / germànic -a.
germinate (to) v. germinar
gerund s. gerundi, m.
gesture s. gest, m., acció, f.
get (to) v. obtenir, adquirir, guanyar / **to... back** v. tornar, retornar / **to... better** v. millorar / **to... down** v. baixar / descavalcar / **to... in** v. entrar, penetrar / **to... into** v. ficar-se, entrar / **to... off** v. baixar, descendir / **to... old** v. envellir / **to... on** v. prosperar / pujar / muntar (un cavall) / **to... out** v. fer sortir, treure /**to... rid of** v. desempallegar-se, / **to... tired** v. cansar-se / **to... up** v. llevar-se, aixecar-se / **to... warm** v. escalfar-se / **to... worse** v. empitjorar-se, agreujar-se.
ghastly a. lívid-a, cadavèric-a / horrible, m.-f. espantós-osa.

ghost s. fantasma, espectre, esperit, m.
giant a. gegantí -ina / s. gegant, m.
giddiness s. vertigen, m. / desvari, m.
gift s. regal, obsequi, m., / ofrena, f.
gild (to) v. daurar, m.
guilt a. daurat-ada.
gill s. brànquia, ganya, f.
gilt a. daurat -ada.
gin s. ginebra, f.
gingerly adv. cautelosament / a. cautelós-osa.
gipsy s. gitano, m.
giraffe s. girafa, f.
girdle s. faixa, f., cenyidor, m.
girl s. nena, minyona, noia, xicota, f.
give v. lliurar, donar / regalar / deixar, cedir / concedir, atorgar / **to... away** v. regalar, desfer-se de / **to... back** v. restituir, tornar / **to... notice** v. despatxar, acomiadar / **to... out** v. exhaurir-se, acabar-se / **to... rise to** v. ocasionar, causar / **to... up** v. abandonar, renunciar / **to... give way** v. cedir, consentir, retre.
giver a. donador -a, donant, m. -f.
glacier s. glacera, gelera, congesta, f.
glad a. content-a, alegre, m.- f., agraït-ïda.
glamour s. encís, embruix, encant, m.
glance s. mirada, llambregada, ullada, f. / **to...** v. mirar, donar una ullada
gland s. glàndula, f.
glare (to) v. enlluernar / resplendir, brillar
glass s. vidre / vas, got, m.
glasses s. ulleres, f. pl.
glide (to) v. lliscar, patinar / planar

glider s. planador, m.
glimpse s. ullada, llambregada, f.
/ to... v. ullar, llambregar,
donar un cop d'ull.
globe s. globus, m.
gloom s. obscuritat, tenebra, f.
gloomy a. tenebrós-osa, llòbrec
-ega
glory s. glòria, magnificència, f.
glove s. guant, m.
glow s. lluïssor, fulgor, resplendor, m. / to... v. lluir, resplendir, irradiar
glue s. cola, f.
go (to) v. anar / anar-se'n, sortir,
marxar, caminar, passejar /
to... about v. anar d'un lloc a
l'altre, emprendre, intentar,
penetrar / to... on v. continuar, avançar, seguir, prosse-
guir / to... out v. sortir / to...
to v. acudir.
goal s. meta, finalitat, f., terme,
objectiu, m. / gol, m. / goalkeeper s. porter (futbol), m.
goat s. cabra, f.
God s. Déu, m. deïtat, f.
godchild s. afillat, fillol, m.
goddaughter s. fillola, afillada, f.
goddess s. deessa, f.
godfather s. padrí, m.
godless a. ateu -a, descregut
-uda
godlike a. diví -ina
godmother s. padrina, f.
godson s. fillol, afillat, m.
gold s. or, m.
golden a. auri -àuria, d'or, daurat
-ada / excel·lent, m.-f.
goldfinch s. cadernera, f.
good a. bo -bona / útil, m.- f.,
apte-a / escaient, m.-f. / s.
avantatge, profit, m. / ...loo-
king a. de bon aspecte, formós
-osa, ben plantat -ada
good-bye interj. adéu, adéu-siau,
m.

goodness s. bondat, benvolença,
f.
goodwill s. bona voluntat, f. /
bon nom, m. / valor del nom
(d'una empresa)
goose s. oca, f.
gorilla s. goril·la, m.
gorse s. argelaga, f.
gospel s. evangeli, m.
gossip s. xerrameca, xafarderia, f.
gout s. gota, f. poagre, m.
gouty a. gotós-osa, poagrós-osa
govern (to) v. governar
governess s. institutriu, f.
government s. govern, m.
governor s. governador, m.
gown s. bata, f., vestit femení, m.
/ toga, f.
grace s. gràcia, mercè, f.
graceful a. graciós-osa, gentil,
m.-f.
gracious a. clement, m.- f., benigne-a, bondadós -osa / graciós
-osa
grade s. grau, m., categoria, f. /
to... v. classificar.
graduate (to) v. graduar.
gradually adv. gradualment, pro-
gressivament
graft s. empelt, m. / to... v. empeltar
grain s. gra, cereal, m.
gram s. gram, m.
grammar s. gramàtica, f.
gramme s. gram, m.
grand a. magnific -a, imponent
m.- f., grandiós -osa
grandchildren s. néts, m. pl.
granddaughter s. néta, f.
grandfather s. avi, m.
grandma s. (fam.) iaia, f.
grandmother s. àvia, f.
grandparents s. avis, m. pl.
grandson s. nét, m.
grandstand s. tribuna, f.
granite s. granit, m.
grant s. concessió, mercè, dona-

ció, f. / to... v. concedir, atorgar / to take for granted deixar ben establert, convenir en ferm.

grape s. raïm, m.

grasp (to) v. agafar, prendre, usurpar.

grass s. herba, gespa, f.

grasshopper s. llagosta f. (insecte)

grateful a. agraït-ïda / grat-grata.

gratify (to) v. acontentar, complaure / gratificar

gratitude s. agraïment, m., gratitud, f.

grave a. important, m. f., / seriós -osa, greu, m.- f., / s. sepultura, f., sepulcre, m.

gravestone s làpida (sepulcral). f.

graveyard s. cementiri, m. / fossa, f., fossar, m.

gravity s. gravetat / seriositat, solemnitat, f.

grease (to) v. greixar.

great a. gran, m.-f., magne -a / important, m.- f. / a ... many adv. molts, moltes

great-aunt s. tia àvia, f.

great-grandfather s. besavi, m.

great-grandmother s. besàvia, f.

greatness s. grandesa / grandiositat, f.

Greek a. i s. grec -grega

green a. verd -a,

greengrocer s. verdulaire, m.-f.

greet (to) v. rebre, acollir, donar la benvinguda, saludar

grenade s. granada, f.

grey a. gris-grisa.

greyhound s. llebrer, m.

grief s. aflicció, tribulació, f.

grievance s. greuge, ultratge, m.

grill s. graella, f.

grimace s. ganyota, carassa, f.

grind (to) v. triturar, moldre, polvoritzar / esmolar, afilar

grip s. agafada / estreta de mà, f.

groan s. gemec, m., queixa, f.

groan (to) v. gemegar, queixar-se

grocer s. botiguer de comestibles, m.

grocery s. adrogueria, botiga, f.

ground s. terra, f., terreny, sòl, m. / base, f.

groundwork s. fonaments, m. pl.

group s. grup, m.

grow (to) v. créixer / cultivar, conrear.

growl (to) v. rondinar, grunyir, botzinar.

grown-up a. adult -a, persona gran

growth s. creixement / desenvolupament /augment, m.

guarantee s. garantia, f. / fiador garant, m. / to... v. garantir

guard s. guarda, revisor, m.

guess s. suposició, f. / to... v endevinar, suposar

guest s. invitat -ada, convida -ada / hoste -essa

guide s. guia, m.-f. / to... v. guiar dirigir.

guild s. gremi, m. / associació corporació, f.

guilt s. culpa, f., delicte, m. / culpabilitat, f.

guilty a. culpable, m.- f., reu -rea

guinea s. guinea, f. (moneda de 21 xílings)

guitar s. guitarra, f.

gulf s. golf, m.

gull (to) v. enganyar, defraudar.

gum s. goma / geniva, f.

gun s. canó, fusell, revòlver, m.

gunman s. pistoler, m.

gunner s. artiller, m.

gunpowder s. pólvora, f.

gust s. ràfega, ventada, f., rampell, m., rauxa, f.

gut s. intestí, m. / (fam.) budells, m., tripa, f.

gutter s. canal, claveguerÃ³, m. / cuneta, f.

gymnasium s. gimnÃ s, m.

gypsy s. gitano -a, zÃngar -a

H

habit s. costum, m., habitud, f. / vestit, m.

habituate (to) v. habituar, acostumar, avesar

haggard a. cansat -ada, las -lassa, decaigut -uda, ullerÃ³s -osa

hail s. calamarsa, f. / salutaciÃ³, f. / **to...** v. calamarsejar, / saludar,

hair s. pÃ¨l, cabell, m.

hairdresser s. perruquer-a, barber, m.

hairdressing s. pentinat, m.

hairy a. pelut -uda, pilÃ³s -osa

hake s. lluÃ§, m.

half a. mig -mitja / s. meitat, f.

hall s. rebedor, vestÃbul / gran salÃ³ m.

hallelujah s. alÂ·leluia, f.

hallo interj. hola!

hallow (to) v. santificar / consagrar.

halt s. parada, f. / a. coix -a / **to...** v. parar, aturar / coixejar

ham s. pernil, m.

hammer s. martell, m. / **to...** v. clavar

hammock s. hamaca, f.

hamper s. panera, cistella, f.

hand s. mÃ , f.

handicraft s. mÃ d'obra, f. / ofici manual, m., artesania, f.

handful s. manat, grapat, m.

handicap s. inconvenient, desavantatge, m.

handkerchief s. mocador, m.

handle (to) v. manejar / s. mÃ nec, m.

handrail s. barana, f., passamÃ ,m.

handshake s. encaixada, f.

handsome a. bell, bonic, elegant, ben plantat, m.

handy a. traÃ§ut-uda, destre-a / manual, manejable, m.- f.

hang (to) v. penjar

hangar s. cobert, porxo, hangar, m.

hanger s. penja-robes, m.

hanging a. penjant, m.- f.

hank s. troca, madeixa, f.

happen (to) v. succeir, esdevenir, ocÃ³rrer

happiness s. felicitat, f.

happy a. feliÃ§, m.- f.

happy-go-lucky a. imprevisor -a, renyat -ada, despreocupat -ada

harass (to) v. molestar, pertorbar

harbour s. port, refugi, m.

hard a. dura, difÃcil, m.-f.

harden (to) v. endurir, enfortir.

hardluck s. mala sort, f.

hardly adv. a penes, tot just, amb prou feines

hardness s. duresa, solidesa / severitat, f.

hardship s. estretor, dificultat, f., privacions, f. pl.

hardy a. robust-a, fort-a / temerari -Ã ria, ardit-ida.

hare s. llebre, f.

harm s. dany, perjudici, perill, m.

harmful a. perjudicial,m.- f., nociu, -iva.

harmless a. inofensiu -iva, anodÃ -ina

harmony s. harmonia, f.

harness s. guarniments, arreus, m. pl.

harp s. arpa, f.

harpoon s. arpÃ³, m.

harrier s. llebrer, m.

harry (to) v. saquejar, devastar

harsh a. aspre-a, dura, esquerp-a.

harvest s. collita, sega, f. / to... v. collir, recol·lectar.

haste s. pressa, urgència, f.

hasten (to) v. donar pressa, fer afanyar

hastily adv. apressadament

hasty a. apressat-ada, precipitat-ada, lleuger-a.

hat s. barret, capell, m.

hatch s. niada, f. / escotilla, f. / escotilló, m. / to... v. covar / sortir de l'ou / idear

hatchet s. destral, f.

hate s. odi, m. / to... v. odiar

hateful a. odiós-osa, rancorós-osa.

hatter s. barretaire, m.

haughty a. altiu-iva, orgullós-osa

haul s. estrebada, estirada, f. / to... estirar, arrossegar

haunt (to) v. freqüentar, rondar

have (to) v. haver, tenir

haven s. port, recer, embarcador, m.

havoc s. destrucció f., estrall, m. ruïna, f. / tala, f. / to... v. assolar, devastar, talar

hawk s. falcó, esparver, m.

hay s. fenc, m.

hayloft s., pallissa, pallera, f.

haystack s. paller, m.

hazard s. atzar, m. / to... v. arriscar, aventurar

hazel s. avellaner, m.

hazelnut s. avellana, f. / color d'avellana, m.

he pron. pers. ell

head s. cap. m. testa, f.

headache s. mal de cap, m., migranya, f., maldecap (preocupació), pl. maldecaps, m.

heading s. títol / encapçalament / epígraf, m.

headlines s. titulars, rètols, m. pl.

headmaster s. director (de col·legi), m.

headmistress s. directora (de col·legi), f.

headquarters s. quarter general, m.

heady a. obstinat-ada / decidit-ida, brau -ava.

heal (to) v. guarir, remeiar, purificar.

health s. salut, sanitat, f.

healthy a. sa-ana, fort-forta

heap s. munt, m., pila, f. / to... v. apilotar, amuntegar, acumular

hear (to) v. oir, sentir, escoltar.

hearer s. oient, m.-f. oïdor -a.

hearing s. oïda, f.

hearth s. llar de foc, xemeneia, f. / llar, casa, f.

heart s. cor / ànim, m.

heartily adv. cordialment

hearty a. cordial,m.- f., sincer-a / robust, -a.

heat s. calor, escalfor, f. / to... v. escalfar

heater s. escalfador, m., estufa, f.

heathen s. i a. pagà -ana, idòla-tra, gentil, m.-f.

heathenism s. paganisme, m.

heather s. bruc, m.

heating s. calefacció, f.

heave (to) v. aixecar / llançar

heaven s. cel, paradís / firmament, m.

heavenly a. celestial, m.- f., divina.

heavy a. pesat-ada, massís-issa.

hedge s. clos, m., bardissa, cleda, f. / to... v. encerclar, tancar amb bardissa

hedgehog s. eriçó, m.

heed (to) v. atendre, observar

heel s. taló, m.

height s. alçària, elevació, f., cim, m.

heinous a. atroç m.- f., malvat-ada, pervers-a.

heinousness s. atrocitat, perversitat, f.

heir s. hereu, m. / **to...** v. heretar

heirdom s. herència, f.

heiress s. hereva, f.

helicopter s. helicòpter, m.

hell s. infern, m.

hello interj. digueu! (per a establir comunicació telefònica)

helm s. timó, governall, m.

helmet s. elm, casc, m.

help s. ajuda, f., ajut, m. / **to...** v. ajudar

helper s. ajudant, assistent, / criat, m.

helpful a. útil, m.- f., profitós-osa.

helpless a. desvalgut -uda, inútil / irremeiable m.- f.

helve s. mànec, m. / **to...** v. manegar

hem s. vora, f., doblec, m.

hen s. gallina, f.

henceforth adv. d'ara endavant, des d'ara

hepatic a. hepàtic -a

her pron. pers. la, li, a ella / ella (després de preposició) / a. possessiu: el seu, la seva, els seus, les seves, d'ella

herald s. herald, missatger, m.

herb s. herba, f.

herbalist s. herbolari -ària / botànic -a.

herd s. ramat, m. / munió, multitud, f.

here adv. aquí, ací

heresy s. heretgia, f.

heretic s. heretge, m.-f.

heritage s. heretatge, m., herència, f.

hermetic a. hermètic -a

hermit s. ermità, m.

hermitage s. ermita, f.

hero s. heroi, campió, m.

heroic a. heroic-a, èpic-a.

heroine s. heroïna, f.

heron s. garsa, f.

herring s. arengada, f., areng, m / **red ...** areng fumat

hers pron. pos. seu -seva, el seu -la seva, els seus -les seves (d'ella); d'ella

herself pron. ella mateixa

hesitate (to) v. dubtar, vacil·lar

hesitation s. indecisió, vacil·lació, f. dubte, m.

hew (to) v. picar, trossejar, desbastar

hewer s. picapedrer, m.

hide s. cuir, pell, f. / **to...** v. amagar

hideous a. horrible, m.- f., espantós -osa / repugnant, m.- f.

hidding place s. amagatall, m.

high a. alt-a, eminent, m.-f.

highness s. alçada, elevació / violència, f.

highway s. carretera, f.

hike s. caminada, f.

hiker s. caminant, excursionista, m.

hill s. turó, pujol, m.

hilly a. muntanyós-osa, abrupte -a

hilt s. puny, m., empunyadura, f.

him pron. pers. m. a ell, el, li, lo

himself pron. ell mateix.

hind s. cérvola, f. / a. posterior, m.-f. darrer-a.

hinder (to) v. obstruir, impedir

hindrance s. impediment, obstacle, m.

hinge s. frontissa, f.

hint (to) v. suggerir, indicar, insinuar

hip s. maluc, m.

hippopotamus s. hipopòtam, m.

hire s. lloguer, m. / **to...** v. llogar

his pron. i adj. pos. m. el seu -la seva, els seus -les seves, seu -seus; d'ell

hiss (to) v. xiuxiuejar / xiular (per protestar)

history s. història, f.

hit (to) v. pegar, copejar / encertar

hive s. rusc, eixam, m.

hoard (to) v. atresorar, acabalar

hoarse a. ronc -a, enrogallat -ada

hobby s. afecció, inclinació, f.

hockey s. hoquei, m.

hod s. gaveta, f.

hoe s. aixada, f., càvec, m.

hoist s. grua, f., elevador, m. / **to...** v. hissar, aixecar.

hold s. subjecció, presa, possesió, f. / mànec, m. / **to...** v. tenir, retenir / aguantar, sostenir.

hole s. forat, m. / **to...** v. foradar

holiday s. festa, festivitat, f.

holidays s. vacances, f. pl.

holiness s. santedat, f.

hollow a. buit -buida, còncau -ava, concavat-ada.

holly s. grèvol, boix grèvol, m.

holy a. sagrat -ada, sant -santa, beneït -ïda.

Holy Ghost s. Esperit Sant, m.

Holy Land s. Terra Santa, f.

Holy Week s. Setmana Santa, f.

Holy Writ s. Sagrades Escriptures, f. pl.

home s. llar, f. domicili, m., casa, f. / pàtria, terra natal f.

home-made a. casolà -ana, de fabricació casolana.

home rule s. autonomia, f.

homeland s. terra nadiua, pàtria, f.

homeless a. sense llar

homesickness s. enyorament, m., enyorança, nostàlgia, f.

homework s. deures, treballs escolars fets a casa, m. pl.

honour s. honor, m.

hook s. ganxo, ham, m. / falç, f.

hoop s. cèrcol, m., rotllana, f.

hop (to) v. saltar, brincar, saltironar, fer saltirons a peu coix

hope s. esperança, f., suport, m. / **to...** v. esperançar, confiar

hopeful a. il·lusionat -ada, esperançat -ada, optimista, m.- f. / esperançador-a, prometedor -a

hopeless a. desesperat -ada, desesperançat -ada / desnonat -ada

horizon s. horitzó, m.

horn s. banya, f.; corn, m.

hornet, s. vespa, tavà, m.

horrible s. horrible, m.- f.

horrid a. horrorós -osa, horrible, m.- f. / hòrrid -a, esglaiador -a

horse s. cavall, m.

horseman s. genet, cavaller, m.

horsepower s. cavall de força, HP, m.

horseshoe s. ferradura, f.

hose s. mànega, f.

hospital s. hospital, m. / **private...**, clínica

Host s. hòstia, f.

host s. hostaler, dispeser, m. / amfitrió, m.

hostage s. ostatge, m.

hostess s. dispesera, hostalera, f.

hot a. calent -a

hotel s. hotel, m. fonda, f.

hotness s. escalfor, calor, f.

household a. domèstic -a, de la llar / s. família, els de casa, m. pl.

houskeeper s. majordona, f.

housemaid s. serventa, f.

hovel s. barraca, cabana, f. / tuguri, barracot, m.

hound s. gos de caça, m.
hour s. hora, f.
house s. casa, f.
how adv. com
however adv. comsevulla que, de totes maneres / conj. no obstant, malgrat
howl s. udol, m. / to... v. udolar
hug s. abraçada, f. / to... v. abraçar, acaronar
hullo! interj. hola!
human a. humà - ana.
humble a. humil, m.- f., modest -a, / to... v. humiliar
humour s. humor, m.
humane a. humà-ana, humanitari-ària, benigne-a.
humankind s. humanitat, f. gènere humà, f.
hump s. gep, m., gepa, f.
hundred a. i s. cent, m., centena, f., centenar, m.
hundredth a i m.- f. centè-centena
Hungarian a. i s. hongarès -esa
hunger s. fam, f.
hungry a. famolenc -a.
hunt (to) v. caçar, perseguir
hunter s. caçador -a / cavall de caça, m.
hunting s. caça, cacera, f.
hurricane s. huracà, m.
hurl (to) v. llançar / disparar, tirar
hurrah interj. visca!
hurry s. pressa, urgència, f. / to... v. apressar, activar, accelerar
hurt s. ferida f., cop, m. / to... v. ferir, ofendre, adolorir
husband s. espòs, marit, m.
hush! interj. silenci! pst! calleu!
hush money s. soborn, m.
hut s. cabana, barraca, f.
hyacinth s. jacint, m.
hymn s. himne, m.
hyphen s. guió, guionet, m. (gram.)

hypnotism s. hipnotisme, m.
hypotenuse s. hipotenusa, f.

I

I pron. pers. jo
ice s. gel, m. / to... v. gelar
iceberg s. iceberg, m.
icebox s. nevera, f., frigorífic, m.
ice cream s. gelat, m.
icicle s. caramell, m.
icy a. gelat-ada, glacial, m. - f.
idea s. idea, f.
ideal a. i s. ideal, m.
identical a. idèntic -a.
identify (to) v. identitat, f. / to... v. identificar.
idiocy s. bajanada, niciesa, f.
idiom s. idioma / modisme, m.
idiot a. idiota, imbècil, m.-f.
idle a. dropo -a, gandul -a / to... v. gandulejar, vagarejar
idleness s. ganduleria, droperia, f.
idly adv. ociosament
idolater s. idòlatra, m.-f.
idolatry s. idolatria, f.
idyll s. idil·li, m.
if conj. si
ignite (to) v. encendre, inflamar
ignition s. ignició, inflamació, f.
ignoble a. innoble, m.- f., indigne -a
ignore (to) v. desconèixer, ignorar
ill a. malalt-a, dolent-a, funest-a / adv. malament
ill-bred a. groller -a, mal educat-ada
ill-breeding s. mala educació, f.
illegal a. il·legal, m.-f.
illiterate a. analfabet -a.
illness s. malaltia, f.

illuminate (to) v. enllumenar, il·luminar

illusion s. il·lusió, f.

illustrate (to) v. il·lustrar, demostrar

illustration s. il·lustració, f., aclariment, m.

image s. imatge, semblança, f.

imagine (to) v. imaginar, suposar, pensar-se

imitate (to) v. imitar

immense a. immens -a.

immoral a. immoral, m.-f.

immortal a. i s. immortal, m.-f.

immovable a. inamovible, m.-f., fixa / immoble, m.-f.

impasse s. carreró, atzucac, cul-de-sac, m.

impeach (to) v. acusar, imputar

impeacher s. acusador, denunciador, m.

impeachment s. acusació, imputació, f.

impeccable a. impecable, m.-f.

impel (to) v. impel·lir

implore (to) v. implorar

imply (to) v. implicar, significar

impolite a. groller -a, descortès -esa

import s. importació, f.

import (to) v. importar

importance s. importància, f.

important a. important, m.-f.

impose (to) v. imposar.

imposing a. imponent, impressionant, m.-f.

impossible a. impossible, m.-f.

impost s. impost, tribut, m.

impress (to) v. impressionar, influir

impressive a. impressionant, m.-f., commovedor -a

imprest s. préstec, emprèstit, m.

imprint (to) v. imprimir

imprison (to) v. empresonar

improper a. impropi -òpia.

improve (to) v. millorar, progressar.

improvement s. millora, f., progrés, m.

improvise (to) v. improvisar

impulse s. impuls, m., embranzida, f.

impute (to) v. imputar, atribuir

in prep. en / adv. dins, dintre

inability s. incapacitat, f.

inaugurate (to) v. inaugurar, iniciar

incentive s. incentiu estímul, m.

inch s. polzada, f.

inclination s. inclinació, f. declivi, m.

incline (to) v. inclinar.

include (to) v. incloure

including a. inclús -usa / adv. àdhuc, fins i tot

income s. renda, f., rèdits, guanys, m. pl. / ...tax impost sobre la renda, m.

incompetency s. incompetència, ineptitud, f.

increase s. augment, engrandiment, increment, m. / to... v. augmentar, engrandir, incrementar

incubate (to) v. incubar, covar

indefatigable a. incansable, m.-f.

indented a. dentat -ada, oscat -ada.

independent a. independent, m.-f.

index s. índex, m.

indicate (to) v. indicar

indicator s. indicador, m.

indifferent a. indiferent, m.-f.

indignation s. indignació, còlera, f., despit, m.

induce (to) v. induir, instigar

indulge (to) v. tolerar, condescendir

indulgence s. indulgència, tolerància, f.

industrious a. treballador -ora, aplicat -ada, diligent, m.-f.
industry s. indústria, f.
infancy s. infantesa, infància, f.
infantry s. infanteria, f.
infect (to) v. infectar, contagiar / corrompre, contaminar
infection s. infecció, f., contagi, m.
inferior s. inferior, m.-f.
influence (to) v. influir
influenza s. grip, f.
inform (to) v. informar
information s. informació, f.
infringe (to) v. infringir
ingenious a. enginyós -osa, hàbil, m.- f. manyós -osa.
inhabit (to) v. habitar, residir, viure
inhale (to) v. aspirar, inhalar
inherit (to) v. heretar
inheritance s. herència, f., patrimoni, m.
iniquity s. iniquitat, f.
initial a. inicial, m.-f.
initiate (to) v. iniciar
inject (to) v. injectar
injured a. injuriat -ada, agreujat-ada, ofès -esa / lesionat -ada, ferit-ida
injury s. injúria, f., mal, perjudici, m. / ferida, lesió, f.
ink s. tinta, f.
inkstand s. tinter, m.
inmost a. íntim -a, profund -a, recòndit -a.
inn s. hostal, m., posada, f.
inner a. interior, m.-f.
innocent a. innocent, m.-f.
inoculate (to) v. inocular
inordinate a. desordenat -ada / immoderat -ada, excessiu -iva
inquire (to) v. preguntar, inquirir
inquiry s. pregunta / indagació, f., investigació, f.

insanity s. demència, bogeria, f.
insect s. insecte, m.
insert s. intercalació, f.
insert (to) v. intercalar, inserir.
inside s. interior, m.- f.
insides s. pl. entranyes, f. pl.
insight s. discerniment, m. / perspicàcia, intuïció, f.
insist (to) v. insistir.
insistence s. insistència, f.
insomnia s. insomni, m.
insomuch conj. fins a tal punt, de tal manera
inspect (to) v. inspeccionar, examinar
inspection s. inspecció, f.
inspector s. inspector, m.
inspire (to) v. inspirar.
install (to) v. instal·lar.
installation s. instal·lació, f.
instance s. exemple, m. / cas, m. / instància, sol·licitud, petició, f.
instant s. instant, moment, m.
instead adv. en canvi, en lloc de
instep s. empenya (del peu), f.
instinct s. instint, m.
institute s. institut, m.
instruct (to) v. instruir, ensenyar
instrument s. instrument, m., eina, f.
insulate (to) v. aïllar, isolar
insult (to) v. insultar
insurance s. assegurança / seguretat, f.
insure (to) v. assegurar, garantir
intelligence s. intel·ligència / compenetració, f., acord, m. / informació, f.
intend (to) v. intentar / proposar-se
intense a. intens -a
interest s. interès, m. / to... v. interessar

interesting a. interessant, m.-f.

interior a. interior, m.- f., intern -a

interpreter s. intèrpret, m.

interrupt (to) v. interrompre

interval s. interval, espai, m., pausa, f.

intervene (to) v. intervenir

interview s. entrevista, f., interviu, m.

intestine s. intestí, m.

intimate a. íntim -a, entranyable, m.- f. / familiar, m.- f.

into prep. en / a dins, cap a dintre

introduce (to) v. introduir

intruder s. intrús, importú, manefla, m.

invade (to) v. envair

invader s. invasor, usurpador, m.

invent (to) v. inventar, crear, idear

invention s. invenció, inventiva, f.

invert (to) v. invertir / capgirar

investigate (to) v. investigar

investment s. inversió, f.

invite (to) v. convidar, invitar

involve (to) v. encloure, implicar

inward a. intern -a, interior, m.- f.

inwards adv. cap a l'interior, cap a dins / interiorment

iris s. iris / arc de Sant Martí, m.

Irish a. i s. irlandès - esa

iron s. ferro, m.

irony s. ironia, f.

irrigate (to) v. regar, irrigar.

irrigation s. regatge, reg / irrigació, f.

island s. illa, f.

islander s. illenc, insular, m.

isolate (to) v. isolar, aïllar / separar / incomunicar

issue s. sortida / emissió, f. / to... v. sortir, eixir / publicar, editar

isthmus s. istme, m.

it pron. ell, ella, el, la, li

Italian a. i s. italià -ana

italics s. itàlic -a / lletra cursiva

itch s. sarna, ronya / picor, f.

item s. notícia, f., assumpte, m., punt, m. / s. paràgraf o article (en un text, document, etc.)

its pron. pos. seu (d'ell, d'ella, d'allò).

itself pron. ell mateix, ella mateixa, allò mateix.

ivory s. vori, ivori, m.

ivy s. heura, f.

J

jab s. punxada, f. / cop violent, m.

jabber s. xerrameca, barbolla, f.

jabberer a. xerraire, barbollaire, m.-f.

jacent a. jacent, m.-f.

jack s. gat, cric. (mec.)

jackdaw s. gralla (ocell), f.

jacket s. jaqueta, americana, f.

jade s. jade, m.

jag s. osca, dent, f.

jaggy a. oscat -ada, dentat -ada

jail s. presó, f.

jailer s. escarceller, m.

jam s. melmelada, confitura, f. / to... v. encallar, embussar

jamboree s. aplec, m., festa popular, f.

January s. gener, m.

Japanese a. i s. japonès -esa

jar s. gerra, f. / pot, m.

jargon s. argot, m.

jasmine s. llessamí, m.
jasper s. jaspi, m.
jaundice s. icterícia, f.
jaundiced a. ictèric -a
javelin s. javelina, f.
jaw s. mandíbula, barra, f.
jay s. gaig (ocell), m.
jealous a. gelós -osa
jealousy s. gelosia, f., recel, m., suspicàcia, f.
jeep s. jeep, m. (automòbil per terrenys difícils)
jeer s. mofa, f.
jelly s. gelea, gelatina, f.
jellyfish s. medusa (ict.), f.
jerk s. sotrac, m. batzegada, f.
jersey s. jersei, m.
jest s. acudit, m., facècia, f.
jester a. faceciós-osa, bromista, m.- f.
jet s. raig, doll, m.
jetty s. moll, desembarcador, m.
jew s. jueu, israelita, m.
jewel s. joiell, m.
jeweller s. joier, m.
jewellery s. joieria, f., joiells, m. pl.
jewess s. jueva, israelita, f.
jewish a. judaic, hebraic, m.
jingle s. dring, tritlleig, m.
job s. feina, ocupació, f. / quefer, negoci, m.
jobber s. agiotista, negociant, m.
jockey s. joquei, lacai, m.
jocund a. alegre, m.- f., divertit-ida.
jog s. empenta, escomesa, f., sacseig, m. / to... v. empentejar, empènyer
joiner s. ebenista, m.
joinery s. ebenisteria, f.
joint s. juntura, unió, f. / to... v. ajuntar, unir, combinar
joist s. biga, f.
joke s. broma, f. / barra, f. / to... v. bromejar

joker a. bromista, m.- f. plaga, m.
jolly a. alegre, m.- f, xalest-a, divertit-ida
jolt s. sotragueig, trontoll, m.
jot s. mica, engruna, f. bri, m.
journal s. diari, periòdic, m. revista, f.
journalist s. periodista, m. -f.
journey s. viatge, m / to... v. viatjar
jowl s. galta, f.
joy s. alegria, f.
joyful a. joiós -osa, gojós-osa, content-a / feliç, m. -f.
jubilee s. jubileu, aniversari, m.
judge s. jutge, m. / to... v. jutjar
judgement s. judici, m.
judicious a. assenyat -ada, entenimentat-ada, sensat-a
jug s. càntir, gerro, m.
juggle s. malabarisme, m.
juggler s. joglar, malabarista, m.
jugular a. jugular, m.- f.
juice s. suc, m., salsa, f.
juicy a. sucós, -osa
July s. juliol, m.
jumble (to) v. barrejar, amalgamar.
jump s. salt, bot, m. / to... v. saltar, botre
jumper s. saltador, m. / jersei, m.
junction s. unió, conjunció, f. / encreuament, m.
June s. juny, m.
jungle s. selva, jungla, f.
junior a. menor, jove, m.-f. / ...than, més jove que / (seguint un nom) fill del qui el porta, gen. abreujat: **Jr.** / subordinat, m.
juniper s. ginebre, ginebró, m.
jurist s. jurista, legista, m.
jury s. jurat / tribunal, m.
just a. just-a, recte-a, justicier-a / adv. justament.
justice s. justícia, f.

justification s. justificació, f.
justificative a. justificatiu -iva, defensiu -iva
justify (to) v. justificar
jut (to) v. sobresortir / projectar-se
juvenile a. jove, m.- f. / galan jove, m. / juvenil, m.- f., jovenívol -a

K

kangaroo s. cangur, m.
keel s. quilla, f.
keen a. agut -uda, penetrant, mordaç, m.- f. / entusiasta, m.- f.
keenly adv. agudament, vivament
keenness s. agudesa, penetració, vivacitat, subtilesa, f. / entusiasme, m.
keep (to) v. guardar, conservar, retenir, mantenir, protegir / reservarse / ... on v. continuar, romandre / ... up v. mantenir-se ferm / conservar.
keeper s. guardià, conserge, defensor, conservador, m.
kennel s. gossera, canera, canilla, f.
kerb s. vorada / voravia, f.
kerchief s. còfia, f. / mocador, m.
kernel s. pinyol, m.
kettle s. olla / caldera, f. / tetera, f.
key s. clau (de pany) / tecla, f. / tornavís, m.
keyboard s. teclat, m.
keyhole s. forat del pany, m.
khaki s. caqui, m.
kick s. xut, m., guitza, potada, f.
kid s. cabrit, m., cabreta, f.

kidnap (to) v. segrestar / plagiar
kidnapper s. segrestador -a.
kidney s. ronyó, m.
kill (to) v. matar
killer s. matador, assassí, m.
kilogram s. quilogram, m.
kilometer s. quilòmetre, m.
kind a. amable, m.- f., benèvol-a / s. gènere, m.
kindergarten s. jardí d'infància / guarderia, f.
kindle (to) v. encendre, enardir, agitar
kindler s. incendiari, agitador, m.
kindliness s. bondat, benvolença, f.
kindly adv. amablement / a. amable, m.- f.
kindness s. amabilitat, bondat, f.
kindred s. afinitat, consanguinitat, f., parentiu, m.
king s. rei, m.
kingdom s. regne, reialme, m.
kingfisher s. martí pescaire, m.
kinglike a. reial, m.- f., august-a, majestuós-a.
kingship s. reialesa, monarquia, f.
kiosk s. quiosc, m.
kiss s. bes, petó, m. / to...v. besar, petonejar
kit s. equip, equipament, m.
kitchen s. cuina, f. fogó, m.
kite s. milà, m. grua, f. / estel, m.
kitten s. gatet -a / felí jove, marruix, m., marruixa, f.
knap (to) v. mossegar, trencar
knave s. bergant, bretol, murri, m.
knavery s. bretolada, picardia, f.
knead (to) v. pastar, amassar
knee s. genoll, m.
kneel (to) v. agenollar-se
knife s. ganivet, m.

knight s. cavaller, m.
knit (to) v. fer mitja
knob s. agafador, pom, m., protuberància, f. / nus a la fusta
knock s. cop, pic, truc, m. / to...
v. pegar / trucar / topar
knocker s. balda, f., trucador,
picaporta, m.
knot s. nus, llaç, m., intriga, f. /
to... v. nuar, lligar, enredar.
know (to) v. conèixer, saber.
knowing a. instruït-ïda, entès -e-
sa, intel·ligent, m.-f.
knowledge s. coneixement,
saber, m.
knuckle s. artell, nus dels dits, m.
/ frontissa, f.
knurled a. nuós -osa

L

label s. etiqueta, f., rètol, m. /
to... v. retolar / classificar
laboratory s. laboratori, m.
laborious a. treballós -osa, ardu
-àrdua / manyós -osa, diligent,
m.- f.
labour s. treball, m., feina, f. /
to... v. treballar
labourer s. treballador -a, jorna-
ler -a
labyrinth s. laberint, dèdal, m.
lace s. cordó m., punta, randa, f.
/ to... v. cordar, lligar
lack s. manca, mancança, f. /
to... v. mancar, escassejar
lackey s. lacai, m.
laconic a. lacònic -a
laconism s. laconisme, m.
lacquer s. laca, f., vernís, m.
lad s. noi, jove, xicot, minyó, bordegàs, m.
ladder s. escala portàtil o de mà,
f.

ladle s. cullerot, m.
ladleful s. cullerada, f.
lady s. senyora, dama, f.
lag (to) v. pr. ressagar -se, endarrerir-se
lagoon s. albufera, llacuna, f.
laic a. i s. llec-llega, seglar, m.- f.
lair s. cau, amagatall, m.
lake s. llac, m.
lamb s. anyell, be, m.
lame s. i a. coix -coixa.
lameness s. coixesa, f
lament (to) v. lamentar, lamen-
tar-se
lamp s. llum, m., llàntia, f.
lampshade s. pantalla, f., pàmpol
(d'un llum), m.
lance s. llança, f.
lancer s. llancer, m.
lancet s. bisturí, m., llanceta, f.
land s. terra, f., sòl, país, m. /
to... v. aterrar, desembarcar
landholder s. terratinent, hisendat, m.
landlady s. hostalera, patrona,
mestressa, f.
landlord s. hostaler, fondista,
amo, m.
landscape s. paisatge, m.
lane s. carreró, corriol, senderó,
m.
language s. idioma, m. llengua,
f.
languette s. llengüeta, f.
languid a. llangorós, -osa, dèbil,
m. -f.
languish (to) v. llanguir,
decaure
languor s. llangor, f., decaïment,
m.
lantern s. llanterna, f., fanal, m.
lap s. falda, faldilla, f. / to... v.
embolicar, enrotllar / llepar
lapel s. solapa, f.
lapidary a. i s. lapidari -ària
lapse s. lapsus, error, m., relliscada, f. / to... v. relliscar

larboard s. babord, m.
lard s. llard, m.
larder s. rebost, m.
larderer s. reboster -a
large a. gran, m.-f., gros-ossa / extens-a.
lark s. alosa, f.
larynx s. larinx, laringe, f.
lash s. xurriaques, f. pl., tralla, f., fuet, m. / to... v. flagel·lar, assotar
lass s. noia, donzella, joveneta, f.
lassitude s. cansament, m. lassitud, f.
last a. darrer -a, últim -a, / to... v. durar, subsistir
latch s. balda, f., baldó, m. / tanca, m.
late adv. tard / a. tardà -ana, lent -a, triganer -a
lately adv. darrerament, últimament
lathe s. torn (màquina), m.
lather s. sabonera, f. / to... v. ensabonar, fer bromera
latin a. llatí -ina
latitude s. latitud, amplària, f.
latrine s. comuna, latrina, f.
latten s. llautó, m.
latter a. posterior, m.- f., darrer-a / més modern-a
laugh s. rialla, f. riure, m. / to... v. riure
laughter s. rialla, riallada, f.
launch s. llanxa, f.
laundress s. bugadera, f.
laundry s. rentador, safareig, m.
laureate a. llorejat -ada
laurel s. llorer, m. / honorança, f.
lavatory s. lavabo, wàter, urinari, m.
lave (to) v. rentar, banyar
lavender s. espígol, m.
lavish a. mà foradada, malversador-a, / to... v. malversar
law s. llei, jurisprudència, f., dret, m.

lawful a. legal, m. -f
lawfulness s. legalitat, legitimitat, f.
lawn s. prat, herbei, m. gespa, f.
lawsuit s. plet, litigi, m.
lawyer s. advocat, jurista, m.
laxative a. laxant, m.- f.
lay a. laic-a, m. / balada, f. / to... v. posar, estendre, tombar
layer s. llit, estrat, m., capa, f. / (gallina) ponedora, f.
lazar a. llebrós, m.
lazaret s. llatzeret, m. llebroseria, f.
laze (to) v. mandrejar, gandulejar
laziness s. mandra, ganduleria, f.
lazy a. mandrós -osa, gandul -a
lead s. direcció, guia, f. / plom, m. / to... v. dirigir, guiar, conduir
leader s. cap, guia, cabdill, m.
leadership s. cabdillatge, m. / direcció, f.
leaf s. fulla, f. / full, m.
league s. lliga, aliança, f.
leaguer s. aliat -ada, col·ligat -ada
leak s. gotera / esquerda, f. / to... v. gotejar, degotar
lean (to) v. recolzar, reclinar / v. pr. repenjar-se
leap s. salt, bot, saltiró, m. / to...v. saltar, botre, botar
leap year s. any bixest, any de traspàs, m.
learn (to) v. aprendre, descobrir
learning s. saber, m., il·lustració, f.
lease s. arrendament, m. / to... v. arrendar
least a. el (o la) menor, el (o la) més petit (petita)
leather s. cuir, m. pell, f.
leave (to) v. deixar, abandonar
leaves s. fulles (bot.) f. pl.

163

lecture s. conferència, lliçó, dissertació, f.
lecturer s. conferenciant / lector, m.
ledge s. prestatge, m. / vora, f.
left a. esquerre-a / s. esquerra, f.
leg s. cama, pota (d'animal, d'un moble), f.
legal a. legal, m.- f., legítim-a,
legality s. legalitat, f.
legend s. llegenda, f.
legion s. legió, f.
legislation s. legislació, f.
legitimate (to) v. legitimar
leisure s. lleure, oci, m.
lemon s. llimona, f.
lend (to) v. deixar, prestar / proporcionar
lender s. prestador -a
lending s. préstec, m.
lenght s. longitud, f.
lengthen (to) v. allargar, prolongar / allargar-se
lens s. lent, f. cristal·lí, m.
Lent s. Quaresma, f.
lentil s. llentia, f.
leopard s. lleopard, m.
leper s. leprós -osa, llebrós -osa
leprosy s. lepra, f.
lesion s. lesió, f.
less adv. menys
lesser a. menor, més petit -a
lesson s. lliçó, f.
lest conj. perquè, a no ser que, per tal que no
let (to) v. permetre, deixar
letter s. carta, lletra, f.
letterbox s. bústia, f.
lettered a. culte -a, instruït -ïda, docte -a / erudit -ita
lettuce s. enciam, m. lletuga, f.
levant s. llevant, orient, m.
level s. nivell, m. / to... v. anivellar, igualar
leveller a. anivellador -a, igualador -a

lever s. palanca, f., alçaprem, elevador, m.
levity s. lleugeresa, f.
liability s. responsabilitat, f. / risc, m.
liable a. subjecte responsable, exposat -ada
liaison s. enllaç, m., connexió, f. / relació extramatrimonial, romanço, embolic
liar s. mentider -a
libel s. libel, m.
libeller a. libel·lista, m.-f., difamador -a
liberality s. liberalitat, generositat, f.
liberate (to) v. alliberar, deslliurar
liberty s. llibertat, f.
librarian s. bibliotecari -ària
library s. biblioteca / circulating o lending... biblioteca circulant
licence o license s. llicència, f., permís, m. / vènia f.
licenciate s. llicenciat -ada
licit a. lícit -a
lick (to) v. llepar, xuclar
lid s. tapadora, f. / parpella, f.
lie s. mentida, f. / to... v. mentir / jeure, ajeure's
lieutenant s. tinent, lloctinent, m.
life s. vida, f.
lifeless a. exànime, insensible, m.-f. / inanimat -ada
lifetime s. vida, f. / tota una vida, curs total d'una vida / eternitat (fig.)
lift s. ascensor, elevador, m. / to... v. enlairar-se, aixecar-se
light s. llum, f. / a. lleuger-a, / to... v. il·luminar, encendre
lighten (to) v. alleugerir (d'un pes, d'una càrrega)
lighter s. encenedor, m.
lighthouse s. far, m.
lightly adv. lleugerament

lightning s. llamp, llampec, m.
like a. similar, semblant, m.-f. /
to... v. plaure, agradar
likely a. probable, m.-f., apropiat-
ada
likeness s. semblança, similitud,
f.
likewise adv. també, igualment,
així mateix
lilac s. lila, f. / lilà, m.
lily s. lliri, m. / flor de llir, f.
limb s. membre, m., extremitat,
f. / to... v. desmembrar
lime s. calç m. / til·ler, m. / llima, f.
lime flower s. til·la, f.
lime juice s. suc de llima
lime tree s. til·ler, m.
limit s. límit, m. to... v. limitar.
limp s. coixesa, f. a. fluix-a, tou
-ova to... v. coixejar.
linden s. til·ler, m.
line s. línia, ratlla, f. / to...v. alinear / ratllar
linen s. lli, fil, m. / llenç, m., tela, f.
liner s. transatlàntic, vaixell de
línia / delineant, m.
link s. baula, malla, anella, f. /
enllaç, m. / to... v. enllaçar,
connectar
lion s. lleó, m.
lioness s. lleona, f.
lip s. llavi, m. vora, f.
liqueur s. licor, m.
liquid a. líquid -a / s. líquid, m.
liquidate (to) v. liquidar
liquor s. licor, m.
list s. llista, f. catàleg, m. / to...v.
allistar
listen (to) v. escoltar, atendre
listener s. escoltador -a, oient,
m.- f.
litany s. lletania, f.
literary a. literari-ària.
literature s. literatura, f.
litre s. litre, m.
litle a. petit -a / una mica f. / poc-
poca.

litter s. llitera, f. / deixalles, dei-
xles, f. pl.
live a. viu-viva, vivent, m.- f.
to... viure
lively a. animat -ada, coratjós
-osa / adv. vigorosament, vivament
liver s. fetge, / vividor, m.
living a. viu -viva vivent, m.- f.
living room s. sala, f.
lizard s. llangardaix, m., sargan-
tana, f.
llama s. (zool.), llama, m.
load s. càrrega, f. to... v. carregar
loaf s. pa, m., peça de pa, fogassa, f.
loan s. préstec emprèstit, m.
on... a crèdit
lobby s. passadís, vestíbul, m.,
galeria, f.
lobster s. llagosta, f.
lock s. pany forrellat, m. resclosa, f. comporta, f. rínxol,
m.
locomotive s. locomotora, f. a.
locomotriu, f.
locust s. cigala, f. llagosta
(insec.) f.
lodge (to) v. allotjar
lodger s. estadant, hoste, m.
loft s. golfes, f. pl.
lofty a. elevat -ada, eminent, m.f.
log s. tronc, tió, m.
logic s. lògica, f.
lone a. sol-a, solter -a (esp. no casat) solitari -ària.
loneliness s. soledat, f. aïlla-
ment, m.
lonely a. solitari -ària, aïllat -ada
log s. tronc, tió, m.
longitude s. longitud, m.
look s. mirada, f. / aspecte, m.
to... v. mirar, esguardar, considerar / to... after v. tenir cura
/ to... for v. cercar / to... in v.
entrar a veure, visitar / to...
like v. assemblar-se a /

to...over v. fullejar / **to... well
bad** v. tenir bon ; mal
aspecte
looking-glass s. espill, mirall,
m.
loom s. teler, m.
loop s. trau, m., bragueta, f. /
...hole s. obertura / espitllera,
f.
loose a. fluixa / **to...** v. afluixar,
deslligar.
loosen (to) v. afluixar, deslligar
separar-se.
looseness s. afluixament, m., re-
laxació, f.
lord s. senyor, amo, patró, m.
títol de respecte (donat a qui
té un títol, l'esposa al marit,
etc.), m. / **Lord** s. Déu, m. / Jesucrist, m. / **Lord's prayer** s.
Parenostre, m.
lorry s. camió, m.
lose (to) v. perdre
loss s. pèrdua, f.
lost a. perdut -uda / esgarriat
-ada, trasparent -ada
lot s. lot, m. / sort, f. / parcel·la, f.
loud a. sorollós -osa, cridaner -a
/ alta, forta / **speaker** s. altaveu, m.
lounge chair s. gandula (moble),
poltrona, butaca, f.
lout a. rústec -ega
loutish a. rústic -a
love s. amor, m. / **to...** v. estimar,
amar / agradar, ésser afeccio-
nat -ada
lovely a. amè -ena, plaent, m. -f.
lover a. enamorat -ada, amant,
m. -f.
low a. baixa / profund -a / dèbil,
m.-f. / roí-ïna.
lower a. inferior, m.-f. / més
baix·a / **to...** v. humiliar, rebaixar
loyalty s. lleialtat, f.
luck s. atzar, m. / sort, f.

luggage s. equipatge, m.
luckily adv. sortosament, afortu-
nadament
lucky a. sortós, -osa, afortunat
-ada
lump s. massa, multitud, f. protuberància, f. terròs, m.
lunch s. dinar, m. / **to...** v. dinar
lung s. pulmó, m.
lute s. llaüt, m.
luxurious a. luxós -osa, sumptuós -osa
luxuriant a. exuberant, m.- f.
pletòric -a/ gemat -ada
luxury s. luxe, m.
lye s. lleixiu, m.
lyre s. lira, f.

M

macaroni s. macarrons, m. pl.
mace s. maça, porra, f.
macerate (to) v. macerar
maceration s. maceració, f.
machine s. màquina, mecànica,
f.
machinery s. maquinària, f.,
mecanisme, m.
mackerel s. verat, m.
mackintosh s. capot impermeable, m.
mad a. boig -boja, enfollonit- ida
madam s. senyora, f.
magazine s. revista, f. /
magatzem, m.
magic s. màgia, màgica, f.
magical a. màgic -a / maravellós
-osa, sobrenatural, m.- f.
magician s. màgic, nigromant,
m.
magisterial a. magistral, m. -f.
magistrate s. magistrat, jutge,
m.
magnanimity s. noblesa, f.

magnanimous a. magnànim -a, noble, m. -f.

magnet s. imant, m.

magnetism s. magnetisme, m.

magnificence s. magnificència, f.

magnificent a. magnífic -a, esplèndid -ida

magnify (to) v. magnificar, exalçar

magnifying glass s. lent d'augment, lupa, f.

magpie s. garsa, f.

maid s. donzella / serventa, f.

maiden s. verge, donzella, f.

mail s. correu, m.

main a. principal, important, major, m.- f.

mainland s. continent, m.

mainly adv. principalment, sobretot

maintain (to) v. mantenir

maintenance s. conservació, f., manteniment, sosteniment, m.

maize s. blat de moro, moresc, m.

majestic a. majestuós -osa

majority s. majoria, majoria d'edat, f.

make s. forma, estructura, fabricació, f. / marca, f. / ...up s. maquillatge / to... v. fer, crear, fabricar, produir / assolir / to... fun v. escarnir, mofar-se / to... out v. desxifrar / to... off v. anar-se'n, tocar el dos (vulg.) / to... over v. traspassar / to... up v. formar, arranjar, inventar / maquillar-se / to... up one's mind v. resoldre's, determinar, decidir

maker s. creador, fabricant, artífex, m.

malapert a. desvergonyit -ida, descarat -ada

malapertness s. impertinència, f.

male s. baró, mascle, m.

malignant a. maligne -a, malèvol -a

mallet s. mall, m., maça, f.

mallow s. malva, f.

mammal a. i s. mamífer, m.

mammoth s. mamut, m. / a. gegantí -ina

manacle (to) v. emmanillar

manacles s. manilles, f. pl.

man s. home, m., individu, m. / humanitat, f. el gènere humà / servent, m. / to... v. tripular, proveir, d'homes (un vaixell / ...-of-war s.vaixell de guerra

manage (to) v. endegar, arreglar, enginyar

management s. direcció, f. maneig, m. / gerència

manager s. gerent, director, empresari, apoderat, m.

mandolin s. mandolina, f.

mane s. crinera, cabellera, f.

manger s. menjadora, f.

mango, s. mango, m.

manhood s. virilitat, valentia, f.

manifold a. múltiple, m.- f. / variat -ada

manifoldness s. multiplicitat, f.

manipulate (to) v. manipular

manipulation s. manipulació, f.

mankind s. humanitat, f. / els homes, m. pl. el gènere humà, m.

manlike a. baronívol, viril, m.

mannequin s. maniquí / model, m.

manner s. manera, .f., costum, m.

manor s. feu, domini, senyoriu, m.

mansion s. casal, palau, m.

mantis s. pregadéu, m.

mantle s. mantell, m. / to... v. enmantellar

manufacture s. manufactura, fàbrica, indústria, f. / to... v. fabricar, manufacturar manufacturer s. fabricant, industrial, m.

manure s. adob, fem, m.

manuscript s. manuscrit, m.

many a. molts, moltes, pl. / a great... moltíssims, moltíssimes, / how...? quants, quantes?

map s. mapa, m.

marbre s. marbre, m. / a. marmori -òria

March s. març, m. / marxa, f. / to... v. marxar

marchioness s. marquesa, f.

mare s. euga, f.

margin s. marge, m. / to... v. marginar

marine a. marí-ina

mariner s. mariner, m.

marionette s. titella, putxinel·li, m.

mark s. marca, senyal, f., traç, m. / to... v. marcar, senyalar

market s. mercat, m. / to... v. mercadejar

marmalade s. melmelada de taronja, f.

maroon s. castanya, marró, m.

marquis s. marquès, m.

marriage s. casament, m., noces, f.

married a. casat -ada / matrimonial, conjugal, m.- f. / to get married v. casar-se.

marrow s. medul·la, f.

marry (to) v. pr. casar-se, maridar-se.

marsh s. aiguamoll, pantà, m.

marshal s. mariscal, m.

marshy a. pantanós -osa

marten s. marta, f.

martyr s. màrtir, m. -f.

martyrdom s. martiri, m.

martyrize (to) v. martiritzar

marvel s. meravella, f. / to... v. meravellar / meravellar-se

marvellous a. meravellós -osa

masculine a. masculí-ina

mash s. pastada, f. / to... v. amassar, pastar, barrejar

mask s. màscara, careta, f.

mason s. paleta / francmaçó, m.

mass s. missa, f. / massa, f., conglomerat, m.

massage s. massatge, m.

massif s. massís, m. serralada, f.

massive a. massís -issa, sòlid -a.

mast s. (mar) pal, m.

master s. amo, mestre, m. / to... v. domesticar, governar

mastery s. superioritat, domini, mestrage, m. / mestria, f.

mastiff s. mastí, m.

mat s. estora, f. / a. mat, m.- f.

match s. partit, combat, m. / llumí, cerilla, f. / to... v. oposar / aparellar, acoblar

mate s. company -a / parella, f., cònjuge, m.- f. / to... v. casar / agermanar, igualar

material a. material, m.- f. / s. material, m.

mathematics s. matemàtiques, f. pl.

matron s. supervisora, superiora / matrona, f.

matter s. matèria, f.

mattock s. aixada, f., picot, m.

mattress s. matalàs, m.

mature a. madur -a / to... v. madurar

matureness s. maduresa, f.

maximum s. màxim, m.

May s. maig, m.

maybe adv. potser

mayonnaise a. i. s. maionesa, f.

mayor s. batlle, alcalde, m.

maze s. laberint, embolic, m., confusió, f. / to... v. confondre, embrollar

me pron. pers. em, me, mi

meadow s. prat, m., prada, f.

meagre a. magre -a, flac -a, desnerit-ida / pobre-a

meal s. àpat, m.,

mean a. d'intermitja categoria / mesquí -ina, humil, m.-f., pobre-a / roí -roïna / to... v. voler dir, donar a entendre, significar

meander s. meandre, m. / to... v. serpentejar

meaning s. significat, m.

meanness s. baixesa, vilesa, f.

means s. mitjans, recursos, m. pl./ by all... de tota manera, sigui com sigui / bv no... de cap manera / by... of mitjançant

meantime adv. mentrestant, interinament

measure s. mida, mesura, f. / to... v. mesurar, ajustar

meat s. carn, / vianda, f.

mechanic s. mecànic, m.

mechanics s. mecànica. f.

medal s. medalla, f.

medical a. mèdic-a

medicine s. medicament, m.

medley s. barreja, mescla, f.

meek a. humil, suau, m.-f., manyac -aga, submís -isa

meekness s. mansuetud, docilitat, f.

meet (to) v. coincidir, trobar / trobar-se, reunir-se

meeting s. reunió, assemblea, f.

mellow a. madur -a / melós -osa, dolç -a / tou-tova / suau, m.-f., tendre-a.

melody s. meló, m.

melon s. meló, m.

melt (to) v. fondre, dissoldre

melter s. fonedor / gresol, m.

melting s. fosa, fusió, f.

member s. membre, m. / soci -sòcia, associat-ada.

membrane s. membrana, f.

memoir s. memòria, relació, f., memòries f. pl.

memory s. memòria, f.

memorize v. aprendre de memòria, aprendre de cor (memoritzar)

menace s. amenaça, f. / to... v. amenaçar

mend (to) v. reparar, adobar, corregir, esmenar / millorar

mention s. menció, al·lusió / to... v. mencionar

menu s. menú, m.

merchand s. comerciant, m.

merchandise s. mercaderia, f.

merciful s. misericordiós -osa

merciless a. cruel, m. -f.

mercy s. compassió, misericòrdia, f. / perdó, m. mercè, f.

merely adv. merament, simplement, solament

merit s. mèrit, m.

merry a. alegre, content-a.

merry-go-round s. cavallets, m. pl.

mesh s. xarxa, malla, trampa, f.

message s. missatge, avís, m.

messenger s. missatger-a.

Messiah s. messies, m.

Messrs s. abrev. de senyors, m. pl.

metal s. metall, m.

metamorphosis s. metamorfosi. f.

meter s. comptador / amidador / metre, m

method s. mètode, m.

methodical a. metòdic -a

metre s. v. **meter**

microphone s. micròfon, m.

microscope s. microscopi, m.

mid a. mig-mitja / prep. enmig

midday s. migdia, m.

middle a. mig -mitja, intermig -itja / s. centre, m. / s. meitat, f. / a. ... aged d'edat madura.

midget s. nan-nana, lil·liputenca.

midnight s. mitjanit, f.

midwife s. llevadora, f.

might s. força, energia, f., poder, m.

mighty a. poderós -osa, fort-forta, potent, m.-f.

migrate (to) v. emigrar.

mild a. manso -a, dòcil, m.-f.

mile s. milla, f.

milestone s. fita, f. molló, m.

militant s. militant, m.- f.

military a. militar, m.- f. / s. tropa, f.

milk s. llet, f. / **to...** v. munyir

mill s. molí, m. / **to...** v. móldre

miller s. moliner -a

milliard s. mil milions

millimetre s. mil·límetre, m.

million s. milió, m.

milliner s. modista de capells, f.

millon s. milió, m.

mind s. ment, intel·ligència, f.

mindful a. acurat -ada, atent -a

mindless a. descurat -ada, deixat -ada

mine pron. meu, meva, meus, meves, s. i pl. / s. mina, f.

miner s. minaire, miner, m.

mingle (to) v. barrejar, mesclar / confondre

minimum s. mínim, m.

mining s. mineria, f.

minister s. ministre, m.

ministry s. ministeri, m.

minor a. menor, m. -f.

minority s. minoria, minoritat, f.

minstrel s. trobador -a, joglar, m.

mint s. menta / secam f. / **to...** v. encunyar

minus a. i prep. menys / a. negatiu -iva

minute s. minut, m.

miracle s. miracle, m.

miraculous a. miraculós -osa

mirage s. miratge, engany, m.

mire s. llot, fang, m.

mirror s. mirall, m.

mirth s. alegria, gaubança, jovialitat, f.

misadventure s. dissort, desgràcia, malaurança, f., contratemps, m.

mischief s. mal, dany, perjudici, m. / entremaliadura, trapelleria, f.

misdeed s. malifeta, f.

misdoer s. malfactor, m.

miser a. avar -a, miserable, m.- f. gasiu -iva

misery s. misèria, roïnesa, f.

misfortune s. desgràcia, f.

mislay (to) v. perdre, esgarriar

mislead (to) v. enganyar, despistar

Miss s. senyoreta, damisel·la, f.

miss (to) v. fallar, perdre (una oportunitat, en una competició)

missile a. llancívol -a / s. projectil, m., esp. el teledirigit

mission s. missió, f.

mist s. boira, f.

mistake s. error, m.

mistaken a. equivocat -ada

mister s. senyor, m.

mistress s. senyora, mestressa, f. / directora / majordona / amistançada, f.

Mistress s. senyora, f.

mistrust s. malfiança, desconfiança, f. / **to...** v. malfiar, desconfiar

misunderstanding s. malentès, m., confusió, f. desavinença, discrepància, f.

mitigate (to) v. mitigar, atenuar barrejar, mesclar

mixed a. barrejat -ada

mixer s. ciment, formigó, m.

mixture s. barreja, mescla, f.

mizzle (to) v. plovisquejar

moan s. gemec, m. / **to...** v. gemegar

mockery s. mofa, befa, f.

mode s. mode, m., manera, f.
model s. model, m. / **to...** v. modelar
modify (to) v. modificar, reformar
moist a. humit -ida
moisture s. humitat / sucositat, f.
moment s. moment, m.
monarch s. monarca, m.
monarchy s. monarquia, f.
monastery s. monestir, m.
monday s. dilluns, m.
money s. diner, m., moneda, f.
monitor s. monitor -a, instructor -a, entrenador -a
monk s. monjo, m.
monkey s. mona, f.
monotony s. monotonia, f.
monsoon s. monsó, m.
monster s. monstre, m.
monstruous a. monstruós -osa
month s. mes, m.
mood s. mode, temperament, caràcter, estat d'ànim, m. / (gram.) mode, m.
moon s. lluna, f.
moonlight s. llum de la lluna, f. / a. il·luminat -ada per la lluna
moor s. fangar, ermot / moro, m.
mop s. fregall, m.
moral s. moral, m.- f., virtuós -osa, recte -a
more adv. més
moreover adv. a més
morning s. matí, m.
morsel s. mossada, menja, f., mos, m.
mortar s. morter, m. / argamassa f.
mortgage s. hipoteca, f.
mosque s. mesquita, f.
mosquito s. mosquit, m.
most a. el (la, els, les) més / la major part de, la majoria
mostly adv. principalment

moth s. arna, f.
mother s. mare, f.
mother-in-law s. sogra, f.
motion s. moviment, m. / moció, f.
motive s. motiu, m. / **to...** v. motivar
motorcar s. automòbil, m.
motorcycle s. motocicleta, f.
motor road s. autopista, f.
motorist s. automobilista, m. -f.
motor ship s. motonau, f.
mould s. motlle, m. / **to...** v. emmotllar, motllurar
mount s. muntanya, f., mont, m. / **to...** v. muntar, pujar
mountain s. muntanya, f.
mourn (to) v. deplorar, lamentar / doldre's / portar dol
mourning s. dol, m., aflicció, f.
mouse s. ratolí, m.
moustache s. bigoti, m.
mouth s. boca, f.
mouthpiece s. broquet, m.
move s. moviment, m., / **to...** v. moure
movies s. cinema, m.
moving s. moviment, m., mudança, f. / a. motriu, f. / commovedor -a, patètic-a
much a. molt -a, abundós -osa
mud s. fang, m.
mudguard s. parafang, m.
muffler s. bufanda, f. / tapaboques, m.
multiply (to) v. multiplicar
mummer s. màscara, careta, f.
mummy s. mamà, f. / mòmia, f.
municipality s. municipi, m.
murder (to) v. assassinar
murderer s. assassí, m.
muscatel s. moscatell, m.
muscle s. múscul, m.
museum s. museu, m.
mushroom s. bolet, m.
music s. música, musica / harmonia, f.

music stand s. faristol, m.
musician s. music, m.
mussel s. musclo, m.
must s. most, m. / floridura, f., verdet, m. / v. haver de, obligar a
mustache s. bigoti, m.
mustard s. mostassa, f.
mute s. mut -uda
mutiny s. motí, m.
mutton s. moltó, m.
mutual a. mutu -mútua
muzzle s. morro, musell, m.
my a. el meu, la meva; els meus, les meves; mon; ma; mos, mes
myrrh s. mirra, f.
myself pron. pers. jo mateix
mystery s. misteri, m.
myth s. mite, m.

N

nacre s. nacre, m.
nag s. haca, f.
naiad s. nàiade, f.
nail s. ungla, f., unglot, m. / clau, m. / to... v. clavar
nailer s. clavetaire, m.
naked a. nu -a, despullat -ada
name s. nom, m. / to... v. anomenar, nomenar
nameless a. innominat -ada
namely adv. és a dir, o sigui
nap s. migdiada, becaina, f.
nape s. clatell, m., nuca, f.
napkin s. tovalló, m.
nappy s. bolquer, bolcall, m.
narcissus s. narcís, m.
narrate (to) v. narrar
narration s. narració, f.
narrow a. estret -a,

narrowness s. estretesa, f.
nasty a. repugnant, m.- f., brut -a / obscè -ena
nates s. natges, f. pl.
nation s. nació, f.
national a. nacional, m. -f.
nationality s. nacionalitat, f.
native s. indígena, m. -f.
natural a. natural, m.- f. / senzill-a
naturally adv. naturalment
nature s. naturalesa, natura, f.
naught s. res, no res/ zero, m.
naughty a. entremaliat -ada
naughtiness s. entremaliadura, f.
navel s. llombrígol, melic, m.
navigate (to) v. navegar
navigation s. navegació, f.
navigator a. navegant, m. -f.
navy s. armada, esquadra, marina, f.
nay adv. no / s. negativa, denegació, f.
near adv. i prep. devora
nearly adv. gairebé, quasi
neat a. net -a, pulcre -a
neatness s. netedat, polidesa, f.
necessary a. necessari -ària
necessity s. necessitat, f.
neck s. coll, m.
necklace s. collaret, m.
necktie s. corbata, f.
need s. necessitat, misèria, f. / to... v. necessitar
needle s. agulla (de cosir), f.
needless s. inútil, m. -f.
negative a. negatiu -iva, / s. negatiu, m. (fotog.) / s. negativa, denegació, f.
neglect s. negligència, f. / to... v. negligir, ometre
negress s. negra, f.
neigh s. renill, m. / to... v. renillar
neighbour s. veí, m.

neighbourhood s. veïnatge / veïnat, m., barriada, f.
neither a. cap, ni l'un ni l'altre / conj. ni, tampoc
nephew s. nebot, m.
nerve s. nervi, m.
nervous a. nerviós-osa, nerviütüda, vigorós -osa
nest s. niu, m.
net s. xarxa, f.
network s. xarxa / retícula, f.
neuter a. neutre -a
neutrality s. neutralitat, f.
neutron s. neutró, m.
never adv. mai, jamai
nevermore adv. mai, jamai
nevertheless adv. nogensmenys, malgrat això, no obstant
new a. nou -nova
newly adv. recentment, novament
news s. notícia, f.
newspaper s. periòdic, diari, m.
next a. pròxim -a, proper -a
nice a. agradable m.-f., delicat -ada, fi -fina, gentil m.-f.
nickel s. níquel, m.
nickname s. motiu, malnom, renom, m.
niece s. neboda, f.
niggardly a. gasiu -iva
night s. nit, f.
nightingale s. rossinyol, m.
nightly a. nocturn -a
nightmare s. malson, m.
nil adv. res, zero
nimble a. àgil, m.-f., lleuger -a, ràpid -a
nine s. i a. nou, m.
nineteen s. i a. dinou, m.
nineteenth a. i m.-f. dinovè-dinovena
ninetieth a. i m.-f. norantè-norantena
ninety s. i a. noranta, m.
ninth a. i m.-f. novè -novena

nip (to) v. pessigar
nitrate s. nitrat, m.
no adv. no
nobility s. noblesa, dignitat, f.
noble a. noble, m. -f.
nobly adv. noblement
nobody pron. ningú
nod (to) v. saludar, assentir, aprovar movent el cap / fer capcinades
noise s. soroll, m.
noisy a. sorollós -osa
nomand s. i a. nòmada, m.-f.
nominate (to) v. nomenar
none pron. ningú, cap
nonsense s. ximpleria, niciesa, f.
noon s. migdia, m.
noose s. llaç, m., llaçada, f.
nor conj. ni
normal a. normal, m. -f.
Norman a. i s. normand, -a.
normally adv. normalment
Norse a. i s. escandinau -ava (llengua, llenguatge) / a. noruec -ega
North s. nord, m.
Norwegian a. i s. noruec -ega
nose s. nas, m.
nostrils s. narius, f. pl.
not adv. no
note s. nota, anotació, f.
notebook s. llibreta, f., bloc de notes, m.
noted a. notable, m.-f., famós-osa
notice s. avís, m. / to... v. advertir, observar
notify (to) v. notificar
notion s. noció, intenció, f.
notoriety s. notorietat, f.
notwithstanding adv. tanmateix, nogensmenys / prep. malgrat que /conj. encara que
nought s. no-res, m.
noun s. nom, sustantiu, m.
nourish (to) v. nodrir

nourishing a. nutritiu -iva
novel s. novel·la, f.
November s. novembre, m.
novelty s. novetat, innovació, f.
novice s. novici -ícia
now adv. ara
nowadays adv. en aquests temps, avui dia
nowhere adv. enlloc
noxious a. nociu -iva
nozzle s. broquet, m.
nuance s. matís, m.
nucleus s. nucli, m.
nude a. nu -a, despullat -ada
nudity s. nuesa, f.
nuisance s. molèstia, incomoditat, f.
null a. nul- nul·la.
nullify (to) v. anul·lar, invalidar
number s. número / nombre, m. / to... v. numerar
numerous a. nombrós -osa.
nun s. monja, f.
nurse s. mainadera, infermera, f.
nut s. nou (fruit), f.
nutcracker s. trencanous, m.
nutritious a. nutritiu -iva
nymph s. nimfa, f.

O

oak s. roure, m.
oar s. rem, m. / to... v. remar, vogar
oarsman s. remer, m.
oasis s. oasi, m.
oat s. civada, f.
oath s. jurament, m.
obdurate a. obstinat -ada, endurit -ida
obedience s. obediència, f.

obedient a. obedient, m. -f.
obelisk s. obelisc, m.
obey (to) v. obeir
object s. objecte, m.
object (to) v. objectar
objection s. objecció, f.
obligation s. obligació, f. / agraïment, m.
oblige (to) v. obligar / complaure
obliging a. servicial, m. -f., obsequiós -osa
obliterate (to) v. esborrar / oblidar
oblivion s. oblit, m.
oblivious a. oblidadís -issa
oblong a. oblong -a
obscure a. obscur -a, fosc -a
obscurity s. foscor, foscúria, fosca, f.
observance s. observança / cerimònia, f.
observant a. observador -a / observant, m. -f.
observation s. observació, f.
observe (to) v. observar
observer a. observador -a
obsolete a. obsolet -a / antiquat -ada
obstacle s. obstacle, m.
obstinacy s. obstinació, f.
obstinate a. obstinat -ada, contumaç, m. -f.
obstruct (to) v. obstruir, barrar / obstaculitzar
obstruction s. obstrucció, f.
obtain (to) v. obtenir, aconseguir
obtainable a. accessible, assolible, m. -f.
obtuse a. obtús -usa
obvious a. evident, m. -f., obvi -òbvia
occasion s. ocasió, f. / to... v. ocasionar.
occasional a. ocasional, casual, m. -f.

occasionally adv. ocasional- ment, de tant en tant

occult a. ocult -a

occupancy s. ocupació, f.

occupation s. ocupació, f.

occupy (to) v. ocupar

occur (to) v. ocórrer, succeir

occurrence s. esdeveniment, m., ocurrència, f.

ocean s. oceà, m. / (fig.) immen- sitat, f.

o'clock loc. hora que marca el rellotge, f., **it is two o'clock**, són les dues

October s. octubre, m.

octopus s. pop, m.

oculist s. oculista, m. -f.

odd a. extravagant, m.-f., estrany -a.

odds s. pl. desigualtat, diferèn- cia, f. / avantatge, m. / possibi- litat, probabilitat, f.

oddity s. extravagància, raresa, f.

odious a. odiós -osa

odorous a. olorós -osa, flairós -osa

odour s. olor, flaire, f.

odourless a. inodor -a

of prep. de, en / **...course** adv. naturalment, és clar

off adv. lluny

offence s. ofensa, f., greuge, m.

offend (to) v. ofendre

offensive a. ofensiu -iva / s. ofen- siva, f.

offer s. oferta, f., oferiment, m. / **to...** v. oferir

office s. oficina, f., despatx, m.

official a. official, m. -f.

officially adv. oficialment

officiate (to) v. oficiar / actuar de, exercir

offset s. compensació, equiva- lència, f. / **to...** compensar, balancejar

offspring s. descèndencia, prole, f., brot, m.

often adv. sovint, freqüentment

oil s. oli, petroli, m. / **to...** v. untar, greixar

oily a. oliós -osa

oinment s. ungüent, untura, f.

old a. vella.

old-fashioned a. passat -ada de moda, antiquat -ada.

oldeness s. vellesa, antiguitat, f.

oligarchy s. oligarquia, f.

olive s. oliva, f. / olivera, f.

olympiad s. olimpíada, f.

omelet s. truita, f.

omen s. presagi, auguri, averany, m.

omission s. omissió, f.

omit (to) v. ometre

on prep. en, sobre, damunt de / adv. endavant, avant / succes- sivament / **... horseback** a cavall

once adv. una vegada / en altre temps / **at...** adv. immediata- ment, al moment, tot seguit

one a. un -una / pron. u, un

onion s. ceba, f.

only adv. solament, sols / a. únic -a

onset s. arrencada, irrupció, f.

onslaught s. escomesa, f., assalt, m.

onward a. avançat -ada, progres- siu -iva / adv. d'ara endevant

ooze (to) v. suar, traspuar / fluir, brollar / s. llim, fang, m.

opacity s. opacitat, f.

opaque a. opac -a

open a. lliure, m.-f., obert-a / **to...** v. obrir, descloure.

opening s. obertura, f.

opera s. òpera, f.

operate (to) v. operar, manejar, actuar

operation s. operació, f.

operator s. operari -ària / maqui- nista, m. -f. / operador -a / agent, m. -f.

opine (to) v. opinar
opinion s. opinió, f.
opponent a. antagonista, oposant, m. -f.
opportune a. oportú -una
opportunity s. oportunitat, f.
oppose (to) v. oposar, objectar
opposite a. oposat -ada / contrari-ària
oppress (to) v. oprimir
oppressive a. opressiu -iva.
opprobrium s. oprobi, m., igno-mínia, f.
optician s. òptic, m.
optimist s. optimista, m. -f.
option s. opció, f.
opulence s. opulència, f.
or conj. o / altrament / ...so adv. tant per tant, més o menys / ... else adv. d'altra manera
oral a. oral, verbal, m. -f.
orange s. taronja, f.
oration s. oració f. / discurs, m.
orator s. orador, m.
oratory s. oratòria, f.
orbit s. òrbita, f.
orchard s. hort, verger, m.
orchestra s. orquestra, f.
orchid s. orquídia, f.
order s. comanda, ordre, f. / to... v. manar, ordenar
orderly a. ordenat -ada
ordinary a. ordinari -ària / vulgar, m. -f.
ore s. mineral, m.
organ s. òrgan / orgue, m.
organization s. organització, f.
organize (to) v. organitzar
origin s. origen, m.
originality s. originalitat, f.
originate (to) v. originar
ornament s. ornament, m. / to... v. ornamentar, guarnir
orphan s. orfe, òrfena
orthography s. ortografia, f.
ocillate (to) v. oscil·lar
ostracism s. ostracisme, m.

ostrich s. estruç, m.
other a. altre -a. altres, m. -f. i pl.
otherwise adv. altrament / si no
ought (to) v. caldre, ésser neces-sari
our a. nostre -a, nostres, m. -f. i pl.
ours s. i, a. el nostre, la nostra, els nostres, pron. pos. nostre, nos-tra, nostres
ourselves pron. nosaltres matei-xos, mateixes
out adv. fora, defora
outcast a. rebutjat -ada, proscrit -a, foragitat -ada
outcome s. resultat, m.
outdoor s. fora, a fora, fora de casa
outdoors adv. fora de casa, a l'aire lliure
outer a. exterior, m.- f. extern -a
outside s. exterior, m. / a. extern -a, fora.
outskirts s. pl. rodalies, f. pl. ravals, m. pl.
outstanding a. destacat -ada, nota-ble / pendent, m. -f.
oval s. oval, m. / oval m. -f., ovalat -ada.
oven s. forn, m.
over adv. i prep. sobre, damunt
overalls s. pl. granota, roba de mecànic, f.
overcast (to) v. pr. enfosquir-se, ennuvolar-se
overcoat s. abric, m.
overland a. i adv. per terra, terres-tre, m. -f.
overlook (to) v. dominar (amb la vista), mirar per sobre / no fer cas de, passar per alt
overtake (to) v. aconseguir / ul-trapassar.
overtime adv. fora de temps / s. hores extraordinàries, f. pl.
overwhelm (to) v. abatre, aclapa-rar
owe (to) v. deure, estar en deute

owl s. òliba, f., duc, m.
own a. propi-pròpia, particular / individual, m. -f. / to... v. posseir
ox s. bou, m.
oxen s. pl. de ox
ownership s. domini, m., propietat, f.
oxygen s. oxigen, m.
oyster s. ostra, f.

P

pace s. pas, m.
pacific a. pacífic -a
pacification s. pacificació, f.
pack s. paquet, fardell, m. / to... v. empaquetar
pact s. pacte, m.
paddock s. clatell, m. / gripau, m. prat, m. cleda, f. / granota, f.
page s. pàgina, f. / patge, m. / to... v. paginar
pageant s. desfilada, cavalcada, f. / trofeu, m. / a. ostentós -osa
pail s. galleda, f., poal, m.
pain s. dolor, m.-f., càstig, m. / to... v. turmentar, castigar.
painful a. dolorós -osa, penós -osa
painstaking a. curós -osa / industriós -osa
paint s. pintura, f. color, m. / to... v. pintar, descriure
painting s. pintura, f., quadre, m.
pair s. parell, m. parella, f. / to... v. aparellar, aparionar
pal s. (vulg.) company, m.
palace s. palau, m.
palate s. paladar, m.
palatial a. palatí- ina, sumptuós -osa
pale a. pàl·lid -a
paleness s. pal·lidesa, f.

palette s. paleta, f.
palm s. palma, palmera, f. / palmell, m.
palsy s. paràlisi, f.
paltry a. mesquí-ina, menyspreable, m.- f.
pamper (to) v. aviciar, consentir
pamphlet s. pamflet, opuscle, m.
pan s. cassola, f. / perol, m. perola, f.
panel s. tauler, plafó, m.
panelled a. i s. enteixinat, m.
pannier s. sàrria, f.
pant s. panteix, m. / to... v pantei-xar
pantry s. rebost, m.
pants s. calçotets, m. pl.
papacy s. papat, pontificat, m.
paper s. paper, m.
papers s. pl. paperam, m., documentació, f.
paprika s. pebre vermell, m.
parable s. paràbola, f.
parabola s. (geom.) paràbola, f.
parachute s. paracaiguda, f.
paradise s. paradís, m.
paragraph s. paràgraf, m.
parallel a. paral·lel -a
paralyzed a. paralitzat -ada
paralysis s. paràlisi, f.
paralytic s. i. a. paralític -a
parasite s. paràsit -a
paratrooper s. paracaigudista, m. -f.
parcel s. parcel·la, porció, f. / paquet, embalum, m. / to... v. parcel·lar, dividir, partir
parch (to) v. ressecar, abrusar / cremar, torrar
parchment s. pergamí, m.
pardon s. perdó, m. / absolució, f. indult, m. / to... v. perdonar, absoldre
parent s. pare, m. / mare, f.
parish s. parròquia, feligresia, f.
park s. parc, m. / to... v. aparcar
parliament s. parlament, m.

parliamentary a. parlamentari -ària

parlour s. locutori, m.

parrot s. papagai, lloro, m.

parse (to) v. (gram.) analitzar

parsley s. julivert, m.

parson s. rector, capellà, m.

part s. part, porció, f. / **to...** v. partir, dividir / separar-se.

partake (to) v. participar, compartir

partaker s. participant, m. -f.

partial a. parcial, m.- f.

participle s. (gram.) partícipi, m.

particle s. partícula, f.

particular a. particular, especial, individual, singular, m.-f.

particulars s. pl. detalls, m

partner s. soci, associat / company, m.

partridge s. perdiu, f.

parturient a. partera, f.

parturition s. part, infantament, m.

party s. partit, bàndol, grup, m. / festa, f.

pasha s. paixà, m.

pass mountain... s. pas de muntanya / **to...** v. passar / travessar / transferir / aprovar un examen.

passage s. pas, passatge, m., travessia, f.

passenger s. passatger -a

passer-by s. transeünt, vianant, m. -f.

passion s. passió, f.

passionate a. apassionat -ada

passaport s. passaport, m.

past s. passat, m.

paste s. pasta, f. / **to...** v. empastar, enganxar

pastime s. passatemps, entreteniment, m.

pastry s. rebosteria, pastisseria, f.

pasty a. pastós -osa

pat s. moixaina, carícia, f. / **to...** v. acaronar, amoixar

patch s. pedaç, parrac, m. / **to...** arreglar, adobar

path s. camí, viarany, m.

pathetic a. patètic -a

patience s. paciència, f.

patient a. pacient -a, sofert -a

patriot s. patriota, m. -f.

patrol s. patrulla, f., escamot, m. / **to...** v. patrullar

patron s. patró, protector, m.

pattern s. model, patró, m., mostra, f. / **to...** v. copiar, imitar

paunch s. panxa, f.

pause s. pausa, f. interval, m. / **to...** v. parar

pave (to) v. empedrar, pavimentar

pavement s. empedrat, paviment, m.

pavilion s. pavelló, m. tenda, f.

paw s. urpa, xarpa, f.

pawnbroker a. prestador-a.

pawn (to) v. empenyorar

pay (to) v. pagar

payment s. pagament, m.

pea s. pèsol, m.

peace s. pau, concòrdia, f.

peach s. préssec, m.

peacock s. paó, m.

peak s. cim, cimal, puig, pic, m.

peanut s. cacauet, m.

pear s. pera, f.

pearl s. perla, f.

peasant s. camperol -a, pagès -esa

pebble s. còdol, palet, m.

pedal s. pedal, m.

peel s. pela, closca, f. / **to...** v. pelar, espellar

peep s. llambregada, f., cop d'ull, m. / ullada d'esquitllentes, f. / **to...** v. mirar d'esquitllentes, de retop

peer s. igual, m. / del mateix grau

(social) / persona d'alt rang (noble, bisbe, etc.), f.
pelvis s. pelvis, f.
pen s. ploma (d'escriure), f.
penalty s. càstig, m.
pencil s. llapis, m.
pendulum s. pèndul, m.
penguin s. pingüí, m.
penicillin s. penicil·lina, f.
penknife s. trempaplomes, m.
penny s. penic, m.
people s. gent, f. poble, m.
pepper s. pebre, m.
perceive (to) v. percebre
perfect a. perfecte -a
perform (to) v. efectuar, complir, portar a cap / interpretar, representar
performance s. composició, execució, f. / representació, f.
perfume s. perfum, m.
perfume (to) v. perfumar.
perhaps adv. tal vegada, potser
peril s. perill, risc, m.
period s. període, m.
periscope s. periscopi, m.
perish (to) v. perir, morir
permanence s. permanència, f.
permission s. permís, m.
permit s. permís, m. / to... v. permetre
permute (to) v. permutar, canviar
perpendicular a. perpendicular, m. -f.
persecution s. persecució, f.
persist (to) v. persistir
person s. persona, f., individu, m.
personate (to) v. personificar, representar
perspective s. perspectiva, f.
perspicacious a. perspicaç, m. -f.
perspire (to) v. transpirar, suar
persuade (to) v. persuadir
persuasion s. persuasió, f.
perturb (to) v. pertorbar

peruse (to) v. llegir amb atenció (com examinant el text)
perusal s. lectura atenta, valorativa, f.
pester (to) v. molestar
pet a. consentit -ida, malcriat-ada, aviciat -ada / s. animal domèstic / to... v. consentir, malcriar.
petal s. pètal, m.
petrol s. benzina, gasolina, f.
petroleum s. petroli, m.
petty a. menut -uda, petit -a
petticoat s. enagos, m. pl.
phantom s. fantasma, m.
pharynx s. faringe, f.
pharmacy s. farmàcia, f.
photography s. fotografia, f., retrat, m. / to... v. fotografiar
pheasant s. faisà m.
phenomenon s. fenomen, m.
phlegm s. flema, f.
phlegmatic a. flemàtic -a, apàtic -a
phone s. (fam.) telèfon, m.
phrase s. frase, f. / to... v. frasejar
physical a. físic -a
physician s. metge, físic, m.
physicist s. físic, m.
physics s. física, f.
physiognomy s. fisonomia, f.
piano s. piano, m.
pick s. pic (eina) m. / el bo i millor, la flor i la nata / to... v. picar / foradar / arrencar (un queixal, etc.) / fer el tastet / ...at v. perseguir, buscar, bronquina / out... v. escollir, triar / **pickup** s. peça que sosté l'agulla en un tocadiscos.
pickle s. escabetx, m. / salmorra f.
picnic s. fontada, berenada al camp, f.
picture s. quadre, m., fotografia, f.
pictures s. pel·lícules, f., films, m. / gravats, m., pintures, f.

picturesque a. pintoresc -a
pie s. empanada, f., bescuit far-
   cit, m. / (orn.), garsa, f.
piece s. tros, m. peça, f.
pierce (to) v. perforar, foradar
pig s. porc, m.
pigeon s. colom, colomí, m.
pile s. pilot, munt, m. / **to...** v.
   amuntegar
pilgrim s. pelegrí, m.
pill s. píndola, f.
pillar s. columna, f., pilar, m.
pillar box s. bústia pública
pillow s. coixí, m.
pilot s. pilot, pràctic, m. / **to...** v.
   menar
pin s. agulla de cap, f.
pincer s. pinça, f.
pinch s. pessic, m. / pinça, f. /
   to... v. pessigar / prémer, oprimir
pineapple s. pinya d'Amèrica, f. /
   ananàs, m.
pine s. pi, m. / **to...away** v. defallir
pine cone s. pinya, f.
pinion s. punta d'ala, f. / (mec.)
   pinyó, m.
pink s. clavell, m. / a. rosat -ada
pint s. pinta, f., petricó, m.
   (mesura de capacitat)
pioneer s. peoner -a, iniciador
   d'una acció, d'una política
pious a. piadós -osa, pietós -osa
pip s. llavor, f. / **to...** v. piular /
   sortir de l'ou
pipe s. pipa, f. tub, m. conducte,
   m. / gaita, f., sac de gemecs,
   m.
piper s. gaiter, m.
pipes s. gaita, f., sac de gemecs,
   m.
pipette s. pipeta, f.
pirate s. pirata, m. / **to...** v. piratejar
pistol s. pistola, f.
piston s. èmbol, pistó, m.

pit s. pou, clot, abisme, m., fossa,
   f. / pinyol, m.
pitcher s. càntir, m. / llançador
   (en el beisbol), m.
pith s. medulla.
pity s. pietat, compassió, llàstima, f. / **to...** v. compadir-se,
   fer pietat, fer llàstima
place s. lloc, indret, m. / **to...** v.
   col·locar
plague s. plaga, f., flagell, m.,
   calamitat, f.
plain s. plana, planúria, f., planell, m. / a. planer -a, llis-a /
   senzill -a
plaint s. plant, plany, m.
plait s. trena, f. / plec, m. / **to...**
   v. trenar / plegar.
plan s. pla, plànol, m.
plane a. pla-plana, planer-a / s. ri-
   bot, m.
planet s. planeta, m.
plank s. flata, f., tauló, m. / **to...**
   v. enllatar, empostissar
plant s. planta, f.
plaster s. guix, morter, m. / a.
   enguixat -ada / **to...** v. enguixar
plate s. xapa, làmina, f.
plateau s. planell, m.
platform s. plataforma, tribuna, f.
platinum s. platí, m.
play s. joc, divertiment, m. / **to...**
   v. jugar
plea s. súplica, al·legació, f., descàrrec, m. / argument, m. /
   to... v. argumentar, excusar
plead (to) v. al·legar, disculpar /
   pledejar
pleasant a. agradable, m.- f., amè
   -ena
please interj. si us plau / feu el
   favor de / **to...** v. plaure, agradar
pleasure s. plaer, goig, m.
pledge (to) v. comprometre's,
   prometre

plenty s. abundància, abundor, f.

pliers s. alicates, estenalles, tenalles, f. pl.

plot s. solar m. / parcel·la f. / argument, m. trama, f. / conspiració f. / to... v. conspirar, intrigar.

plotter s. conspirador, m.

plough s. arada, rella, f. / to... v. llaurar

ploughman s. llaurador, m.

pluck s. valor, ànim, coratge, m. / entranyes, f. pl. menuts, m. pl. (d'un animal mort) / to... v. arrencar, collir / plomar

plucky a. coratjós -osa, animós -osa

plug s. tac, tascó, m., tap, m.

plum s. pruna / prunera, f.

plumber s. lampista, m.

plume s. ploma, f. / plomall, flocall, m.

plunge s. cabussada, f. / to... v. cabussar

plump a. gras-assa, rodanxó-o-na.

plum tree s. pruner, m., prunera, f.

pluperfect s. plusquamperfet, m.

plural a. i s. plural, m.

plus adv. més / sobre zero, positiu

pocket s. butxaca, f.

pod s. (bot.) beina, tavella / càpsula, f.

poem s. poema, m., poesia, f.

poet s. poeta, m.

poetess s. poetessa, f.

poetry s. poesia / poètica, f.

point s. punt, m., punta, f.

pointer s. índex / apuntador / punter, m.

poison s. verí m., metzina, f. / to... v. emmetzinar

pole s. pol, m. / vara, f.

police s. policia, f.

policeman s. guàrdia, policia, m.

policy s. política, f. pla d'acció, m. / pòlissa, f.

polish s. vernís, poliment, m. / to... v. polir

polite a. cortès -esa

politeness s. cortesia, urbanitat, f.

political a. polític, m.

politician s. polític, estadista, m.

politics s. política, f.

poll s. cens electoral, padró, m. / votació, f., escrutini, m. / to... v. votar, escrutar

pond s. estany, m. bassa, f. / abeurador, m.

pontiff s. pontífex, m.

pony s. haca, f.

pool s. toll, estany, bassiol, m. / unió d'interessos, f. / cert joc (de billar), m.

poop s. popa, f.

poor a. pobre -a.

pope s. papa, pontífex, m.

population s. poblament, m.

porcelain s. porcellana, f.

porch s. pòrtic, vestíbul, m. / porxo, m.

pore s. porus, m.

pork s. carn de porc, f.

porridge s. farinetes, f. pl.

porter s. portador, camàlic, m. / porter, m. / cervesa negra, f.

portfolio s. cartera, carpeta, f.

portrait s. retrat, m.

position s. posició, situació, f.

positive a. positiu -iva.

possess (to) v. posseir

possessive a. possessiu -iva

possible a. possible, m. -f.

possibly adv. possiblement, tal vegada

post s. pla, pilar, m. / lloc de treball, m. / correu, m. / to... v. enviar per correu / enganxar cartells

postage s. franqueig, m.
postcard s. postal, f.
poster s. cartell, m.
posterity s. posteritat, f.
postman s. carter, m.
postmark s. mata-segells, m.
post office s. estafeta, f.
post-paid s. correu pagat, m.
postpone (to) v. ajornar, diferir, posposar
pot s. pot m. / olla, f. / gibrelleta, f., orinal, m.
potato s. patata, f.
pouch s. saquet, sarró, m. bossa, f. / to... v. embossar / empassar
pottery s. terrisseria, f., plats-i-olles, m. / ceràmica, f.
poultice s. cataplasma, pegat, m.
poultry s. aviram, f.
pound s. lliura, f.
pour (to) v. vessar, abocar / fluir / ploure a bots i barrals
powder s. pols / pólvora, f.
power s. força f., poder, m.
powerful a. poderós -osa
practical a. pràctic -a.
practice s. pràctica, f.
practise (to) v. practicar, exercir, professar
prairie s. prada, f., prat, m.
praise s. lloança f. / to... v. lloar
praiseworthy a. elogiable, lloable, m.- f., meritori -òria
prawn s. llagostí, m. / gamba, f.
pray (to) v. resar, pregar
prayer s. oració, f.
preach (to) v. predicar
preacher s. predicador, m.
precocius a. precoç, m.- f.
predict (to) v. predir, vaticinar, profetitzar
preface s. prefaci, pròleg, m.
prefer (to) v. preferir
pregnant a. embarassada, prenys, gràvida, f.
prejudice a. prevenció, preocupació f. prejudici, m.

premium s. premi, m. / prima, f., incentiu, m.
prepare (to) v. preparar
preposition s. preposició, f.
present a. present, actual, m.-f. / s. present, regal, m. / el present, m.
present (to) v. presentar / regalar.
presently adv. aviat, d'ací a poc / (dial. i Amèr.) ara / tot seguit
preserve s. conserva, f./pot de llauna, m. / vedat, m. / to... v. conservar, preservar
president s. president, m.
press s. premsa, f. / to... v. premsar, prèmer
pressure s. pressió, f.
prestige s. prestigi, m.
pretty s. bonic -a. xamós -osa.
prevailing a. predominant, m.- f.
prevent (to) v. prevenir, evitar / impedir
prevention s. prevenció, f., impediment / destorb, m.
previous a. previ -prèvia
price s. preu, m.
prick s. punxó, m. / picada, punxada, f. / to... v. punxar, picar, estimular
pride s. orgull, m.
priest s. sacerdot, prevere, m.
prime a. primer -a, principal, m.-f. / selecte -a, escollit -ida / primicer -a /tendral, m.- f. / s. flor de la joventut, plenitud de la vida / la crema, la nata, la flor (d'alguna cosa)
prince s. príncep, m.
princess s. princesa, f.
principally adv. principalment
principle s. principi, origen, m. / on... loc. per principi
print (to) v. imprimir
printer s. impressor, m.
printing s. impremta, f.

prison s. presó, f. / **to...** v. empresonar

prisoner s. pres, presoner, m.

privacy s. retir, recés, m. / retraïment, m.

private a. privat-ada, reservat-ada, secret-a.

privately adv. secretament.

privilege s. privilegi, m.

prize s. premi, guardó, m.

probability s. probabilitat, f.

probable a. probable, m. -f.

problem s. problema, m.

procedure s. procediment, m.

proceeding s. procediment, tràmit, m.

process s. procés, m.

produce (to) v. produir

product s. producte, m.

production s. producció, f.

profess (to) v. professar / declarar, confessar

profession s. professió f.

professor s. professor, m., catedràtic, m.

profile s. perfil, m., silueta, f.

profit s. profit, m. / **to...** v. aprofitar

profound a. profund -a, pregonona.

programme s. programa, m.

progress s. progrés, m.

progress (to) v. progressar, millorar.

prohibit (to) v. prohibir

project s. projecte, m.

project (to) v. projectar, esbossar

projector s. projector, m.

promenade s. passeig, m.

promise s. promesa, f.

prone a. bocaterrós -osa, inclinat -ada / propens-a.

pronoun s. pronom, m.

proof s. prova, f., assaig, experiment, m.

propaganda s. propaganda, f.

propel (to) v. propulsar, impulsar, impel·lir

propeller s. impulsor, propulsor, m. / hèlice, f.

proper a. propi -pròpia, adequat -ada.

property s. propietat, f.

prophecy s. profecia, f. / averany, m.

proposal s. proposta, proposició, f.

propose (to) v. proposar / proposar-se

propriety s. propietat f. / decència, correcció, f.

prorogue (to) v. diferir, prorrogar

prose s. prosa, f.

prospective a. anticipat -ada, esperat -ada, possible, m.- f.

prosper (to) v. prosperar, millorar, progressar

prosperous a. pròsper -a / propici-ícia

prosy a. prosaic -a

protect (to) v. protegir / defensar

protection s. protecció, f.

protest s. protesta, f.

protest (to) v. protestar.

protractor s. extensor -a / transportador -a.

proud a. orgullós -osa, soberg -a

prove (to) v. provar, justificar / experimentar

proverb s. refrany, proverbi, m.

provide (to) v. proveir, abastir, subministrar

province s. província, f.

prow s. proa f., tallamar, m.

prudent a. prudent, m.- f.

prune s. pruna seca, f. / **to...** v. podar, esporgar

psychology s. psicologia, f.

pub s. taverna / cerveseria, f.

public a. públic -a / s. públic, m.

publican s. taverner, m.

public-house s. taverna, f. / bar, m.

publish (to) v. publicar / divulgar, propagar / **publishing house** s. casa editorial f.

publisher s. editor -a

pudding s. púding (pastís de farina i fruita seca,) m.

puff s. buf, esbufec, m., alenada, f.

pulpit s. púlpit, m., trona, f.

pull s. estirada, sacsejada, f.

pullover s. jersei, m.

pulse s. pols, m., pulsació, f.

pump s. bomba (de líquids), f.

pumkin s. carbassa, f.

punch s. punxó, trepant, m. / cop de puny, m. / **to...** v. punxar, trepar / apunyegar

punctuate (to) v. puntuar

punishment s. càstig, m.

pupil s. alumne, deixeble, m.

puppet s. titella, m. / nina, f.

puppy s. cadell, gosset, m.

purchase s. compra, f. / **to...** v. comprar

purchaser s. comprador -a

pure a. pur -a.

purgative a. purgant, m.- f.

purgatory s. purgatori, m.

purge s. purga, f. / **to...** v. purgar

purify (to) v. purificar

purity a. puresa, puritat, f.

purple a. purpuri-úria

purpose s. propòsit, m. / **to...** v. proposar, tenir la intenció, intentar

purse s. portamonedes, m., bossa, f.

pursue (to) v. perseguir, encalçar

push s. empenta, f. / **to...** v. empènyer

put (to) v. posar, col·locar

puzzle s. endevinalla, f. / trencaclosques, m. / **to...** v. embrollar, embullar, enredar

pyjamas, s. pijama, m.

pyramid s. piràmide, f.

Q

quack a. i s. xerraire

quadrate a. quadrat-ada

quadrille s. contradansa, f. / escamot, m. / quadrícula, f.

quail s. guatlla, f. / **to...** v. recular / acovardir-se

quaint s. rar -a., original, m.- f.

quake s. tremolor, m., trepidació, f. / **to...** v. tremolar, trontollar.

quaker s. quàquer -a / a. tremolós -osa,

qualification s. qualificació, f.

qualify (to) v. qualificar.

quality a. qualitat, f.

quantity s. quantitat, f.

quarantine s. quarantena, f.

quarrel s. baralla, brega, f. / **to...** v. barallar-se

quarrier s. picapedrer, m.

quarry s. pedrera, f.

quarter s. quart / trimestre / barri, m.

quartely a. trimestral, m.- f. / adv. trimestralment.

quash (to) v. reprimir / invalidar.

quay s. moll, desembarcador, m.

queasiness s. nàusea, basca, f.

queasy a. nauseabund -a, fastigós -osa

queen s. reina, f.

queer a. estrany -a, misteriós -osa

queerness s. raresa, f.

quell (to) v. reprimir / apaivagar.

quench (to) v. apagar, extingir.

query s. interrogant, m. / interrogació, f. dubte, m.
quest s. recerca, f.
question s. qüestió, interrogació, f.
queue s. cua / renglera / trena, f.
quick a. ràpid -a, llest -a
quickly adv. ràpidament.
quicken (to) v. accelerar, apressar.
quicksilver s. argent viu, mercuri, m.
quiet a. tranquil -il·la, silenciós -osa / s. silenci, m., tranquil·litat, f.
quilt s. cobrellit m.
quilter s. matalasser -a
quince s. codony / codonyer, m.
quit a. absolt -a, lliure, m.- f., quiti -quítia / to... v. marxar, renunciar, desistir.
quite adv. completament.
quoin s. falca, f. / cantó m., cantonada, f. / to... v. falcar.
quota s. quota, f., contingent m.
quotation s. citació, cita / cotització, f.
quotation marks s. cometes, f. pl.
quote s. menció, cita, f. / to... v. mencionar, esmentar, citar.
quotidian a. quotidià, -ana
quotient s. quocient, m.

R

rabbit s. conill, m.
rabble s. gentussa, xusma, f.
rabid a. rabiós -osa, rabiüt -üda
rabies s. ràbia, f.
race s. raça / arrel / cursa, f.
rack s. penjador, prestatge, m. / xarxa, f. / turment, m.
racket s. aldarull, m / raqueta, f. / trampa, f.

radiate (to) v. irradiar, radiar, il·luminar
radiator s. radiador, m.
radication s. radicació, f.
radio s. radio, f. / ...set s. ràdio-receptor, m.
radish s. rave, m.
radium s. radi (metall), m.
radius s. radi (geom.) m.
raffle, s. rifa, f., sorteig, m. / to.. v. rifar.
raft s. rai, m.
rafter s. cabiró, m. biga, f.
rag s. parrac, drap, m.
rage s. ràbia, f.
ragged a. esparracat -ada, espellifat -ada
raging a. rabiós -osa
ragman s. drapaire, m. -f.
raid s. incursió, irrupció, f. / to... v. irrompre
rail s. rail, carril / passamà, m.
railing s. barana, reixa, f.
railway s. ferrocarril, m.
rain s. pluja, f. / to... v. ploure
rainbow s. arc iris, arc de Sant Martí, m.
rainfall s. xàfec, m.
rainy a. plujós -osa
raise (to) v. aixecar, elevar.
raisin s. pansa, f.
rake s. rasclet, m. / to... v. rasclar
rally s. reunió, concentració, f. / to... v. reunir, concentrar
ram s. ariet, martinet, esperó / boc, m.
ramble (to) v. rondar, passejar.
ramification s. ramificació, f.
ramp s. rampa f., declivi, m.
rampart s. baluard, m.
rancour s. rancor, m.
rancorous a. rancorós -osa
random a. fortuït-a, impensat-ada m/s. atzar, m.
range s. serralada / renglera /

sèrie, f. / to... v. arrenglerar /
col·locar
ranger s. guardabosc, m.
rank s. rang, grau, m.
ransom s. rescat, m. / to... v. rescatar
rap (to) v. trucar, picar.
rapacity s. rapacitat, f.
rapid a. ràpid -a
rapine s. rapinya, f.
rapt a. encisat -ada, embadalit
-ida
rarity s. raresa / curiositat, f.
rascal s. bergant, brivall, m.
rash a. irreflexiu -iva, imprudent,
m.- f.
rashnness s. temeritat, irreflexió,
rauxa, f.
rat s. rata, f.
rate s. tarifa / proporció, f.
rather adv. més aviat, més bé /
tal vegada.
ratification s. ratificació, f.
ratify (to) v. ratificar, confirmar.
ration s. ració, f. / to... v. racionar.
rational a. racional /raonable,
m.- f.
rattle s. grinyol, carrisqueig /
brunzit, m. / xerrameca, f.
ravage s. estrall, saqueig, m. /
to... v. saquejar, destruir.
rave (to) v. delirar, desvariejar.
raven s. corb, m.
ravening a. rapaç, salvatge, m.- f.
ravenous a. famolenc -a, voraç
rapaç, m.- f.
ravine s. barranc, m., fondalada, f.
ravish (to) v. arrabassar.
raw a. cru -a, descarnat -ada
ray s. llamp, raig, m.
raze (to) v. arrasar, enderrocar /
esborrar
razor s. navalla, f.
reach (to) v. abastar, aconseguir

react (to) v. reaccionar
reaction s. reacció, f.
read (to) v. llegir, desxifrar
reader s. lector -a
reading s. lectura / lliçó, f.
ready a. enllestit -ida, disposat
-ada, / ...made, de confecció /
to be.. to v. estar a punt de
real a. real, veritable, m.- f.
reality s. realitat, f.
realize (to) v. realitzar, efectuar
/ adonar-se
really adv. realment
realm s. reialme, m.
ream s. raima, f.
reap (to) v. segar, collir
reaper s. segador -a
reaping s. sega, collita, f.
reappear (to) v. reaparèixer
rear a. posterior, m. -f. / to... v.
criar, cultivar / erigir, alçar
reason s. raó, causa, f. / to... v.
raonar, discutir
rebate (to) v. rebaixar, descomp-
tar
rebel s. rebel, m.- f. / to... v. rebe-
lar- se, revoltar-se
rebellion s. rebel·lió, revolta, f.
rebound s. rebot m., repercussió, f. / to... v. rebotre, repercutir
rebuff s. rebuig, m., denegació, f.
rebuke s. censura, reprensió, f.
rebut (to) v. refutar, rebatre
recall (to) v. anul·lar, retirar /
recordar
receipt s. rebut, m.
receipts s. ingressos, m. pl.
receive (to) v. rebre, acollir.
receiver s. receptor -a, dipositari-
ària
receptionist s. recepcionista,
m.-f.
reception s. recepció, f. / acolliment, m.
recipe s. recepta (mèdica), f.
reciprocity s. reciprocitat, f.

recite (to) v. recitar, relatar
reckon (to) v. comptar, calcular, considerar, tenir per
reclaim (to) v. reclamar
reclamation s. reclamació, f.
recline (to) v. reclinar, recolzar
recognition s. reconeixement, m.
recognize (to) v. reconèixer
recoil s. retrocés m. / to... v. recular, retrocedir
recollect (to) v. recordar / recollir, reunir
recollection s. record, m.
recomend (to) v. recomanar
recommendation s. recomanació, f.
recompense s. recompensa, compensació, f. / to... v. recompensar, compensar
reconcile (to) v. reconciliar
reconciliation s. reconciliació, f.
reconnoitre (to) v. explorar, reconèixer
record s. acta, f., registre , m. / disc (de gramòfon), m.
record (to) v. inscriure, enregistrar
recorder s. registrador / comptador, m.
record player s. tocadiscos, m.
recount (to) v. narrar, referir
recourse s. recurs, m.
recover (to) v. recuperar, restablir
recovery s. recuperació, f.
recreation s. esbargiment, m.
recruit s. recluta, m. / to... v. reclutar, enrolar
rectangle s. rectangle, m.
rectification s. rectificació, f.
recumbent a. ajagut -uda, ajaçat -ada
recuperate (to) v. recuperar / v. pr. recuperar-se, recobrar-se
recurrence s. repetició, f. / recurs, m.

red a. roig -roja, vermell -a
redden (to) v. enrogir
reddish a. vermellós -osa
redeem (to) v. redimir
redeemer s. redemptor -a
redness s. vermellor, f.
redolent a. fragant, m.- f., olorós -osa
redoubtable a. formidable, m. -f.
redress s. esmena, f., remei, m. / to... v. remeiar, redreçar.
reduce (to) v. reduir.
reduction s. reducció / rebaixa, f.
reed s. canya, f.
reef s. escull, rompent, m.
reeky a. fumat -ada
reel s. rodet, m., debanadora, f.
refer (to) v. al·ludir, atribuir, adreçar
referable a. atribuïble, imputable, m.- f.
referee s. àrbitre, m.
reference s. referència, f.
refine (to) v. refinar
refinement s. distinció, f., refinament, m.
refinery s. refineria, f.
refit (to) v. reajustar, reparar
reflect (to) v. reflectir
reflector s. reflector, m.
reform (to) v. reformar
reformation s. reforma, f.
refresh (to) v. refrescar / renovellar
refreshment s. refresc, refrigeri, m.
refrigerator s. refrigerador, m., nevera, f.
refuge s. refugi, aixopluc, m.
refund (to) v. reintegrar, restituir
refusal s. negativa, f.
refuse s. rebuig, m., / deixalles, f. pl.
refuse (to) v. refusar, denegar.

regal a. regi -règia, reial, m.- f.

regard s. mirada, f. / mirament, m., consideració, f. / to... v. mirar, observar / considerar

regarding prep. en relació a, respecte a, quant a

regards s. records, m. pl., salutacions, f. pl.

regenerate a. regenerat -ada, / to... v. regenerar

régime s. règim, m.

region s. regió, f.

register s. registre, arxiu, m. / to... v. enregistrar, certificar, inscriure

registered a. certificat-ada / a. patentat -ada

regret s. remordiment, penediment, m. / enyorança f. / to... v. lamentar, enyorar-se, penedir-se

regrettable a. lamentable, deplorable, m. -f.

regular a. regular, m.-f. / metòdic-a.

regulate (to) v. regularitzar, regular.

regulation s. regulació, f., mètode, m.

rehearsal s. assaig, m.

rehearse (to) v. assajar, recitar (per a memoritzar)

reign s. regnat, m. / to... v. regnar

rein s. regna, brida, f.

reindeer s. ren, m.

reinforce (to) v. reforçar

reins s. ronyons, m. pl.

reinsurance s. reassegurança, f.

reject (to) v. rebutjar / refusar

rejection s. rebuig / refús, m.

rejoice (to) v. alegrar / alegrar-se

relapse (to) v. recaure / reincidir

relate (to) v. relatar, narrar / emparentar

relation s. parent, m. / relació, f.

relationship s. parentiu, m.

relative a. relatiu -iva / s. parent -a

relax (to) v. relaxar, afluixar, cedir

relay s. relleu, m. / reposició, f. / to... v. rellevar / (ràdio) retransmetre

release s. alliberament, m., / to... v. alliberar

reliable a. fidedigne-a, segur-a,

reliance s. confiança. f.

relic s. relíquia, f.

relief s. conhort, alleujament, m. / desgreuge, m. / relleu, m.

relieve (to) v. rellevar / socórrer

religion s. religió, f.

religious a. i s. religiós -osa

relish s. condiment, amaniment, m.

relishable a. gustós -osa, saborós -osa

rely (to) v. confiar / fiar-se

remain (to) v. romandre, restar

remainder s. resta, romanalla, f.

remake (to) v. refer

remark s. remarca, observació f. / to... v. remarcar, observar

remedy s. remei, medicament, m. / to... v. curar, remeiar

remember (to) v. recordar

remembrance s. record, m., recordança, f.

remind (to) v. recordar, fer present

remit (to) v. trametre, enviar

reminder s. advertiment, recordatori, m.

remittance s. tramesa, remesa, f.

remnant s. resta, f., residu, retall, m.

remonstrate (to) v. protestar

remorse s. remordiment, m.

removal s. trasllat, m., remoció, f.

remove (to) v. remoure, treure
remunerate (to) v. retribuir
rend (to) v. dividir, separar, esquinçar
render (to) v. rendir, restituir / prestar ajut, serveis
renew (to) v. renovar, recomençar
renewal s. renovació, pròrroga, f.
renounce (to) v. renunciar
renovation s. renovació, f.
renown s. renom, m., reputació, f.
renowned a. famós -osa, notable, remarcable, m.- f.
rent s. lloguer,m. / to... v. arrendar, llogar
reorganize (to) v. reorganitzar
repair s. reparació, f., adob, m. / to... v. reparar, adobar
repay (to) v. restituir, reintegrar
repeal (to) v. derogar, abolir
repeat (to) v. repetició, f. / to... v. repetir
repel (to) v. repel·lir, rebutjar
repellent a. repel·lent, m.- f
repent (to) v. pr. penedir-se
replace (to) v. reemplaçar, substituir / tornar a col·locar
reply s. resposta, rèplica, f. / to... v. respondre, replicar
report s. informe, m. / to... v. informar
reporter s. repòrter, periodista, m.
repose (to) v. descansar, reposar
reprehend (to) v. reprendre, renyar, reprovar
represent (to) v. representar
representative s. representant, m. / a. representatiu -iva
repress (to) v. reprimir / dominar
repression s. repressió, f.
reprieve s. dilació, f., ajornament, m. / suspensió, f.

reprisal s. represàlia, f.
reproach s. retret, blasme, m. / to... v. blasmar
reproval s. reprovació, f., reny, m.
reprove (to) v. renyar, reprovar
reproduce (to) v. reproduir
reptile a. i s. rèptil, m.- f.
republic s. república, f.
repudiate (to) v. repudiar
repulsion s. repulsió, repugnància, f.
reputable a. honrat-ada, estimable, m.- f.
request s. requesta, petició, f. / to... v. demanar, sol·licitar / apel·lar
require (to) v. exigir, requerir
requite (to) v. correspondre, compensar, recompensar
reredos s. retaule, m.
rescue s. rescat, salvament, m. / to... v. rescatar, salvar
research s. recerca, investigació f. / to... v. recercar, investigar
resemblance s. semblança, f.
resemble (to) v. pr. assemblar-se
resent (to) v. ressentir-se, ofendre's
resentment s. ressentiment, m.
reserve s. reserva, f. / to... v. reservar
reservoir s. dipòsit, embassament, m.
reside (to) v. residir
residue s. residu, m., resta, f.
resign (to) v. renunciar, cedir, dimitir
resignation s. resignació / dimissió, f.
resin s. resina, f.
resist (to) v. resistir
resistance s. resistència / oposició, f.
resolution s. resolució, decisió, f.

resolve s. resolució, f. / **to...** v. resoldre

resort s. recurs, refugi, m. / punt de reunió, m.

respect s. respecte, m. / **to...** v. respectar

respite s. treva, f., respir, m.

respond (to) v. respondre, correspondre

response s. resposta, contestació, f.

responsible a. responsable, m.-f.

rest s. repòs, m., pausa, f., / resta, f., romanent, m. / **to...** v. reposar, romandre

restful a. assossegat-ada, quiet-a, m. -f.

restless a. inquiet-a, neguitós-osa.

restore (to) v. restablir, restaurar / restituir.

restrain (to) v. restringir, refrenar

restrict (to) v. restringir, reduir, disminuir

result s. conseqüència, f., resultat, m. / **to...** v. resultar.

resume (to) v. resumir, reprendre, continuar.

resurrection s. resurrecció, f.

retail s. venda al detall, a la menuda, f.

retailer s. botiguer, revenedor, m.

retain (to) v. retenir, conservar

retard s. retard, m., dilació, f. / **to...** v. retardar, diferir

retire (to) v. retrocedir / jubilar-se

retouch s. retoc, m. / **to...** v. retocar

retract (to) v. retractar / estrènyer, contreure

retribution s. retribució, f.

return s. recompensa, f. / ...tic-

ket s. bitllet d'anar i tornar, m. / **(to)** v. retornar, tornar

reveal (to) v. revelar, descobrir

revelation s. revelació, f.

revelry s. gresca, xerinola, disbauxa, f.

revels s. festes, f. pl.

revenge s. venjança, f. / **to...** v. venjar, venjar-se

revenue s. renda, f., benefici, m. / ingressos del govern, m. pl.

revere (to) v. reverenciar, venerar

reverie s. somni, somieig / embaladiment, m. / fantasia, f.

revers s. solapa, gira, f.

reverse s. revés, oposat, contratemps, m.

review s. revista, revisio, inspecció, f.

revise (to) v. revisar, repassar

revival s. renaixement, restabliment, m.

revive (to) v. reanimar, revifar

revocation s. revocació, f.

revolt s. revolta, f.

revolve (to) v. girar, rodar / giravoltar

revolver s. revòlver, m.

revolving a. giratori -òria

revue s. revista, f.

reward s. recompensa, f. / **to...**: v. recompensar, premiar

rhinoceros s. rinoceront, m.

rhyme s. rima, f. / vers, m.

rhythm s. ritme, m.

rib s. costella, f.

ribbon s. cinta, veta, f.

rice s. arròs, m.

rich a. ric -rica

richness s. riquesa, fertilitat, f.

rickets s. raquitisme, m.

rickety a. raquític -a, esquifit -ida

riddle s. enigma, m., endevinalla, f.

ride (to) v. cavalcar, muntar
rider s. genet / ciclista, m.
ridge s. serralada, carena, f.
ridicule a. ridícul -a / to... v. ridiculitzar
rifeness s. abundància, abundor, f.
rifle s. fusell, m. carrabina, f.
right a. dret-dreta, recte-a, justa, correcte-a / to be... encertar, tenir raó.
righteous a. justa, honrat -ada.
righteousness s. rèctitud, equitat, f.
rigid a. rígid -a
rigidity s. rigidesa, austeritat, f.
rind s. escorça, clofolla, f.
ring s. cercle, anell, cèrcol / circ, m.
rinse (to) v. rentar, esbaldir
riot s. aldarull, avalot, motí, m.
rip s. laceració, esquinçada, f. / to... v. esquinçar, trencar
ripe a. madur -a
ripen (to) v. madurar
rise s. pujada, f., ascens, m. / to... v. ascendir, pujar
rising s. aixecament, m., insurrecció, f. / a. naixement, ascendent, m.-f.
risk s. risc, perill, m. / to... v. arriscar, perillar.
risky a. arriscat -ada, atzarós -osa
rite s. ritu, m.
rival a. i s. rival, m.- f. / to... v. rivalitzar
rivalry s. rivalitat, f.
river s. riu, m.
rivet s. rebló, m. / to... v. reblar
road s. carretera, f.
roadway s. calçada, f.
roar s. bramul, rugit, m. / to... v. bramular, rugir
roast a. rostit -ida / to... v. rostir

rob (to) v. robar, furtar
robber s. lladre, m.
robbery s. robatori, furt, m.
robe s. túnica, toga, f. / vestit, m.
rock s. roca, f., penyal, m.
rocket s. coet, m.
rocking chair s. balancí, m.
rocky a. rocós -osa, petri -pètria / endurit -ida
rod s. vara, vareta / canya de pescar, f.
rogue s. bergant, brivall, m.
roguery s. picardia, berganteria, f.
roister (to) v. fanfarronejar
roll s. panet / llonguet, m. / rotllo, rotlle, m. / balanceig, m. / to... v. rodar, rodolar / balancejar-se
roller s. roleu, cilindre, m.
romance s. novel·la, f. / romanç, m.
rood s. crucifix, m.
roof s. teulada, f.
rook s. cornella, graula, f. / (escacs) torre, f.
rookie s. novell-a, principiant, m.- f., novici-ícia
room s. cambra, habitació, f.
rooster s. gall, pollastre, m.
root s. arrel, rel, f. / to... v. arrelar
rope s. corda, f.
rose s. rosa, f., roser, m.
rosebush s. roser, m.
rose tree s. roser, m.
rosemary s. romaní, m.
rot s. podridura, f., podriment, m. / càries, f. / to... v. podrir, podrir-se, corrompre
rotary a. giratori -òria, rotatiu -iva / s. rotativa, f.
rotten a. podrit -ida.
rough a. basta, groller -a.
roughly adv. aproximadament / asprament.

round a. rodó-ona, circular, m.-f.

roundabout a. indirecte -a, desviat -ada

rouse (to) v. despertar / v. pr. despertar-se.

rout s. derrota, fugida, f. / to... v. derrotar.

route s. ruta, f.

rove (to) v. vagar, divagar.

row s. filera, renglera, f.

royal a. reial, m.- f., regi- règia

royalty s. reialesa, f.

rub s. fregament, frec, m.

rub out (to) v. esborrar

rubber s. cautxú, m.

rubbish s. escombraries, f. pl.

ruby s. robí, m.

rucksack s. motxilla, f. / morral, m.

rude s. rude m.-f., groller-a, basta.

rug s. estoreta, f.

ruin (to) v. arruïnar, malmetre.

ruins s. ruïnes / runes, f. pl.

rule s. regla, f., estatut, reglament, m. / to... v. regir, governar

ruler s. governador, m. / regla, f.

rum s. rom (alcohol), f.

rumble s. remor, f. brogit, m.

ruminant a. i s. remugant, ruminant, m.

run s. cursa, f. / recorregut, m. / to... v. córrer

rung s. llistó, barrot, m.

runner s. corredor -a, missatger -a

running s. cursa, correguda, f.

rupture s. ruptura / hèrnia, trencadura, f.

rush s. pressa, precipitació, escomesa, f. / to... v. precipitar / v. pr. abalançar-se

rust s. rovell, òxid, verdet, m. / to... v. rovellar, oxidar

rusty a. rovellat-ada, oxidat-ada

rut s. rodera, f.

ruthless a. cruel, insensible, m.-f.

ruthlessness s. crueltat, f.

rye s. sègol, m.

S

sabot s. esclop, m.

sabre s. sabre, m.

sack s. sac / saqueig, m. / to... v. ensacar / saquejar

sacred a. sagrat-ada,

sacredness s. santedat, f.

sacrifice s. sacrifici, m. / to... v. sacrificar

sad a. trist-trista.

sadden (to) v. entristir, entristir-se.

saddle s. sella, f. / to... v. ensellar

saddler s. baster, guarnimenter, guarnicioner, m.

sadness s. tristesa, f.

safe a. segur-a, il·lès-esa, intacte-a / s. caixa de cabals, f. / ...and sound a. sa. i estalvi, m.

safeguard s. salvaguarda, f. / to... v. salvaguardar.

safety s. seguretat, f.

safety pin s. imperdible, agulla imperdible, f.

safety razor s. màquina d'afaitar, f.

saffron s. safrà, m.

sagacious a. sagaç, m.- f.

sage s. savi, filòsof, m., / sàlvia, f.

sail s. vela, f. / to... v. navegar,

sailing ship s. veler, vaixell de vela, m.

sailor s. mariner, m.

saint a. i s. santa.

sake s. causa, f., motiu, fi, objecte, m.
salable a. vendible / venal, m.-f.
salad s. amanida, f.
salamander s. salamandra, f.
salary s. sou, salari, m.
sale s. venda, f.
sallow a. pàl·lid-a, lívid-a, esgroguelt-ïda
sally s. sortida, passejada, excursió / rauxa, f.
salmon s. salmó, m.
saloon s. saló / cafè, bar, m.
salt s. sal, f. / to... v. salar.
salutation s. salutació, f.
salute (to) v. saludar.
salvage s. salvament, m.
salvation s. salvació, f.
salve s. ungüent, bàlsam, m., pomada, f. / to... v. untar.
salver s. safata, plàtera, f.
same a. mateix-a, semblant, m.-f.
sample s. mostra, f. / to... v. mostrar, provar.
sanctify (to) v. santificar.
sanctuary s. santuari, m.
sand s. sorra, arena, f.
sandal s. sandàlia, f.
sandwich s. entrepà, emparedat, m.
sane a. entenimentat-ada, assenyat-ada,
sanity s. sensatesa, f., seny, m.
sap s. saba, f. / sapa, mina, f. // to... v. soscavar, minar.
sapphire s. safir, m.
Saracen a. i s. sarraí-ïna,
sardine s. sardina, f.
sash s. banda, faixa, f.
sateen s. setí, m.
satellite s. satèl·lit, m.
satiate a. saciat-ada, satisfet-a (fam.) tip-a, / to... v. saciar, atipar (vulg.) afartar
satisfaction s. satisfacció, f.

satisfied a. satisfet-a,
satisfy (to) v. satisfer.
Saturday s. dissabte, m.
sauce s. salsa, f.
saucepan s. cassola, f.
saucer s. platet, m. / **flying**... platet, m. volador
sauciness s. desvergonyiment, m. insolència, f.
saucy a. descarat-ada
sausage s. salsitxa, f.
savage s. salvatge, m.- f.
save (to) v. salvar / estalviar / evitar.
Saviour s. salvador, m.
savour s. sabor, m.
savoury a. saborós-osa,
saw s. serra, f. / proverbi, m. / to... v. serrar.
sawdust s. serradures, f. pl.
saxophone s. saxofon, m.
say (to) v. dir.
saying s. dita, f., adagi, m.
scab s. crosta, ronya, f.
scabbard s. beina, f.
scaffold s. bastida, f., cadafal, m.
scaffolding s. bastida, bastimentada / carcassa, f.
scald s. escaldada, cremada, f. / to... v. escaldar
scale s. balança, bàscula / escala, graduació / escama, crosta, f. / to... v. escalar, graduar, pesar
scales s. balances, f. pl.
scamper s. corredissa, fugida, f. / to... v. fugir / v. pr. escapar-se
scan (to) v. escrutar, examinar
scandal s. escàndol, m.
Scandinavian a. i s. escandinau-ava
scantiness s. estretor, misèria, f.
scanty a. escàs-assa, insuficient, m.- f.
scar s. cicatriu, f.

scarce a. rar -a, escàs -assa

scarcely adv. escassament

scare (to) v. esglaiar, espantar

scarf s. bufanda, f., tapaboques, m.

scarlet a. escarlata

scarlet fever s. escarlatina, f.

scatter (to) v. espargir, escampar

scavenger s. escombriaire, m.

scene s. escena, f.

scenery s. perspectiva, f., paisatge, m. / decoració, f.

scent s. olor, flaire, f.

scepter s. ceptre, m.

sceptic a. i s. escèptic -a

sceptre s. ceptre, m.

schedule s. cèdula, f. / programa, horari, m. / llista, f.

scheme s. esquema, m.

scholar s. escolar, m. -f. / docte -a, erudit -a

school s. escola, f.

schoolfellow s. condeixeble-a

schoolmate s. company d'escola, m.

schooner s. goleta f.

science s. ciència, f.

scientific a. científic-a

scientist s. científic (home de ciència), m.

scintilla s. guspira, espurna, f.

scintillate (to) v. centellejar, espurnejar

scissors s. tisores, f. pl.

scope s. abast, m. / gamma, f. / camp d'actuació, m.

scorch (to) v. socarrimar, socarrar / emmusteir-se

score s. osca, incisió / marca, f., marcador, m.

scorn s. menyspreu, m. / to... v. menyspreuar

scornful a. desdenyós -osa

scorpion s. escorpí, m.

Scotch o Scottish a. i s. escocès -esa

scoundrel s. bergant, brivall, canalla, m.

scour (to) v. polir, fregar, brunyir

scourer s. desengreixador, m.

scout s. explorador, m. / to... v. explorar

scrap s. bocí, rosegó, m., deixalla, f.

scrape (to) v. rascar, raspar, gratar /esgarrapar

scratch s. esgarrapada, rascada, f. / to... v. rascar, esgarrapar, escarbotar

screak s. grinyol, xerric, m. / to... v. grinyolar, xerricar

scream s. crit, xiscle, m. / to... v. cridar, xisclar

screen s. mampara, pantalla, persiana, f.

screw s. cargol (mec.), m. / to... v. cargolar

screwdriver s. tornavís, m.

scribe s. cal·lígraf, escrivent, m.

scrimp a. escàs -assa / to... v. escatimar.

scrub (to) v. fregar, refregar.

scruple s. escrúpol, m.

sculpture s. escultura, f.

scrutiny s. escrutini / recompte, m.

scum a. escuma, f.

scurf s. crosta, caspa, f.

scythe s. dalla, f.

sea s. mar, m. -f.

seabord s. costa, f., litoral, m.

seagull s. gavina, f.

seal s. segell, precinte, m. / to... v. segellar, precintar

seam s. costura, sutura, f.

search s. percaça, recerca, f. / to... v. escorcollar, investigar

seasick a. marejat -ada

seasickness s. mareig, m.

seasonable a. oportú -una / propi del temps.

season-ticket s. abonament de temporada, m.
seat s. seient, lloc, m. / to... v. seure
sea wall s. escullera, f.
seaweed s. alga, f.
secede (to) v. pr. separar-se
seclude (to) v. recloure, tancar / apartar.
second a. i m.- f. segon-a / s. segon, m.
secret a. secret -a / s. secret, m.
secretary a. secretari-ària.
secretary's office o secretariship s. secretaria, f.
section s. secció, divisió, f.
secular a. seglar
secure a. segur-a, ferm-a, / to... v. assegurar, afermar.
sedate a. assossegat -ada
seduce (to) v. seduir.
seduction s. seducció, f.
sedulity s. assiduïtat, f.
see (to) v. veure.
seed s. llavor, semença, f.
seek (to) v. cercar.
seem (to) v. semblar
seeming s. aparença, f. / a. aparent, m. -f.
seer s. profeta, vident, m.
seesaw s. balancí, gronxador, m.
segment s. segment, m.
seize (to) v. agafar, subjectar / embargar.
seldom adv. rarament, poques vegades.
select a. selecte-a, escollit-ida / to... v. escollir, seleccionar.
selection s. selecció, f.
self a. mateix -a, propi -pròpia / command s. domini d'un mateix, m. / ...-denial s. abnegació, f., altruisme, m. / ...-important a. presumit-ida, superbiós-osa / selfish a. egoista, m.- f. / ...-made a.

autodidacte / ...-willed a. obstinat-ada
sell (to) v. vendre.
seller s. venedor, m.
semicolon s. punt i coma, m.
senate s. senat, m.
send (to) v. trametre, enviar.
sender s. remitent, m. -f.
senior a. i s. gran, antic, pare, degà, m.
sensation s. sensació, f.
sense s. sentit / enteniment, m.
senseless a. insensible, m.- f. / desbaratat -ada
sensitive a. sensitiu -iva, sensible, m. -f.
sentence s. oració, proposició / sentència, f.
sentinel o sentry s. sentinella, m.
separate (to) v. separar, allunyar.
September s. setembre, m.
sepulchre s. sepulcre, m.
sequel s. seqüela, conseqüència, f.
sequent a. següent, m.- f.
sequestrate (to) v. segrestar / embargar, confiscar.
seraph s. serafí, m.
sere a. sec-a, marcit-ida
serenade a. serenata, f.
serf s. serf, esclau, m.
sergeant s. sergent, m.
series s. sèrie, f.
serious a. seriós -osa, sever -a
sermon s. sermó, m., prèdica, f.
serpent (to) v. serpejar, serpentejar
servant s. criat, servent, m.
serve (to) v. servir
service s. servei, m.
servitude s. servitud, f.
session s. sessió, junta, f.
set s. assortit, joc, m., col·lecció, sèrie, f. / posta de sol, f. / set back s. retrocés, m. / adversi-

tat, f. / ...square cartabó, m. / to ...forth v. manifestar, exposar / to ...off v. emprendre la marxa / compensar / to ...on fire v. calar foc / to ...out v. partir, anar-se'n.

settle s. escó, m. / to... v. decidir, determinar / v. pr. posar-se, afermar-se, establirse / establir, col·locar, fixar, colonitzar / ... down (to) v. establir-se.

settkenebt s. establiment, m., instal·lació, f. / colònia, f. col·locació, f.

seven a. i s. set m.

seventeen a. i s. disset. m.

seventeenth a. i m.- f. dissetè-dissetena

seventh a. i m.- f. setè -ena

seventieth a. i m.- f. setantè-setantena

severe a. sever -a

several a. pl. alguns-algunes

sew s. (to) v. cosir

sewer s. claveguera, f.

sewing s. costura, f.

sex s. sexe, m.

shabbiness s. malendreç, m.

shabby a. malendreçat-ada / usat -ada

shackles s. manilles, f. pl., grillons, m. pl.

shade s. ombra, f. matís, m. / to... v. ombrejar, matisar.

shadow s. ombra, f., espectre, m.

shady a. ombriu -iva, obac -aga, ombrejat -ada

shaft s. sageta, fletxa, f. / mànec, m. / obertura, boca de mina, f. / tronc, m. / ...of light s. raig de llum, m.

shafting s. transmissió, f.

shaggy a. pelut -uda / apelfat -ada

shah s. xa, m.

shake (to) v. sacsejar, remenar / estrènyer (la mà).

shallow s. som-soma, de poca fondària / superficial, m.-f.

sham s. fingiment, m. / a. fals-falsa, postís-issa / to... v. simular, fingir.

shame s. vergonya, f., deshonor, m. / to... v. avergonyir

shameful a. vergonyós-osa

shameless a. desvergonyit -ida.

shank s. canyella (cama), f.

shanty s. cabana, barraca, f.

shape s. forma, figura, f., model, m. / to... v. modelar, afaiçonar

shapeless a. deforme, m. -f.

shapely a. ben format -ada, ben fet-feta.

share s. part, porció, f. / to... v. compartir, dividir.

shareholder s. accionista, m. -f.

shark s. tauró / estafador, m.

sharp a. agut -uda, punxegut -uda

sharpen (to) v. esmolar, afilar, agusar

shave (to) v. afaitar.

shaving-brush s. brotxa d'afaitar, f.

shawl s. xal, m.

she pron. ella, f.

sheaf s. garba, f., feix, m.

shear (to) v. esquilar, tondre, xollar.

shearer s. esquilador, xollador, m.

sheep s. be, moltó, m.

sheepdog s. gos de pastor, m.

sheer a. escarpat -ada, abrupte-a pur-pura / fi-fina.

sheet s. llençol / full, m. / làmina, f.

shelf s. prestatge, m., lleixa, f.

shell s. closca, clofolla, / petxina / conquilla, f.

shepherd s. pastor, m.

shepherdess s. pastora, f.

sheriff a. algutzir, m.
shield s. escut / to... v. protegir, defensar.
shift s. torn, m., tanda, f. / to... v. mudar (de lloc) / v. pr. desplaçar-se.
shilling s. xíling, m.
shine (to) v. lluir, brillar.
ship s. vaixell, m. / to... v. embarcar.
shirk (to) v. eludir, defugir, esquivar.
shirt s. camisa, f.
shock s. xoc, m., topada, f.
shoe s. sabata, f.
shoemaker s. sabater, m.
shoot (to) v. disparar / ferir o matar (amb arma de foc) / afusellar
shooter s. tirador, m.
shop s. botiga, f.
shopkeeper s. botiguer-a.
shore s. riba, ribera, costa, f.
short a. curt-curta, escas -assa / in... en resum.
shortage s. escassetat, escassesa, mancança, f.
shorten (to) v. escurçar, abreujar.
shoulder s. espatlla, f., muscle, m.
shove s. empenta, f. / to... v. empentar.
shovel s. pala, f.
show s. espectacle, m., exhibició, f. / to... v. exhibir, exposar, mostrar.
shower (to) v. regar, vessar, ploure.
showman s. empresari, m.
shrewd a. astut-a / subtil, m.-f.
shrub s. arbust, m., mata, f.
shut (to) v. tancar, tancar-se.
shutter s. tancador / finestró / obturador (fotog.), m.
shuttle s. llançadora, f.

sick a. malalt -a
sicken (to) v. emmalaltir.
sickness s. malaltia, f.
side s. costat, m.
side face s. perfil, m.
sidewalk s. vorera, andana, f.
sieve s. garbell, sedàs, m.
sift (to) v. garbellar
sigh s. sospir, m. / to... v. sospirar
sight s. vista, visió, f. / to... v. albirar, distingir
sightless a. cec-cega.
sign s. signe, m. signatura, firma, f. / to... v., signar, firmar.
signal s. senyal, m.
signature s. signatura, firma, f.
signify (to) v. significar
silence s. silenci, m.
silent a. silenciós -osa
silk s. seda, f.
sill s. llindar, marxapeu, m.
silver s. argent, m., plata, f.
silversmith a. argenter, m.
similar a. semblant, similar, m.-f.
simmer (to) v. bullir o estar-ne a punt, xauxinar
simple a. i. s. simple m.- f.
simplify (to) v. simplificar.
sin s. pecat, m. / to... v. pecar
since prep. des de, d'ençà.
sincere a. sincer-a
sincerity s. sinceritat, f.
sinew s. tendó, m. / fortalesa, fortitud, f.
sinewy a. fibrós-osa / vigorós-osa, robust-a
sinful a. pecador-a.
sing (to) v. cantar.
singer s. cantaire, cantant, m.-f.
singing s. cant, m.
single a. senzill-a / individual, m.-f. / solter-a.
sinister a. sinistre-a / esquerre-a / funest-a.

197

sink s. aigüera, f. / **to...** v. enfonsar, enfonsar-se.
sinner a. i m. pecador-a.
sip s. glop, xarrup, m. / **to...** v. xarrupar.
sir s. senyor, m. / títol honorífic (a Anglaterra).
sirup s. xarop, m.
sister s. germana, f.
sister-in-law s. cunyada, f.
sit (to) v. seure / posar-se / covar (les aus).
sit down (to) v. seure / **to sit oneself down**, asseure's.
site s. lloc, indret, m.
situation s. situació, orientació, f.
six a. i s. sis, m.
sixteen a. i s. setze, m.
sixteenth a. i m.- f. setzè-setzena
sixth a. i m.- f. sisè-sisena
sixtieth a. i m.- f. seixantè-seixantena
sixty a. i s. seixanta, m.
size s. mida, dimensió f.
sizy a. enganxós-osa
skate s. patí, m. / **to...** v. patinar
skater s. patinador-a
skeleton s. esquelet, m.
sketch s. disseny, croquis / sainet, m.
ski s. esquí, m. / **to...** v. esquiar
skid (to) v. lliscar, relliscar, patinar.
skier s. esquiador-a.
skilful a. hàbil, m.-f. destre-a.
skill s. habilitat, traça, f.
skilled a. expert-a, destre-a, experimentat-ada
skim (to) v. desnatar, escumar.
skin s. pell / pellofa, f. / **to...** v. pelar
skip s. salt, bot, m. cabriola, f. / omissió, f. / **to...** v. saltar, triscar / ometre

skipper s. patró d'un vaixell.
skirt s. faldilles, f. pl.
skull s. crani, m., calavera, f.
sky s. cel, firmament, m.
slack a. fluix-a, negligent m.-f. lent-lenta.
slam s. cop de porta, m. / **to...** v. tancar de cop.
slander s. calúmnia, f. / **to...** v. calumniar
slang s. argot, m., llenguatge xaró
slap s. bufetada, f.
slash (to) v. acoltellar, tallar / fuetejar.
slate s. pissarra, f.
slaughter s. matança, mortaldat, f. / **to...** v. matar, sacrificar
Slav a. i s. eslau-ava
slave s. esclau-ava
slavery s. esclavitud, f., esclavatge, m.
slavish a. servil, m.- f. / esclavitzat-ada.
slay (to) v. occir, assassinar.
sledge s. trineu, m.
sleep (to) v. dormir.
sleeper s. màniga, f., mànega (d'un vestit).
slender a. prim-prima, delicat-a-da, dèbil, m.-f.
slice s. llesca, tallada, penca, f. / **to...** v. llescar.
slide (to) v. relliscar.
sliding-door s. porta corredissa, f.
slim a. prim-a, esvelt-a.
sling s. fona, f., mandró, m. / cabestrell / portafusell, m.
slipper s. sabatilla, babutxa, f.
slip s. relliscada / error, m. / tira de paper, f. / **to...** v. relliscar / esmunyir-se / equivocar-se.
slobber s. bava, f. / **to...** v. bavejar.
slogan s. mot o refrany publicitari.

slop (to) v. vessar, sobreeixir.
slope s. desnivell, m.
sloppy a. mullat-ada, enfangat-ada.
sloth s. mandra, ganduleria, f.
slow a. lent-lenta, calmós-osa.
slowly adv. poc a poc.
slowness s. lentitud, apatia, f.
sluggish a. indolent, m.-f. apàtic-a
sluice s. resclosa, f.
slum s. suburbi, m.
smack s. sabor, gust, m. / manotada, f. / bes sonor// to... v. besar sonorament / xerricar.
small a. petit-a, mesquí-ína, esquifit-ida / ... **change** s. canvi, m. / xavalla f.
smart a. elegant, m.-f., polit-ida, eixerit-ida / s. coïssor, f.
smash s. ruïna, fallida, f. / to... v. trencar, aixafar.
smell (to) v. olorar, flairar.
smile s. somrís, m. / to... v. somriure.
smith s. forjador / artífex, m.
smithy s. forja, farga, fornal, f.
smog s. boira (f.) espessa i fum (m.) barrejats.
smoke s. fum, m. / to... v. fumar
smooth a. suau, m.-f., llisa.
smother (to) v. ofegar, apagar / dissimular.
smuggler s. contrabandista, m.
smuggling s. contraban, m.
snack s. mossada, queixalada, f. refrigeri, m.
snail v. cargol (de terra) / llimac, m.
snake s. serp, serpent, f.
snapshot s. instantània (fotog.), f.
snare s. parany, m. trampa, f.
snarl s. regany, gruny, m. / to... v. rondinar, grunyir, remugar

sneeze s. esternut, m. / to... v. esternudar.
snob s. fatxenda, fanfarró, m.
snooze (to) v. dormisquejar.
snore (to) v. roncar.
snort (to) v. esbufegar, bufar
snout s. morro, musell, m.
snow s. neu, f. / to... v. nevar
snowfall s. nevada, f.
snowflake s. borralló, m. (de neu)
snuffle (to) v. parlar amb veu de nas / s. catarro nasal, m.
snug a. arrecerat -ada, còmode -a
so adv. així
soak s. remull, m., remullada, f.
soap s. sabó, m. / to... v. ensabonar
soar (to) v. enlairar-se, ascendir
sob (to) v. sanglotar
social a. social, m. -f.
socket s. punta, randa, f. / endoll, m.
soda s. soda / sosa, f.
soda water s. aigua carbònica, f. de sifó
soulful a. commovedor-a / espiritual, m.- f.
sofa a. sofà
soft a. tou -tova, tendre -a
softness s. blanor, blanesa, suavitat, f.
softly adv. suaument
soil s. sòl, terreny, m., terra, f.
soldier s. soldat, m.
sole s. planta del peu / sola (de sabata), f., llenguado (ict.), m. / a. un -a. únic -a / absolut -a
solid a. i s. sòlid -a
solidify (to) v. solidificar
solution s. solució, f.
solve (to) v. resoldre
solvent a. solvent, m.- f. / a. i s. dissolvent, m.
sombre a. obac -aga, ombríu -iva, ombrívol -a

199   **sombre**

some a. algun-a
somebody pron. algú
somehow adv. d'alguna manera, d'una manera o altra
someone a. algú / pron. algun -a
something pron. quelcom.
sometimes adv. de vegades, algunes vegades
son s. fill, m.
song s. cançó, f., cant, m.
son-in-law s. gendre, m.
sonnet s. sonet, m.
soon adv. aviat, prompte
sorcerer s. bruixot, m.
sorceress s. bruixa, fetillera, f.
sore a. adolorit -ida / macat -ada, / inflamat -ada, nafrat -ada / s. plaga, úlcera, nafra, f.
sorrow s. dolor, preocupació, aflicció, f.
sorrowful a. afligit-ida, apresarat -ada
sorry a. trist-a, apesarat-ada
sort s. espècie, classe / manera, f.
soul s. ànima, f.
sound s. so, m. / a. sa-sana, sòlid-a, / to... v. sonar
soup s. sopa, f.
sour a. agre-a, aspre-a, àcid-a / to... v. agrejar, amargar
south s. sud, m.
south-east s. sud-est, m.
southern a. meridional, austral, m.- f., del sud
south-west s. sud-oest, m.
souvenir s. recordatori, record, m.
sovereign s. i a. sobirà-ana
sow s. truja, f.
soya s. soja, f.
space s. espai, m.
spade s. pala, aixada, f. / espases (del joc de cartes), f.
Spanish a. espanyol -a
spanner s. (mec.) clau, f.
spare (to) v. excusar, escatimar

sparger s. regadora, f.
spark s. espurna, guspira, f.
sparkle s. centelleig, m., espurna, f. / to... v. centellejar, llampeguejar
sparrow s. pardal, m.
spatial a. espacial, m.- f.
speak (to) v. parlar
speaker s. orador / president d'algun cos legislatiu, m.
special a. especial, m. -f.
specify (to) v. especificar
specimen s. espècimen, exemplar, m., mostra, f.
spectacles s. ulleres, f. pl.
spectator s. espectador -a
spectre s. espectre, fantasma, m.
speech s. discurs, m.
speed s. velocitat, rapidesa, f. / to... v. pr. afanyar -se
speedy a. ràpid -a, accelerat -ada,
spell (to) v. lletrejar / encisar
spend (to) v. despendre, gastar
sphere s. esfera, f.
spice s. espècia, f.
spider s. aranya, f.
spin (to) v. filar
spine s. espinada / espina, f.
spinster s. soltera, conca, f.
spiral a. i s. espiral m.-f.
spire s. agulla, cúspide (arq.), f.
spirit s. esperit, m.
spit s. ast, rostidor, m. / saliva, f., esput, m. / to... v. escopir
spite s. rancor, despit, m.
spittle s. saliva, bava, f.
spittoon s. escopidora, f.
splotch s. taca, f. / to... v. tacar
spoil (to) v. malmetre, corrompre / espoliar
sponge s. esponja, f.
sponsor s. patrocinador, m. / padrí -ina, fiador-a
spontaneous a. espontani -ània
spoon s. cullera, f.

spoonful s. cullerada, f.

sport s. esport, m.

sportsman s. esportista, m.

spot s. lloc, indret, m.

spout s. canella, f., galet, m. / brollador, m. / aixeta, f. / raig, m.

spray s. escuma, ruixada, f. / polvoritzador, m. / to... v. polvoritzar

spread s. extensió, propagació, difusió, f. / to... v. estendre, propagar, estirar, desplegar

spring (to) v. sorgir, brollar, néixer, saltar

spring s. primavera, f. / ... **mattress** s. somier, m.

sprinkle s. ruixada, remullada, f. to... v. ruixar, remullar / espargir / plovisquejar

sprint s. esprint, m.

sprout (to) v. brotar, rebrotar

spy s. espia, m.- f. / to... v. espiar

square s. quadrat, quadre, m.

squash s. suc (de taronja, llimona, etc.) m. / to... v. esprémer, reprimir, suprimir, sofocar

squint-eyed a. guenyo -a, guerxo-a

squirrel a. esquirol, m.

stadium s. estadi, m.

stage s. escena, f., escenari, m. / grau, estat, m. / grada, f.

stain s. taca, f., tint, m. / to... v. tacar, acolorir, tenyir

stainless a. net-a / inoxidable, m.- f.

stair s. esglaó, graó, m.

staircase s. escala, f.

stalk s. tija, f. / to... v. caçar

stammer s. quequeig, m. / to... v. quequejar

stammerer s. quec -a

stamp s. segell de correus, timbre, m. / to... v. segellar, estampillar

stand s. lloc, m. / posició, f. / pedestal, m. / estrada / parada, tribuna, f. sòcol, peu, m. / resistència, f.

stand (to) v. tolerar, aguantar, suportar / to... for v. estar per, significar / to... up to v. defensar, recolzar / v. posar dempeus

standard s. norma, mesura, f., patró, contrast, m. / estendard, m., senyera, f.

standing a. dret -a, vertical, m.- f. / s. posició, situació, categoria, f.

staple s. grapa, f. / article principal, m. / primera matèria, f., rengló, m.

star s. estel, m., estrella, f.

starboard s. estribord, m.

starch s. midó, m. / to... v. emmidonar

stare s. mirada insistent, f. / to... v. mirar fixament

starfish s. estrella de mar, f.

start s. ensurt, sobresalt, esglai, m. / punt de partida / to... v. causar, provocar / començar / esglaiar-se

starvation s. fam, inanició, privació, f.

state s. estat, m. / to... v. manifestar, proposar.

statement s. declaració, relació, f. estat, m. / informe, m.

statesman s. estadista, m.

station s. lloc, post, m. / estació, f.

stationary a. estacionari -ària, immòbil, m.- f.

stationer s. paperer, llibreter, m.

stationery s. papereria, venda d'articles d'escriptori, f.

statue s. estàtua, f.

statuesque a. estatuari -ària / escultural, m.- f.

status s. posició, categoria, f., estat legal, m.

statute s. estatut, m., llei, f.
statutory a. estatutari -ària / legal, m.- f.
steady a. ferma, segur-a, estable, uniforme, m.-f.
steadily adv. fermament, de manera estable.
steak s. bistec, tall de carn, m.
steal (to) v. robar
steam s. vapor, m.
steamship s. vapor, vaixell de vapor, m.
steamer s. vaixell a vapor, m.
steel s. acer, m.
steelyard s. romana (balança), f.
steer (to) v. guiar, dirigir, conduir
steersman s. timoner, m.
stem s. tija, f., tany, pecíol, m.
step s. pas, llindar, graó, esglaó, m.
stepbrother s. germanastre, m.
stepdaughter s. fillastra, f.
stepfather s. padrastre, m.
stepmother s. madrastra, f.
stepsister s. germanastra, f.
stepson s. fillastre, m.
sterling a. veritable, excel·lent, m.- f. / **pound ...** s. lliura esterlina, f.
stern s. popa, f. / a. auster-a, sever-a, rígid -a
sterness s. severitat, austeritat, duresa, f.
stethoscope s. estetoscopi, m.
stew a. cuit-a, estofat-ada / **to...** v. estofar, guisar
steward s. administrador, majordom, m.
stewardess s. cambrera, assistenta, hostessa (de l'aire), f.
stick s. pal, bastó, m. / **to...** v. pegar, copejar
sticking plaster s. esparadrap, m.
sticky a. enganxós-osa, viscós-osa
stiff a. rígid -a, tor-forta, dur-dura, sòlid-a, encarcarat-ada.

stiffen (to) v. endurir, reforçar, endurir-se
still a. immòbil,m.- f., tranquil -il·la,, silenciós-osa, quiet-a / s. silenci, m., quietud, f. / adv. encara, si més no. / **to...** v. calmar, assossegar
stimulate (to) v. estimular
sting (to) v. picar, punxar
stir s. moviment, m., excitació, f. / aldarull, m. / **to...** v. agitar, remoure
stirring a. commovedor-a, impressionant, m.-f.
stirrup s. estrep, m.
stitch (to) v. cosir, embastar
stock s. soca, f., tronc, cep, m. / existències, f. pl. / **capital comercial**, m. / **... exchange** s. borsa, f.
stocking s. mitja, f.
stomach s. estómac, m.
stone s. pedra, f.
stool s. banc, tamboret, m. / inodor, m. / reclam, m.
stoop (to) v. pr. ajupir-se
stop s. parada, detenció, f. / **to...** v. detenir, deturar, parar-se.
storage s. magatzematge, dipòsit, m.
store s. botiga, f. magatzem, m. / **to...** v. emmagatzemar
storeroom s. rebost, m.
storied a. historiat -ada
stork s. cigonya, f.
storm s. tempesta, f.
story s. conte, m., faula, f. argument, m.
stout a. robust-a, corpulent-a
stove s. estufa, f., fogó, m.
stowaway s. polissó -ona
straight a. recte-a, dret-dreta.
strain s. tensió, f. / **to...** v. esforçar, apretar, prémer.
strainer s. colador, m.
strand s. platja, ribera, f. / ramal, m., trena, fibra, f.

strange a. estrany-a, rar-a / foraster-a

stranger s. estranger, estrany, foraster, m.

strangle (to) v. escanyar, estrangular

strap s. corretja, f.

straw s. palla, f.

strawberry s. maduixa, f.

stray a. esgarriat -ada, perdut -uda

streak s. ratlla, llista, f. / veta, f.

stream s. corrent / rierol, m., riera, f.

street s. carrer, m.

strength s. força, resistència, intensitat, f., vigor, m.

strengthen (to) v. enfortir, consolidar, reforçar

stress s. tensió, f. / accent, m. / to... v. accentuar, fer pressió

stretch s. extensió, f., eixamplament, m. / to... v. estirar, estendre

stretcher s. estirador, m. / llitera, f.

strict a. estricte -a

strike s. cop, m. / vaga, f.

striker a. vaguista, m.- f.

string s. cordó, cordill, enfilall, m.

strip (to) v. despullar, desvestir

stripe s. ratlla, llista, franja, f. / (mil.) galó, m.

strong a. fort -a, vigorós -osa

structure s. estructura, f. / edifici, m.

struggle s. lluita, f. / to... v. lluitar, pugnar

stub s. soca, f., rabassot, m. / punta de cigar, f.

student s. estudiant, m.

study s. estudi m. / to... v. estudiar

stuff (to) v. farcir, embotir, omplir

stumble s. ensopegada, f. / to... v. ensopegar, trompassar

stupid a. estúpid -a, atordit -ida, atabalat -ada

style s. estil, m., manera, f.

stylish a. elegant, m.- f., a la moda

subdue (to) v. subjugar, conquerir, sotmetre

subject s. súbdit / subjecte / assumpte, tema, m.

submarine s. submarí, m.

submit (to) v. sotmetre, rendir / presentar, exposar, oferir (una teoria, tesi)

substance s. substància, f.

substitute (to) v. substituir, suplir

subtle a. subtil, m. -f.

subtract (to) v. restar, sostreure

subtraction s. substracció, resta, f.

suburb s. suburbi, m.

succeed (to) v. reeixir, triomfar / succeir

success s. èxit, triomf, m.

such a. aital, semblant, m. -f. / pron. tal, un tal, m. / adv. tan

suck (to) v. xuclar

suckle (to) v. alletar

suckling s. nodrissó, lactant, m.

sudden a. sobtat -ada, de sobte

suffer (to) v. sofrir

suffice (to) v. bastar, satisfer

sufficient a. suficient, bastant, m.- f.

suffix s. sufix, m.

suffrage s. sufragi, vot, m.

sugar s. sucre, m.

suggest (to) v. suggerir, insinuar, aconsellar

suggestion s. suggestió, f. / suggeriment, m.

suit s. petició, f. / galanteig, m. / litigi, m. / vestit d'home, m.

suitable a. convenient, m.- f.

suiting s. roba per a vestits, f.

suitor s. pretendent-a / demandant, aspirant, m. -f.

sullen a. malagradós -osa, ressentit -ida, taciturn -a, insociable, m.- f.

sulphur s. sofre, m.

sulphureous a. sulfurós-osa

sum s. suma, quantitat, f. / to... v. sumar

summary s. resum, sumari, m.

summer s. estiu, m.

summit s. cim, m., cúspide, f.

sun s. sol, m.

Sunday s. diumenge, m.

sunder v. separació, f. / to... v. separar, apartar

sundial s. rellotge de sol, m.

sunflower s. gira-sol, m.

sunrise s. sortida (f.) del sol

sunset s. posta (f.) del sol

superior a. i s. superior / s. superior-ora

superiority s. superioritat, f.

supermarket s. supermercat, m.

supper s. sopar, m.

supply (to) v. proveir, fornir / suplir

support (to) v. recolzar, ajudar

supporter a. partidari-ària, sostenidor -a

suppose (to) v. suposar

suppress (to) v. suprimir, reprimir

sure a. cert -a, segur-a. / adv. certament

surely adv. certament, seguramment

surety s. seguretat, garantia, f.

surf s. ressaca, maror, marejada, f., tràngol, m.

surface s. superfície, f.

surgeon s. cirurgià, m.

surgery s. cirurgia, f.

surly a. malagradós -osa, malcarat -ada, sorrut- uda, aspre-a

surmount (to) v. superar, vèncer

surname s. cognom, m.

surpass (to) v. excedir, superar, eclipsar

surprise s. sorpresa, f.

surrender (to) v. rendir, lliurar

surround (to) v. rodejar, encerclar

surrounding a. circumdant, m.- f.

surroundings s. pl. rodalies, f., pl., encontorns, voltants, m. pl. / ambient, m.

survive (to) v. sobreviure / durar, perdurar

survivor a. i s. supervivent, sobrevivent, m. -f.

suspect (to) v. sospitar, recelar

suspend (to) v. suspendre

suspenders s. pl. lligacama, f., / elàstics, m. pl.

suspense s. incertesa, angoixa, f., dubte, m.

suspicious a. recelós-osa, sospitós-osa

sustain (to) v. recolzar / sustentar

swallow s. bocí, m., mossegada, f. / (orn.) oreneta, f. / (to) v. engolir, empassar-se

swamp s. pantà, aiguamoll, m.

swan s. cigne, m.

swarm s. eixam, formiguer, m.

swear (to) v. jurar / blasfemar

sweat s. suor, f. / to... v. suar

sweater s. suèter, m.

Sweden s. Suècia, f.

Swedish a. i s. suec -a

sweep (to) v. escombrar

sweepings s. escombraries, deixalles, f. pl.

sweet a. dolç -a

sweeten (to) v. ensucrar, endolcir

sweetness s. dolcesa, suavitat, f.

swell (to) v. inflar / embotir / v. pr. inflar-se / envanir-se, presumir

swelling s. inflor, protuberància, f., bony, m.

swift a. veloç, m.- f., ràpid-a
swim (to) v. nedar
swimmer s. nedador-a
swimming pool s. piscina, f.
swindle (to) v. estafar
swine s. porc, m. / brètol, bergant, m.
swing s. balanceig, gronxament, m., oscil·lació, f.
Swiss a. i s. suís -ïssa
switch s. vara, vareta, f. / trena, f. / interruptor, commutador, m. / agulla ferroviària, f. / to... v. desviar / commutar. / to... off v. desconnectar, apagar (un llum) / to... on v. encendre, connectar
swoon s. desmai, síncope, m.
swop s. bescanvi, intercanvi, m. / to... v. canviar, intercanviar, baratar
sword s. espasa, f.
swordfish s. peix espasa, m.
syllable s. síl·laba, f.
symbol s. símbol, m.
sympathetic a. simpàtic-a, compassiu-iva
sympathy s. simpatia, f. / compassió, condolença, f.
symphony s. simfonia, f.
symptom s. símptoma, indici, m.
syntax s. sintaxi, f.
synthesis s. síntesi, f.
syringe s. xeringa, f. / to... v. xeringar, injectar
syrup s. xarop, m.
system s. sistema, m.

T

table s. taula, f., tauler, m. / altiplà, planell, m. / ...-cloth s. estovalles, f. pl. / ...-linen s. joc de taula, m. / ...-tennis s. ping-pong, m.
tablespoon s. cullera, f.
tablet s. pastilla, f.
tack s. xinxeta, f. / to... v. embastar, cosir, unir
tact s. tacte, m., discreció, f.
tactics s. tàctica, f.
tactile a. palpable, tocable, m. f.
tadpole s. cap-gros, m.
tail s. cua, f.
tailor s. sastre, m.
tailoring s. sastreria, f.
taint s. taca, tara, f.
take (to) v. agafar, prendre / conquistar, ocupar / guanyar / to... advantage v. beneficiar-se, aprofitar-se / to... cover v. arrecerar, emparar / to... down v. baixar, despenjar / desmuntar / anotar / to... off v. marxar / arrencar, enlairar-se (un avió), treure's (la roba)
taking a. encisador -a, atractiu-iva, / s. afecció, inclinació, f..
talc s. talc, m.
tale s. conte, m.
talk s. conversa, xerrada, f., col·loqui, m. / to... v. parlar, conversar, xerrar
talkative a. parlador -a, xerraire, m.-f.
tall a. alt-alta, espigat -ada.
tallness s. talla, alçada, f.
tame a. domesticat -ada, mans-a / to... v. domesticar, amansir.
tamper (to) v. potinejar, tafanejar, espatllar / subornar.
tan a. cobrat -ada, torrat -ada / to... v. adobar, assaonar, / bronzejar.
tangerine s. mandarina, f.
tangle s. embolic, embull, m. / to... v. embolicar, embullar
tank s. tanc, dipòsit, m. / cisterna, f.

tankard s. catúfol, m.

tanner s. assaonador, adobador, m.

tantalize (to) v. temptar / fer gruar amb promeses impossibles

tap s. aixeta, f.

tape s. cinta, veta, f. / esparadrap, m. / ...measure s. cinta mètrica f. /... recorder s. magnetòfon, m.

taper s. espelma / candela, f., ciri, m.

tapestry s. tapís, m., tapisseria, f. / to... v. entapissar

tar s. quitrà, m. / to... v. enquitranar

tardy a. tardà -ana, lent -a

target s. blanc (de tir), objectiu, m.

tariff s. tarifa, f.

tarnish (to) v. deslluir, desenllustrar, entelar

tarry a. enquitranat -ada

tart a. àcid-a, agre -a, aspre -a / s. coca, f., pastís (de fruita), m. / amistançada, f.

task s. tasca, feina, f., / treball, m.

tasty a. saborós -osa, apetitós -osa

taste s. gust, m., sabor, m.-f., tast, tastet, m. / to... v. tastar

tasteful s. elegant, m. -f.

tavern s. taverna, f.

tax s. impost, m.

taxation s. tributació, f.

tea s. te, m.

teach (to) v. ensenyar, instruir

teacher s. mestre, professor, m.

teachings s. pl. ensenyament, m., doctrina, f.

team s. tir, tronc (de cavalls, etc.) / equip / grup, m.

teapot s. tetera, f.

tear s. llàgrima, f. / plor, m. / to... v. esquinçar, estripar,

esgarrapar / to... up v. trencar

tearful a. plorós-osa

tease s. burleta, m. / to... v. prendre el pèl

teaspoon s. cullareta, f.

teat s. mugró, m. / mamella, f.

technical a. tècnic -a

technician s. tècnic -a, especialista, m.- f., expert-a

teething s. dentició, f.

teetotaler a. abstemi -èmia

telegraph s. telègraf, m. / to... v. telegrafiar

telephone s. telèfon, m. / to... v. telefonar

telescope s. telescopi, m.

television s. televisió, f.

tell (to) v. dir, relatar

telling a. eficaç, notable, m. -f.

temerity s. temeritat, f.

temper s. geni, humor, tremp, m.

temperance s. moderació, temperança, f.

temperate a. moderat -ada, temperat -ada

temperature s. temperatura, f.

tempest s. tempesta, tempestat, f.

temple s. temple, m.

temporary a. temporer -a

temporize (to) v. temporitzar, contemporitzar

tempt (to) v. temptar, incitar, induir

temptation s. temptació, f.

tempter a. temptador -a

ten a. i s. deu, m. / desena, f.

tenacious a. tenaç, m. -f.

tenant s. resident, m. / llogater, arrendatari, m.

tend (to) v. tendir / atendre, tenir cura

tendency s. tendència, f.

tendentious a. tendenciós -osa

tender a. tendre-a, delicat -ada,

afectuós -osa. / to... v. entendrir, oferir

tenderness s. tendresa, delicadesa, f.

tendon s. tendó, m.

tennis s. tennis, m.

tense a. tibant, m.- f., tens -a, rígid -a/ s. temps (gram.), m.

tension s. tensió, f.

tent s. tenda (de càmping), f.

tentacle s. tentacle, m.

tentative s. temptativa, f.

tentatively adv. provisionalment / temptejant, experimentalment

tenuous a. tènue, subtil, m.- f.

tenth a. i m.- f. desè-ena / s. delme, m.

tepid a. tebi -tèbia

tergiversation s. tergiversació, f.

term s. terme, curs, període, m. / (gram.) terme, m. / to... v. donar nom

terminate (to) v. acabar, finir

termite s. tèrmits, m. pl.

termless a. il·limitat -ada

terrace s. terrat, m. / terrassa, f. / terraplè, m.

terrestrial a. terrestre, m.- f.

tertiary a. terciari -ària

terrible a. terrible, m. -f.

terribly adv. terriblement

territory s. territori, m.

terror s. terror, m.

test s. prova, f., assaig, experiment, m. / to... v. provar, assajar

testify (to) v. testificar.

testimony s. testimoni, m. / declaració, f.

test tube s. proveta, f.

text s. text / lema, m.

textbook s. llibre de text, m.

textile a. tèxtil, m. -f.

than conj. que

thank (to) v. agrair, regraciar

thankful a. agraït -ida

thankfulness s. agraïment, m., gratitud, f.

thanks s. gràcies, mercès, f. pl.

thanksgiving s. regraciament, m. / acció de gràcies, f.

that a. aqueix, aqueixa / aquell, aquella

thaw s. desglaç m. / to... v. desglaçar

the art. el, la, els, les, m. -f. sing. i pl.

theatre s. teatre, m.

theirs pron. pos. el seu, la seva, els seus, les seves, d'ells, d'elles, m. -f. sing. i pl.

them pron. els, les

theme s. tema, m.

themselves pron. ells mateixos, elles mateixes / si mateixos, si mateixes

then adv. aleshores, llavors

thence adv. d'allí, des d'allí / per conseqüent, per tal raó

theology s. teologia, f.

theorem s. teorema, m.

theoretical a. teòric -a

theoretically adv. teòricament, en teoria

theorist s. teòric -a

theory s. teoria, f.

therapeutics s. terapèutica, f.

there adv. aquí, ací, allí, allà

thereof adv. d'això, del mateix

thereupon adv. llavors / per tant, per conseqüent

thermometer s. termòmetre, m.

thesaurus s. tresor, m.

these pron. i adj. aquesta, aquestes, m. -f. pl.

thesis m. tesi, f.

they pron. ell, elles, m.-f. pl.

thick a. espès -essa, dens -a, gruixut -uda

thicken (to) v. espesseir

thickness s. espessor, f. gruix, m.

thief s. lladre, m.

thieve (to) v. robar, furtar
thigh s. cuixa, f.
thimble s. didal, m.
thin a. prim-a, subtil, m.- f.
thine pron. pos. teu, teva, teus, teves, m. -f., sing. i pl.
thing s. cosa, f., objecte, m.
think (to) v. pensar, reflexionar
thinker s. pensador, m.
third a. i m.- f. tercer -a
thirst s. set, f. / desig, anhel, m.
thirsty a. assedegat -ada
thirteen a. i s. tretze, m.
thirteenth a. i m.- f. tretzè-tretzena
thirty a. i s. trenta, m.
thirtieth a. i. m.- f., trentè-trentena
this pron. aquest, aquesta, m. -f.
thorn s. espina, punxa, f.
thorough a. complet -a, sencer -a
thoroughfare s. via pública, f., pas públic, m.
those pron. i adj. aquells, aquelles, m. -f. pl.
thou pron. tu
though conj. encara que, si bé
thoughtful a. pensarós -osa, seriós -osa
thought s. pensament, m.
thousand a. i. s. mil, m.- f.
thousandth a. i. s. m.- f. milè-milena
thrash (to) v. desgranar, batre / apallissar, fustigar
thread s. fil, m., fibra, f. / to... v. enfilar
threat s. amenaça, f.
threaten (to) v. amenaçar
three a. i s. tres, m.
threshold s. llindar, marxapeu, m.
thrift s. economia, sobrietat, f.
thrifty a. estalviador -a, sobri -sòbria
thrill s. emoció, f. estremiment,

m. / to... v. emocionar, estremir
thriller s. novel·la (f.) de gran emoció o misteri
thrilling a. emocionant m.- f., commovedor -a, apassionant, m.- f.
thrive (to) v. prosperar, créixer
throat s. gola, gorja, gargamella, f.
throb (to) v. bategar
thrombosis s. trombosi, f.
throne s. tron, m., corona, reialesa, f.
throng s. multitud, gentada, f.
throttle s. gargamella, f., ganyot, m. / to.. v. ofegar, escanyar, estrangular
through a. totalment, de cap a cap/ adv. a través, fins al final / prep. per, per mitjà de
throughout av. arreu, pertot, pertot arreu
throw (to) v. llençar
thumb s. polze, m.
thump s. trompada, patacada, f.
thunder s. tro / estrèpit, m. / to... v. tronar
thunderstorm s. tronada, tempesta, f.
Thursday s. dijous, m.
thyme s. farigola, f.
ticket s. bitllet, m.
tickle (to) v. pessigollejar /tenir pessigolles
tickling s. pessigolles, f. pl.
tidiness s. endreç, m., netedat, pulcritud, f.
tidings s. pl. notícies, noves, f. pl., informes
tidy a. net -a / polit -ida / pulcre-a / to... v. netejar, endreçar
tie s. corbata, f.
tie (to) v. destorbar, limitar, restringir / lligar, enllaçar / to... a bow v. fer un llaç.

tiger s. tigre, m.

tight a. compacte-a estret -a, ata-peït-ïda

tightness s. tensió / estretor / impermeabilitat, f.

tighten (to) v. tibar, estrènyer, tensar

tile s. teula / rajola, f.

till prep. fins / conj. fins que / to... v. llaurar, conrear

tilt (to) v. inclinar, decantar

timber s. fusta, f. / fustam, m.

time s. temps, m.

timetable s. horari, m. / programa (m.) esmentant dies i hores

tin s. estany, m. / llauna, f.

tingle s. frisança, f. / to... v. sentir formigueig / v. pr. esgarrifar-se.

tinker s. llauner, estanyador, m.

tinkle s. tritlleig, m., dringadissa, f.

tinplate s. llauna, f.

tinsel s. oripell, m., quincalla, f.

tint s. tint, matís / color, m. / mitja tinta, f. / to... v. tenir / matisar.

tiptoe s. punta del peu, m. / adv. de puntetes.

tire (to) v. fastiguejar, enfastidir

tired a. cansat -ada

tiredness s. cansament, m.

tireless a. incansable, infatigable, m.- f.

tiring a. molestós-osa, fatigós -osa, esgotador -a

tissue s. teixit, m.

title s. títol, m., inscripció, f. / to... v. titular

to prep. a, envers, cap a, vers / per a

toad s. gripau, m.

toast (to) v. brindar / torrar

tobacco s. tabac, m.

tobacconist s. estanquer -a. / venedor de tabac.

toboggan s. tobogan, m.

today adv. avui

toddle s. tentines, f., pl. / to... v. tentinejar

toe s. dit del peu, m. / ungla, f., unglot, m.

together adv. juntament / ensems

toil s. treball, m. / fatiga, f. / to... v. treballar durament / atrafegar-se, escarrassar-se

toilet s. toaleta, f. / pentinat, m. / torrent, m. / torrentada, f. escorredor, m.

token s. senyal, detall, indici, m. / penyora, f.

tolerance s. tolerància, f.

tolerate (to) v. tolerar

toll s. peatge, m.

tomato s. tornàquet, m.

tomb s. tomba, f. / to... v. enterrar, soterrar.

tomorrow adv. demà

ton s. tona, f.

tonality s. tonalitat, f.

tone s. to, m. / matís, m., tonalitat, f.

tongs s. pl. tenalles, f. pl. / molls, m. pl. / pinces, f. pl.

tongue s. llengua, f. / idioma, m.

tonight adv. anit, aquesta nit

tonnage s. tonatge, m.

tonsils s. amígdales, f. pl.

too adv. massa, excessivament / també

tool s. eina, f.

tooth s. dent, f., queixal, m.

toothache s. mal de queixal, m.

toothbrush s. raspallet per a les dents, m.

top s. cap, cim, m. / punta, f.

topaz s. topazi, m.

top hat s. copalta, barret, barret de copa, m.

topic s. assumpte, tema, m., qüestió a tractar, f.

topple (to) v. enderrocar / v. pr. enderrocar-se

torch s. torxa, atxa, f.

torment s. turment, m.

torment (to) v. turmentar

tornado s. tornado, m.

torpedo s. torpede, m.

torpid a. apàtic -a, ensopit -ida / parat -ada, aturat -ada

tortoise s. tortuga, f.

torrent s. torrent, m. / torrentada, f.

torture (to) v. torturar

toss (to) v. sacsejar, batzegar, sotragar / llançar enlaire

total a. i s. total, tot, m., / s. suma, f.

totalitarian a. totalitari -ària

totally adv. totalment, completament

totter (to) v. trontollar, tentinejar

touch s. toc, tacte, contacte, m. / to ...v. tocar, palpar

touching a. patètic -a, commovedor -a

touchy a. primmirat-ada, susceptible, m. -f.

tough a. fort -a / resistent, m. -f. / dur -a / rude, m. -f.

toughen (to) v. endurir, enfortir / enfortir-se

toughness s. tenacitat, resistència, duresa, f.

tour s. viatge, m. / excursió / sortida, f. / visita, inspecció, f. / to... v. viatjar

tourism s. turisme, m.

tourist s. turista, m.-f.

tourney s. torneig, m.

tow (to) v. remolcar

towards prep. envers, devers, cap a

towel s. tovallola, f.

tower s. torre, f.

town s. ciutat, vila, població f. / ...council s. ajuntament, con-

sell municipal, m., municipalitat, f. / ...hall s. casa de la ciutat, alcaldia, f.

townsfolk s. pl. ciutadans, veïns d'un poble, m. pl.

toy s. joguina, f.

trace s. rastre m., emprempta, petja, f. / to ...v. rastrejar

trachea s. tràquea, f.

track s. empremta, petjada / pista, sendera, f.

traction s. tracció, f.

tractor s. tractor, m.

trade s. comerç / ofici, gremi, m.

trader s. comerciant, tractant, m.

tradesman s. botiguer, comerciant, m.

trade-union s. sindicat, gremi, m.

tradition s. tradició, f.

traduce (to) v. calumniar, difamar

traffic s. circulació, f. / tràfic, moviment, m. / ...lights s. pl. semàfors, m. pl.

tragedy s. tragèdia, f.

trail s. rastre, m. pista, f. / sendera, f.

trailer s. remolc, m.

trainer s. entrenador, preparador / domador, m.

train s. tren / seguici, m. / to... v. entrenar, ensinistrar

training s. ensinistrament, entrenament, m., preparació, f.

trait s. tret, caràcter, m. / particularitat, f.

traitor s. traïdor-a

tram, tramway s. tramvia, m.

tramp s. caminada, f. / vagabund, m.

trance s. èxtasi, embadaliment, m. / hipnosi, f.

transfer s. transferència, f. / traspàs, m.

transfer (to) v. transferir, traspassar, cedir

transit s. trànsit, m.

translate (to) v. traduir, interpretar

translation s. traducció, f.

translator s. traductor-a

transmit (to) v. transmetre

transport s. transport, m., /

transport (to) v. transportar

transporter a. transportador -a.

transubstantiation s. transsubstanciació, f.

transverse a. transversal, m. -f., transvers-a

trapeze s. trapezi (gimn.), gronxador, m.

trap s. trampa, f., parany, m.

trapezium s. trapezi (mat.), m.

trash s. fullaraca, f. / endergues, f. pl.

travel s. viatge, m. / to... v. viatjar

traveller s. viatger-a

traverse s. travessia, travessada, f. / to... v. travessar, creuar

tray s. safata, f.

treachery s. traïció, traïdoria, falsedat, f.

tread s. trepig, m. / to... v. trepitjar

treadle s. pedal, m.

treason s. traïció, f.

treasure s. tresor, m.

treasurer s. tresorer-a

treasury s. erari, m., tresoreria, f., finances, f. pl.

treat s. homenatge, obsequi, convit, m. / to... v. tractar, convidar, obsequiar

treatise s.tractat, m.

treatment s. tracte, tractament, m.

treaty s. tractat, conveni, m.

treble a. triple, s. / (mús.) tiple, f. / to... v. triplicar

tree s. arbre, m.

tremble (to) v. tremolar, estremir-se

trench s. fossat, m., rasa, f. / (mil.) trinxera, f.

trend s. tendència / direcció, f., curs, m.

trespass s. infracció, culpa, f. / to... v. infringir, delinquir

trial s. procés, judici, m. / prova, f., assaig, m

triangle s. triangle, m.

tribe s. tribu, casta, f.

tribune s. tribuna, f. / tribú, m.

tribute s. tribut, m. / homenatge, elogi, m.

trick s. trampa, emboscada, f. / parany, giny, m. / truc, m., enganyifa, f.

tricycle s. tricicle, m.

trickle s. regalim, rajolí, m. / to... v. regalimar, degotar

tripod s. trespeus, trípode, m.

trifle s. bagatel·la, fotesa, f.

trifling a. insignificant, m. -f. sense importància

trigger s. gallet, disparador, m.

trill s. refilet, m. / to... v. refilar

trillion s. trilió, m.

trimester s. trimestre, m.

triumph s. triomf, m. / to... v. triomfar

trivet s. trespeus, trípode, m.

trolley s. trolei, m. / tauleta de rodes, f. / carret, m.

trolley bus s. troleibús, m.

trolley car s. tramvia, m.

trombone s. trombó, m.

troop s. tropa, f., escamot, m.

trophy s. trofeu, m.

tropics s. pl. tròpics, m. pl. / zona tropical, f.

troth s. veritat, fidelitat, f. / esposalles, f. pl.

troubadour s. trobador, m.

trouble s, molèstia, f., enuig, m. / to... v. molestar, enutjar

troubler s. pertorbador -a

troublesome a. molestós -osa enutjós -osa, empipador -a

trousers s. pantalons, m. pl
trowel s. remolinador, m.
truant a. gandul -a, dropo -a / s. truà, m.- f. bergant-a
truck s. carro, camió / canvi, intercanvi, bescanvi, m.
true a. veritable, m. -f. vertader -a, sincer -a
truffle s. tòfona, trufa, f.
truly adv. exactament, fidelment
trumpet s. trompeta, f.
truncheon s. garrot, m., porra, f. / bastó de comandament, m.
trunk s. tronc, m. / bagul, m. / trompa (de l'elefant), f.
trust s. confiança, f. / trust, m. / to... v. confiar
trusty a. fidel, lleial, íntegre-a
truth s. veritat, realitat, f.
truthful a. verídic -a, exacte -a / veraç, m. -f.
try (to) provar, intentar
tube s. tub / metro, ferrocarril subterrani, m.
tuber s. tubercle, tubèrcul, m.
tubing s. canalització, canonada, f.
Tuesday s. dimarts, m.
tug s. estrebada, estirada, f. / to... v. arrossegar, remolcar
tulip s. tulipa, f.
tumour s. tumor, m.
tune s. tonada, melodia f. / to ... v. entonar, afinar
tuner s. afinador, m.
tunic s. túnica, f.
tunnel s. túnel / embut, m.
tunny s. tonyina, f.
turbine s. turbina, f.
tureen s. sopera, f.
turf s. gespa / torba, f.
turkey s. gall dindi, m.
Turkish a. i s. turc -a
turmoil s. confusió, f., desordre, aldarull, m.
turn s. tomb, volt, passeig, m. / to... v. tombar, girar

turnip s. nap, m.
turnsole s. gira-sol, m.
turtle s. tortuga de mar, f.
turtledove s. tórtora, f.
tusk s. ullal (d'elefant, senglar o foca), m.
tweezers s. pl. pinces, f. pl.
twelfth a. i m. -f. dotzè -dotzena
twelve a. i s. dotze, m.
twentieth a. i. m. -f., vintè-vintena
twenty a. i s. vint, m.
twice adv. dos cops, dues vegades
twig s. branqueta, vareta, f.
twilight s. crepuscle, capvespre, m.
twin a. i s. bessó-ona
twinge s. punxada, f., dolor agut, m. / remordiment, m.
twinkle (to) v. centellejar, parpellejar, titil·lar
twist s. torsió, f. / to... v. trenar, tòrcer
twitter s. piuladissa, f. / agitació, inquietud, f. / to... v. piular, xerrotejar / agitar-se.
two a. i s. dos-dues
type s. tipus, m.
typewriter s. màquina d'escriure, f.
typhoon s. tifó, m.
typical s. típic -a, característic -a.
typist s. mecanògraf -a
typography s. tipografia, f.
tyrannize (to) v. tiranitzar.
tyranny s. tirania, f.
tyrant s. tirà, m.
tyre s. pneumàtic, m.
tzar s. tsar, m.

U

ugly a. lleig -lletja, malcarat -ada
ulcer s. úlcera, plaga, f.
ulcerous a. ulcerós -osa
ululate (to) v. ulular, udolar.
umbrella s. paraigües, m.
unable a. incapaç, m.-f.
unacceptable a. inacceptable, m. -f.
unaccountable a. inexplicable, m. -f.
unanimous a. unànime, m. -f.
unaptness s. ineptitud, f.
unarmed a. indefens -a, inerme, m.-f.
unavoidable a. inevitable, m.-f.
unaware a. ignorant / inconscient, m. -f.
unawares adv. d'improvís, inesperadament
unbearable a. insuportable, intolerable, m.-f.
unbeliever s. incrèdul-a, descregut -uda
unbending a. inflexible, m.-f.
unbroken a. intacte -a / inviolat -ada
uncanny a. misteriós -osa
uncertain a. incert -a
unclad a. despullat -ada, desvestit -ida
uncle s. oncle, m.
unclose (to) v. obrir / revelar
unconscious a. inconscient, m. -f.
uncover (to) v. destapar, descobrir
unction s. unció, f. / ungüent, m.
undamaged a. il.lès -esa, indemne, m.-f.
undaunted a. impàvid -a, impertèrrit -a

undecided a. indecís -isa, dubtós -osa
under adv. sota, dessota / a. inferior, m. -f. / ...aged a. menor d'edat
underclothes s. roba interior, f.
undercover a. secret -a / clandestí -ina
undergo (to) v. aguantar, soportar
underground s. metro, m. / a. subterrani -ània
underline (to) v. subratllar
undersign (to) v. sotasignar.
undersigned a. sotasignat -ada.
undershirt s. samarreta, f.
understand (to) v. capir, comprendre, entendre
understanding s. comprensió, f.
undertake (to) v. emprendre, intentar
underwear s. roba interior, f.
underwood s. sotabosc, m., brossa, malesa, f.
underworld s. infern, m. / xusma, f., baixos fons, m. pl.
undesirable a. indesitjable, m.-f.
undisputed a. evident, incontestable, m.-f.
undivided a. indivís -isa
undo (to) v. desfer, deslligar / anul·lar / destruir
undoing s. ruïna, perdició, f.
undue a. indegut -uda, il·lícit -a
undulate (to) v. ondular / fluctuar
unearthly a. sobrenatural, m. -f.
uneasiness s. inquietud, f.
uneasy a. inquiet -a, incòmode -a
unending a. inacabable, m. -f.
unequal a. desigual, m. -f.
unfold (to) v. desplegar
unglued a. desenganxat -ada, desencolat -ada
ungodly a. impiu -ia, impiadós -osa

unguarded a. indefens -a, desguarnit -ida
unhappy a. infeliç, m. -f., dissortat-ada
unhealthful a. insà-ana, malsà -ana
unhealthy a. malaltís -issa
uniform a. i s. uniforme, m.
unguent s. ungüent, m., untura, f. /
uninjured a. il·lès -esa, indemne, m.-f.
union s. unió, f.
unique a. únic -a
unit s. unitat, f.
unite (to) v. unir, ajuntar
unity s. unitat / unió, f.
universal a. universal, m.-f.
universe s. univers, m.
university s. universitat, f.
unkempt a. despentinat -ada, escabellat -ada
unkind a. adust -a, aspre -a, esquerp -a
unknown a. inconegut -uda, ignorat-ada
unless conj. llevat que, a menys que
unlike a. desigual, m. -f.
unlikely a. inversembl improbable, m.-f.
unload (to) v. descarregar, alleugerir
unmannered a. groller -a, rude, m. -f.
unmoved a. impassible, inalterable, indiferent, inamovible, m. -f.
unpick (to) v. descosir.
unpleasant a. desagradable, m. f.
unrest s. neguit, malestar, desassossec, m.
unsafe a. insegur -a
unsalable a. invendible, m.-f.
unseen a. invisible, m.-f.
untidy a. malendreçat-ada / brut-bruta.

until prep. fins.
untold a. desmesurat -ada, incalculable, m.-f.
untruth s. falsedat, infidelitat, f.
untutored a. inculte, m.-f.
unwell a. malaltís -issa / que no està gaire fr.
unworthy a. indigne -a.
up adv. dalt, amunt / up and down loc. adv. amunt i avall / pertot arreu / adv. cap amunt.
upkeep s. manteniment, conservació, f.
uplift (to) v. elevar, aixecar
upon prep. sobre, damunt, amb, de, prop de
upper a. superior, m.- f., més alt, m., més amunt
uproar s. gatzara, f., cridòria, f., enrenou, m.
uproot (to) v. desarrelar, extirpar
upset (to) v. bolcar, capgirar
upside-down a. a l'inrevés, de cap per avall, capgirat-ada
upstairs adv. a dalt, cap a dalt
upstream adv. riu amunt, aigua amunt
up-to-date a. modern -a, actual, m.-f.
upward a. ascendent, m.-f.
upwards adv. cap amunt, cara enlaire
uranium s. urani, m.
urban a. urbà-ana
urchin s. pillet, murri, m. / eriçó, m.
urge (to) v. apressar, urgir
urgency s. urgència, f.
urinal s. orinal, m., gibrelleta, f.
urinary s. orinador, urinari, m.
urine s. orina, f. / orins, m. pl.
urn s. urna, f.
us pron. ens, nos / nosaltres
usage s. tracte, m. / habitud, f.

use s. ús, costum, hàbit, m. / **to...**
v. usar, utilitzar, emprar / **to...**
up v. despendre, exhaurir.
useful a. útil, m.-f.
useless a. inútil, m. -f., inepte -a
usher s. uixer, conserge / acomo-
dador, m.
usurp (to) v. usurpar
usurpation s. usurpació, f.
usury s. usura, f.
utility s. utilitat, f.
utilize (to) v. utilitzar
utmost a. major m. -f., suprem -a,
el que més
utter a. complet- a, total m. -f.,
absolut -a
utterance s. pronunciació,
expressió, f.

V

vacancy s. buit / oci, lleure, m.
vacant a. vacant m. -f., buit-buida
/ disponible, lliure, m. -f.
vacation s. vacances, f. pl.
vaccinate (to) v. vacunar
vaccine s. vacuna, f.
vacillate (to) v. vacil·lar
vacillation s. vacil·lació f.
vacuity s. vacuitat, buidor, f.
vacuum a. vacu-vàcua, buit-buida
/ s. buit, m.
vagabond a. vagabund, m.
vagary s. capríci, m., extravagància, f.
vague a. vague - vaga, indetermi-
nat -ada
vagueness s. vaguetat, f.
vain a. va -vana / vanitós -osa /
fatxenda, m. / inútil, m. -f.
vainly adv. vanament
valet s. servent, m.
valiant a. valent -a, intrèpid -a.

valid a. vàlid -a.
validity s. validesa, f.
valise s. maleta, valisa, f.
valley s. vall, f.
valour s. valor, coratge, m.
valuable a. valuós -osa
value s. vàlua. f., preu, m. / **to...** v.
avaluar.
valuer s. taxador-a.
valve s. vàlvula, f.
vamp s. empenya, pala del calçat,
f. / s. vampiressa, f. / **to...** v. flir-
tejar.
vampire s. vampir, m.
van s. camioneta, f., furgoneta,
f.
vane s. penell, gallet, m.
vanguard s. avantguarda, f.
vanilla s. vainilla, f.
vanish (to) v. esfumar-se, desaparèixer
vanity s. vanitat, f.
vanquish (to) v. conquerir, vèncer, sotmetre
vanquisher s. vencedor, m.
vantage s. avantatge, m.
vaporous a. vaporós -osa
vapour s. vapor, m.
variable a. variable, m.- f.
variably adv. variablement
variance s. discòrdia, desavinença, f.
variation s. variació, f.
variegated a. bigarrat -ada, jas-
piat -ada
variety s. varietat, f. assortit, m.
variola s. verola, f.
various a. vari -vària, divers -a
diferent, m. -f.
varnish s. vernís m. / **to...** v.
envernissar
varnisher s. envernissador -a
vary (to) v. variar / discrepar
vase s. gerro, pitxer, m.
vaseline s. vaselina, f.
vassal s. vassall, m.
vast a. vast-vasta, immens-a.

vastness s. vastitud, immensitat, f.

vault s. cripta, f., soterrani, m. / volta, f., arc, m.

veal s. vedella (vianda), f.

vegetable a. vegetal, m.- f. / verdura, f. / llegum, m.

vegetarian a. vegetarià -ana

vegetate (to) v. vegetar

vegetation s. vegetació, f.

vehemence s. vehemència, f.

vehicle s. vehicle, m.

veil s. vel, m.

vein s. vena, f.

velleity s. vel·leïtat, f.

velocity s. velocitat, f.

velvet s. vellut, m.

velvety a. vellutat -ada

venality s. venalitat, f.

vendue s. subhasta, f.

venerate (to) v. venerar

veneration s. veneració, f.

vengeance s. venjança, f.

vengeful a. venjatiu -iva

venom s. metzina, f., verí, m.

vent s. respirall, m., sortida, f.

ventilate (to) v. ventilar

ventilation s. ventilació, f.

ventilator s. ventilador, m.

venture s. aventura, f. / to... v. aventurar, arriscar

venturer s. aventurer -a

veracious a. verídic -a, veritable, m.-f.

veracity s. veracitat, f.

verandah s. galeria, terrassa / veranda, f.

verbatim a. i adv. paraula per paraula, literalment.

verdancy s. verdor, f.

verdict s. veredicte, m.

verdure s. verdura, verdor, f.

verge s. marge, límit, m., vora, f.

verification s. verificació, f.

verify (to) v. verificar, comprovar

veritable a. veritable, m.-f.

verity s. veritat / realitat, f.

vermicelli s. fideus, m. pl.

vermin s. vermina, f. / paràsits, m. pl., munió d'insectes, f.

vermouth s. vermut, m.

vernal a. vernal, primaveral, m. -f.

versatile a. versàtil / adaptable, flexible, m. -f. / polifacètic -a

verse s. vers / versicle, m.

versed a. versat -ada, coneixedor -a.

versify (to) v. versificar

version s. versió, traducció, f.

versus prep. contra / vers, devers

vertebrate a. vertebrat -ada

vertex s. vèrtex, m.

vertical a. vertical, m. -f.

vertically adv. verticalment

vertiginous a. vertiginós -osa

very adv. molt / a. idèntic -a / ... much loc. adv. moltíssim.

vespers s. vespres, f. pl., vigília, vetlla, f.

vessel s. vaixell / vas, atuell, m.

vest s. armilla, jaqueta, f.

vestry s. sagristia, f.

veteran a. i s. veterà -ana.

veterinary a. i s. veterinari -ària

vex (to) v. vexar, fastiguejar

vexatious a. vexatori -òria, provocatiu -iva

viaduct s. viaducte, m.

vial s. flascó, m. ampolleta, f.

viands s. pl. viandes, menjars selectes, m. pl.

vibrate (to) v. vibrar

vibration s. vibració, f.

vicar s. vicari, m.

vicarage s. vicaria, f.

vice s. vici, defecte, m.

viceroy s. virrei, m.

vicinity s. veïnatge, m., proximitat, rodalia, f.

vicious a. viciós -osa, pervers -a, depravat -ada

vicissitude s. vicissitud, peripè-
cia, f.
victim s. víctima, f.
victor s. vencedor -a
victorious a. victoriós -osa
victory s. victòria, f.
victual s. vitualles, f. pl. to... v. avituallar.
victuals s. vitualles, f. pl.
view s. vista, perspectiva, f., paisatge, panorama, m. / to... v.
mirar, examinar
vigil s. vetlla, vigília, f.
vigilance s. vigilància, f.
vigour s. vigor, m.
vile a. vil, m. -f., pervers -a
vileness s. vilesa, f.
vilify (to) v. difamar
villa s. vil·la, f., xalet, m.
village s. poble, llogaret, m.
vindicate (to) v. vindicar
vine s. cep, m., parra, f. / (bot.)
enfiladissa, f.
vinegar s. vinagre, m.
vineyard s. cep, m., vinya, f.
vintage s. verema, f.
vintner s. vinater -a, taverner -a
viol s. (mús.) viola, f.
violate (to) v. violar
violence s. violència, f.
violent a. violent -a
violet a. i s. violeta, m.-f.
violin s. violí, m.
violinist s. violinista, m.-f.
violoncello s. violoncel, m.
viper s. escurçó, m., víbra, f.
virgin s. verge, donzella, f.
virous a. verinós -osa
virtue s. virtut, f.
virtuous a. virtuós -osa
virtuoso s. virtuós (mús.), m.
visa s. visat, m.
viscount s. vescomte, m.
visible a. visible, m. -f.
visibility s. visibilitat, f.
visit s. visita, f. / to... v. visitar
visitor s. visitant, m. -f.

visor s. visera, f.
vitality s. vitalitat, f.
vitally adv. vitalment, essencial-
ment
vitals s. pl. parts vitals, f. pl.
vitamin a. vitamínic -a. / s. vitamina f.
vitreous a. vidriós -osa, vítric
-a
vitrify (to) v. vitrificar.
vituperation s. vituperi, blasme,
m.
viz (abr. de videlicet) adv. és a dir,
a saber.
vizor s. visera, f.
vocabulary s. vocabulary, m.
vocal a. vocal, oral, m.-f.
vocation s. vocació, f.
vocative s. vocatiu.
vogue s. moda, f.
voice s. veu, f.
void a. buit -buida, vacant, m. -f.
/ nul -nul·la, invàlid -a
volcano s. volcà, m.
volition s. volició, voluntat, f.
volley s. descàrrega (d'armes de
foc), salva, f.
voltage a. voltatge, m.
voluble a. parlador -a, xerraire,
m.- f.
volume s. volum, m.
voluntary a. voluntari -ària,
espontani -ània
volunteer s. voluntari -ària
voluptuous a. voluptuós -osa
voracious a. voraç, m. -f.
vortex s. vòrtex, remolí, m.
votary a. devot -a
vote s. vot, parer, m. / to... v.
votar
voter s. elector -a
voting s. votació, f.
votive a. votiu-iva
vouch (to) v. testimoniar, certificar
voucher s. comprovant, res-
guard, m.

vow s. vot, m., prometença, f.
vowel a. vocal, m.-f. / s. vocal, f.
voyage (to) v. viatjar, navegar
voyager s. vitager -a, viatjant, m.
-f.
vulgarity s. vulgaritat, f.
vulture s. voltor, m.

W

wabble s. balanceig, balandreig, m.
wad s. borra, buata, f.
wadding s. entretela, f., contrafort, m.
wag (to) v. remenar, moure
wager s. aposta, juguesca, f. / to... v. apostar
wages s. salari, sou, m. / honoraris, m. pl.
wagon s. carro, vagó, m
waggon s. vagó, m.
wail (to) v. deplorar, lamentar
waist s. cintura, f.
waistcoat s. armilla, f.
wait (to) v. esperar.
waiter s. cambrer, mosso m.
waiting s. espera, f.
waiting room s. sala d'espera, antesala, f.
waitress s. cambrera, f.
waive (to) v. renunciar, repudiar
wake (to) v. desvetllar, excitar
walk s. passeig, m., caminada, f. / to ... v. passejar, caminar
walker s. passejant, vianant, m.-f.
wall s. paret, f., mur, m.
wallet s. sarró, m., alforja, f. / cartera, f.
walnut s. nou / noguera, f.
walrus s. morsa, f.
waltz s. vals, m. / to... v. valsar
wan a. pàl·lid-a, descolorit -ida
wand s. vareta, batuta, f.

wander (to) v. vagar, rondar.
wanderer s. vagabund, rodamón. m.
wane s. minva, decadència, f. / to... v. minvar
want s. necessitat, manca, f. / to... v. voler / tenir mancança de
wanton a. enjogassat -ada, entremaliat -ada / desenfrenat -ada / pervers-a, insensible, cruel, m.- f.
war s. guerra, f.
warble (to) v. refilar, trinar
ward s. pupil, m. / barri, m. barriada, f. / sector (en un hospital) guarda, custòdia, f. / to... v. guardar, custodiar
warder s. escarceller, m.
wardrobe s. guarda-roba, armari, m.
wardship s. tutela, f., pupil·latge, m.
ware s. vaixella, pisa, f.
warehouse s. magatzem, dipòsit, m.
wares s. pl. mercaderies, f. pl.
warlike a. guerrer-a, bèl·lic-a, militar, marcial, m.- f.
warm a. calent -a, càlid -a / to... v. escalfar.
warming pan s. escalfador, escalfallits, m.
warmly adv. efusivament, afectuosament, amb entusiasme
warmth s. calor, escalfor, f. / efusió, f., afecte, m.
warn (to) v. avisar, prevenir / amonestar
warning s. avís, m., amonestació, advertència, f.
warrant s. ordre judicial / lliurament, m. / to... v. garantir, autoritzar
warranty s. garantia, f.
warren s. conillera, lludriguera, f.
warrior s. guerrer, m.

warship s. vaixell de guerra, m.
wart s. berruga, f.
wary a. caut-a, cautelós -osa, prudent, m.- f.
wash (to) v. rentar / banyar / regar
washer s. rentador, m. / (mec.) arandela, virolla, f.
washerwoman s. rentadora, bugadera, f.
washing place s. safareig / rentador, m.
washstand s. lavabo, m.
washy a. aigualit -ida, diluït -ida
wasp s. vespa, f.
waste (to) v. malgastar, dilapidar
waste s. rebuig, m., rampoina, f. / a. desolat -ada, arruïnat -ada / s. malversació, pèrdua, f.
wasteful a. dilapidador -a / ruïnós-osa, antieconòmic -a
wastefulness s. prodigalitat, malversació, f.
waste pipe s. tub de desguàs, m., canonada, f.
waster s. article defectuós, rebuig, m. / malgastador -a
wastrel s. perdut -uda, dilapidador-a
watch s. guarda, guàrdia, vigilància, f. / rellotge de butxaca, de polsera, m. / to... v. vigilar, observar
watchful a. vigilant, m.- f. observador -a / desvetllat -ada
watchmaker s. rellotger, m.
watchman s. vigilant, guarda, guardià, m.
water s. aigua, f. / to... v. regar / abeurar
water bottle s. cantimplora, f.
watercolour s. aquarel·la, f.
waterfall s. cascada, f., saltant, m.
watering s. regatge, reg, m., irrigació, f.

watering can s. regadora, f.
water lily s. nenúfar, m.
waterman s. barquer, m.
watermelon s. síndria, f.
water pipe s. canella, f., canonada, conducció d'aigua, f.
waterproof a. i s. impermeable, m. -f.
waterwheel s. sínia, roda hidràulica, f.
watery a. aquós-osa / aigualit-ida.
watt s. vat, m.
wave s. ona, onada, f. / to.. v. onejar
waver (to) v. oscil·lar
wax s. cera, f.
wax paper s. paper encerat, parafinat, m.
way s. via, f., camí, m.
wayside s. vora del camí, vorera, f.
wayward a. volenterós -osa / entremaliat -ada, rebel.m.- f.
we pron. nosaltres, m.-f., pl.
weak a. dèbil, m.- f., delicat -ada
weaken (to) v. debilitar
weakness s. debilitat, fluixedat, f.
weal s. benestar, m.
wealth s. riquesa, opulència, f.
wealthy a.
wean (to) v. deslletar, desmamar
weapon s. arma, f.
wear (to) v. usar, portar, fer servir / deteriorar, desgastar
weariness s. cansament, m.
weary a. cansat -ada, fastiguejat -ada. / to... v. cansar, fastiguejar
weasand s. gargamella, f.
weasel s. mostela, f.
weather s. temps (meteor.), m.
weather vane s. girell, penell, m.
weave (to) v. teixir, trenar
weaver s. teixidor-a

web s. tela, xarxa, f./ rotlle (de paper), m.
wed (to) v. casar / v. pr. casar-se.
wedding s. boda, noces, f.
wedge s. falca, f., tascó, m.
wedlock s. matrimoni, m.
Wednesday s. dimecres, m.
wee a. petit-a, menut -uda, diminut -a
weed s. mala herba, cugula, f.
week s. setmana, f.
weekday s. dia feiner, laborable, m.
weekend s. fi de setmana, cap de setmana, m.
weep (to) v. plorar.
weft s. trama (d'un teixit) / (fig.) xarxa, f.
weigh (to) v. pesar, sospesar
weight s. pes, m., càrrega, f. / to... v. carregar
weir s. resclosa, presa, f.
weird a. sobrenatural, m.- f., fantàstic -a
welcome s. benvinguda, f.
weld (to) v. soldar / unir.
welding s. soldadura, f.
welfare s. benestar, m., prosperitat, f.
well adv. bé, ben / s. pou, m.
wellingtons s. botes de goma, f. pl.
Welsh a. i s. gal·lès -esa
wen s. llúpia, f.
west s. oest, ponent, occident, m.
western a. occidental, m.- f.
westwards adv. cap a l'oest, a l'oest
wet a. humit -ida, mullat -ada, / to... v. humitejar, mullar
wetness s. humitat, f.
whale s. balena, f.
whaler s. balener, m.
wharf s. dàrsena, f. / moll / embarcador, m.

what? pron. què?
whatever pron. qualsevol
wheat s. blat, m.
wheedle (to) v. afalagar
wheel s. roda, f. / disc, m. / to... v. rodar
wheelbarrow s. bolquet, carretó, m.
wheelman s. timoner, m.
wheelwright s. carreter, m.
wheeze (to) v. panteixar
wheezing s. panteix, m.
whelp s. cadell, m.
when adv. quan, on
whence adv. d'on, des d'on / de què, de qui
whenever adv. quan calgui que, sempre que, sempre que calgui
where? adv. on?
whereas conj. considerant, mentre que, ensems que / contràriament
wherefore adv. per què / per tant
wherever adv. on sigui que, onsevulla que.
whet (to) v. esmolar, afilar.
which pron. qui, quin -a, pron. rel. que, el qual, els quals, les quals
whichever a. qualsevol, qualsevulla
whiff s. bufada / alenada, f.
while adv. mentre / s. estona, f.
whilst a. estona, f., temps, m. / conj. mentre, encara que
whim s. caprici, antull, m., fal·lera, f., rampell, m.
whimsical a. capriciós -osa
whine s. gemec, ploricó, m. / to... v. gemegar, ploriquejar
whinny s. renill, m. / to... v. renillar
whip s. fuet, m., tralla, f., xurriaques, f. pl. / to... v. fuetejar, assotar

whirl s. giravolt, remolí, m. / to...
v. giravoltar

whirlpool s. terbolí, remolí,
xuclador, m.

whisk s. batedor, remenador, m.

whiskers s. patilles, f. pl. / bigo-
tis, m. pl.

whisky s. whisky, m.

whisper s. xiuxiueig, murmuri,
m. / to... v. xiuxiuejar, mormo-
lar

whistle s. xiulet, m. / to... v. xiular

white a. blanc-blanca.

whiten (to) v. emblanquir, emblanquinar.

whiteness s. blancor, f.

whither adv. a on?, cap a on?,
fins a on?

whitlow s. voltadits, panadís, m.

Whitsuntide s. Pentecosta, f.

who pron. qui

whoever pron. qualsevol que /
quisvulla que.

whole a. tot-tota m.-f., sencer -a /
s. totalitat, f.

wholesale s. venda (f.) al major,
a l'engròs

wholesome a. sa -ana / saludable
m.- f., salutífer-a, sanitós-osa

wholly adv. totalment, completament

whose pron. del qual, de la qual,
de qui, de quina, m.-f.

why? conj. per què?

wick s. ble, m.

wicked a. pervers -a, malvat
-ada

wickedness s. maldat, impietat,
f.

wicker s. vímet, m.

wicket s. finestreta, portella, f.

wide a. ample-a, extens-a, vast.

widespread a. ample-a, estès-
-esa

widely adv. àmpliament, extensa-
ment

widen (to) v. eixamplar, estendre

wideness s. amplària, f.

widow s. vídua, f.

widower s. vidu, m.

width s. amplada, extensió,
amplària, f.

wield (to) v. manejar / manar

wife s. esposa, muller, f.

wig s. perruca, f.

wild s. salvatge, m.- f., agrest -a

wilderness s. desert, erm, m. /
soledat, f.

wiles s. pl. enganys, ardits, artifi-
cis, fraus, m. pl.

wilful a. volenterós -osa / tossut
-uda

will s. voluntat / resolució, f.

willing a. servicial, complaent,
amatent, m.- f.

willingly, adv. de bon grat, gustosament, volenterosament

willow s. salze, m.

win (to) v. vèncer, triomfar,
guanyar

wind s. vent / alè, m. / respir /
esbufec, m. / to... v. ventilar,
bufar / debanar

windig staircase s. escala de cargol, f.

window s. finestra / vidriera,
f.

windmill s. molí de vent / molinet, m.

wind up (to) v. donar voltes, cargolar / donar corda al
rellotge

wine s. vi, m.

wing s. ala, f.

wink s. parpelleig, m. / to... v.
parpellejar

winner s. guanyador -a, vencedor -a

winning s. guany, m.

winnow (to) v. ventar, ventejar

winsome a. atractiu -iva, encisador -a

winter s. hivern, m.

wipe (to) v. eixugar / assecar

wire s. filferro, m., fil (m.) o corda (f.) metàl·lics / telègraf, telegrama, m. / to... v. telegrafiar

wireless s. telegrafia sense fils, ràdio, f.

wisdom s. saviesa, f. seny, m.

wise s. savi-sàvia, assenyat -ada

wisely adv. assenyadament, prudentment, raonablement

wish s. desig, deler, m. / to... v. desitjar.

wistful a. trista / pensarós -osa, f.

wit s. enginy, sentit, m., gràcia, f.

witch s. bruixa, f. / to... v. embruixar

with prep. amb

withdraw (to) v. retirar

withdrawal s. retirada, f.

wither (to) v. marcir-se

withhold (to) v. retenir, reprimir, suspendre

within prep. dintre de

without prep. sense

withstand (to) v. resistir, oposar

witness s. testimoni, m. -f. / to... v. testimoniar, atestar

witty a. enginyós -osa, faceciós -osa

wizard s. bruixot, m.

woe s. dolor, m.-f., aflicció, f.

wolf s. llop, m.

woman s. dona, f.

womb s. matriu, f., úter, m. / si, m.

wonder s. meravella, f. / to... v. meravellar-se

wonderer s. admirador -a.

wonderful a. meravellós -osa.

woo (to) v. festejar, galantejar

wood s. fusta, llenya, f. / bosc, m., forest, f.

woodman s. llenyataire, guardabosc, m.

wooer s. galantejador, pretendent, m.

wool s. llana, f.

woolen a. de llana

woolly a. llanut -uda

word s. paraula, f., mot, m.

work s. obra, f., treball, m. / to... v. treballar

workable a. pràctic -a, factible, m.- f.

workday s. dia feiner, laborable

worker s. treballador -a, obrer -a, productor -a

workshop s. obrador, taller, m.

world s. món, m., terra, f. / ...wide a. mundial, universal, m.- f.

worm s. cuc, verm, m.

worry s. preocupació, inquietud / angoixa, f. / to... v. preocupar, capficar-se

worried a. angoixat -ada, preocupat -ada

worse adv. pitjor.

worship (to) v. adorar, venerar

worst a. pèssim-a, dolentíssim-a, / adv. pèssimament

worth s. mèrit, preu, m., vàlua, importància, f.

worthily adv. dignament, merescudament

worthy a. digne -a, mereixedor -a /adient, m.- f.

worthless a. indigne-a, menyspreable, inútil, m.- f.

worthwhile a. valuós -osa, útil, m.- f., digne-a de consideració

wound s. ferida, ofensa, f. / to... v. ferir / ofendre

wounding a. mordaç, m.- f,. feridor -a, ofensiu -iva

wrap s. cobertor, m. / sobrecoberta (de llibre), f. / to... v. cobrir / embolicar

wrath s. ira, ràbia, f.

wreath s. corona de flors, garlanda, f.

wreck s. naufragi, m. / to... v. naufragar

wrench a. arrencada, estrebada, torçada, f. / clau anglesa, f. / to... v. arrencar, tòrcer, dislocar

wrest (to) v. arrabassar, arrencar

wrestle (to) v. lluitar, disputar

wrestler s. lluitador, m.

wrestling s. lluita lliure, f.

wretch s. infeliç, m.- f., dissortat -ada

wretched a. infeliç, m.- f., dissortat-ada, m.- f.,

wriggle (to) v. serpejar, serpentejar / desplaçar-se sinuosament

wright s. artífex, artesà -ana

wring (to) v. retòrcer, recargolar / esprémer, escórrer

wrinkle s. arruga, f., plec, séc, m. / idea, noció, f.

wrist s. canell, m.

write (to) v. escriure, redactar

writer s. escriptor -a

writing s. lletra, escriptura, f. / escrit, m.

wrong a. falsa, injusta, equivocat-ada.

wrought a. forjat -ada, obrat -ada, afaiçonat -ada

wry a. torçat -ada, tergiversat -ada

wryface s. ganyota, f.

X

xanthic a. xàntic -a.

xebec s. xabec, m.

xerophtalmia s. xeroftalmia, f.

xiphias s. sípia, f.

Xmas s. Nadal (abreviatura), m.

xylography s. xilografia, f.

xylophone s. xilofon, m.

Y

yacht s. iot, m.

yam s. nyam, m.

yank (to) v. estrebar, estirar

yankee a. i s. ianqui

yap (to) v. lladrar, bordar

yard s. pati, corral, clos, m. / iarda, f.

yarn s. filassa, f., fil, filat, m.

yawl s. iol, bot, m.

yawn s. badall, m. / to... v. badallar.

yawner s. badallaire, m.-f.

yawning s. badall, m. / badallera, f.

year s. any, m.

yearling a. primal -a

yearly a. anual, m.-f. / adv. anualment

yearn (to) v. anhelar, desitjar

yearning s. anhel, m.

yeast s. llevat, ferment, m.

yell s. crit / udol / alarit, m. / to... vociferar / bramar (fig.) / udolar

yellow a. groc -groga,

yellowish a. grogós -osa,

yelping s. grinyol, m.

yeoman s. camperol, pagès (propietari de la terra que treballa) / hisendat / alabarder, m.

yes adv. si.

yesterday s. i adv. ahir.

yet adv. encara / conj. no obstant, així i tot.

yew s. teix, m.

yield s. rendiment, m. / to... v. rendir, produir

yoghourt s. iogurt, m.

yoke s. jou, m. / to... v. subjugar

yolk s. rovell d'ou, m.

yonder adv. allà, allí

yore adv. antany

you pron. pers. tu, vós, vosaltres

young s. jove, m.-f.

your pron. el teu, la teva, els teus, les teves, el vostre, les vostres

yours pron. teu -teves, seu -seves, vostre -a, vostres

yourself pron. per. vós mateix -vós mateixa, tu mateix - tu mateixa

yourselves pron. pers. vosaltres mateixos, vosaltres mateixes

youth s. joventut, jovenesa, f.

youthful a. jove, jovençà -ana / juvenil, m.- f., jovenívol -a

yucca s. iuca, f.

Z

zany s. joglar, pallaso, m.

zeal s. zel, fervor, m.

zealot s. fanàtic, entusiasta, m.

zebra s. zebra, f.

zebu s. zebú, m.

zenith s. zenit, m.

zephyr s. zèfir, m.

zero s. zero, m.

zest s. delit, gaudi, m.

zigzag s. ziga-zaga, f. / to... v. zig-zaguejar

zinc s. zenc, zinc, m.

zither s. cítara, f.

zodiac s. zodíac, m.

zone s. zona, f.

zoo s. parc zoològic, zoo, m.

zoological a. zoològic -a

zoology s. zoologia, f.

zoom s. brunzit, m.

Spanish and Latin American Interest Titles
from Hippocrene Books...

LANGUAGE GUIDES

Spanish-English/English-Spanish
Practical Dictionary
**35,000 entries • 338 pages • 5 x 8 • 0-7818-0179-6 • $9.95pb •
(211)**

Spanish-English/English-Spanish Concise
Dictionary (Latin American)
**8,000 entries • 500 pages • 4 x 6 • 0-7818-0261-X • $11.95pb •
(258)**

Spanish Handy Dictionary
**3,800 entries • 120 pages • 5 x 7 • 0-7818-0012-9 • $8.95pb •
(189)**

Hippocrene Children's Illustrated
Spanish Dictionary
English-Spanish/Spanish-English
**500 entries • 94 pages • 8 x 11 • 0-7818-0733-6 • $14.95hc •
(206)**

Beginner's Spanish
330 pages • 5 ½ x 8 ½ • 0-7818-0840-5 • $14.95pb • (225)

Mastering Spanish
338 pages • 5 x 8 • 0-87052-059-8 • $11.95pb • (527)
2 cassettes: ca. 2 hours • 0-87052-067-9 • $12.95 • (528)

Mastering Advanced Spanish
326 pages • 5 x 8 • 0-7818-0081-1 • $14.95pb • (413)
2 cassettes: ca. 2 hours • 0-7818-0089-7 • $12.95 • (426)

Spanish Grammar
224 pages • 5 x 8 • 0-87052-893-9 • $12.95pb • (273)

Spanish Verbs: Ser and Estar
220 pages • 5 x 8 • 0-7818-0024-2 • $8.95pb • (292)

Dictionary of 1,000 Spanish Proverbs: Bilingual
131 pages • 5 x 8 • 0-7818-0412-4 • $11.95pb • (254)

Spanish Proverbs, Idioms and Slang
350 pages • 6 x 9 • 0-7818-0675-5 • $14.95pb • (760)

Dictionary of Latin American Spanish Phrases and Expressions
1,200 entries • 150 pages • 5 ½ x 8 ½ • 0-7818-0865-0 • $14.95pb • (286)

Language and Travel Guide to Mexico
224 pages • 5 x 8 • 0-87052-622-7 • $14.95pb • (503)

Basque-English/English-Basque
Dictionary and Phrasebook
**1,500 entries • 240 pages • 3 x 7 • 0-7818-0622-4 •
$11.95pb • (751)**

Galician-English/English-Galician
Concise Dictionary
**10,000 entries • 600 pages • 4 x 6 • 0-7818-0776-X •
$14.95pb • (58)**

Maya-English/English-Maya
Dictionary and Phrasebook (Yucatec)
**1,500 entries • 180 pages • 3¾ x 7 • 0-7818-0859-6 •
$12.95pb • (244)**

Portuguese Handy Dictionary
**15,000 entries • 120 pages • 5 x 7 • 0-87052-053-9 •
$8.95pb • (324)**

Portuguese-English/English-Portuguese
Practical Dictionary
**3,000 entries • 426 pages • 4 x 7 • 0-87052-980-3 •
$19.95pb • (477)**

HISTORY

Mexico: An Illustrated History
**150 pages • 5 x 7 • 50 illustrations • 0-7818-0690-9 • $11.95pb
• (585)**

Spain: An Illustrated History
150 pages • 5 x 7 • 50 b/w photos/illus./maps •
0-7818-0836-7 • $14.95hc • (113)

Tikal: An Illustrated History of the
Ancient Maya Capital
150 pages • 5 x 7 • 50 b/w photos/illus./maps •
0-7818-0853-7 • $12.95pb • (101)

BILINGUAL POETRY

Treasury of Spanish Love Poems, Quotations
and Proverbs: Bilingual
128 pages • 5 x 7 • 0-7818-0358-6 • $11.95 • (589)
2 cassettes: ca. 2 hours • $12.95 • (584) •
0-7818-0365-9

Treasury of Spanish Love Short Stories
in Spanish and English
157 pages • 5 x 7 • 0-7818-0298-9 • $11.95 • (604)

FOLK TALES

Folk Tales from Chile
121 pages • 5 x 8 • 15 illustrations • 0-7818-0712-3 •
$12.50hc • (785)

COOKBOOKS

Argentina Cooks!: Treasured Recipes from the
Nine Regions of Argentina
300 pages • 6 x 9 • 0-7818-0829-4 • $24.95hc • (85)

Cuisines of Portuguese Encounters
260 pages • 6 x 9 • 0-7818-083106 • $24.95hc • (91)

Old Havana Cookbook (Bilingual)
Cuban Recipes in Spanish and English
**128 pages • 5 x 7 • illustrations • 0-7818-0767-0 •
$11.95hc • (590)**

A Spanish Family Cookbook, Revised Edition
244 pages • 5 x 8 • 0-7818-0546-5 • $11.95pb • (642)

Art of South American Cookery
**266 pages • 5 x 8 • b/w line drawings • 0-7818-0485-X •
$11.95pb • (423)**

The Art of Brazilian Cookery
240 pages • 5½ x 8½ • 0-7818-0130-3 • $11.95pb • (250)

Prices subject to change without prior notice. To order
Hippocrene Books, contact your local bookstore, call (718)
454-2366, visit www.hippocrenebooks.com, or write to:
Hippocrene Books, 171 Madison Avenue, New York, NY
10016. Please enclose check or money order adding $5.00
shipping (UPS) for the first book and $.50 for each addi-
tional title.